THE POLITICS OF PARADISE

George Gordon (Lord) Byron
© *National Portrait Gallery*

William Hazlitt
© *Witt Library*

THE POLITICS
OF
PARADISE

A Vindication of Byron

MICHAEL FOOT

COLLINS
8 Grafton Street, London W1
1988

William Collins Sons and Co. Ltd
London · Glasgow · Sydney · Auckland
Toronto · Johannesburg

First published 1988
Reprinted 1988
Copyright © Michael Foot 1988

BRITISH LIBRARY CATALOGUING IN PUBLICATION DATA

Foot, Michael
The politics of paradise: a vindication
of Byron.
1. Byron, George Gordon Byron, *Baron*—
Criticism and interpretation
I. Title
821'.7   PR4388

ISBN 0-00-217255-0

Set in Digitek Meridien by Ace Filmsetting Ltd, Frome, Somerset
Made and printed in Great Britain by
T.J. Press (Padstow) Ltd, Padstow, Cornwall

To Jill

who has had to endure intensifying signs of Byron-mania for the past ten years, and has borne it with great patience and sympathy.

To

the electors of Blaenau Gwent who have always shown that they know the meaning of Byronic resistance to Toryism, ancient and modern, and all its works.

To

all my friends among the race of second-hand booksellers who have given me a lifetime of help and enjoyment, headed by Sam Joseph and David Low who first introduced me to the delights of the Charing Cross Road, Peter Eaton, who had always a wisdom all his own, and Alan Hancox of Cheltenham, the most generous of them all.

CONTENTS

ACKNOWLEDGEMENTS

I wish to put on record my thanks to two sets of writers and publishers in particular, who granted me permission to quote from their publications. I am grateful to Leslie A. Marchand and John Murray for the extensive quotations from their edition of *Byron's Letters and Journals*; as the reader can easily see, the debt to this edition of Byron's letters is outstanding. And a similar expression of gratitude must be made to Jerome J. McGann and the Oxford University Press for the quotations from *Lord Byron: The Complete Poetical Works*.

Most of the other acknowledgements – some of them also to John Murray and to the Oxford University Press – appear in the elaborate footnotes which, I trust, may serve the double purpose of guiding readers to my sources and encouraging them to read further.

I owe a special debt to Enid Hutchinson for the patience, skill and hard work which she has shown in making the production of this book possible. She in turn has had invaluable assistance from Una Cooze and from Elizabeth Thomas in compiling the index.

Part One

THE SOIL
FOR DISSENT

A cold, calculating indifference in matters of taste is generally the effect of want of feeling; as affected moderation in politics is (nine times out of ten) a cloak for want of principle.

Hazlitt's essay on Sismondi's
'Literature of the South', June 1815

ONE

A Cavanagh of a Critic

His blows were not undecided and ineffectual
– lumbering like Mr Wordsworth's epic
poetry, nor wavering like Mr Coleridge's
lyric prose, nor short of the mark like Mr
Brougham's speeches, nor wide of it like Mr
Canning's wit, nor foul like the *Quarterly*, nor
let balls like the *Edinburgh Review*. Cobbett
and Junius together would have made a
Cavanagh. He was the best *up-hill* player in the
world.

Hazlitt on Cavanagh, the fives player,
from the essay 'The Indian Jugglers'

William Hazlitt was my guide.* No would-be reader and writer,
no democratic socialist could wish for a better one. For him, the
paths of politics and literature crossed and re-crossed in an endless interweaving; each could lead to fulfilment in the other,

* As for most others, my first biographical guide to William Hazlitt was
supplied by P. P. Howe in his *Life*, first published by Martin Secker in 1922,
and reissued by J. M. Dent in 1940, and still in so many respects the best. I
started reading Hazlitt himself in the excellent Everyman editions; one,
The Plain Speaker, with a P. P. Howe introduction. Then I bought (the best
purchase of my life) the P. P. Howe–J. M. Dent twenty-one volumes, from
which all the Hazlitt quotations here are taken. 'He lived in spirit with
Hazlitt,' wrote Howe's own lifelong friend, Frank Swinnerton. No other
volumes are as precious as his, but a few win their place on the same shelf:
David Bromwich's *Hazlitt: The Mind of a Critic*; Ronald Blyth's splendid
Selected Writings in the Penguin English Library and Charles Morgan's
1948 *Liber Amoris*. Above all, I am grateful to Stanley Jones, both for his
encouragement and for an invaluable correspondence. My debt to him
can be compared with my debt to Howe, and I am certain that his forth-
coming book will mark a new departure in Hazlitt scholarship.

13

and each without sustenance from the other could prove bitter and abortive. Of course, in Hazlitt's time the word 'socialist' had not even been invented, and even the word 'democracy' had acquired little of its modern connotation. No matter: it was part of Hazlitt's genius that he anticipated so much of the revolutionary impulse of the subsequent century; that he presented the true manner in which men and women should speak and act if they were to treasure what was good from the past and win the people's battles for the future. The word 'people' too will need some definition, but Hazlitt, unlike many of his romantic contemporaries, never wished to shelter in rhapsody or verbiage. For all his faith in the imagination as the great liberating force for individuals and societies, he took pride also in his own unrelenting realism. His politics were gripped by the contest between rich and poor, and he looked for no nostalgic or Utopian escape.

In the year 1789, when the French Revolution started to shake the foundations of his world, he was eleven years old, the zestful, observant, but still not notably precocious son of a loving, Dissenting household. Most of the Dissenters then, and all the Unitarians it may be imagined, shared the bliss of that Paris dawn. When he died in 1830, just as the news of a lesser French revolution reached his bedside, he had witnessed the rise and destruction of all his political aspirations; the new flicker from France was no more than just that. But he had witnessed also, during those forty-odd years, the mightiest awakening of the human mind at least since the age of the Renaissance. He called it himself 'an apocalyptical chapter in the history of human nature'. He had seen it with his own eyes and heard it with his own ears, and had marked the pre-eminent role played by the England he both loved and hated. The turmoil in his mind had never been subdued, though a later generation sought to bury him under a tombstone which read succinctly 'painter, critic, essayist'. Hazlitt could not have quarrelled with any of those titles, but he would have unleashed a ferocious counter-assault against all who sought to debase his revolutionary doctrines or to deny the means whereby they could be translated into deeds.

He was born ten years before Lord Byron; he lived six years

longer. They looked out on the same revolutionary world, shared many of the same intellectual excitements, devoured the same authors; they were indeed both bookworms, whatever other pastimes were allowed to intrude. Yet there was between them, at first sight or first reading, an imperfect sympathy which could turn to something truly fierce. Hazlitt introduced me, most guardedly, to Byron. His credentials as the greatest of all literary critics are worth fresh examination on their own, but they point also, as I hope to prove, to a new, modern estimate of Byron.

Considering how straight and narrow was the path mapped out for Hazlitt by his descent and upbringing, the remarkable fact is how he seemed to find his own route to unexpected, spacious fields of intellectual inquiry. But much of the drive came from that very upbringing, from just that old Dissenting source. Hazlitt's father, the Reverend William, was a man accustomed to risking his own comfort for his principles. A founder of the American Unitarian Church during a four-year transatlantic mission, the sturdy Nonconformist had drawn cries of 'beware the black rebel' on the streets of his native Ireland for befriending ill-used American prisoners during the War of Independence and for preaching the cause of American freedom from his pulpit. His famous son William was born and mostly bred in England, but it should not be forgotten how strong was the Irish streak. He was, from his mother's womb and his father's knee, a Celtic Dissenter.

William, like his father, had been destined for the Dissenting Ministry. He had been despatched at the age of fourteen, in the fateful year 1793, to the Unitarian New College at Hackney, to be instructed in the doctrine which enabled good Unitarians to escape from crude Presbyterian clutches, and he had returned home three years later, not lapsing back into Calvinist reveries, but, as one observer claimed – probably overstating the case – an 'avowed infidel'. He himself said he wanted only to be satisfied of 'the reason of things'. He could feel occasional stabs of bitterness that his perfect sympathy with such a father might be put

15

in peril by 'a veering point of theology, the officious meddling political critics'. But no lasting estrangement was conceivable; rather the tact of father and son was such that not so much as a shadow was allowed to fall across their relationship, and for two men so lacking in the sneaking virtue of discretion, it was a wonderful achievement. William returned home with his religious allegiance shaken, his political passions stirred and yet having his first taste of other delights which captured his heart and mind in a manner to shape his whole life. 'Happy are they', he wrote years later, 'who live in the dream of their own existence, and see all things in the light of their own minds; who walk by faith and hope; to whom the guiding star of their youth still shines from afar, and into whom the spirit of the world has not entered! They have not been "hurt by the archers" nor has the iron entered their souls. The world has no hand on them.'

Roughly between the years 1795 and 1800, when Hazlitt in his late teens and early twenties was still arguing with himself about what occupation he would seek to follow, he read the books which moulded his mind. Constantly throughout the rest of his life he would return to themes which had made the deepest impression then. Of course, it would be absurd to suppose that all the later elaborations of these themes presented themselves at the first hearing or reading. But with Hazlitt especially, the opposite supposition would be much more likely to mislead. First impressions with him could be indelible. He could fall in love with authors at first reading, and never fall out again, and his haphazard choice of favourites was not at all that which might be expected to be easily available in a strict, God-fearing non-conformist home.

'The greatest pleasure in life', he wrote years later in *The Plain Speaker*, 'is that of reading, while we are young', and his memory alighted at once on the English novelists, starting with Henry Fielding's *Tom Jones*. 'I would like to devote a year to a course of them and perhaps add that old sly knave, Sir Walter [Scott] to the end of the list.' The novelists exerted their influence before anyone else; a point of some interest, apart from any other, since Hazlitt became the very first critic who ever treated the novel as a serious form of art. Maybe we anticipate in some degree the later Hazlitt. Some of these other master spirits could even match Fielding – Cervantes, in particular, although it is invidious to make any selection from such a list. Fielding, Sterne, Smollett, Richardson, Steele, Le Sage were all competing for his favour when he was still fifteen.

While he was living at Hackney, he sank himself in metaphysical studies which left another mark, English and French philosophers who got him 'entangled in the briars and thorns of subtle distinctions. . . . I did arrive at some very satisfactory and potent conclusions; nor will I go so far, however ungrateful the subject might seem, as to exclaim with Marlowe's Faustus – "Would I had never seen Wittenberg, never read a book" – that is, never studied such authors as Hartley, Hume, Berkeley, etc.' But he was near it. His study of these established authorities pointed to what he believed was an original philosophical discovery of his own, one not unconnected with his political discoveries, and, with the return to Wem especially, a new dimension was opened. He started to read some of the poets who later became favourites but not at all with full appreciation. 'For I would have the reader understand,' he remarked (incredibly, as all his readers must suppose), 'I am deficient in the faculty of imagination.' He read Chaucer for the first time, Spenser with 'a sort of voluptuous indolence', Pope, Dryden, Goldsmith, not Milton nor Shakespeare yet. Poetry had not yet touched his heart as Fielding or Cervantes did. It was another combination of discoveries which truly changed his course. 'My three favourite writers about the time I speak of were Burke, Junius and Rousseau. I was never weary of admiring and wondering . . . I laid the book down to find out the secret of so much strength and beauty, and took it up again to read and admire. So I passed whole days, months and, I may add, years.' And two of these remained the most potent influences upon him thereafter. Junius must be excluded from that company, although, since the ever-magnanimous Hazlitt was always eager to acknowledge his literary debts, his place of honour cannot be altogether overlooked. Junius helped to shape Hazlitt's eventually much superior gift for sharp sentences, epigrammatic force, political invective off the leash; Junius showed why it was worth polishing the point of the dagger. But it was the other two, Burke and Rousseau, who more than any others made Hazlitt the unique political figure that he became, and remains. He applied his mind *all his life* – yes, the claim is not too high – to the task of seeking a synthesis between them.

He seems to have plunged into reading Burke and Rousseau indiscriminately. Each became entangled with the other, and few of the individual writings of each of them could be set aside. With both, between man and book – and from Hazlitt this was a high compliment – no distinction need be drawn.

> Let me then conjure the gentle reader who has ever felt an attachment to books, not heartily to divorce them from their authors. Whatever love or reverence may be done to the one, is equally owing to the other. To cherish the work and *damn* the author is as if the traveller who slakes his thirst at the running stream, should revile the spring-head from which it gushes.

For that century, and for Hazlitt, Rousseau was the challenger. Let us take him first.

The very first book by Rousseau which came Hazlitt's way was a coarse leathern-covered copy of *The Social Contract* picked off some bookstall in London. He carried it home and was thrilled by the opening sentences:

> I mean to inquire if, in the civil order, there can be any sure and legitimate rule of administration, men being taken as they are and laws as they might be . . . I shall be asked if I am a prince or a legislator, to write on politics. I answer that I am neither, and that is why I do so. If I were a prince or a legislator, I should not waste time in saying what wants doing; I should do it and hold my peace . . . I am happy when I reflect upon governments, to find my inquiries always furnish me with reasons for loving that of my own country.

And then the trumpet blast, familiar and unfamiliar:

> Man is born free; and everywhere he is in chains. One
> thinks himself the master of others, and still remains a
> greater slave than they. How did this change come about, I
> do not know. What can make it legitimate? That question I
> think I can answer.

Soon, very soon, Hazlitt had moved to 'the best of all his
works', the *Confessions*: 'He makes us enter into his feelings as if
they were his own and we seem to remember every incident
and circumstance of his life as if it had happened to ourselves.
We are never tired of his work, for it everywhere presents us
with pictures which we fancy to be counterparts of our own
existence.' It was by this delicate path that he was led to Rousseau's *La Nouvelle Héloïse*:* 'There are no passages in the *New
Eloise* of equal force and beauty with the best descriptions in the
Confessions, if we except the excursion on the water, Julia's last
letter to St Preux, and his letter recalling the days of their first
loves.' Some exception indeed! 'We spent two whole years reading these two works; and (gentle reader, it was when we were
young) in shedding tears over them – as fast as the Arabian trees
their medicinal gums. They were the happiest years of my life.'
And this same man, this same Rousseau, brought passion into
politics as no one had ever done.

> He did more [said Hazlitt] toward the French Revolution
> than any other man. Voltaire, by his wit and penetration,
> had rendered superstition contemptible and tyranny
> odious, but it was Rousseau who brought the feeling of
> irreconcilable enmity to rank and privileges, *above humanity*,
> home to the bosom of every man, – identified it with all the
> pride of intellect, and with the deepest yearning of the
> human heart.

---

* We shall come across this title so often in reference to other readers, such
as Byron, that the French title seems better, whatever the inconsistencies.

And then again, in Hazlitt's words but with a true Dantonesque audacity:

> He was the founder of Jacobinism which disclaims the division of the species into two classes, the one the property of the other. It was of the disciples of this school, where principle is converted into passion, that Mr Burke said, and said truly – 'Once a Jacobin, always a Jacobin'. The adept in this school does not so much consider the political injury as the personal insult. This is the way to put the case, to see the revolutionary leaven, the self-love which is at the bottom of every heart, and this was the way in which Rousseau put it. It then becomes a question between man and man, which there is but one way of deciding.

This was the Rousseau who had stirred revolutionary multitudes, as he stirred Hazlitt. He was truly the foremost engineer of the Revolution; only a giant could stand across his path.*

How Hazlitt, the great rebel, the arch-defender of Rousseau, the English writer of the age who, above any other and with fuller justification, gloried in the title of Jacobin, could revere Burke, the great apostate, is one of the combined mysteries and miracles of our literature. One explanation, no doubt, affecting others beside Hazlitt, was the persuasive power of the other, earlier Burke, the great exponent of liberal causes who had defended the Americans in their war of independence and defied George III. But Hazlitt, it seems, only came to these writings later. The first book he carried home in triumph from

---

* I cannot resist quoting a sentence from an essay on Burke written by G. M. Young in 1948, 'Today and Yesterday':

> Like his Americans, Burke had sniffed the tainted gale: he had felt the hot breath of Rousseau. I have often thought that if there was one man in Europe who really understood the Genevan, it was the Irishman, and the understanding reveals itself as much in their conflicts and recoils as in their approximations and intersections. 'The wild beast of the desert shall also meet with the wild beast of the island: and the satyr shall cry to his fellow.'

Shrewsbury to Wem, the *Letter to a Noble Lord*, was written in Burke's full anti-Revolution period, and the other writings to which he speedily turned were directly aimed at the very heart of the political creed he was shaping for himself, yet he discovered Burke for himself too. 'His words are most like things; his style is the most strictly suited to the subject.' Hazlitt's own style owed more to Burke's than to anybody's, but he was never primarily a student of style, despite his many apposite remarks upon it. The thing mattered more than the word. Literature was not something removed from life. Books were weapons in the cause of human freedom. No one ever accepted that proposition more eagerly than Hazlitt. So was not this Edmund Burke to be found guilty of amassing a great arsenal *against* the greatest cause?

But Hazlitt would not be deterred. Thirty years later, in *The Plain Speaker*, he recalled:

I had reason for my prejudice in favour of this author. To understand an adversary is some praise: to admire him is more. I thought I did both; I knew I did one. From the first time I ever cast my eyes on anything of Burke's . . . I said to myself, 'This is true eloquence: this is a man pouring out his mind on paper.' All other styles seemed to me pedantic and impertinent. Dr Johnson's was walking on stilts, and even Junius's (who was at that time a favourite with me), with all his terseness, shrunk up into little antithetic points and well-trimmed sentences. But Burke's style was forked and playful as the lightning, crested like the serpent. He delivered plain things on a plain ground; but when he rose, there was no end of his flights and circumgyrations – and in this very Letter, 'he like an eagle in a dove-cote, fluttered his Volcians' (the Duke of Bedford and the Earl of Lauderdale) 'in Corioli.' I did not care for his doctrines. I was then, and am still, proof against their contagion; but I admired the author, and was considered a not very staunch partisan of the opposite side, though I thought myself that an abstract proposition was one thing – a masterly transition, a brilliant metaphor, another. I conceived too that he might be wrong

21

in his main argument, and yet deliver fifty truths in arriving at a false conclusion.

And if anyone doubts the Hazlitt claim, if anyone still questions his allegiance to the Jacobin's cause, let them read Burke, as Hazlitt did. Hazlitt saw the truth and force of so much that Burke was saying; no man could write like that and tell lies. Burke's understanding of mankind, he said, was 'inexhaustible as the human heart, and various as the sources of nature'. Yet this mighty intellect had somehow been used to persuade the people of England that 'liberty was an illiberal, hollow sound; that humanity was a barbarous modern invention; that prejudices were the test of truth, that reason was a strumpet and right a fiction;' that the whole Rousseauan dream was a monstrous threat to the human spirit. To explain the phenomenon, the mechanism of politics must be taken to pieces, but, imperatively, Burke must be answered. 'He presents to you', said Hazlitt, 'one view of the face of society. Let him who thinks he can, give the reverse side with equal force, beauty and clearness . . .' And indeed Hazlitt's life work was his great reply. He gave to the English Left a perspective and philosophy as widely ranging as Burke had given to the English Right.

No one could ever remove Burke from his place in Hazlitt's Valhalla; no prose writer was ever regarded as his equal. Coleridge once tried to persuade him that Wordsworth could be regarded as a rival in this field, but Hazlitt scorned the comparison. 'I am too old to be a convert to a new mythology of genius. The niches are occupied, the tables are full.' It is true that Hazlitt preferred to honour the dead; time, in his reckoning, was incomparably the best critic. Yet even his selection of the greatest prose writers in the past showed his power of discrimination and was seemingly divorced from his own political predilections. He could write of Jeremy Taylor and Thomas Browne as well as any lover of times past. He folded Montaigne to his bosom as no English writer had done before, and he rescued Jonathan Swift from the defamatory clutches of Tory and Whig alike, but possibly in these instances their common strand of scepticism made a special appeal to him. He was, as we have mentioned, the first writer to treat the English novelists, starting with Defoe, as serious artists. He looked back to the past, but not to accept other men's verdicts. Such a stance made it all the more remarkable that, in dealing with his own time, he could displace Dr Johnson from his pedestal and put Burke there instead. And Burke, be it not forgotten, was something of a philosopher, and so, most assuredly, was Hazlitt. His first vain exertions to write at all were to produce what he believed to be an original philosophical treatise, and the subject never lost its magnetism. His extensive knowledge and persistent interest gave a fresh dimension to his aesthetic judgements, although he could never quite shed an ambivalent attitude towards them. At one moment he would applaud the suggestion that Shakespeare was as much a metaphysician as a poet. At the next he would gleefully record how 'Homer's poetical world has outlived Plato's philosophical Republic.' Hazlitt and the prose writers is a simple enough study compared with Hazlitt and the poets.

He once remarked, as we noted before, on his own deficient imagination; it is impossible to accept, the more so when we recall how often he stressed the word in his own essay 'On Poetry in General'. But what is true is that his imaginative appreciation of poetry had been painfully acquired. 'I believe', he himself acknowledged years later, 'I may date my insight into the mysteries of poetry from my acquaintance with the authors of the *Lyrical Ballads*; at least, my discrimination of the richer sorts – not my predilection for such writers as Goldsmith or Pope . . .' Coleridge and Wordsworth were something fresher and greater than he had ever known before, and he described the experience in 'My First Acquaintance with Poets'. There he recalled, with an exhilaration which still tingles in every sentence, all his richest memories, his youth, his father, those first books he had read, the first meeting with Coleridge, the visit to Llangollen, 'the cradle of a new existence', the journey to Nether Stowey, the first hearing of the *Lyrical Ballads* from the lips of Wordsworth himself, and 'the sense of a new spirit in poetry came over me'. One large part of Hazlitt's life thereafter was his response to that moment. While much of his mental energy was to be devoted to answering Burke, room was evidently left – or perhaps the activities were combined – to comprehend the new mystery now unfolded before him. No critic (except perhaps a few fellow poets, and not many of them) ever heard the strange language of a new school of poetry with such an alert sympathy, and certainly no critic ever welcomed the innovation with greater daring and, despite all subsequent political feuds, with more steadfastness and warmth.

He returned to these themes again and again, to Wordsworth's 'originality' and to the light which Coleridge had brought into his life, never wavering in his acceptance that the new school of poetry had its own special greatness, though they helped primarily to introduce him to something greater still. Considering how significant for Hazlitt were his first impressions and how he remembered so well how he had first stumbled on Rousseau's *La Nouvelle Héloïse* or his other favourites, it is surprising that he cannot be equally specific in recalling his first acquaintance with Shakespeare. The time came when, for Hazlitt, Shakespeare established a pre-eminence over everyone else, although here too, it must be hastily added, he made his own discoveries. He did not accept the verdict of other critics, Dr Johnson or Coleridge. He made his own discoveries, with the assistance of a few others such as Edmund Kean, as we shall see. Eventually, maybe, he would have found his own path to Shakespeare, but it was the journey to Nether Stowey that put him on the path to poetry, and without that awakening there would be no Hazlitt. Not even Rousseau and Burke together could have achieved the feat.

The year of Coleridge's visit to Wem, and of Hazlitt's journey to Nether Stowey, 1798, was the year to which he himself traced the awakening of his mind and spirit: 'the figures that compose that date', he said, quoting *Paradise Lost*, 'are to me like "the dreaded name of Demogorgon" '. But, even then, it was no sudden revelation, releasing at once his creative powers. He still could not write himself; instead tears flooded the blank page before him. Not until nineteen years later did he first incorporate those precious and explosive memories in the form of an essay, and not until a full twenty-five years later had he elaborated them finally in 'My First Acquaintance with Poets'. Some of these exertions in writing and re-writing were dictated by the pressure to earn his living as a journalist. It took him years to learn the trade, and he never achieved financial security. All the more noteworthy is the deliberation and poise which he showed in judging his contemporaries. He reached his conclusions cautiously, for himself, and was therefore the more entitled to insist that he would not be shifted from them once they had been established and stated. These were never the verdicts of a stubborn, closed, dogmatic mind; they had been shaped by rich reflection, and this applied especially, it must be noted, to his judgements on the poets. His first acquaintance with them was in 1798; his first critical writings about them were not attempted until 1814.

The intervening years could properly be regarded as the most momentous of modern times, second only in earth-shattering significance, if subordinate at all, to the revolutionary epoch after 1789 which set these later convulsions in motion. They witnessed the rise and fall of Napoleon, the lightning campaigns across the plains of Lombardy, Marengo, Austerlitz, Jena, Trafalgar, the invasion of Spain, the retreat from Moscow, the first European war of full continental dimensions, conducted without restraint or pity. 1798 itself saw the conflict coming much nearer home to English hearths and homes than most observers had thought possible. A French army made the attempt to land in Ireland to back a truly Irish revolution, and in London the war hysteria prompted Parliament to suspend Habeas Corpus and proscribe such incipient working-class organizations as the Corresponding Society as hotbeds of high treason. It would be a mistake to identify the national mood with that which prevailed, say, in 1914 or 1940; a large section of the politically articulate community had opposed, and still opposed, the war with France and indeed regarded the English party of William Pitt as the aggressor or at least the ally of the aggressors. Charles James Fox still voiced these views in the House of Commons or outside. Quite a number of truly patriotic

English citizens, Hazlitt included, were proud to call themselves Jacobins or Jacobin sympathizers. But the courage required for such resistance to the popular wartime mood was becoming more testing, month by month. Even down in the secluded shade of Nether Stowey, a spy was allocated to mark the activities of such erstwhile French sympathizers as Wordsworth and Coleridge.

Not so much of the conversation on that Nether Stowey visit can have been directly political, for by that time Wordsworth and Coleridge were already beginning to temper their early revolutionary enthusiasms, whereas their young disciple would not have approved even the mildest signs of wavering. Hazlitt was much more of a political thinker already than some of his later writing might indicate. Rousseau, Burke and Junius still retained their place of dominance, even if the poets must be allowed their share of devotion and the painters too. His brother had become a painter and he himself showed considerable aptitude. He was still uncertain about his own future, even though his political convictions had already taken firm root.

One day, either in late December of that same auspicious 1798 or in the early months of 1799, he strolled into a picture sale in Pall Mall, an exhibition of old Italian masters. It was his first sight of Titian and Raphael, and for a while not only the poets but even politics seemed cast out from his mind.

> I was staggered when I saw the works there collected, and looked at them with wondering and with longing eyes. A mist passed away from my sight; the scales fell off. A new sense came upon me, a new heaven and a new earth stood before me . . . From that time I lived in a world of pictures. Battles, sieges, speeches in Parliament seemed mere idle noise and fury, 'signifying nothing', compared with these mighty works that spoke to me in the eternal silence of thought.

Moreover, soon after, in the spring of May 1802, the battles and sieges had actually been suspended momentarily, and, thanks to the Peace of Amiens, he was able in two capacities, as an

aspiring young painter and a true friend of the French Revolution, to visit Paris, Napoleon's Paris, and the Louvre which
Napoleon had enriched with his Italian spoils. He wrote back to
his father some ecstatic accounts of the pictures he had seen, the
Titians he attempted to copy, and one of his letters contained a
breathless postscript: 'I saw Bonaparte.'

On his return to England, he soon renewed his acquaintance
with the poets. He paid two lively visits to Wordsworth and
Coleridge at their newly-adopted homes in the Lakes, chiefly
for the purpose of securing their support for him in his would-
be profession as a painter, either as sitters themselves or
through their aid in getting commissions from their patron, Sir
George Beaumont. But there was plenty of opportunity for argument, and Hazlitt was no longer the timid, bashful, adoring
pupil. He had views of his own, not only about politics, but on
philosophy and religion, and in some of these disputes he found
himself on Wordsworth's side against a growingly devout Coleridge. Wordsworth sailed with him on Grasmere Lake, tramped
the hills with him and read from his unpublished works, such
as *The Borderers*, which, amazingly, Hazlitt could quote and mis-
quote twenty-five years later. But sometimes he argued with
Wordsworth too, and the portrait he painted of him was so for-
bidding that, with a little encouragement from Southey, he
destroyed it himself.

However, despite a strange tale from de Quincey that he had
actually proposed marriage to Dorothy, and despite some
obscure escapade with a girl at Keswick, his relations with
Wordsworth remained tolerably good till his departure and
beyond. With Coleridge some strains appeared, but they were
nowhere near breaking point. A friend of Coleridge, Tom
Wedgwood, had asked about Hazlitt's qualifications as a possible companion on a continental tour, and Coleridge replied
sharply but in a way which showed clearly his fascination with
the young man. Despite Hazlitt's intellectual and artistic gifts
and his kind ways with children he was said to be

jealous, gloomy and of an irritable Pride – and addicted to
women, as objects of sexual Indulgence. With all this, there

is much good in him – he is disinterested, an enthusiastic
Lover of the great men, who have been before us – he says
things that are his own in a way of his own – and tho' from
habitual Shyness and the Outside and bearskin at least of
misanthropy, he is strangely confused and dark in his conversation and delivers himself of almost all his conceptions
with a Forceps, yet he says more than any man, I ever knew,
yourself only excepted, that is his own in a way of his own –
and oftentimes when he has warmed his mind, and the
synovial juice has come out and spread over his joints, he
will gallop, for half an hour together with real Eloquence.
He sends well-headed and well-feathered Thoughts straight
forwards to the mark with a Twang of the Bow-string. If you
could recommend him, as a Portrait-painter, I should be
glad. To be your Companion he is, in my opinion, utterly
unfit. His own Health is fitful.

By any reckoning whatever, this was an astonishing judgement for Coleridge to make about a Hazlitt who had written
little and published nothing. It was an indication of Coleridge's
insight, but an indication too of his readiness to sway with passing pressures. It might have been a verdict which he could
have passed at the end of Hazlitt's life, not the beginning.
Clearly, the arguments in which Hazlitt had engaged on his two
visits to the Lakes must have been much more entrancing and
extensive than the brief records left us suggest. Hazlitt was no
longer overawed in that company; he could be bold, eloquent,
original in his talk. Possibly, too, he did show Coleridge the
draft of his philosophical essay which he carried around with
him so proudly or defiantly, and possibly some drafts of his first
attempts at political controversy. For had not Coleridge himself
set the example with a splendid invective against William Pitt,
the Prime Minister, and the war he seemed resolved to pursue
to the bitter end? The point can be underlined: Hazlitt admired,
loved, honoured and would even for a decade or so still sit
quietly at the feet of the poets. About philosophy or politics, he
felt qualified to hold his own with them or anyone else.

Hazlitt's first publication, *Essay on the Principles of Human*

Action, to which are added 'Some Remarks on the Systems of Hartley and Helvetius', was published (anonymously) in 1805. His second, 'Advice to a Patriot' in a letter addressed 'To A Member of the Old Opposition' was published (also anonymously and at the author's expense) in 1806. Consider the first targets against which he directed his assault: no other writer of the time had the same interest and aim. He made his entry, even this student of Wordsworth and Coleridge, as a philosopher-politician-journalist. Rousseau and Burke were still his mentors and models. Rousseau was still his treasured ally, Burke his honoured opponent, and he set about the task of fighting his political betters where they must always be fought, not to the music of some distant drum, but here and now, in the burning controversies of the hour.

Of this first batch, Hazlitt's own favourite was undoubtedly his little-read and not easily readable *Essay on the Principles of Human Action*, his most painfully delivered first child. It comprises a careful, reasoned, well-argued analysis of what he described as the balance between self-love and benevolence. He was not afraid to argue with Bacon and Hobbes and Locke and Berkeley: so why later should he cower beneath the high-pitched tirades of Coleridge and the rest? He was shaping his own syntheses between reason and imagination, thought and action. Sometimes and mostly in his early writings, he could only find his way by means of an argument which needed to seek diversions. Later he would transform some of his most hardly-fashioned ideas into aphorisms: 'The seat of knowledge is in the head; of wisdom, in the heart. We are sure to judge wrong, if we do not feel right.' Curiously, both Rousseau and Burke understood that, in their utterly divergent manners. Hazlitt accepted to the full the reformers' doctrine that men do not become what by nature they are meant to be, but what society makes them. And society could be transformed: the French Revolution looked like romance in action. But the deed could not be done by Utopians who would not soil their hands, nor by an arid appeal to reason alone, nor by the economists and utilitarians who inherited the tattered mantle of the revolutionaries. He was a passionate believer in man's benevolence and his perfectibility but one who could not deny, had no wish to deny, Burke's insistence that passion and prejudice could not easily be uprooted from the human heart. Since the passions could be good, since the heart and the imagination exercised their right to govern, since the best traditions, and, not least, the wonderful tradition of dissent, should be revered, why should they not be? They too could be enlisted in the Good Cause. These were themes which Hazlitt went on elaborating all through his life. Most remarkable of all perhaps was how much of his thought was compressed into these first sturdy, if tentative, exercises in independence.

'Advice to a Patriot' was an anti-war tract directed against a particular warmaker. It was paid for by the author (much to the horror of a new and true friend, Charles Lamb), produced by an unknown printer in Shoe Lane, and rarely noticed thereafter. But it boils with the true Hazlittean passion, one who would not 'blow the blast of war for a livelihood' or be content to echo the popular cry. Had the war against France been renewed on a great principle? It was rather 'a diplomatic ambiguity', a breach of the peace treaty in fact enacted by us and not our enemies.

> It is no part of wisdom to hang the fate of kingdoms in the balance with straws. It is no part of courage to fight, to show that you are not afraid of fighting. Calm steady courage does not distrust itself; nor is it afraid that by giving up a trifling or doubtful point, it may afterwards be bullied into dangerous compliances . . . It is therefore of the highest consequence to ascertain the true grounds and motives of a war, to know the spirit and sentiments by which it is brought about . . . It is not from loud boasting, from what we think or say of ourselves, but from what we really are . . . Here then was a war voluntarily undertaken for its own sake, peace studiously shunned, and all the evils consequent upon such a step incurred, for the sake of making one more desperate effort to reduce the power of France, and humble it with the dust.

And all done to defend ourselves, of course: 'Of the necessity of this defence there can be but one opinion. But to confound this with the necessity of the war itself or to argue as if the discontinuance of the war would increase the dangers arising from it,' such was Government logic which drew forth his bitterest derision.

> It seems Malta was the enchanted island into which Buonaparte was to convey himself by stealth, and thence passing easily into Egypt was, at another vast stride, to come down *souse* upon our possessions in India. With these resting places, and the help of the thousand-league boots which our imagination had lent him, the political magician was to take but a hop, step and a jump, from one hemisphere into the other.

So the argument was mounted, and an awkward question was posed about who was the real aggressor. Hazlitt urged that we should be eager to accept that test, a good one for civilized standards between states, but even if this latest war unleashed by an English aggression were merged into the earlier one which had shaken Europe, what was our case? 'The gigantic strength and towering greatness of France had arisen from her convulsive struggles for existence, and in the cause of that liberty which was denied her. They, who had insulted her weakness and blasted her hopes, had no right to complain of her strength or her despair.' Thus the French case was presented brazenly and bravely, yet braver still and more apposite was the exposure of England's war leader William Pitt, and the distortions and subjugations he felt it necessary to impose on English society, the wanton destruction of English liberties combined with the elevation of the money-makers in all their squalor and greed. 'You give a manifest advantage to the enemy if you in any way lessen the sources of enthusiasm, or in any way check the ardour, confine the energy, degrade the sentiments, or discountenance the erect, manly, independent spirit of your country.' And no substitute for such a spirit, in Hazlitt's eyes, could come from those inspired by the love of gain.

31

They will defend England as connected with her colonies, with her proud canopies of Eastern state, her distant spicy groves and the rich spoils of her Western isles; but will they defend her as she is England, as their country? . . . They would defend their country not as her children, but as her masters; as a property, not as a state . . . As they believe money to be the only substantial good, they are also persuaded that it is the only instrument of power . . . I therefore think there ought to be as little connection as possible between the measures of government and the maxims of the Exchange, and that the interests of a great empire ought not to be managed by a company of factors.

Thus, in the peroration, the echo from Edmund Burke became more exact than ever, and Hazlitt would yield to no one in his love of England. 'Advice to a Patriot' was an attempt to summon afresh the old magnificent Foxite opposition to the war, in the name of liberty – just at the moment when Fox himself was no longer there to sustain the cause.

Perhaps the most awesome of all Hazlitt's polemical assaults was launched not at a poet or a politician, but rather a priest, the Reverend Thomas Robert Malthus, author of the *Essay on the Principle of Population*. Hazlitt saw at once, and more clearly than anyone else, the full menacing nature of the apparition, how surely was here offered a philosophy for the rich, an economic textbook for Tories, a faith as firm as a mathematical equation which could salve their consciences and cast the cloak of religion over the whole scene of human wretchedness.

I shall dispute Mr Malthus's right to thrust the poor man out of existence because there is no room for him 'at nature's mighty feast,' till he can give some better reason for it than that there is not room for an *unlimited number*! – The maintainance of the needy poor is a tax on the inequality of conditions and the luxuries of the rich, which they could not enjoy but in consequence of that general depression of the lower classes which continually subjects them to difficulties and want. It is a *douceur* to keep them quiet, and prevent them from enforcing those more solid, and important claims, not interfering with the right of property, but a direct consequence of the right of personal freedom, and of their right to set their own price on their own exertions, which would raise them above the reach of want, and enable them to maintain their own *poor*. But they cannot do this without a general combination of the labouring part of the community; and if any thing of this kind were to be attempted, the legislature we know would instantly interfere to prevent it. I know indeed that the legislature assumes a right to prevent combinations of the poor to keep themselves above want, though they *disclaim* any right to meddle with monopolies of corn, or other combinations *in the regular course of trade*, by which the rich and thriving endeavour to grind the poor. But though the men of property have thus retained the legislature on their side, Mr Malthus does not think this practical security sufficient: he thinks it absolutely necessary to recur to first principles; and that they may see how well qualified he is to act as chamber counsel in the business, he makes them a present of his Essay, written expressly for the purpose, and containing a new institute of the laws of nature, and a complete theory of population, in which it is clearly proved that the poor have no right to live any longer than the rich will let them. In this work which those to whom it is addressed should have bound in morocco, and constantly lying by them as a textbook to refer to in all cases of difficulty, it is shewn that there is no injustice in forcing the poorer classes to work almost for nothing, because they have no right to the produce of their labour, and no inhumanity in denying them assistance when they happen to be in want, because they ought not to be encouraged in idleness. Thus armed with 'metaphysical aid', and conscience-proof, the rich will I should think be able very successfully to resist the unjust claims of the poor – to a subsistence!

Hazlitt sensed better than most other articulate observers what was happening to *the people*, the bulk of them, in the England of his age. His politics were not rooted in theory although he did not despise theories. They were founded on what he saw and felt, and how, as with Edmund Burke, the passions and the imagination were unloosed to do their work. And yet again, agonizing as it must have been, the Hazlitt who had just found his voice still was compelled to speak anonymously. Partly this was due to the practice of the times and the force and unpopularity of his opinions, but it meant for Hazlitt that he could not carry his hardly-gained reputation in one field into another. None but a very few close friends would detect his talents. No contemporary reader of the day, neither Coleridge, Byron nor anyone else could read the Hazlitt we know with all his catholic tastes and emotional sympathies and complex political judgements. He took a particular pride in his own portraits of the four statesmen who had dominated the parliamentary stage in the age just before his own – Chatham, William Pitt, Edmund Burke, and Charles James Fox. Long buried in dusty cellars, these may be cleaned, after the modern fashion, to present the work of a political Rembrandt. Hazlitt in fact of course had never heard any of them speak, but he could record their individual arguments and accents, as he could those of Coleridge. It is curious that their value was not immediately appreciated, but Hazlitt valued them himself.*

The Hazlitt who had unloosed his onslaught against Malthus and all his pieties – it was renewed with sustained ferocity from year to year – had discovered his true mission; he had constructed an inner political citadel of conviction which he could guard against all comers for the rest of his life and from which he could make his forays in all directions thereafter. Politics *did* govern his mind; but politics should never be allowed to block

* These four first appeared in his two-volume *The Eloquence of the British Senate*, with Notes Biographical, Critical and Explanatory by William Hazlitt in 1807. He happily reprinted them in his *Political Essays*, published in 1819, and chunks of them in other places, but they have not been reprinted together anywhere else since, except in the full collected editions.

his search for truth and his search for beauty. These other quests need not be distracting: each could encourage the others, each without the others would prove vain. This was Hazlitt's peculiar faith which sometimes disrupted his dealing with the poets or the politicians or the journalists or some of his other chosen companions of the moment, and which, maybe, accounts for the comparatively slow awakening of his own literary genius.

Even after the considerable exertions of 1805, 1806 and 1807, no assured outlet for his writings opened before him. He was plunged into the political-cum-journalistic life of London but was by no reckoning a leading figure within it. He made firm friends with Charles and Mary Lamb, the most precious of his life, and married one of their company, Sarah Stoddard. He was friendly, too, with William Godwin, as he had been since the 1790s, and wrote an English grammar for Godwin to publish. One notorious figure of the Godwin circle was Thomas Holcroft, who had been among those tried for high treason in 1794 and acquitted thanks partly to Godwin's intervention. Holcroft died in 1808, and Hazlitt undertook the task of assembling his papers and writing his life. It was not an easy assignment, and his work upon it was described by Lamb as the Life Everlasting (it was actually published in 1816). But in 1812 and the years that followed his literary luck began to turn. He got a job as a parliamentary reporter for the *Morning Chronicle*, the leading Whig journal of the day, and was soon branching out in those columns into other fields. He delivered a series of lectures on his long-favoured, if abstruse, theme of English philosophy. He followed with sympathy and excitement the trial of Leigh Hunt, editor of the *Examiner*, tried and convicted for insulting the Prince Regent.

Leigh Hunt was another of the friends he had made at Lamb's fireside, and he proudly went to call on him at the Surrey Gaol. A few others, truly famous men, headed by Lord Byron and Jeremy Bentham, paid their visits too, but Hazlitt and Byron, alas, never bumped into one another. It was here, wrote Leigh Hunt (much later in his *Autobiography*) that 'Hazlitt first did me the honour of a visit, and would stand interchanging amenities at the threshold, which I had great difficulty in making him

pass. I know not which kept his hat off with the greater pertina-
city of deference, I to the diffident cutter-up of Tory dukes and
kings, or he to the amazing prisoner and invalid who issued out
of a bower of roses.' Hunt had decorated his prison room with
some flamboyance, and he was still able to edit his paper from
his commodious prison cell, but some other items in his recollection may be exaggerated. Hazlitt had not yet had the chance
to cut up kings and Tories with all the fine relish he was later to
display. He had only just started his career, as a fully-fledged
political and literary commentator, at the age of thirty-five, and
at this very moment, when he got his real first chance, the
national and international skies, for him, an opponent of the
war, grew darker month by month.

Yet 1814 was for Hazlitt a kind of *annus mirabilis*. It was the
year in which, in open defiance of the political defeats and
defeatism which engulfed him, he declared his own faith without qualification or restraint. It was the year in which he
denounced the whole war against France: 'a war of proscription
against a great and powerful state, for having set the example of
a people ridding itself of an odious and despicable tyranny. It
was the question of the balance of power between kings and
people; a question, compared with which the balance of power
in Europe is petty and insignificant.' It was the year in which he
went to see Edmund Kean perform as Shylock at the Drury
Lane Theatre – a momentous occasion, for Kean, for theatre
criticism, for Shakespearean criticism, for the Jewish people.
For the first two hundred years or so in which *The Merchant of
Venice* was performed, Shylock was the villainous and malignant Jew, without any heroic appeal whatever. Kean and
Hazlitt together ensured that thereafter he should acquire a new
character. Even those who never saw the one and never read
the other would not be able to escape the consequences. Hazlitt
went away and read the play with new eyes; Kean stepped to
glory with a single stride. The London of that age, even the
London of the England at war with Napoleon, bowed before
them – and both, be it not forgotten, were novices in their
respective trades.

Above all, 1814 was the year in which he first delivered his judgement on the great spirits who dominated his intellectual world. As we have seen from the lengthy apprenticeship he had served to reach this moment of opportunity, no one could accuse him of making up his mind flippantly. If it was a great event in the history of the English theatre when Edmund Kean first performed for William Hazlitt, it was no less an event in the history of English literature when William Hazlitt wrote his first criticism of William Wordsworth. For in 1814, Words-worth was not in any sense an established poet, and the poem he published in that year brought no swift alteration in his reputation; indeed it was furiously denounced – it was the one which Francis Jeffrey, in the formidable *Edinburgh Review*, said would *never do*.

Hazlitt had first heard the new poetry recited by Wordsworth himself, at Nether Stowey in 1798. He heard it again five years later on Grasmere Lake. He had read the book of Wordsworth's poems published in 1807. His ear was better attuned to the new tones than anyone else's. Yet to express an original judgement, openly and extensively – the review extended over three issues of the *Examiner* – was to attempt a feat of a quite different order. 'In power of intellect, in lofty conception in the depth of feeling, at once simple and sublime which pervades every part of it and which gives to every object an almost preternatural and preterhuman interest, this work has seldom been surpassed.' That was the opening salvo, and in all the pages and qualifications which followed it lost nothing of its impact. No great poet was ever heralded by a more discriminating critic, and of course the discrimination enhances the praise. It is hard to know which to admire the more – the rejection of current fashion with which the poem was being damned elsewhere, the whole spacious context in which the poem is placed, the flow of sensitive individual perceptions, even the delicacy of the rebuke for calling Voltaire 'dull': 'We can assure Mr Words-worth that we would not have bestowed so much on a single voluntary perversion of language but that our respect for his character makes us jealous of his smallest faults!' There, for sure, was a touch of sarcasm. Hazlitt did not always treat Wordsworth in so tender a tone, and perhaps he was already nursing in his subconscious the tremendous anti-Wordsworthian political philippics to which he would later give utterance. At the time he wrote it, *The Excursion* was much the most ambitious poem Wordsworth had attempted. Hazlitt's judgement of it was considered the bravest and best at the time, and has indeed been so considered ever since. He quoted at one stage the famous passage, or rather a passage which he made famous by his constant reiteration:

> At this day,
> When a Tartarian darkness overspreads
> The groaning nations; when the Impious rule,
> By will or by established ordinance,
> Their own dire agents, and constrain the Good
> To acts which they abhor; though I bewail
> This triumph, yet the pity of my heart
> Prevents me not from owning that the law,
> By which mankind now suffers, is most just.
> For by superior energies; more strict
> Affiance in each other; faith more firm
> In their unhallowed principles, the Bad
> Have fairly earned a victory o'er the weak,
> The vacillating, inconsistent Good.

Hazlitt indeed accepted the passion of that appeal. He made it part of his politics, and was entitled to add:

In the application of these memorable lines we should perhaps differ a little from Mr Wordsworth; nor can we indulge with him in the fond conclusion afterwards hinted at, that one day *our* triumph, the triumph of virtue and liberty, may be complete. For this purpose, we think several things necessary which are impossible. It is a consummation which cannot happen till the nature of things is changed, till the many become as the *one*, till romantic generosity shall be as common as gross selfishness, till reason shall have acquired the obstinate blindness of prejudice, till the love of power and of change shall no longer goad man on to restless action, till passion and will, hope and fear, love and hatred, and the objects proper to excite them, that is, alternate good and evil, shall no longer sway the bosoms and businesses of men. All things move not in progress, but in a ceaseless round; our strength lies in our weakness; our virtues are built on our vices; our faculties are as limited as our being; nor can we lift man above his nature more than above the earth he treads. But though we cannot weave over again the airy, unsubstantial dream, which reason and experience have dispelled –

'What though the radiance, which was once so bright
Be now for ever taken from our sight,
Though nothing can bring back the hour
Of glory in the grass, of splendour in the flower . . .'

– yet we will never cease, nor be prevented from returning on the wings of imagination to that bright dream of our youth; that glad dawn of the day-star of liberty; that springtime of the world, in which the hopes and expectations of the human race seemed opening in the same gay career with our own; when France called her children to partake her equal blessings under her laughing skies; when the stranger was met in all her villages with dance and festive songs, in celebration of a new and golden era; and when, to the retired and contemplative student, the prospects of human happiness and glory were seen ascending, like the steps of Jacob's ladder, in bright and never-ending succession. The dawn of that day was suddenly over-cast; that season of hope is past; it is fled with the other dreams of our youth, which we cannot recall, but has left behind it traces, which are not to be effaced by birth-day odes, or the chaunting of *Te Deums* in all the churches of Christendom. To those hopes eternal regrets are due; to those who maliciously and wilfully blasted them, in the fear that they might be accomplished, we feel no less what we owe – hatred and scorn as lasting.

Yet even that, his grand and legitimate political response, was not the end. He, first and foremost, saw Wordsworth as a true inheritor of the greatest English tradition, of Chaucer, Spenser, Shakespeare and Milton.

As he himself informs us, and as we can easily believe,

> ' – The meanest flow'r that blows can give
> Thoughts that do often lie too deep for tears.'

The extreme simplicity which some persons have objected to in Mr Wordworth's poetry is to be found only in the subject and the style; the sentiments are subtle and profound . . . His poems bear a distant resemblance to some of Rembrandt's landscapes . . . He has described the love of nature better than any other poet . . . We take Mr Wordsworth himself for a great poet, a fine moralist, and a deep philosopher . . . We conceive that about as many fine things have passed through Mr Wordsworth's mind as, with five or six exceptions, through any human mind whatever . . . It is not in our power to add to, or take away from the pretensions of a poem like the present, but if our opinion or wishes could have the least weight, we would take our leave of it by saying – *Esto perpetua!*

These were the final words, and these were the calculated, crushing encomiums which Hazlitt heaped on Wordsworth's head, interwoven it is true with some diversions and criticisms, mostly political, but none detracting one jot from the mighty, ecstatic conclusion.*

---

* Much the best modern comment upon Hazlitt's review of *The Excursion* is contained in David Bromwich's *Hazlitt: The Mind of a Critic*. Indeed, page after page in his book, author after author with whom he deals, prompts the same reference. 'Any author whom we love must be another self,' says Bromwich. Hazlitt might have said it. In this instance the phrase was provoked by Hazlitt on Rousseau; but it might as easily have been provoked by Hazlitt on Wordsworth. Moreover, David Bromwich shows by argument and illustration, how necessary it is to quote Hazlitt *at length*. I have

This was Hazlitt on *The Excursion*. What would he have written if he had ever been able to read *The Prelude*! It would have been a new 'Acquaintance with Poets', and as memorable for Wordsworth's fame as the other was for Coleridge's. One of Wordsworth's poems which he *was* able to read – written in 1814, as it happens – became a Hazlitt favourite, the exquisite *Laodamia*; it

> breathes the pure spirit of the finest fragments of antiquity – the sweetness, the gravity, the strength, the beauty and the languor of death –

> 'Calm contemplation and majestic pains.'

> Its glossy brilliancy arises from the perfection of the finishing, like that of a careful sculpture, not from gaudy colouring. The texture of the thoughts has the smoothness and solidity of marble. It is a poem that might be read aloud in Elysium, and the spirits and sages would gather round to listen to it!*

Hazlitt never abandoned or abated his faith in Wordsworth's originality and genius as a poet – for him the two words always overlapped and intermingled. After some fearful vicissitudes, the faith emerged stronger than ever. But there were good reasons, political and personal, why he felt compelled to quarrel

* Alas, it must be recorded that the solid marble so much admired by Hazlitt was chipped away in the most awkward place by the sculptor himself. For in later years Wordsworth returned to the 1815 edition which Hazlitt must surely have read and which was certainly the one he recommended for reading in the Elysian fields and substituted a much fiercer moral judgement upon Laodamia's passion: 'Ah, judge her gently who so deeply loved' was the earlier Wordsworth verdict, even in 1814. By 1827, it was altered: 'By no weak pity might the gods be moved.'

followed his example. Hazlitt, like not so many prose writers, is equally proficient in the abundance of his sharp aphorisms and the mounting, rhetorical outbursts which need space.

with Wordsworth, even while he honoured him. How he retained his objective attitude amid such tests is the most truly admirable of all his qualities, as a critic and as a man; it was part of that same faculty which enabled him to hold two competing truths in his mind at the same time, and to force from them not a wretched compromise, but a synthesis. And the provocation, against him, from Wordsworth's side, was truly severe.

One story which reached Hazlitt's ears later, and which he mockingly recapitulated, purported to tell how Wordsworth had read the *Examiner* reviews of *The Excursion* before he knew that Hazlitt was the author. He first objected that 'it was presumption in the highest degree for these Cockney writers to pretend to criticize a Lake poet'. But as the reading continued the scorn subsided: 'Ha, there's some sense in this fellow too,' Wordsworth was supposed to have remarked; 'the Dog writes strong.' But when the author's identity was revealed he was thrown into 'a fit of outrageous incredulity'. So beautiful an irony is hard to accept in every particular, but apart even from the evidence offered by the actual content of the review, there is plentiful proof that other readers were impelled towards similar conclusions. Crabb Robinson wrote in his diary (15 October): 'I read almost the whole day with interest the *Examiner* for the last three months. They contain an excellent review of Wordsworth's poem by Hazlitt.' Charles Lamb assured Coleridge that when Hazlitt 'sat down to write a critique of the *Excursion* he actually cried because he was disappointed and could not praise it as it deserved'. Crabb Robinson doubted the tears, but not the enthusiasm. A youthful John Keats, either then or soon afterwards, after reading that review and the poem or the two together, started to open for himself a new realm of gold. And, most tellingly of all, when Wordsworth himself came to London a few months later, having sent a presentation copy of his latest poems in advance, he made a special point of calling on Leigh Hunt to thank him for 'the zeal I had shown in advocating the cause of his genius'. The meeting between Hunt and Wordsworth was not entirely a happy one; Hunt knew that Wordsworth, like Southey and Coleridge, 'have both accepted office under Government, of such a nature as absolutely ties up their independence', and he could not help noting the egotism and vanity upon which Hazlitt so often remarked.

On that same fateful day, 11 June 1815, the *Examiner* had carried not the review of his new book of poems which Words-worth might have hoped for, but a review of a performance of Milton's *Comus* which Hazlitt had contributed, and in which he had extolled Milton both as a poet and a patriot:

> He did not retract his defence of the people of England; he did not say that his sonnets to Vane or Cromwell were meant ironically; he was not appointed Poet Laureate to a Court which he had reviled and insulted; he accepted nei-ther place nor pension; nor did he write paltry sonnets upon the 'Royal Fortitude' of the House of Stuart.

And then followed the footnote:

> In the last edition of the works of a modern poet, there is a sonnet to the King complimenting him on his 'royal fortitude'. The story of the Female Vagrant, which very beautifully and affectingly describes the miseries brought on the lower classes by war, in bearing which the said 'royal fortitude' is so nobly exercised, is very properly struck out from the collection.

In fact, the 'Female Vagrant' poem did appear in that same vol-ume in a somewhat different form – so in this criticism Hazlitt had been careless. But the accompanying sonnet to the King was there in all its shame and sycophancy. It was the war, then mounting to its climax at Waterloo, which had cut the gulf between them so deep. If Wordsworth and Coleridge too had kept their polemics on this plane, the contest would have been more creditable to their fame. It would have been enough, if they had so wished, to pillory Hazlitt for his Bonapartist hero-worship and the shattering defeat he and his hero had shared.

A week after the meeting between Wordsworth and Leigh Hunt, Wordsworth discussed the matter with Crabb Robinson, and described how Hunt had 'disclaimed the article', that is, the one containing the comparison with Milton. 'This led', the diarist recorded, and the words should always be recorded carefully since this was the first account from Wordsworth's own lips of what had allegedly happened fourteen years before:

> This led to W.'s mentioning the cause of his coolness towards H. It appears that H. when at Keswick narrowly escaped being ducked by the populace and probably sent to prison for some gross attacks on women. (Here follow half a dozen words in the diarist's not infrequent shorthand, the key to which is lacking.) The populace were incensed against him and pursued him, but he escaped to W. who took him into his house at midnight, gave him clothes and money (from 3 to 5 pounds). Since that time W. though he never refused to meet W. [sic] when by accident they came together did not choose that with his knowledge he should be invited. In consequence Lamb never asked H. when he was in town, which probably provoked H. and which Lamb himself disapproved of. But L. who needs very little indulgence for himself is very indulgent towards others, and rather reproaches W. for being inveterate against H.

This then was the first Wordsworth account of the so-called Keswick affair. A second account was given by Wordsworth to Robert Haydon as they strolled down Pall Mall a few days later:

> He was relating to me with great horror Hazlitt's licentious conduct to the girls of the Lake, and that no woman could walk after dark, 'for his Satyr and *beastly* appetites'. Some girl called him a black-faced rascal when Hazlitt enraged pushed her down, 'and because, Sir,' said Wordsworth, 'she refused to gratify his abominable and devilish propensities', he lifted up her petticoats and *smote* her *on the bottom*.

A third account was given by Coleridge, some months later again, who spoke of Hazlitt as one 'whom Southey and myself at our own hazard saved from infamy and transportation in return for his having done his best by the most loathsome conduct (known to all the neighbourhood of Keswick and Grasmere but ourselves and the Wordsworths) to bring disgrace on our names and families'. These shattering revelations take no account of the friendly exchanges between Wordsworth and Hazlitt after he had left Grasmere and after the whole countryside was supposedly astir with news of his misdemeanours. But these were hysterical times. The atmosphere of wartime, even a wartime not so afflicted with totalitarian culture as our century has known, could turn even poets into pitiless, embittered propagandists.

Hazlitt was devastated by the news of Napoleon's defeat (infinitely more so, it seems, than by the Keswick gossip now filtering out, since he never troubled to make any direct rebuttal of the charges). He grieved long and hard and, if Haydon is to be believed, plunged into a drunken stupor which led him to his resolution never to drink again. But he was in no mood for political weakness or retreat, in any form whatever, and even if he had ever been tempted in this direction, the monstrous nature and scale of the counter-revolution, led sometimes by the poets, guided him back into the political arena. Robert Southey, the newly appointed Poet Laureate, would have consigned some of his fellow journalists to Botany Bay. Coleridge addressed Lord Liverpool, the Prime Minister: 'It is high time, my Lord, that the subjects of Christian Governments should be taught that neither historically or morally, in fact or by right, have men made the state; but that the state, and that alone, makes them men.' Here was the ancient Tory doctrine of Edmund Burke sharpened into an implement of tyranny such as Burke would never have dared to express. And Wordsworth had come to London with his Thanksgiving Odes, celebrating not only the victory but the war itself, reminding the Deity that

> Thy most dreaded instrument,
> In working out a pure intent,
> Is Man – arrayed for mutual slaughter,
> – Yea, Carnage is thy daughter!

Before that piece of blasphemy, the Christians were subdued, the infidels were outraged, even the author – at a much later date – felt a spasm of remorse.

If 1814 was Hazlitt's *Annus Mirabilis*, the miracle was repeated in each of the five years from 1815 to 1820. Throughout the whole period, he was swimming against the current. His political essays found their way month by month into the few journals which would dare to print them; they started to provide the answer of English radicalism to Edmund Burke but they also touched on the raw of most of the immediate controversies. He wrote regular theatre criticisms, almost week by week; he wrote of the characters in Shakespeare's plays in a way which opened a new vista in Shakespearean criticism; he got published, at last, his 'everlasting' life of Holcroft; he found his way into new fields, among the Elizabethan or Restoration playwrights or the English comic writers. He pondered most deeply on the English poets, past and present, and was prepared to deliver his iconoclastic judgements, even at the moment when the political storms were blowing most fiercely. Even when his political dreams seemed so nearly crushed for ever, he conducted his high critical debates with Coleridge, Wordsworth, Burke, Byron and several more of hardly lesser stature. He was accused of letting his politics sour his literary judgement. The opposite was much truer; he proved his disinterestedness and the absolute integrity of his judgements, as few other critics have done before or since. It was the age of Waterloo and Peterloo, of a war which brought glory and fame for the few, but bitter humiliation and hardship for the mass of the people. An English radical, in such an age, could be congratulated, or forgiven, if, like Thomas Paine or William Cobbett, he chose to devote all his exertions to politics. But Hazlitt would not, or could not, follow that example; that would mean the forfeit of the whole cultural tradition of the nation into the care of Wordsworth, Coleridge and the rest, yes with Edmund Burke at their head. That would be an eternal, irredeemable betrayal, and Hazlitt knew that here he had his own special role to play. But the apparent alternative, to leave politics to the politicians, to withdraw into some poet's haven or ivory tower, to stifle his rising fury, Hazlitt would have none of that either. He knew that the intellectual field should never, could never, be left to others. Sometimes it has been alleged, quite falsely and mostly by accusers who had the advantage of delivering the indictment when he was safely in his grave, that he did turn aside from the rough political arena to follow his other joyous pursuits of painting, poetry, philosophy and the rest. His *Political Essays**, produced in this period, are there to kill the charge. He carried that same political faith and judgement wherever he went. One of the editors for whom he worked at this time, John Scott of the *London Magazine*, said that he took his politics around with him like a giant mastiff, and, 'love me, love my dog' was his motto.

Thus his invectives in those political essays comprehend the whole array of the establishment of his day, the 'Thing', as his fellow practitioner, William Cobbett, used to call it:

THE KING: 'The ancients sometimes worshipped the sun or stars, or deified heroes and great men: the moderns have found out the image of the divinity in Louis XVIII.'

THE TORIES: 'A Tory is one who is governed by sense and habit alone . . . His principle is to follow the leader; and this is the infallible rule to have numbers and success on your side, to be on the side of success and numbers.'

THE WHIGS: 'A Whig is properly what is called a Trimmer – that is, a coward to both sides of a question, who dare not be a knave nor an honest man, but is a sort of whiffling, snuffling, cunning, silly, contemptible negation of the two.'

THE DIPLOMATS: 'This question of Africa, being considered as an idle question, in which neither courts nor ministers

---

* The *Political Essays*, published in 1819, have been republished in the collected editions, but never as a separate product. Perhaps that is one explanation of the false perception of his all-embracing politics.

were concerned, would be naturally left as a sort of *carte-blanche* for all the flourishes of national *politesse*, as a kind of *no man's ground* for a trial of diplomatic skill and complaisance. So Lord Castlereagh, drawing on his gloves, hemmed once or twice, while the French minister carelessly took snuff: he then introduced the question with a smile, which was answered by a more gracious smile from M. Talleyrand; his Lordship then bowed, as if to bespeak attention; but the Prince of Benevento bowing still lower, prevented what he had to say; and the cries of Africa were lost amidst the nods and smiles and shrugs of these demi-puppets.'

THE PHILANTHROPISTS: 'The great problem of our great problem-finders appears to be, *to take nothing from the rich, and give it to the poor.'*

THE LAWYERS: 'The opinions of the gentlemen of the bar go for nothing in the House of Commons: but their votes tell; and are always sure – in the end.'

THE PARSONS: 'They therefore venture out into the streets with this gratuitous obtrusion of opinion and unwarrantable assumption of character wrapped about them, ticketted and labelled with the Thirty-nine Articles, St. Athanasius's Creed, and the Ten Commandments, – with the Cardinal Virtues and the Apostolic Faith sticking out of every corner of their dress, and angling for the applause or contempt of the multitude. A full-dressed ecclesiastic is a sort of go-cart of divinity; an ethical automaton. A clerical prig is, in general, a very dangerous as well as contemptible character. The utmost that those who thus habitually confound their opinions and sentiments with the outside coverings of their bodies can aspire to, is a negative and neutral character, like wax-work figures, where the dress is done as much to the life as the man, and where both are respectable pieces of pasteboard, or harmless compositions of fleecy hosiery.'

THE EDITORS (of *The Times* especially 'ever strong on the stronger side'): 'In 1792 Mr. Thomas Paine was outlawed for his *Rights of Man*. Since that period, the press has been "the great enemy of freedom".'

He attacked the whole establishment but the individuals too; since Hazlitt certainly could not be accused of any cowardly resort to concealment:

ROBERT SOUTHEY: 'Poor Bob Southey! how they laugh at him! What are the abuse and contumely which we are in the habit of bestowing upon him, compared with the cordial contempt, the flickering sneers, that play round the lips of his new-fangled friends, when they see "the Man of Humanity" decked out in the trappings of his prostitution, and feel the rankling venom of their hearts soothed by the flattering reflection that virtue and genius are mere marketable commodities! What a squeeze must that be which Mr. Canning gives the hand that wrote the Sonnet to Old Sarum, and the Defence of Rotten Boroughs in the Quarterly Review! . . . As some persons bequeath their bodies to the surgeons to be dissected after their death, Mr. Southey publicly exposes his mind to be anatomized while he is living. He lays open his character to the scalping-knife, guides the philosophic hand in its painful researches, and on the bald crown of our *petit tondu*, in vain concealed under withered bay-leaves and a few contemptible grey hairs, you see the organ of vanity triumphant – sleek, smooth, round, perfect, polished, horned, and shining, as it were in a transparency.'

So Hazlitt would fight his enemies – and ours, the people's enemies throughout the ages. The same Hazlitt had comprehended for himself what poetry was and why this knowledge, like his political understanding, must be shared with his friends and allies. 'Poetry is the universal language which the heart holds with nature and itself. He who has a contempt for poetry, cannot have much respect for himself, or for anything else. It is not a mere frivolous accomplishment . . . it has been the study and delight of mankind in all ages.' These were some of his first sentences when he rose to deliver the lectures at the Surrey Institution, Great Surrey Street, near Blackfriars Bridge, during January and February 1818. In that opening lecture 'On Poetry in General', the passion infuses every paragraph. 'Man is a poetical animal . . . Poetry puts a spirit of life and motion into the universe . . . It is the language of the imagination.' No one can doubt how devoted he was to this cause too. Whatever he thought of the poets, no one except the poets themselves had ever exulted in their art with the same gusto.

> The poetical impression of any object is that uneasy exquisite sense of beauty or power that cannot be contained within itself; that is impatient of all limit; that (as flame bends to flame) strives to link itself to some other image of kindred beauty or grandeur; to enshrine itself as it were, in the highest forms of fancy, and to relieve the aching sense of pleasure by expressing it in the boldest manner.

It was an essay on the imagination: the word mentioned thirty-seven times in this first lecture. And the boldness with which he spoke was matched by the freshness with which he was ready to summon the very greatest names: 'Homer's poetical world has outlived Plato's philosophical Republic . . . The tragedy of Shakespeare which is true poetry stirs our inmost affections; abstracts evil from itself by combining with it all the forms of imagination, and with the deepest workings of the heart and rouses the whole man within us'; and the poetry of the Bible: 'Jacob's dream arose out of this intimate communion between heaven and earth . . . The story of Ruth, again, is as if all the depth of natural affection in the human race was involved in her breast'; and Dante: 'He stood bewildered, not appalled, on that dark shore which separates the ancient and the modern world . . . He is power, passion, self-will personified.' Who could ever be expected to compete with such giants? John Bunyan, maybe: 'His pilgrims walk above the earth, and yet are on it.'

Hazlitt was fit to judge, no one could doubt it. No one could question his disinterestedness. Had he not himself acquired something of Shakespeare's imagination which 'unites the most opposite extremes', the genius which shines 'on the evil and the good, on the wise and the foolish, the monarch and the beggar'? Of course, he never made such a claim on his own behalf; indeed he persistently denied it. Yet his lecture 'On Poetry in General' is a poem, like Bunyan's, a new Jacob's dream. 'Poetry is only the highest eloquence of passion, the most vivid form of expression that can be given to our conception of anything, whether pleasurable or painful, mean or dignified, delightful or distressing. It is the perfect coincidence of the image and the words.' So he lectured on Shakespeare and Milton, on Dryden and Pope, on Donne, Waller, Marvel, Butler, Rochester, Suckling, on Thomson and Cowper, on Swift, Young, Gray, Collins, Prior, Johnson, Chatterton and Robert Burns. It was a comprehensive and, in one sense, an orthodox list; most of the most famous names in our literary history appeared on it. Hazlitt revered the judgements of the past, but he never failed to offer his own view which could sometimes shatter previous perceptions. He contrasted, for example, the style of the writing of the age of Queen Anne and the style of Dr Johnson: 'The one is English and the other is not.' Hazlitt was the first critic who dared to question the ascendancy which Dr Johnson had so recently and near-fatally established, and he did it with a flair and a daring which still can make us gasp:

> Dr. Johnson takes the first English word that offers, and by translating it at a venture into the first Greek or Latin word he can think of, only retaining the English termination, produces an extraordinary effect upon the reader by much the same sort of mechanical process that Trim converted the old jack-boots into a pair of new mortars. Dr. Johnson was a lazy learned man who liked to think and talk better than to read or write; who, however, wrote much and well, but too often by rote.

Quite an attack, from an unknown man on the great presiding panjandrum of English letters, and in those same lectures, we

51

should remember and celebrate too, he restored the poetry and prose of the Queen Anne period to its proper place and in particular put Jonathan Swift back on the pedestal from which Dr Johnson had sought to displace him, and to defame him in the process. It is often forgotten now how far the defamation of Swift had proceeded before Hazlitt came to his aid. Hazlitt indeed extolled Swift as a poet, as a prose writer, and, maybe above all, as a man. 'There is nothing more likely to drive a man mad than the being made to get rid of the idea of the distinction between right and wrong, and an obstinate, constitutional preference of the true to the agreeable.' Hazlitt, it may be said, anticipated the twentieth-century view of the sanity of Swift, when if we had been forced to rely on Dr Johnson's Christian mercies, he would be left to swing as 'a driveller and show'. And the same discernment and generosity was applied to a much more modern figure, not at that date yet accorded his national and international reputation, Robert Burns. In defiance of popular opinion, Hazlitt could delineate Burns's virtues as surely as he could Swift's:

> He had a strong mind and a strong body, the fellow to it. He had a real heart of flesh and blood beating in his bosom – you can almost hear it throb . . . He was not like Shakespeare in the range of his genius; but there is something of the same magnanimity, directness and unaffected character about him . . . He has made us as well acquainted with himself as it is possible to be.

And thus, with a side glance at Wordsworth who had 'missed the chance of doing Burns justice and himself honour', he came to modern times, to the living poets, in judgement of whom the reputation of critics, if not poets, must rest. He had trained himself for the task. He was ready for the test.

Here, too, we must emphasize how legitimate it is to combine what Hazlitt said about the living poets in 1818 with his continued comments upon them through the next few years, culminating in *The Spirit of the Age* Essays in 1824, in which most of the same poets took their place. His verdicts were softened somewhat, or rather became more subtle and synthetized, during this intervening period, but his consistency remained. The intervening years saw him emerge more as an essayist than a critic, not that he himself ever drew any sharp distinction between the two functions. They saw too his famous or infamous love affair with Sarah Walker which he enshrined in his anonymous *Liber Amoris*, of which everyone knew him to be the author and the victim. Whatever else that affair did, he had momentarily played into the hands of his political enemies, and this was the crime he found it hard to forgive himself. Even *The Spirit of the Age*, his next volume, comprising some of the greatest essays in the language, had to be anonymous too. But the Hazlitt style was now unmistakeable and inimitable. It is hard to believe that he censored or even softened a single word in deference to the host of literary enemies whom he had mobilized against him by one means or another. He truly treasured his own judgement, his anticipations of posterity's judgement.

The 'Living Poets' lecture was chiefly concerned with five of his leading contemporaries – Scott, Wordsworth, Coleridge, Southey and Byron. But his glances at some of the others are too good to be missed altogether. He made a gracious but not too flattering bow towards some of the poetesses, Mrs Barbauld, Mrs Hannah More, Miss Bailie, and then attempted the not very difficult transition to Samuel Rogers; 'he is a very ladylike poet . . . full of enigmas with no meaning . . . the whole frittered away into an appearance of the most evanescent brilliancy and tremulous imbecility'. Considering how high Samuel Rogers stood in the estimate of others, Byron for example, not to mention his own, this was a bold declaration. The next on his list was the well-established Thomas Campbell – 'Lest he should wander irretrievably from the right path, he stands still.' Mr Campbell liked to be popular: but 'it is the business of reviewers to watch poets, not of poets to watch reviewers'. Thomas Moore was a more considerable figure, and the 1818 version acclaimed his wit, even when it displayed 'a certain sickliness of pretension'. But by 1824 the verdict here had become deadly: 'he cloys with sweetness; he obscures with splendour; he fatigues with gaiety. We are stifled in beds of roses. We literally lie "on the rack of restless ecstasy".' And most damning of all, on his *Irish Melodies*: 'If these national airs do indeed express the soul of impassioned feeling in his countrymen, the case of Ireland is hopeless . . . There are here no tones to waken Liberty, to console Humanity. Mr. Moore converts the wild harp of Erin into a musical snuff-box.' When Hazlitt dared to strike that blow, Thomas Moore was still a general favourite, and the same applied to Walter Scott, 'the most popular of all the poets of the present day and deservedly so'. With him, Hazlitt was much less fierce but no less discriminating. He admired Scott as a novelist almost beyond his own powers of description, and yet he deftly detected Scott's weaknesses as a poet when this was still his chief claim to fame – 'It is history or tradition in masquerade. Not only the crust of old words and images is worn off with time – the substance is grown comparatively light and worthless.' A great poet must have more and much more. 'A great mind is one that moulds the minds of others.'

The poet who best fitted this last supreme requirement in Hazlitt's estimate was Wordsworth, and no listener at those lectures could doubt the pre-eminence accorded him. He was 'the most original poet now living'. He 'opened a finer and deeper vein of thought and feeling than any poet in modern times has done, or attempted. He has produced a deeper impression, and on a smaller circle, than any other of his contemporaries.' And yet there were weaknesses, and he added hastily and justly: 'I am not, however, one of those who laugh at the attempts or failures of men of genius.' Hazlitt did not use that last word lightly, yet it was never far from his lips when he spoke of Wordsworth. He hated to see how some of Wordsworth's particular poems had been garbled in their presentation for the public, and he attempted an immediate remedy by reading the whole of 'Hart-Leap Well', leading to its lovely climax:

> One lesson, Shepherd, let us two divide,
> Taught both by what she shews, and what conceals,
> Never to blend our pleasure or our pride
> With sorrow of the meanest thing that feels.

So Hazlitt let Wordsworth speak for himself (quite an agreeable change from 'Carnage is thy daughter'!) but he also felt entitled to recall what was one of the origins of the Lake school of poetry of which Wordsworth was the undoubted head. It was born of the French Revolution, of a mighty ferment in the heads of statesmen and poets, kings and people. 'They founded the new school of poetry on a principle of sheer humanity, on pure nature void of art.' So far, so good, and then followed, here and his other critical pieces, a brilliant twist in the argument. Somehow the revolutionary zeal which they abandoned became transmuted into an uncontrolled egotism. Hazlitt adored the one, and despised the other, and was infuriated even more when he detected the connection.

> They took the same method in their new-fangled 'metre ballad-mongering' scheme, which Rousseau did in his prose paradoxes – of exciting attention by reversing the established standards of opinion and estimation in the world. They were for bringing poetry back to its primitive simplicity and state of nature, as he was for bringing society back to the savage state: so that the only thing remarkable left in the world by this change, would be the persons who had produced it. A thorough adept in this school of poetry and philanthropy is jealous of all excellence but his own. He does not even like to share his reputation with his subject; for he would have it all proceed from his own power and originality of mind. Such a one is slow to admire any thing that is admirable; feels no interest in what is most interesting to others, no grandeur in any thing grand, no beauty in anything beautiful. He tolerates only what he himself creates; he sympathizes only with what can enter into no competition with him, with 'the bare trees and mountains bare, and grass in the green field'. He sees nothing but himself and the universe. He hates all greatness and all pretensions to it, whether well or ill-founded. His egotism is in some respects a madness; for he scorns even the admiration of himself, thinking it a presumption in any one to suppose that he has taste or sense enough to understand

him. He hates all science and all art; he hates chemistry, he hates conchology; he hates Voltaire; he hates Sir Isaac New-ton; he hates wisdom; he hates wit; he hates metaphysics, which he says are unintelligible, and yet he would be thought to understand them; he hates prose; he hates all poetry but his own; he hates the dialogues in Shakespeare; he hates music, dancing, and painting; he hates Rubens, he hates Rembrandt; he hates Raphael, he hates Titian; he hates Vandyke; he hates the antique; he hates the Apollo Belvidere; he hates the Venus of Medicis. This is the reason that so few people take an interest in his writings, because he takes an interest in nothing that others do! – The effect has been perceived as something odd; but the cause or prin-ciple has never been distinctly traced to its source before, as far as I know. The proofs are to be found every where – in Mr. Southey's Botany Bay Eclogues, in his book of Songs and Sonnets, his Odes and Inscriptions, so well parodied in the Anti-Jacobin Review, in his Joan of Arc, and last, though not least, in his Wat Tyler:

'When Adam delved, and Eve span,
Where was then the gentleman?'

(– or the poet laureat either, we may ask?) – In Mr. Cole-ridge's Ode to an Ass's Foal, in his Lines to Sarah, his Reli-gious Musings; and in his and Mr. Wordsworth's Lyrical Ballads, *passim*.

This was one of the very rare passages in his writings for which Hazlitt felt it necessary to make some sort of apology. 'Mere epigrams and jeux d'esprit, as far from the truth as they are free from malice.' But that was a reference to some of the embellishments of his general thesis, not to the thesis itself. He would not modify his exposure of one aspect of Wordsworth's poetry, his absorption with himself, 'the egotistical sublime', but he felt it all the more necessary to explain – and he did it bet-ter than anyone else, better than Coleridge who never showed the same understanding or generosity in his critical writings –

why the new poetry had been heard, way back in 1798 and ever since, with such tingling excitement. Hazlitt certainly achieved this again in *The Spirit of the Age*, with most of the distraction removed. For truly, as he said, Wordsworth was for him 'a pure emanation of the Spirit of the Age' . . .

It is one of the innovations of the time. It partakes of, and is carried along with, the revolutionary movement of our age: the political changes of the day were the model on which he formed and conducted his poetical experiments. His Muse (it cannot be denied, and without this we cannot explain its character at all) is a levelling one. It proceeds on a principle of equality, and strives to reduce all things to the same standard. It is distinguished by a proud humility. It relies upon its own resources, and disdains external show and relief. It takes the commonest events and objects, as a test to prove that nature is always interesting from its inherent truth and beauty, without any of the ornaments of dress or pomp of circumstances to set it off. . . No one has shown the same imagination in raising trifles into importance: no one has displayed the same pathos in treating of the simplest feelings of the heart. Reserved, yet haughty, having no unruly or violent passions (or those passions having been early suppressed), Mr. Wordsworth has passed his life in solitary musing or in daily converse with the face of nature. He exemplifies in an eminent degree the power of *association*; for his poetry has no other source or character. He has dwelt among pastoral scenes, till each object has become connected with a thousand feelings, a link in the chain of thought, a fibre of his own heart. Every one is by habit and familiarity strongly attached to the place of his birth, or to objects that recall the most pleasing and eventful circumstances of his life. But to the author of the *Lyrical Ballads* nature is a kind of home; and he may be said to take a personal interest in the universe. There is no image so insignificant that it has not in some mood or other found the way into his heart: no sound that does not awaken the memory of other years. –

'To him the meanest flower that blows can give
Thoughts that do often lie too deep for tears.'

The daisy looks up to him with sparkling eye as an old acquaintance: the cuckoo haunts him with sounds of early youth not to be expressed: a linnet's nest startles him with boyish delight: an old withered thorn is weighed down with a heap of recollections: a grey cloak, seen on some wild moor, torn by the wind or drenched in the rain, afterwards becomes an object of imagination to him: even the lichens on the rock have a life and being in his thoughts. He has described all these objects in a way and with an intensity of feeling that no one else had done before him, and has given a new view or aspect of nature. He is in this sense the most original poet now living, and the one whose writings could the least be spared: for they have no substitute elsewhere.

None of the others tested Hazlitt's combined critical judgement and magnanimity as Wordsworth did, but the manner in which he treated them never lost its interest. Robert Southey he brushed aside with some derision in the lectures, and since the newly elected Poet Laureate was still in his 'Botany Bay' mood, no excuse needs to be offered. His innocence had its attractions, 'while the light of the French Revolution beamed into his soul . . .' but when his chimeras and golden dreams of human perfectibility vanished from him, he turned suddenly round and maintained that:

'whatever is, is right. Mr. Southey has not fortitude of mind, has not patience to think that evil is inseparable from the nature of things. His irritable sense rejects the alternative altogether, as a weak stomach rejects the food that is distasteful to it. He hopes on against hope: he believes in all unbelief. He must either repose on actual or on an imaginary good. He missed his way in *Utopia*: he has found it at Old Sarum . . .'

So Southey could be scorned, and sometimes Coleridge

deserved the same treatment, and if Hazlitt had been interested in personal vendettas he might have dealt with Coleridge in the same manner. But whenever he heard the name, he heard the voice too, and even in his most iconoclastic moods he would become captivated again. He would never forget, as we too can never forget, his first meetings at Shrewsbury and Wem and Nether Stowey.

> He is the only person I ever knew who answered to the idea of a man of genius . . . He was the first poet I ever knew. His genius at that time had angelic wings, and fed on manna. He talked on for ever; and you wished him to talk on for ever. His thoughts did not seem to come with labour and effort; but as if borne on the gusts of genius, and as if the wings of his imagination lifted him from off his feet. . . You then saw the process of human happiness and liberty and never ending succession, like the steps of Jacob's ladder.

Yes, it was Coleridge it seems, who gave Hazlitt that most indelible of his political visions, and who could still repeat the feat. Coleridge's talk was, for sure, one of the wonders of the age, and Hazlitt could recall it better than anyone:

> One of the finest and rarest parts of Mr. Coleridge's conversation is, when he expatiates on the Greek tragedians (not that he is not well acquainted, when he pleases, with the epic poets, or the philosophers, or orators, or historians of antiquity) – on the subtle reasonings and melting pathos of Euripides, on the harmonious gracefulness of Sophocles, tuning his love-laboured song, like sweetest warblings from a sacred grove; on the high-wrought, trumpet-tongued eloquence of Æschylus, whose Prometheus, above all, is like an Ode to Fate and a pleading with Providence, his thoughts being let loose as his body is chained on his solitary rock, and his afflicted will (the emblem of mortality)

> Struggling in vain with ruthless destiny.

59

As the impassioned critic speaks and rises in his theme, you would think you heard the voice of the Man hated by the Gods, contending with the wild winds as they roar; and his eye glitters with the spirit of Antiquity!

Only by a severe wrench – in the *Spirit of the Age* essay – could Hazlitt return from the voice to the writings.

Of all Mr. Coleridge's productions, the *Ancient Mariner* is the only one that we could with confidence put into any person's hands, on whom we wished to impress a favourable idea of his extraordinary powers, but whatever other objections be put to it, it is unquestionably a work of genius – of wild, irregular overwhelming imagination, and has that rich varied movement in the verse which gives a distant idea of the lofty or changeful tones of Mr. Coleridge's voice.'

There again the voice: Hazlitt never ceased to hear it, even when he believed it had been used to betray the cause of those who had kindled their affections at the blaze of the French Revolution:

It was a misfortune to any man of talent to be born in the latter end of the last century. Genius stopped the way of Legitimacy, and therefore it was to be abated, crushed, or set aside as a nuisance. The spirit of the monarchy was at variance with the spirit of the age. The flame of liberty, the light of intellect, was to be extinguished with the sword – or with slander, whose edge is sharper than the sword. The war between power and reason was carried on by the first of these abroad, by the last at home. No quarter was given (then or now) by the Government-critics, the authorized censors of the press, to those who followed the dictates of independence, who listened to the voice of the tempter, Fancy. Instead of gathering fruits and flowers, immortal fruits and amaranthine flowers, they soon found themselves beset not only by a host of prejudices, but assailed with all the engines of power: by nicknames, by lies, by all the arts of malice, interest and hypocrisy, without the possibility of their defending themselves 'from the pelting of the pitiless storm' that poured down upon them from the strongholds of corruption and authority.

The philosophers, the dry abstract reasoners, submitted to this reverse pretty well, and armed themselves with patience 'as with triple steel', to bear discomfiture, persecution, and disgrace. But the poets, the creatures of sympathy, could not stand the frowns both of king and people. They did not like to be shut out when places and pensions, when the critic's praises, and the laurel wreath were about to be distributed. They did not stomach being *sent to Coventry*, and Mr. Coleridge sounded a retreat for them by the help of casuistry and a musical voice. – 'His words were hollow, but they pleased the ear' of his friends of the Lake School, who turned back disgusted and panic-struck from the dry desert of unpopularity, like Hassan the camel-driver,

> 'And curs'd the hour, and curs'd the luckless day,
> When first from Shiraz' walls they bent their way.'

They are safely inclosed there. But Mr. Coleridge did not enter with them; pitching his tent upon the barren waste without, and having no abiding place nor city of refuge.

Wordsworth and Coleridge were the two living poets who made the deepest imprint on Hazlitt's mind; nothing could erase the memory of 1798. But they both became political enemies, and these ruptures could never be repaired, however much he still resolved to retain his awareness of their genius. But he also had political friends or potential political friends among the poets. The test for his integrity and intelligence, in judging them, was more subtle and severe.

Leigh Hunt was one with whom, after a few years, he established both a 'personal intimacy' and a form of political-cum-literary alliance, and he was eager to acclaim his friend's talents. He praised sections of Hunt's *Story of Rimini* for its 'charm and elegance and natural feeling', picked out his

'Epistle to Lord Byron' on his going abroad, as 'a masterpiece', and praised too the 'light, familiar grace, and mild unpretending pathos' of many of his other writings. Yet his tribute to the poet was constrained, and he eagerly asserted: 'The author translates admirably into the man', and the phrase was intended as the surest of tributes: 'Indeed the very faults of his style are virtues in the individual. His natural gaiety and sprightliness of manner, his high animal spirits, and the *vinous* quality of his mind, produce an immediate fascination and intoxication in those who come in contact with him.' Such was the exhilaration of the Hampstead fireside which Leigh Hunt offered to his friends. Hazlitt, like some others, appreciated it all the more since the welcome was given before he had achieved any real fame of his own and when political hostility from other quarters was at its fiercest.

It was here too, in Leigh Hunt's Hampstead cottage, that he first met John Keats before he had even started on his poetical career, and the companionship, intellectual rather than personal, between them became one of the profoundest influences on Keats's life and, moreover, on the whole development of English poetry. Henceforth Hazlitt's ideas were reflected in Keats's poetry but even more indelibly in his letters which came to be regarded as the most revealing ever written by an English poet. It was Hazlitt in those lectures on the English poets at the Surrey Institution, or Hazlitt talking on the walk to Hampstead or Hazlitt writing in Leigh Hunt's *Examiner* who was responsible for most of the introductions which made Keats the poet he became – to Shakespeare, to Wordsworth and several more. In particular it was Hazlitt's *Excursion* article, written at the time when Wordsworth was still rejected or neglected in fashionable quarters, which caught Keats's imagination; it was Hazlitt's 'disinterestedness' which Keats so much admired and emulated, and truly, on his side, the debt was fully understood and expressed: 'I know he thinks himself not estimated by ten people in the world. I wish I knew he is . . . he is your only good damner. . . He hath a demon, as he himself says of Lord Byron.'

But what was Hazlitt's view of his young disciple? Many have been puzzled why he did not write more extensively on

Keats, a full-scale essay instead of the gleaming, tantalizing single sentences and paragraphs that were not Hazlitt's usual way of letting a subject rest. Keats was not included among the living poets in the lecture (he was there in the audience instead), and by the time *The Spirit of the Age* was published he was dead. We have to be content with half glimpses. In the Cockney School battles, against 'the jackals from the North', Hazlitt happily clasped Keats to his bosom as a brother in arms:

> Mr. Keats, whose misfortune and crime it is, like Milton, to have been born in London is a much better poet than Mr. Wilson, or his Patroclus, Mr. Lockart; nay, further, if Sir Walter Scott (the sly Ulysses of the Auld Reekie School) had written many of the passages in Mr. Keats's poems, they would have been quoted as the most beautiful of his works.

And such tributes, it should be especially noted, must have been written before Keats's assailants or his defender had had the chance of reading his final and greatest poems. The same point about timing seems to apply to the oft-quoted criticism which he did write.

> I cannot help thinking that the fault of Mr. Keats's poems was a deficiency in masculine energy of style. He had beauty, tenderness, delicacy, in an uncommon degree, but there was a want of strength and substance. His Endymion is a very delightful description of the illusions of a youthful imagination, given up to airy dreams – we have flowers, clouds, rainbows, moonlight, all sweet sounds and smells, and Oreads and Dryads flitting by – but there is nothing tangible in it, nothing marked or palpable – we have none of the hardy spirit or rigid forms of antiquity. He painted his own thoughts and character; and did not transport himself into the fabulous and heroic ages. There is a want of action, of character, and so far, of imagination, but there is exquisite fancy. All is soft and fleshy, without bone or muscle. We see in him the youth, without the manhood of poetry. His genius breathed 'vernal delight and joy'. – 'Like Maia's son

he stood and shook his plumes,' with fragrance filled. His mind was redolent of spring. He had not the fierceness of summer, nor the richness of autumn, sad winter he seemed not to have known, till he felt the icy hand of death!

Those last words sound final indeed. But a few others shine even more sharply: 'The reading of Mr. Keats's Eve of St. Agnes lately', he wrote, 'made me regret that I was not young again', and for Hazlitt, who honoured the memory of his youth, a higher tribute was scarcely imaginable. When a year or two later again, he produced his anthology of the poets, including the modern ones, he spoke of Keats as one who 'gave the greatest promise of genius of any poet of his day'. This was the phrase he used in his critical list of authors from his *Select British Poets*, the anthology he compiled in 1824, and he then continued: 'he displayed extreme tenderness, beauty, originality, and delicacy of fancy; all he wanted was manly strength and fortitude to reject the temptations of singularity in sentiment and expression. Some of his shorter and later pieces are, however, as free from faults as they are full of beauties.' This surely was almost as good as a full treatment of his genius. Others might use that word lightly, but not Hazlitt.*

He did apply the same term – 'a man of genius' – to Shelley, but here the qualifications attracted much more interest than the tributes. How often he and Shelley met each other, how much of Shelley's early poetry he had read, how their clash of temperament and ideas developed year by year – so much in their relationship is infuriatingly unknown. Nothing of the personal intimacy between Hazlitt and Hunt or the intellectual intimacy between Hazlitt and Keats existed between them. Hazlitt never formed the habit of quoting Shelley constantly as

* The best account of the Keats–Hazlitt relationship is given by David Bromwich in his *Hazlitt: The Mind of a Critic*. 'No other encounter between poet and critic', he says, 'has been so fortunate for our literature.' He also observes that 'Hazlitt seemed to Keats almost an embodiment of the modern idea of genius.' And that was Keats's estimate round about the year 1819, before the writing of what a later age would reckon as at least half of the greatest Hazlitt essays.

he did Keats and of course, much more so, Wordsworth and Coleridge. All, or almost all, we know about what happened between them must be deduced from two major essays on the subject which Hazlitt wrote. They did meet, quite frequently it seems from Mary Shelley's report, in Leigh Hunt's cottage in 1817 and, quite possibly, they had done so before at Godwin's house in 1812. On one occasion, at least, Hazlitt had found himself on the same side as Shelley in an argument about republicanism. But these recordings are transient glimpses and cannot be properly used to allot full-scale attitudes to one side or another. One resonant recollection is left of those meetings: what Hazlitt called 'the incessant, alarming whirl of Shelley's Voltaic battery'. This was more a judgement on Shelley's argumentative manner, on his politics rather than his poetry. He is describing how Shelley talked, and, as we have seen in the case of Coleridge, he had mastered this particular art. Approached from this angle, the first major comment which Hazlitt wrote about Shelley may be seen to have had a purpose quite distinct from a poetical criticism. It was much more a political riposte in a major debate.

The passage occurs in an essay called 'On Paradox and Common Place', which was incorporated in his *Table Talk*, published in 1821, and it is by no means certain that when he started writing it, Hazlitt intended to become involved in drawing so elaborate a portrait. His aim was rather to explore afresh the idea of how the old and the new in art and most other fields of human activity should be honoured together, not the one always set to challenge the other. It was part of the same theme which had made him respect both Rousseau and Burke, and he never ceased to return to it. 'Originality implies independence of opinion', he wrote at the beginning of the essay, 'but differs as widely from mere singularity as from the tritest truism. It consists in seeing and thinking for one's self.' For Hazlitt, that would always be the highest virtue. But it must also always be distinguished most sharply from a mere love of contradicting others or despising the past. 'The wisdom of the ancients, the doctrines of the learned, the law of nations, the common sentiments of mortality, are (for some people) like a bundle of old almanacs. As the modern politician always asks for this day's paper, the modern sciolist always inquires after the latest paradox. With him instinct is a dotard, nature a changeling and common sense a discarded bye-word.' But Hazlitt wanted to recruit instinct, nature, commonsense as his allies in the political battleground. It was in this context that Hazlitt recalled Shelley, and it is notable, we must insist again, that these brilliant paragraphs on Shelley's manner contained not a single line or inflection from his poetry. Here was a political debate.

> The author of Prometheus Unbound (to take an individual instance of the last character) has a fire in his eye, a fever in his blood, a maggot in his brain, a hectic flutter in his speech, which mark out the philosophic fanatic. He is sanguine-complexioned, and shrill-voiced. As is often observable in the case of religious enthusiasts, there is a slenderness of constitutional *stamina*, which renders the flesh no match for the spirit. His bending, flexible form appears to take no strong hold of things, does not grapple with the world about him, but slides from it like a river –

> 'And in its liquid texture mortal wound
> Receives no more than can the fluid air.'*

> The shock of accident, the weight of authority make no impression on his opinions, which retire like a feather, or rise from the encounter unhurt, through their own buoyancy. He is clogged by no dull system of realities, no earthbound feelings, no rooted prejudices, by nothing that belongs to the mighty trunk and hard husk of nature and habit, but is drawn up by irresistible levity to the regions of mere speculation and fancy, to the sphere of air and fire, where his delighted spirit floats in 'seas of pearl and clouds of amber'. There is no *caput mortuum* or worn-out, threadbare experience to serve as ballast to his mind; it is all volatile intellectual salt of tartar, that refuses to combine its evanescent, inflammable essence with any thing solid or

* From John Milton's *Paradise Lost.*

any thing lasting. Bubbles are to him the only realities: – touch them, and they vanish. Curiosity is the only proper category of his mind, and though a man of knowledge, he is a child in feeling. Hence he puts every thing into a metaphysical crucible to judge of it himself and exhibit it to others as a subject of interesting experiment, without first making it over to the ordeal of his common sense or trying it on his heart. This faculty of speculating at random on all questions may in its overgrown and uninformed state do much mischief without intending it, like an overgrown child with the power of a man. Mr. Shelley has been accused of vanity – I think he is chargeable with extreme levity; but this levity is so great, that I do not believe he is sensible of its consequences. He strives to overturn all established creeds and systems: but this is in him an effect of constitution. He runs before the most extravagant opinions, but this is because he is held back by none of the merely mechanical checks of sympathy and habit. He tampers with all sorts of obnoxious subjects, but it is less because he is gratified with the rankness of the taint, than captivated with the intellectual phosphoric light they emit. It would seem that he wished not so much to convince or inform as to shock the public by the tenor of his productions, but I suspect he is more intent upon startling himself with his electrical experiments in morals and philosophy; and though they may scorch other people, they are to him harmless amusements, the coruscations of an Aurora Borealis, that 'play round the head, but do not reach the heart.' . . . To win over the public opinion by fair means is to them an insipid, common-place made of popularity: they would either force it by harsh methods, or seduce it by intoxicating potions. Egotism, petulance, licentiousness, levity of principle (whatever be the source) is a bad thing in any one, and most of all, in a philosophical reformer. Their humanity, their wisdom is always 'at the horizon'. Any thing new, any thing remote, any thing questionable, comes to them in a shape that is sure of a cordial welcome – a welcome cordial in proportion as the object is new, as it is apparently

impracticable, as it is a doubt whether it is at all desirable
. . . Fine words butter no parsnips, says the proverb. 'While
you are talking of marrying, I am thinking of hanging,' says
Captain Macheath. Of all people the most tormenting are
those who bid you hope in the midst of despair, who, by
never caring about any thing but their own sanguine, hair-
brained Utopian schemes, have at no time any particular
cause for embarrassment and despondency because they
have never the least chance of success, and who by including whatever does not hit their idle fancy, kings, priests,
religion, government, public abuses or private morals, in
the same sweeping clause of ban and anathema, do all they
can to combine all parties in a common cause against them,
and to prevent every one else from advancing one step
farther in the career of practical improvement than they do
in that of imaginary and unattainable perfection.

Later in that same essay Hazlitt turned his fury and his eloquence against the upholders of the opposite doctrine, those
who used their smooth, verbal reasoning to defend all the
unfairness of the past, and he chose as his most representative
figure, the most powerful politician of the day, Mr. George
Canning, sometimes hailed then and thereafter as a progressive
Tory, but one who never escaped Hazlitt's exposure whenever
opportunity occurred. Canning maybe knew better than his col-
leagues, but that made all the more inexcusable his resort to
rotund parliamentary subterfuges and conditional clauses, his
belief that we must always act

> from the obsolete inferences of past periods, not from the
> living impulse of existing circumstances, and the consoli-
> dated force of the knowledge and reflection of ages . . . He
> had been so long kept in the solitary confinement of his
> prejudices, and the dark cells of his interest and vanity, that
> he is afraid of being dashed to pieces if he makes a single
> false step, to the right or the left, from his dangerous and
> crooked policy.

How Hazlitt understood the self-imposed compulsions whereby politicians restrict their choice of action and vision. But these revelations were for another day, maybe another age. Immediately, it was the attack on Shelley which drew blood, or, worse still, a cry of anguish.

Leigh Hunt wrote at once (a few much milder criticisms of himself had also been included in some of the other *Table Talk* essays):

> I think, Mr. Hazlitt, you might have found a better time, and place too, for assaulting me and my friends in this bitter manner. A criticism on *Table Talk* was to appear in next Sunday's *Examiner*, but I have thought it best, upon the whole, not to let it appear, for I must have added a quarrelsome note to it; and the sight of acquaintances and brother-reformers cutting and carbonadoing one another in public is, I conceive, no advancement to the cause of Liberal opinion, however you may think they injure it in other respects. In God's name, why could you not tell Mr. Shelley in a pleasant manner of what you dislike in him? If it is not mere spleen, you make a gross mistake in thinking that he is not open to advice, or so wilfully in love with himself and his opinions. His spirit is worthy of his great talents. Besides, do you think that nobody has thought or suffered, or come to conclusions through thought or suffering, but yourself?

And much more of the same force. The friendship, personal and political, between Hunt and 'Mr. Hazlitt' could have been sundered there and then, and most of the just grievance would have been on Hunt's – and Shelley's – side. But Hazlitt wrote such a swift, winning and heart-warming reply, and Hunt replied in turn no less swiftly and warmly, that the tragedy of rupture between them was averted, and they became even stronger friends and allies in the years ahead. Hunt noted his own conclusion: 'I really believe Hazlitt to be a disinterested and suffering man, who feels public calamities as other men do private ones.' But in his letter to Hazlitt he made one plea: 'Oblige me in one matter and one matter only, and take some early opportunity of doing justice to the talents and *generous qualities* of Shelley, whatever you may think of his mistakes in using them.'

The opportunity came in circumstances of unforeseeable tragedy, and in the spacious review of *Posthumous Poems of Percy Bysshe Shelley* which Hazlitt wrote for the *Edinburgh Review* (in July 1824) he had no difficulty in writing about the man; he did so in phrases which paint the portrait as perceptively as any of his closest friends:

> Mr. Shelley was a remarkable man. His person was a type and shadow of his genius. His complexion, fair, golden, freckled, seemed transparent with an inward light, and his spirit with him

> – 'so divinely wrought,
> That you might almost say his body thought.'

He reminded those who saw him of some of Ovid's fables. His form, graceful and slender, drooped like a flower in the breeze . . . Mr. Shelley was an honest man. His unbelief and his presumption were parts of a disease, which was not combined in him either with indifference to human happiness, or contempt for human infirmities. There was neither selfishness nor malice at the bottom of his illusions. He was sincere in all his professions; and he practised what he preached – to his own sufficient cost. He followed up the letter and the spirit of his theoretical principles in his own person, and was ready to share both the benefit and the penalty with others. He thought and acted logically, and was what he professed to be, a sincere lover of truth, of nature, and of human kind. To all the rage of paradox, he united an unaccountable candour and severity of reasoning: in spite of an aristocratic education, he retained in his manners the simplicity of a primitive apostle. An Epicurean in his sentiments, he lived with the frugality and abstemiousness of an ascetick. His fault was, that he had no deference for the opinions of others, too little sympathy with their feelings (which he thought he had a right to sacrifice, as well as his own, to a grand ethical experiment) – and trusted too implicitly to the light of his own mind, and to the warmth of his own impulses.

So much for the man: what of the poet and the politician? Hazlitt could not be swayed from opinions which he had not adopted lightly. But now no one could doubt that he had read the poems – for example, *Julian and Maddalo*, the conversation piece between Shelley and Byron, the poem written in Venice, in 'that paradise of exiles, Italy'. It was a tale of thoughtful and romantic humanity yet veiled in obscurity. Hazlitt struggled to discern the meaning as others have since, but few have been able to escape Hazlitt's conclusion: 'The depth and tenderness of his feelings seems often to have interfered with the expression of them, as the sight becomes blind with tears.' And what of Shelley's politics? Hazlitt could not be shifted and of course he embraced many others besides Shelley in his verdict:

The principles of sound morality, liberty and humanity, are not to be found only in a few recent writers, who have discovered the secret of the greatest happiness to the greatest numbers, but are truths as old as the creation. To be convinced of the existence of wrong, we should read history rather than poetry: the levers with which we must work out our regeneration are not the cobwebs of the brain, but the warm, palpitating fibres of the human heart. It is the collision of passions and interests, the petulance of party-spirit, and the perversities of self-will and self-opinion that have been the great obstacles to social improvement – not stupidity or ignorance; and the caricaturing one side of the question and shocking the most pardonable prejudices on the other, is not the way to allay heats or produce unanimity. By flying to the extremes of scepticism, we make others shrink back, and shut themselves up in the strongholds of bigotry and superstition – by mixing up doubtful or offensive matters with salutary and demonstrable truths, we bring the whole into question, fly-blow the cause, risk the principle,

and give a handle and a pretext to the enemy to treat all
philosophy and all reform as a compost of crude, chaotic,
and monstrous absurdities. We thus arm the virtues as well
as the vices of the community against us . . .

The politics in which Hazlitt believed, indeed the system of
thought which embraced his art, poetry as well as politics, was a
faith which could appeal to the virtues and the passions of the
people. Such was the kind of faith needed to answer Edmund
Burke.

Wordsworth's genius, Hazlitt never ceased to insist, was 'a
pure emanation of the Spirit of the Age'. He could not bring
himself to make a comparable claim about the genius of Byron,
and indeed there was one sense in which Byron's capacities
fitted into a quite different category. If Wordsworth's poetry
was 'founded on setting up an opposition between the natural
and the artificial', if his muse was so much 'a levelling one',
then it was true that Byron must be allocated almost to an opposite pole. For Byron paraded his allegiance to the classical,
artificial standards of the Augustan age, of Alexander Pope in
particular; his muse, like his manners, revealed no levelling
propensities whatever. Childe Harold, the Corsair, the Giaour,
Lara all conducted themselves with an aristocratic flourish and
disdain. It is hard to mention Wordsworth's chosen subjects in
the same breath; they seem like creatures from a different
planet. And yet The Spirit of the Age, the title Hazlitt chose, with
the capitals he supplied, was the flag of revolutionary freedom,
borne in the hearts of men and women, and carried flaming
across Europe, the vision of human hope ascending like Jacob's
ladder. Byron became the embodiment of that spirit. But, for
Hazlitt, this was not a sudden, flashing discovery or revelation.

Hazlitt was ten years older than Byron, and when, with the
publication of Childe Harold in 1812 Byron woke one morning to
find himself famous, almost world-famous, Hazlitt had still not
yet been able to write and publish his first essay in poetical criticism, his 1814 essay for the Examiner. He had some kindred
understanding, therefore, of what Wordsworth must have felt
when he found it so hard to win an early recognition and when

even the meagre portion first gained seemed to be snatched from him: 'To have produced works of genius, and to find them neglected or treated with scorn, is one of the heaviest trials of human patience.' By contrast, Byron's spectacular luck and glory made Hazlitt jealous for others and, maybe, himself too. He read the Noble Lord's elaborate sneers against some of his betters in *English Bards and Scotch Reviewers*, and was not impressed by his satiric gift. He read the first two cantos of *Childe Harold*, and the successors such as *The Corsair*, and thought they were 'all the same person, and all apparently himself'. Here was an egotism to match Wordsworth's, and it had not the excuse of originality; the egotistical obsessions seemed much more evident than any creative revolutionary force. These immediate impressions left their imprint on Hazlitt's mind for the rest of his life. The first Byron he encountered was certainly not Shelley's pilgrim of eternity, not the champion of the revolution, not even the unwavering defender of his own hero, Napoleon Bonaparte. Hazlitt's disappointment was deeply founded, and yet even in the face of it, he strove faithfully and fairly to apply his critical faculty. 'It is not,' he felt bound to insist, 'the passion of a mind struggling with misfortune, or the hopelessness of its desires, but of a mind preying on itself and disgusted with, or indifferent to all other things.' A harsh indictment for sure, but still there was something else there.

Still there is power; and power rivets attention and forces admiration. 'He hath a demon': and that is the next thing to being full of the God . . . Within the contracted range of his imagination, he has great unity and truth of keeping . . . He gives the tumultuous eagerness of action, and the fixed despair of thought. In vigour of style and force of conception, he in one sense surpasses every writer of the present day. His indignant apothegms are like oracles of misanthropy. He who wishes for 'a curse to kill with', may find it in Lord Byron's writings. Yet he has beauty lurking underneath his strength, tenderness sometimes joined with the phrenzy of despair. A flash of sudden light sometimes follows from a stroke of his pencil, like a falling meteor . . .

Such was the poet he presented in his 1818 lectures; not the Byron acclaimed or outlawed by his contemporaries; a profile, not a portrait; the outline of a character, not a specimen of flesh and blood. Hazlitt was puzzled by his own inhibitions. He and Byron shared the same cause, the same hatreds, the same enemies, the same political aspirations; yet he could not or would not speak of him as a comrade-in-arms. The lordly pretensions and posturings seemed to make that impossible. A heavy loss for his contemporaries, for subsequent generations, for English literature, derived from the sad fact that Hazlitt had never heard Byron talk. We know how alertly he could listen, to Coleridge, to Shelley, to Wordsworth and the 'rugged harmony in the tones of his voice'. Byron's voice, according to Coleridge, was angelic – or demon-like; it was the voice with which the serpent tempted Eve. If Hazlitt had had the chance to fall beneath the spell, as Shelley did, or Sheridan or how many others, the common sympathies between them would have been stirred. Instead, insofar as they communicated at all, it was done through intermediaries: Thomas Moore, Leigh Hunt or John Scott. The last of these, incidentally, although a fine and friendly editor from Hazlitt's point of view, was also the editor who, by a most brazen breach of faith, published Byron's farewell poems on his wife, just after he had left the country, thus helping to damn the heartless Byron in the eyes of his own generation.

Altogether, Hazlitt watched Byron's performance from a deceptive distance. He saw him floundering in a controversy about the merits of Pope and was not impressed by what he saw here of Byron's prose style. (He knew nothing, of course, of Byron as a letter-writer.) He was implicated directly with Leigh Hunt and Thomas Moore and Byron in the production of a journal *The Liberal* and was fed with a series of wretched half-truths about Byron's lukewarm aid for the project and for his Cockney associates. He read and reviewed many (but by no reckoning all) of the poems and plays which flowed abundantly from Byron's pen. One picture became embedded in his mind: 'the spoiled child of fortune'; 'the pampered egotist'; 'a coxcomb even though a provoking and sublime one.' The word 'coxcomb' was an important one in Hazlitt's vocabulary. It meant a foolish, foppish, conceited person, vain of his accomplishments or dress, and Hazlitt *did* dare to apply it to Byron. A coxcomb, he once said in another, non-Byronic connection, could not be a genius. Geniuses were unconscious of their powers; they were always thinking of something greater than themselves. The coxcomb, by the same reckoning, was always excruciatingly aware of himself, would preen himself on his least estimable or significant qualities.

When in April 1824, Hazlitt set about writing his Lord Byron essay for *The Spirit of the Age* volume, he seemed to strive not for a finely-balanced final verdict – that was rarely his aim – nor even for the synthesis or the marriage of extremes which better suited his turn of mind but for a more serene and polished invective than any of his previous criticisms on the same subject, and, even while these scarcely forgiveable phrases about the coxcomb were included, it is impossible to deny how subtle and sweeping was the attack. Moreover, the best Hazlitt essays had a momentum of their own; they unleashed his imagination in a manner quite unexpected in the first paragraphs. Nor must it be overlooked, in Hazlitt's defence, that he thought he was directing his fire against one who was still extolled as a glittering success. 'Lord Byron and Sir Walter Scott', he asserted, without any fear of contradiction, in the very first sentence, 'are among writers now living the two who would carry away a majority of suffrages as the greatest geniuses of the age.' So Hazlitt supposed he was seeking to challenge a popular judgement. That was surely the case when, as he usually did, he elevated Wordsworth to the highest pinnacle. However, in this instance, the contrast also between Scott and Byron was drawn all in Scott's favour:

If Sir Walter Scott may be thought by some to have been

'Born universal heir to all humanity,'

it is plain Lord Byron can set up no such pretension. He is, in a striking degree, the creature of his own will. He holds no

communion with his kind, but stands alone without mate
or fellow –

'As if a man were author of himself,
And owned no other kin.'

He is like a solitary peak, all access to which is cut off not
more by elevation than distance. He is seated on a lofty
eminence, 'cloud-capt', or reflecting the last rays of setting
suns, and in his poetical moods reminds us of the fabled
Titans, retired to a ridgy steep, playing on their Pan's-pipes,
and taking up ordinary men and things in their hands with
haughty indifference. He raises his subject to himself, or
tramples on it; he neither stoops to, nor loses himself in it.
He exists not by sympathy, but by antipathy. He scorns all
things, even himself. Nature must come to him to sit for her
picture: he does not go to her. She must consult his time, his
convenience and his humour, and wear a *sombre* or fantastic
garb, or his Lordship turns his back upon her. There is no
ease, no unaffected simplicity of manner, no 'golden mean'.
All is strained, or petulant in the extreme. His thoughts are
sphered and crystalline; his style 'prouder than when blue
Iris bends'; his spirit fiery, impatient, wayward, indefati-
gable. Instead of taking his impressions from without, in
entire and almost unimpaired masses, he moulds them
according to his own temperament, and heats the materials
of his imagination in the furnace of his passions. Lord
Byron's verse glows like a flame, consuming everything in
its way; Sir Walter Scott's glides like a river: clear, gentle,
harmless. The poetry of the first scorches, that of the last
scarcely warms. The light of the one proceeds from an internal source, ensanguined, sullen, fixed; the other reflects the
hues of Heaven or the face of nature, glancing, vivid and
various.

So the indictment mounts:

The genius of Sir Walter is essentially imitative, or 'denotes a foregone conclusion'; that of Lord Byron is self-dependent or at least requires no aid, is governed by no law but the impulses of its own will. We confess, however much we may admire independence of feeling and erectness of spirit in general or practical questions, yet in works of genius we prefer him who bows to the authority of nature, who appeals to actual objects, to mouldering superstitions, to history, observation and tradition, before him who only consults the pragmatical and restless workings of his own breast, and gives them out as oracles to the world. We like a writer (whether poet or prose writer) who takes in (or is willing to take in) the range of half the universe in feeling, character, description, much better than we do one who obstinately and invariably shuts himself up in the Bastile of his own ruling passions. In short, we had rather be Sir Walter Scott (meaning thereby the author of *Waverley*) than Lord Byron a hundred times over, and for the reason just given, namely, that he casts his descriptions in the mould of nature, ever-varying, never tiresome, always interesting and always instructive, instead of casting them constantly in the mould of his own individual impressions.

He gives us man as he is, or as he was, in almost every variety of situation, action and feeling. Lord Byron makes a man after his own image, woman after his own heart; the one is a capricious tyrant, the other a yielding slave; he gives us the misanthrope and the voluptuary by turns; and with these two characters, burning or melting in their own fires, he makes out everlasting centos of himself. He hangs the cloud, the film of his existence over all outward things, sits in the centre of his thoughts, and enjoys dark night, bright day, the glitter and the gloom 'in cell monastic'. We see the mournful pall, the crucifix, the death's-heads, the faded chaplet of flowers, the gleaming tapers, the agonized brow of genius, the wasted form of beauty; but we are still imprisoned in a dungeon; a curtain intercepts our view; we do not breathe freely the air of nature or of our own thoughts. The other admired author draws aside the curtain, and the veil of egotism is rent; and he shows us the crowd of living men and women, the endless groups, the landscape background, the cloud and the rainbow, and enriches our imaginations and relieves one passion by another, and expands and lightens reflection, and takes away that tightness at the breast which arises from thinking or wishing to think that there is nothing in the world out of a man's self!

In this point of view, the author of *Waverley* is one of the greatest teachers of morality that ever lived, by emancipating the mind from petty, narrow, and bigoted prejudices: Lord Byron is the greatest pamperer of those prejudices, by seeming to think there is nothing else worth encouraging but the seeds or the full luxuriant growth of dogmatism and self-conceit. In reading the Scotch Novels, we never think about the author, except from a feeling of curiosity respecting our unknown benefactor: in reading Lord Byron's works, he himself is never absent from our minds. The colouring of Lord Byron's style, however rich and dipped in Tyrian dyes, is nevertheless opaque, is in itself an object of delight and wonder: Sir Walter Scott's is perfectly transparent. In studying the one, you seem to gaze at the figures cut in stained glass, which exclude the view beyond, and where the pure light of Heaven is only a means of setting off the gorgeousness of art: in reading the other, you look through a noble window at the clear and varied landscape without. Or to sum up the distinction in one word, Sir Walter Scott is the most *dramatic* writer now living, and Lord Byron is the least so.

Some of these hard judgements, it has seemed from earlier indications, were based primarily on Hazlitt's reading of Byron's earlier poems, and the supposition is underlined by the hint that the later cantos of *Childe Harold* – which Hazlitt could not have read until after those 1818 lectures – were starting to induce a change of critical mood:

He assumes a lofty and philosophic tone, and 'reasons high of providence, fore-knowledge, will, and fate.' He takes the highest points in the history of the world, and comments on them from a more commanding eminence. He shows us the crumbling monuments of time; he invokes the great names, the mighty spirit of antiquity. The universe is changed into a stately mausoleum: in solemn measures he chaunts a hymn to fame. Lord Byron has strength and elevation enough to fill up the moulds of our classical and time-hallowed recollections, and to rekindle the earliest aspirations of the mind after greatness and true glory with a pen of fire. The names of Tasso, or Ariosto, of Dante, of Cincinnatus, of Caesar, or Scipio, lose nothing of their pomp or their lustres in his hands, and when he begins and continues a strain of panegyric on such subjects we indeed sit down with him to a banquet of rich praise, brooding over imperishable glories,

'Till Contemplation has her fill'.

Some of the late poems indeed aroused almost unqualified praise, not *Manfred* nor *Cain* nor even *Don Juan*, and not Byron's plays which he condemned as unpardonably undramatic, but *Heaven and Earth* for example: 'the space between Heaven and Earth, the stage on which his characters have to pass to and fro, seems to fill his Lordship's imagination; and the Deluge which he has so finely described, may be said to have drowned all his own idle humour.' Even his praise could be grudging: it was the inordinate egotism of the Byronic odyssey which Hazlitt abhorred and as the essay proceeded, the attack on the poet merged into the attack on the man:

He has a seat in the House of Lords, a niche in the Temple of Fame. Every-day mortals, opinions, things are not good enough for him to touch or think of. A mere nobleman is, in his estimation, but 'the tenth transmitter of a foolish face': a mere man of genius is no better than a worm. His muse is also a lady of quality. The people are not polite enough for him; the Court is not sufficiently intellectual. He hates the one and despises the other. By hating and despising others, he does not learn to be satisfied with himself. A fastidious man soon grows querulous and splenetic. If there is nobody but ourselves to come up to our idea of fancied perfection, we easily get tired of our idol.

When a man is tired of what he is, by a natural perversity he sets up for what he is not. If he is a poet, he pretends to be a metaphysician: if he is a patrician in rank and feeling, he would fain be one of the people. His ruling motive is not the love of the people, but of distinction: not of truth, but of singularity. He patronizes men of letters out of vanity, and deserts them from caprice or from the advice of friends. He embarks in an obnoxious publication to provoke censure, and leaves it to shift for itself for fear of scandal. We do not like Sir Walter's gratuitous servility: we like Lord Byron's preposterous *liberalism* little better. He may affect the principles of equality, but he resumes his privilege of peerage, upon occasion. His Lordship has made great offers of service to the Greeks – money and horses. He is at present in Cephalonia, waiting the event!

Thus the essay was mounting to a mighty derisive climax, when the real news from Greece reached Hazlitt:

We had written thus far when news came of the death of Lord Byron, and put an end at once to a strain of somewhat peevish invective, which was intended to meet his eye, not to insult his memory. Had we known that we were writing his epitaph, we must have done it with a different feeling. As it is, we think it better and more like himself, to let what we had written stand, than to take up our leaden shafts, and try to melt them into 'tears of sensibility', or mould them into dull praise and an affected show of candour. We were not silent during the author's lifetime, either for his reproof or encouragement (such as we could give, and *he* did not disdain to accept) nor can we now turn undertakers' men to fix the glittering plate upon his coffin, or fall into the procession of popular woe. Death cancels every thing but truth, and strips a man of every thing but genius and virtue. It is a sort of natural canonization. It makes the meanest of us sacred; it installs the poet in his immortality, and lifts him to the skies. Death is the greatest assayer of the sterling ore of talent. At his touch the drossy particles fall off, the irritable, the personal, the gross, and mingle with the dust – the finer and more ethereal part mounts with winged spirit to watch over our latest memory, and protect our bones from insult. We consign the least worthy qualities to oblivion, and cherish the nobler and imperishable nature with double pride and fondness.

Nothing could show the real superiority of genius in a more striking point of view than the idle contests and the public indifference about the place of Lord Byron's interment, whether in Westminster Abbey or his own family vault. A king must have a coronation – a nobleman a funeral procession. The man is nothing without the pageant. The poet's cemetery is the human mind, in which he sows the seeds of never-ending thought, his monument is to be found in his works:

> 'Nothing can cover his high fame but Heaven;
> No pyramids set off his memory,
> But the eternal substance of his greatness.'

Lord Byron is dead: he also died a martyr to his zeal in the cause of freedom, for the last, best hopes of man. Let that be his excuse and his epitaph!

But which is the true Byron, the Byron of the essay or the Byron of the epitaph? It may be that Hazlitt, for all his insight and honesty, had not taken the full measure of his man or of his demon. It is instructive that Keats should have applied that same term, 'demon', both to his bosom friend, Hazlitt, and to his supposed enemy, Byron. At least we may be sure: demons cannot be coxcombs.

Part Two

THE POET
OF THE
REVOLUTION

God will not be always a Tory . . .

Letter to Murray, 2 February 1821

TWO

Aberdeen

I was bred a canny Scot till ten-years old.

Letter to Walter Scott, 12 January 1822

Where did Byron learn the liberal ideas, the burning passion, which made him the poet of the Revolution? Such a mighty flood could never be traced to a single source, and the full momentum was accumulated only after many years and trials. But, in his own age and thereafter, the combination of word and deed which he fashioned made his faith more potent than that of any of his great contemporaries.

This actual title – the poet of the Revolution – was bestowed upon him by John Morley in a famous lecture delivered in 1870, but Byron's claim to it derived from his life and works. The most notable modern editor of his poetry describes his culminating achievement, *Don Juan*, as 'a conscious attempt to explain critically the meaning of the entire period in Europe stretching from 1789 to 1823'.* He also describes, with more assurance than ever before, how many of Byron's writings, even before *Don Juan*, contributed to this same vision of a universe in tumult; how his appreciation of its portentous scale was not so different from Hazlitt's phrase of 'an apocalyptical chapter in the history of human nature'.

As I seek to present a real argument about him, I shall indicate the various companions, critics, scholars and commentators, ancient and modern, who have shepherded me along my path, sometimes pointing the way to unexpected heights and

---

* This sentence appears in Jerome J. McGann's Introduction to his *Byron*, in the Oxford Authors series, published in 1986. See page 95 below.

glories, sometimes to blind alleys and wasted heaths. The range of commentary about him is inexhaustible; I give the names of those who have guided or misguided me in the text or the footnotes. 'Everybody fell out with everybody else about Byron,' wrote John Drinkwater, who himself wrote about him one of the best polemical biographies in the language.* But Byron himself is the chief guide; he alone can meet and repel the full force of the Hazlittean invectives or those delivered from so many other quarters.

He had, as we shall see, a special brand of self-awareness which was truly not to be confused with egotism. He was, like Jonathan Swift, a kind of inverted hypocrite who was often too proud to repudiate the charges levelled against him by outright enemies or wayward friends. He could always take refuge behind those ample shields, his humour, his wit, and his restless courage. He would happily pretend that poetry, his own and other people's, meant little to him, and was possibly amused when these protestations were taken at their face value. In his world, in his language, in his political creed, words were things. This was Hazlitt's creed too which he had claimed to learn from Edmund Burke; so the disharmony between them appears all the more unexpected and inexplicable.† We must look further to see the quite different route whereby Byron reached his own destination of romantic realism. The origins of his political faith are well worth examination in themselves, and they naturally help to explain his relations with his fellow reformers and revolutionaries.

* John Drinkwater's *The Pilgrim of Eternity. Byron – A Conflict* was published by Hodder & Stoughton in 1925. The reason for the polemical nature of the book was that just a few years before (in 1921) Lord Lovelace, Byron's descendant, had privately republished a new edition of *Astarte*, first privately published in 1907. Both of these volumes had revived, in a more formidable form than ever before, the accusation that Byron had been guilty of committing incest with his half-sister, Augusta. John Drinkwater sought to repudiate this accusation but also to repudiate a whole range of other anti-Byronic themes at the same time.
† In a letter dated 27 February 1814, Byron stated that the phrase 'words are things' came from Mirabeau. Maybe they all got it from that reputable source.

Despite the vast array of material on the subject, nothing truly significant in this field can be deduced from his famous or infamous line of ancestors, the Byrons or the Gordons, whose deeds and misdeeds are recounted for quite different purposes. On his father's side he could look back to the Norman conquerors and on his mother's to the Scottish kings. Considering how passionately Scottish were the Gordons and how the Byrons married and intermarried with Trevanions in Cornwall, Byron was much more a pure Celt than was usually appreciated. He could, like many Celts, come to regard the English as a foreign race, even when he was happy to use their facilities and their language. Thomas Moore, his first biographer,* asserted that Byron himself was much obsessed with these questions of high birth and lineage, and John Cam Hobhouse who knew another part of him promptly denied it. Unlike some of the great Whig families into whose homes Byron later stepped so readily, the Byrons of previous centuries had never found themselves ranged on the anti-royalist side or even riven by dissensions of principle within the family. Eight Byrons, it was reckoned, fought at the battle of Edgehill – all of them on the wrong side. Whatever their other eccentricities, they had chosen to conform with the political institutions and interests of the English state, as interpreted by the reigning English monarch. No amount of nonsense about Byron's aristocratic tastes could ever explain how he could come to see himself 'born for opposition'.

* Thomas Moore's *The Life, Letters and Journals of Lord Byron*, the first and most famous of all the biographies, was published (by John Murray, of course) in 1830. All the references here are taken from the 1866 new and complete edition which contained commentaries from Sir Walter Scott, Lord Jeffrey, Professor Wilson, Thomas Moore himself, William Gifford, Revd George Crabbe, Bishop Hever, J. G. Lockhart, Lord Broughton and Thomas Campbell. 'This volume', wrote Harold Nicolson, no mean authority himself, 'has not, I think, been accorded the praise that it deserves. Within the limit of his regard for Byron's executors and relations, Moore did essay, if not to tell the truth, then at least to avoid untruth; and in this endeavour he was skilful, courageous, and persistent. The book is vivid and agreeable and went far to destroy the wholly false impression of Byron which had been founded on his earlier poems . . .' Enough for now. Both Moore and Nicolson must be revisited later.

A more pressing influence than the family heritage was the financial insecurity, to use no fiercer term, which seemed an essential part of it. Captain John Byron, the poet's father, compressed his life into thirty-five years of fevered romance and dissipation. Born in Plymouth in 1756, he was guided away from his own father's naval career and was pushed instead, with the aid of parental money, into the Guards. He served in the American war, but by the age of twenty-two was back in London drawing rooms able to pursue his own special aptitude for conquering new loves or reconquering old ones. He ran off with one rich and beautiful heiress, and when she died in childbirth, ran off with another not so rich and beautiful. The first of these lovely creatures was the Marchioness Lady Carmarthen, and her daughter who survived was Augusta. The second was Catherine Gordon, Byron's mother. Captain John married her in 1786. Byron was born two years later. There was just time for a few quarrels between father and son, and a few more tempestuous ones between husband and wife, before Captain John departed with most of Catherine's cash for Paris, where he died in 1791. 'It is true that he was a very handsome man, which goes a great way', wrote the son who would never say a word against his father and never pretended to have learnt anything from him either. The impeachment was much too soft. Captain Byron – quite unbeknown to his son, of course – was a sponger, a rogue, a cheat, a liar, a whorer as well as a mere spendthrift. It is lucky Byron was spared the truth.

Byron was 'half a Scot by birth, and bred/A whole one.' That was his own laughing admission but it contains too the proper assertion of his mother's pre-eminent place in his life. Catherine Gordon* counted for more than all the sequence of

---

* Much the fullest and best account of Byron's mother is given by Doris Langley Moore in her *Lord Byron: Accounts Rendered* published by John Murray in 1974. The same volume also contains much the fullest and best account of Jack Byron, her husband. Indeed the volume offers more indispensable biographical material than any other since Thomas Moore's. Further indications of what is owed to all Mrs Langley Moore's volumes will appear later. Immediately, it is worth noting that she acknowledges her debt to J. D. Symon in his *Byron in Perspective* whom she describes as

mad, wicked or eccentric figures on the other side of the family. Too much attention has sometimes been directed to the quarrels which broke out between mother and son, as revealed in Byron's own letters, or to the impression conveyed by the one familiar, blowsy, overblown portrait of her painted in her later years. Both these indications are unfair or misleading since they distract from the indisputable facts of the case and Byron's own awareness of them.

The birth took place at some rented furnished rooms at 16 Holles Street, London on 22 January 1788, and the christening a month later at Marylebone parish church just round the corner. She called him George Gordon, after her own father. Whether Captain John was in attendance at either of these occasions is unknown; he was being chased by claims for debt and could not stay long in one place. A year later she set off, without his company, for Aberdeen where she hoped no doubt to find some comfort among her own countrymen and where she calculated that her own fortune could be eked out more sensibly. Captain John followed them a few months later, more in pursuit of cash than any acknowledgement of domestic ties. She loved him but could never hold him. Mad Jack, as he was commonly nicknamed, had something like an hypnotic power over her: 'Mrs Byron', it was said to an intermediary obviously on her admonition, 'is afraid that she has not the resolution to refuse any request Mr Byron may make to her personally.' He never loved her and rarely troubled to conceal his waywardness. He made his last escape to his sisters in Paris where he died in August 1791, at the age of thirty-five. Young George was three and a

---

'one of her [Mrs Byron's] first defenders'. Yet Symon's book, with this first defence, was published only in 1924 – a hundred years after his death when, as we shall see, the new wave of Byronic studies was by no means moving in his favour. These references to Doris Langley Moore's biographical writings, by the way, are not intended as a reflection on the other most excellent modern Byronic biographers – Leslie Marchand, Peter Quennell, John Drinkwater and some more. Every Byronic reader must start somewhere but all must agree, I would suppose, that the fresh material offered by her, so skilfully, so wittily, so Byronically, has altered the whole picture.

half, but not too young to record years later: 'I was not so young when my father died, but I perfectly remember him; and had very early a horror of matrimony, from the sight of domestic broils.' Catherine was twenty-six and broken hearted. She was the one who had truly had to suffer the domestic broils. Her temper was said to be fierce and, being so much alone in the world with such a burden to bear, she had good reason. Moreover, most painful of all perhaps, the son she loved, the son of the ne'er-do-well husband she loved, was born lame in one foot. The medicine of the time, even the Scottish medicine, did not know what was the cause or cure for such an impediment. It is not fanciful to suppose that the mother suffered on this account as much as her son; according to the strict Calvinistic doctrine of the time or even the orthodox Christianity still accepted without question, such visitations on little children were all part of the divine vengeance for the sins of the fathers or mothers.

The Aberdeen where the Byrons settled was soon entranced by the startling, momentous news from France, Aberdeen more even than other British cities thanks to long-standing French affinities. The *Aberdeen Journal* offered faithful accounts of the fall of the Bastille, the Royal flight to Varennes, the speeches of Danton. Byron's mother must certainly have been fascinated by what she read and heard from that quarter, partly because her husband had escaped and died there, but for other less accidental reasons too. Her half-sister-in-law Mrs Leigh was living in Valenciennes and she invited Mrs Byron to visit her there, but on 29 November 1792 she wrote from Aberdeen thus:

> I wish very much to be with you, but I should not like to go abroad at present, in the state they are in, even if I had money to go, and I suppose you do not think of it. I am very much interested about the French, but I fancy you and I are on different sides, for I am quite a Democrat and I do not think the King, after his treachery and perjury, deserves to be restored. To be sure there has been horrid things done by the People, but if the other party had been successful, there would have been as great cruelty committed by them.

You will see by the papers the riots that has been in this country. I am told the south of Scotland is in a tumult. There has been none here yet, but it is feared there will be. In the principal towns there is societys [sic] of the Friends of the People as they call themselves. I suppose you have heard of the news paper that came out at Edinr, that Government wants so much to suppress. If Mr Dundas had gone to the Perth races as he intended for he was one of the Stewarts [sic] he would certainly have . . .

Here the letter is torn, but the event described gives its own indication of the temper of the times. Mr Dundas, afterwards Lord Melville, was the hated Tory tyrant of Scotland who had sold his cause and country to serve the repressive Pittite regime in London, and he deserved to be paraded in effigy bearing on his breast the legend: 'Haman betrayed his enemies and I have betrayed my friends.' As one who had Stuart blood in her own veins, Mrs Byron might have been expected to show some sympathy for monarchs and their backers on the run in Paris or Perth, but she was already moving on her own account to the side of the people and their friends.

Her connections were Whiggish, and most of the Whig leaders, it should be recalled, headed by Charles James Fox himself, were strong supporters of all the first manifestations of revolution in France. But to use the rare, explosive word 'democrat' with such readiness revealed an even stronger bent in her political temperament. She would gladly join the anti-Haman demonstrations.

She was also a great reader, and not only of the newspapers. A fastidious friend of her husband had once been shocked to see a copy of *La Nouvelle Héloïse* on her dressing table. A new circulating library had been established in Aberdeen, and she must have become a subscriber. The boy was soon learning much at the school where he was sent before he was five but it is well-nigh certain that he learnt much more at home; he was a bookish boy, almost a bookworm from infancy.

But let Byron himself tell some of the tale. He did not write both directly and extensively about Aberdeen, but the references are all the more to be noted on that account. Here is what he wrote in one of his first attempts at a memoir:*

For several years of my earliest childhood I was in that City – but have never revisited it since I was ten years old. – I was sent at five years old or earlier to a School kept by a Mr. Bowers – who was called '*Bodsy* Bowers' by reason of his dapperness. – It was a School for both sexes – I learned little there – except to repeat by rote the first lesson of Monosyllables – 'God made man – let us love him' by hearing it often repeated – without acquiring a letter. – Whenever proof was made of my progress at home – I repeated these words with the most rapid fluency, but on turning over a new leaf – I continued to repeat them – so that the narrow boundaries of my first year's accomplishments were detected – my ears boxed – (which they did not deserve – seeing that it was by *ear* only that I had acquired my letters) – and my intellects consigned to a new preceptor. – He was a very decent – clever – little Clergyman – named Ross – afterwards Minister of one of the kirks (*East* I think) [;] under *him* – I made an astonishing progress – and I recollect to this day his mild manners & good-natured painstaking. – The moment I could read – my grand passion was *history* – and why I know not – but I was particularly taken with the battle near the Lake Regillus in the Roman History – put into my hands the first. — Four years ago when standing on the heights of Tusculum – & looking down upon the little round Lake that was once Regillus & which dots the immense expanse below – I remembered my young enthusiasm & my old instructor. — Afterwards I had a very serious – saturnine – but kind young man named Paterson for a Tutor – he was

* *Byron's Letters and Journals*, edited by Leslie A. Marchand (published, of course, by John Murray) in eleven volumes are, alongside various editions of the poems, the most indispensable source of all. And hardly less indispensable are the other Marchand volumes: the three-volume *Byron: A Biography* published in 1957; the one-volume *Byron: A Portrait*, published in 1971; and, best of all in my book, *Byron's Poetry: A Critical Introduction*, published in 1966.

the son of my Shoemaker – but a good Scholar as is common with the Scotch. – He was a rigid Presbyterian also. – With him I began Latin in Ruddiman's Grammar – & continued till I went to the 'Grammar School' (*Scotice 'Schule'* – *Aberdonice 'Squeel'*) where I threaded all the Classes to the *fourth* – when I was re-called to England (where I had been hatched) by the demise of my Uncle. – I acquired this hand-writing which I can hardly read myself under the fair copies of Mr Duncan of the same city. – I don't think that he would plume himself upon my progress. – However I wrote much better then than I have ever done since; – haste and agitation of one kind or another have quite spoilt as pretty a scrawl as ever scratched over a frank.

Two necessary additions must be made to Byron's own list of the books which spurred his intellectual development. His own last record is considerably abbreviated; elsewhere he made other references, and as J. D. Symon records:

The list of books he had read before he left Aberdeen, at ten years old, is extraordinary for so young a boy. They were Rycaut's 'History of the Turks'; the Turkish histories of Mignet (Hawkins's translation) and Knolles; Cantemir's 'History of the Ottoman Empire'; De Tott's 'Memoirs,' which are alluded to in 'Don Juan'; 'Lady Mary Wortley Montagu,' 'Don Quixote,' Smollett's 'Roderick Random,' and a Roman History. We know also that he had read Solomon Gessner's 'Death of Abel,' which was one of young Walter Scott's permitted Sunday books, and is trebly classic as the book read by the schoolboy in Hood's 'Eugene Aram'.

However, even at that early age the excursion into Roman or Turkish history may have been undertaken on something like his own initiative. An even earlier, deeper and indelible impression was made by his religious instruction, whether it came from his mother, his nurse, his school teachers or the clergymen in the Church itself or all combined together. 'I was cudgelled to Church for the first ten years of my life,' he wrote, and he never escaped from those belabourings. He knew his

Bible as well as any other great English poet, not excluding Milton, but the effect of the instruction became the opposite of that which all the priests and preachers had intended. He was smitten by the injustice, the horror, the cruelty of what his Christian tutors sought to teach him. The revolt was so violent and persistent in his case that it is hard to believe it did not start there and then when his sense of justice, as a child, was so deeply shaken. Sometimes it is suggested that most of his terrifying religious indoctrination came from his nurse Agnes May – one claimant of this view was her sister May. At a very early age she taught him to recite some psalms, and before he was eight he claimed to have read most of the Bible 'through and through – that is to say, the Old Testament, for the New struck me as a task, but the other as a pleasure. I speak as a boy from the recollected impression of that period at Aberdeen in 1796.' He read about Adam and Eve until he knew every twist in the story, and then about Cain and Abel, all before he was eight. He felt for the sheep and goats so blood-thirstily offered as sacrifice by Abel, and he started to feel his own peculiar sympathy with Cain. The Garden of Eden was as much a real place to him as the mountains and seashores where his mother took him; but where had he learnt his ceaseless questionings and doubts? It is the Byronic scepticism, from his earliest childhood, which is the greatest mystery of all.*

Sometimes the blaze of anger about what he was taught

---

* Often it took a Scotsman to understand Byron's religious revolt and its central place in his life. One of the most perceptive whose comments we shall meet frequently was Professor Sir Herbert Grierson, of Edinburgh University, who wrote about Byron as brilliantly as any critic in any age. In his 'Byron and English Society', his Byron Foundation Lecture delivered at Nottingham in 1923, he wrote:

> To say that Byron was touched by the sweep of the Evangelical wave may seem strange but it is true. His early years had been spent, not in aristocratic but in middle class and pious circles. At Aberdeen he acquired the elements of that intimate knowledge of the Bible which he manifested throughout his life and imbibed the Calvinist doctrine of predestination. For him, to be religious meant to be Evangelical or Methodist.

becomes so destructive that it might be supposed it had consumed his whole being. And yet, as the few pages from his Journal indicate, he had happy memories too. Occasionally he might object when people told him that he spoke with a Scottish, or Aberdonian, accent, but at the next moment in another mood he would recall the excursions on which his mother took him, the first mountains he saw, the first sight of the sea, the first songs he heard. Each were to become famous.

Several of his moods could claim a Scottish ancestry. One of his most famous Scottish poems, 'Lachin y Gair', offered an idealized view, doubtless derived directly from his mother, of his Scottish inheritance. He either did not know or did not care to recall that the Gordons of Gight had, as Leslie Marchand put it, 'a record of violence and banditry, of feuding and murder which pales into insignificance the peccadilloes of the Byrons'.

Away, ye gay landscapes! ye gardens of roses!
  In you let the minions of luxury rove;
Restore me the rocks, where the snow-flake reposes,
  Though still they are sacred to freedom and love:
Yet, Caledonia! belov'd are thy mountains,
  Round their white summits though elements war,
Though cataracts foam, 'stead of smooth flowing fountains,
  I sigh, for the valley of dark Loch na Garr.

. . .

Years have roll'd on, Loch na Garr, since I left you,
  Years must elapse, e'er I tread you again;
Nature of verdure and flowers has bereft you,
  Yet still are you dearer than Albion's plain:
England! thy beauties are tame and domestic,
  To one, who has rov'd on the mountains afar;
Oh! for the crags that are wild and majestic,
  The steep, frowning glories of dark Loch na Garr.*

* Jerome J. McGann's *Lord Byron: The Complete Poetical Works* (Oxford University Press). It is now the most up-to-date, best annotated, splendid and indispensable of all the editions of the poems. It is used here in all the volumes so far published.

A similar recollection could, as T. S. Eliot claimed, break the turgidness of *Childe Harold* like a blast from a bagpipe – the reference was intended as a compliment.*

> And wild and high the 'Cameron's gathering' rose!
> The war-note of Lochiel, which Albyn's hills
> Have heard, and heard, too, have her Saxon foes; –
> How in the noon of night that pibroch thrills,
> Savage and shrill! But with the breath which fills
> Their mountain-pipe, so fill the mountaineers
> With the fierce native daring which instils
> The stirring memory of a thousand years,
> And Ewan's, Donald's fame rings in each clansman's ears!

And then another echo from those Aberdeen days:

> We'll gang nae mair a-rovin,
>   A-rovin in the nicht . . .

*For T. S. Eliot's observations I am indebted to *Byron: Wrath and Rhyme*, edited by Alan Bold and published in 1983, containing an excellent series of new essays on various Byronic themes, including one which makes reference to the famous lyric quoted here (see page 201).

THREE

Newstead

I would be a citizen of the world.

Letter home, 23 June 1810

Byron wrote several thousands of lines of verse, almost all of them imitative in manner or matter or both together – as much almost as Keats was able to complete in his whole life – before he started to strike a vein of his own. He showed how readily he could write, how studious he could be, how much he respected the learning of others, how much he wanted, despite all protestations to the contrary, to be a poet. But he gave scarcely a hint of the great themes which later stirred him. Even the burning memories of Calvinistic hellfire retained from his Aberdonian childhood, even the more tepid 'democratic' debate in which his argumentative mother would indulge, seemed to become obliterated.

When he was just turning eleven years old the momentous news reached mother and son in Aberdeen that his uncle had died, that he had therefore become the sixth Baron Byron of Rochdale, and that Newstead Abbey, the family seat near Nottingham, awaited his arrival. Twenty-four hours later he is said to have asked his mother whether she perceived any difference in him since he had been made a lord, as he perceived none himself. The show of modesty, whether real or contrived, was not supposed to be characteristic, but during the next few years quite a number of his associates testified to his readiness to conform with prevailing customs and fashions, his strong streak of shyness and, above all perhaps, his eagerness to learn. He was sent for a while to a school in Dulwich under the tutelage of Dr Glennie whose testimony to his character is truly striking:

I found him enter upon his tasks with alacrity and success. He was playful, good humoured, and beloved by his companions. His reading in history and poetry was far beyond the usual standard of his age, and in my study he found many books open to him, both to please his taste and gratify his curiosity; among others a set of our poets from Chaucer to Churchill, which I am almost tempted to say he had more than once perused from beginning to end. He showed at this age an intimate acquaintance with the historical parts of the Holy Scriptures, upon which he seemed delighted to converse with me, especially after our religious exercises of a Sunday evening; when he would reason upon the facts contained in the Sacred Volume with every appearance of belief in the divine truths which they unfold.

Always as a child, he had been particularly inquisitive and puzzled about religion. That part of the story cannot be doubted. We may wonder whether his enthusiasm for Chaucer or Churchill may not have been ante-dated, but there too Dr Glennie's guidance is worth weighing carefully.

For a few years mother and child could not inhabit the old abbey of Newstead itself; the house was dilapidated and they had not the resources to maintain it; so they had to make do in some by no means incommodious accommodation in nearby Southwell. But he was soon ready for entry into Harrow, where once again he was most fortunate in those charged with his education. Dr Joseph, the headmaster, felt after one of their early encounters 'that his education had been neglected; that he was ill prepared for a public school', and his own testimony was that for the first year and a half he 'hated Harrow'. The solitary upbringing, the lame foot, no doubt combined to make a double impediment for a naturally shy schoolboy. But Dr Drury had always discerned that 'there was a cleverness about him', and he quickly won his way into the young Byron's trust. Was there ever a more touching tribute from pupil to master than that which Byron paid: in 'Dr Drury whom I plagued sufficiently too, was the best, the kindest (and yet strict, too,) friend I ever had – and I look upon him still as a father'. He soon made himself popular with his fellow pupils; none of the indignities and imbecilities of the public school system were sufficient to cow him. His schooling was certainly no drudgery or penance. Dr Drury was struck more by his gift for declamation than any hint of other capacities. 'My first Harrow verses [that is, English, as exercises, a translation of a chorus from the Prometheus of Aeschylus] were received by him [by Dr Drury] but coolly. No one had the least notion that I should subside into poesy.' It was once again his own reading which left the sharpest mark on his own recollection. 'The truth is,' he himself asserted, 'that I read eating, read in bed, read when no one else read, and had read all sorts of reading since I was five years old.' Years later (on 9 June 1820) to Thomas Moore he wrote: 'I have just been turning over Little, which I knew by heart in 1803, being then in my fifteenth summer. Heigho! I believe all the mischief I have ever done or sung, has been owing to that confounded book of yours.' Over the years Byron often taunted Thomas Moore with responsibility for his own sexual misdemeanours and adventures, an especially flattering charge since, years later too, Byron would protest with vociferous assurance that his *Don Juan*, at its most lascivious, never could actually induce real seduction. *The Poetical Works of the Late Thomas Little*, published in 1801 and reaching nine editions by 1806, were neither more nor less effective or aphrodisiacal. Another writer to whom he introduced himself at this same age had a more lasting influence. In that same year, 1803, he started to read Alexander Pope, and he never stopped.

Of course, the young Bryon had love affairs, platonic but none the less passionate, all memorable much more because of what happened to him later than because they suddenly changed his life. In Aberdeen, at the age of eight he was in love with a distant cousin of his own age, Mary Duff. At the age of twelve he fell for another cousin, Margaret Parker. During the summer vacation he fell even more deeply for Mary Chaworth of Annesley Hall, near Newstead. Another favourite, although not similarly loved, was Elizabeth Pigot, a neighbour across the road at Southwell, the first of the mother confessors with whom he found it easier to banter and brag than with girls of his own age. Byron could adopt the tone of his correspondence to suit each individual recipient, and Elizabeth was the first on whom he sought to practise his enchanting art.

One of the best of his early poems which he wrote a few years later (on 23 December 1806 to be exact), just after he left Harrow, was 'The First Kiss of Love'.

> Away, with your fictions of flimsy romance,
>   Those tissues of falsehood which Folly has wove;
> Give me the mild beam of the soul-breathing glance,
>   Or the rapture, which dwells on the first kiss of love.
>
> . . .
>
> Oh! cease to affirm, that man, since his birth,
>   From Adam, till now, has with wretchedness strove;
> Some portion of Paradise still is on earth,
>   And Eden revives, in the first kiss of love.
>
> When age chills the blood, when our pleasures are past,
>   For years fleet away with the wings of the dove;
> The dearest remembrance will still be the last,
>   Our sweetest memorial, the first kiss of love.

Presumably one of the four cited above must have been the giver or receiver of this first kiss, but neither he nor anyone else has recorded which.

The boy also started to write those letters, quite good ones but not yet of his own individual brand of later years which would make him the greatest letter-writer in the language. The adolescent prodigy did not acquire this touch all at once;* only after a

---

* I happily quote in confirmation of my view what Doris Langley Moore wrote (in the *Sunday Times*, 16 September 1973, reviewing the first five volumes of Marchand's *Letters and Journals*):

> 'My dear Hobhouse – In the gentle dulness of a summer voyage I shall converse with you for half an hour.' Thus Byron's pre-eminent gift as a letter-writer is captured in five words: 'I shall converse with you.' He becomes a voice, intimate, arresting, unguarded, with a tone in which, although it sometimes grows peremptory, sometimes a shade

while, in his first confessions to his half-sister Augusta, did he give glimpses of what was to come, and perhaps in this sense hindsight about their later relationship bestows a glint of excitement on the world-weary schoolboy of sixteen who told her: 'I am not old enough or goose enough to be in love, or, more conclusively, love, in my humble opinion, is utter nonsense, a mere jargon of compliments, romance and deceit.' Even at Cambridge, a year or two later, the easy flow of wit and ridicule ('the only weapon the English climate cannot rust', as he later insisted) had not yet developed, although there were signs:

> This place [he told his confessor back in Southwell] is wretched enough, a villainous Chaos of dice and Drunkenness, nothing but Hazard and Burgundy, Hunting, Mathematics and Newmarket, Riot and Racing, yet it is a Paradise compared with the eternal dullness of Southwell Oh! the misery of doing nothing but make *Love, enemies,* and *Verses* . . . I have got a new friend, the finest in the world a *tame Bear*; when I brought him here they asked me what I meant to do with him, and my reply was, 'he should sit for a Fellowship'.

Both at Harrow and at Cambridge he gathered around him a high-spirited bunch of companions, some of whom remained his firm friends for the rest of his life. With two or three of these,

---

contentious, gaiety is the most haunting quality. There is not a trace of consciousness that any recipient of his letters might be keeping them. Their self- revelation is artless, their gossip about others almost as exuberant. Such ease of manner, much rarer in his day than in ours, was not attained without a few false starts, and in the first of these two volumes, we find occasional heroics and affectedness, but this phase passes rapidly, and, while still in his teens, he begins to express himself with an entirely individual humour and simplicity. For us then on, he goes from good to better.

The heroics and affectedness remained, it cannot be denied, for some years still, characteristics of the poet. The revelations in his letter-writing underline how we can know Byron so much better than his contemporaries and certainly those who knew him only in public controversy.

evidently enough, the interest had some homosexual strand woven within it, but Byron himself at the time never stressed the matter and scholarly, prurient investigation has not been able to add any clinching conclusions.* When he had reached the ripe age of twenty, it was still not clear, despite some homosexual disappointments and a few others of a more orthodox character, what had occurred to cramp his natural gaiety, and often indeed the affectations of melancholy gave way to bursts of laughter and wit. 'I am a very unlucky fellow, for I had naturally not a bad heart, but it has been so bent, twisted and trampled on, that it has now become as hard as a Highlander's heel piece.' What happened to that heart, and how it went on beating until it had captivated a continent, is the true Byron story. It is evident from this self-revealing sentence that he himself knew how soft that heart truly was; how deeply it could be moved.

Just occasionally in his first prolific efforts to write poetry – or most rarely, it might be more proper to insist – he could strike a note like 'The First Kiss of Love'. Much more often he found

* And this sentence, too, is not written in the expectation that it can conclude the matter. A huge literature on its own has been devoted to examinations of Byron's alleged homosexuality, started in some instances by Professor Wilson Knight's studies and concluding most recently with *Byron & Greek Love* by Louis Crompton, a serious and original investigation of the matter. His book opens sensationally with an horrific account of the shameful cruelty inflicted on homosexuals in the England of Byron's time: evidence based on a passionate outburst against these horrors by one not previously associated with such a protest: Jeremy Bentham. The Benthamite broadside against this persecution deserves to take its place alongside the greatest philippics against other persecutions; the pogroms against the Jews, against witches, against all the other victims of religious persecution. Madame de Staël, perceptive and generous woman that she could often be, thought that the era in which she lived should be called not the age of Napoleon, nor the age of Byron, nor even the age of Madame de Staël, but the age of Bentham. Louis Crompton's book offers evidence of the first importance why that judgement should be respected. So his view deserves respect in other matters too. Even so, I believe his conclusion about Byron's homosexuality is vastly overstated. The Doris Langley Moore balance on this matter as on so many is the more legitimate and judicious one.

himself grappling with obstacles which seemed to overwhelm him. He wrote a tribute to Newstead and his ancestors in which traitors were arraigned with ponderous orthodoxy. He wrote (in 1806) 'The Prayer of Nature' modelled on another prayer by Pope in which, however, no trace of Popeian optimism was allowed to relieve the Calvinistic gloom; he still had not felt the revolutionary stirrings which Pope could help to instil. He had prepared ready for the press and soon actually printed some love poems, modelled maybe on Thomas Little, which one of his bunch of parson friends advised him to suppress. One portrait in the poems was, according to the Reverend John Becher, 'too warmly drawn'; so all copies were destroyed except four – one fortunately retained by the self-same fastidious John Becher.* The revised volume was, as Byron protested, 'miraculously chaste', and, considering his morals at the time, wretchedly bowdlerized. Most serious of all, he published in July 1807, with a pretentious preface, his first substantial volume, *Hours of Idleness*, and provoked with it one of the most famous critical assaults in our literary history. The assailant was the great Whig journal, the *Edinburgh Review*, in the person, as was revealed years later, of Henry Brougham.†

* John Becher exerted his influence on the young Byron on an even more important matter. See page 128.
† *Hours of Idleness* attracts attention chiefly for the part it played in Byron's own life; none of the criticisms equal in significance those, such as Brougham's, which were provoked at the time. But some of the modern criticisms still have an interest; for instance, those which Jerome McGann offered in his book on Byron, *Fiery Dust*. McGann refers to a fragment of manuscript preserved in the Beinecke Rare Book Library at Yale University and reproduced in *Fiery Dust* which must have been written before 1812, probably in 1809.

> In it Byron asks a series of rhetorical questions about a liberator of Greece. Five times he asks a variant of the question of who will finally set Greece free, and five times the answer to that question – not publicly recorded – is dashed across the page in his bold script: 'Byron'. The scrap of MS is a graphic reminder not only of Byron's heroic pretensions, but of his tendency to refute the distinction between his life in history and his life in art.

Despite all his protestations to the contrary, Byron was deeply hurt. Thomas Moore gives the most authentic account of the moment.

> We have seen [he says] with what feverish anxiety he awaited the verdicts of all minor Reviews, and, from his sensibility to the praise of the meanest of these censors, may guess how painfully he must have writhed under the sneers of the highest. A friend, who found him in the first moments of excitement after reading the article, inquired anxiously whether he had just received a challenge, – not knowing how else to account for the fierce defiance of his looks . . . His pride had been wounded to the quick, and his ambition humbled; but this feeling of humiliation lasted but for a moment. The very reaction of his spirit against aggression forced him to full consciousness of his own powers; and the pain and the shame of the injury were forgotten in the proud certainty of revenge.

He was spurred most perhaps by the knowledge that his mother would feel the blow, and she certainly must have approved the preparations for a counter-attack no less famous than the original assault.

Another report at this anxious moment in his life shows how deep was the wound and how varied the remedies he sought to apply. He wrote to John Cam Hobhouse, one of the closest of his Cambridge friends:

> Dear Hobhouse, – I write to you to explain a foolish circumstance, which has arisen from some words uttered by me . . . when I was devoured with Chagrin, and almost insane with the fumes of, not 'last night's Punch' but that evening's wine. – [In] consequence of a misconception of something on my part, I mentioned an intention of withdrawing my name from the Whig Club, this I hear has been broached, and perhaps in a moment of Intoxication and passion such might be my idea, but *soberly* I have no such design, particularly as I could not abandon my principles, even if I

renounced the society with whom I have the honour to be united in sentiments which I never will disavow. – This I beg you will explain to the members as publicly as possible, but should this not be sufficient, and they think proper to erase my name, be it so, I only request that in this case they will recollect, I shall become a *Tory of their own making*. I shall expect your answer on this point with some impatience, now a few words on the subject of my own conduct. – I am buried in an abyss of Sensuality, I have renounced *hazard* however, but I am given to Harlots, and live in a state of Concubinage, I am at this moment under a course of restoration by Pearsons's prescription, for a debility occasioned by too frequent Connection. – Pearson sayeth, I have done sufficient with[in?] this last ten days, to undermine my Constitution, I hope however all will soon be well. – As an author, I am cut to atoms by the E[dinburgh] Review, it is just out, and has completely demolished my little fabric of fame, this is rather scurvy treatment from a Whig Review, but politics and poetry are different things, and I am no adept in either, I therefore submit in Silence.

The full revenge, *English Bards and Scotch Reviewers*, published in March 1809, certainly presented to the world a new Byron, the belligerent Byron who would never yield an inch to his enemies in political combat, but it was still a Byron content to imitate his tutors, patrons and opponents. *English Bards and Scotch Reviewers* was a satire after the manner of Pope without the grace and precision of the master; but, much more remarkably, it lacked the venom and fury of Pope. It was satire directed not against carefully selected opponents but against an array of random targets. Few who knew him intimately could doubt that there were within him great resources of devilry and passion. But *English Bards and Scotch Reviewers* did not unleash them.* He could not yet – most strangely in view of what came

* The publication of the first volume of Jerome J. McGann's *Lord Byron: The Complete Poetical Works* in January 1981, produced, in the columns of the *Times Literary Supplement* of 23 January, an anti-Byron tirade from Lorna Sage. Intermittently the protest purported to be aimed at some

later – laugh at himself, although was there not just one hint of it?

> And every brother Rake will smile to see
> That miracle, a Moralist in me.

Moreover, this controversy unloosed by his own *Hours of Idleness* dispelled the interest in some other of his poems. It is sometimes overlooked how he was starting to combine his lascivious wit, his lightness of touch, with his serious ambition:

The Farewell to a Lady

> When man expell'd from Eden's bowers,
> A moment linger'd near the gate,
> Each scene recall'd the vanish'd hours,
> And bade him curse his future fate.

---

typographical or textual errors on the part of the editor and the printers; but her real aim was directed at Byron himself, at what she called 'an old question; just how did the fat boy from Harrow turn himself into a poet?' Others before her, as she well knew, had answered the question with the simple retort that he never did. It was not at all clear, after several columns of invective, that she did not reach the same conclusion. 'The flab', she insisted at once with reference to her chosen fat boy, 'is even more in evidence this time round with thirty-five previously uncollected bits and pieces . . .' So she moved from his 'dreadful juvenilia' to the 'silly jauntiness and the arrogant parade of ancestors' in his *Hours of Idleness*. Later she continued: 'His snobbish squirming and his wincing tenderness for his work elicited a corresponding sycophancy from the first reviewers' until the Edinburgh reviewer did his 'splendid if slightly belated job of destruction on the whole production . . .' Brougham, she implied, would have been even more justly severe if he had ever had the bad fortune to set eyes on the young Byron's earlier libertine lyrics to girl and boy loves.

Enough quoted, I trust, to give a hint of the intensity of this particular diatribe, and this much validity in it must be acknowledged: with a few exceptions, Byron's earlier poetry – right up to 1812 – did not show even a glimmer of genius. The question where he got it from becomes all the more fascinating.

But wandering on through distant climes,
    He learnt to bear his load of grief;
Just gave a sigh to other times,
    And found in busier scenes relief.

Thus, lady! will it be with me,
    And I must view thy charms no more;
For while I linger near to thee
    I sigh for all I knew before.

In flight I shall be surely wise,
    Escaping from temptation's snare;
I cannot view my Paradise
    Without the wish of dwelling there.

This lady too is unidentified. He was content to add his own note: 'You perceive the last lines – the "Double Entendre" – are a little too much in English poesy.' And the Garden of Eden still had for him some of its old traditional uses and charm. He did not yet see it only as a place of infamy where the politics of hypocrisy and betrayal had first been practised.

One strong recurrent theme in his conversation with most of his closest companions in those first years found only a pallid reflection in his poetry. But no doubt is possible about the way in which his full mind could become absorbed. 'With him', recorded Thomas Moore, 'the canker showed itself "in the morn and dew of youth" when the effect of such "blastments" is, for every reason, most fatal, – and, in addition to the real misfortune of being an unbeliever at any age he exhibited the rare and melancholy spectacle of an unbelieving schoolboy.' And, most lamentably, according to Moore's account, just at the time when counter-action might have been taken to relieve the affliction, he fell beneath the influence of Charles Skinner Mathews at Cambridge. 'By singular ill fortune, the individual who, among all his college friends had taken the strongest hold on his admiration and affection, and whose loss he afterwards lamented with brotherly tenderness, was, to the same extent as himself, if not more strongly, a sceptic.'

He was willing to debate the subject with all comers,

especially those among his friends whose religious convictions were tempting them to become parsons of one brand or another. He wrote to one old school friend, Edward Noel Long, in April 1807:

> . . . To be plain with Regard to myself. Nature stampt me in the Die of *Indifference*. I consider myself as destined never to be happy, although in some instances fortunate. I am an isolated Being on the Earth, without a Tie to attach me to life, except a few School-fellows, and a *score of females*. Let me but 'hear my fame on the winds' and the song of the Bards in my Norman house, I ask no more and don't expect so much. Of Religion I know nothing, at least in its *favour*. We have *fools* in all sects and impostors in most; why should I believe mysteries no one understands, because written by men who chose to mistake madness for Inspiration, and style themselves *Evangelicals*? However enough on this subject. Your *piety* will be *aghast*, and I wish for no proselytes. This much I will venture to affirm, that all the virtues and pious *Deeds* performed on Earth can never entitle a man to Everlasting happiness in a future State; nor on the other hand can such a Scene as a Seat of eternal punishment exist, it is incompatible with the benign attributes of a Deity to suppose so; I am surrounded here by parsons & Methodists, but, as you will perceive not infected with the *Mania*, I have lived a *Deist*, what I shall die I know not – however come what may, '*ridens moriar*' . . .

And then a year later to Robert Charles Dallas, another dedicated would-be churchman; who can resist the young Byron in such a mood? And this, by the way, is still the emotional dandy of Lorna Sage's caricature.*

> Whenever Leisure and Inclination permit me the pleasure of a visit, I shall feel truly gratified in a personal acquaintance with one, whose mind has been long known to me in his Writings. – You are so far correct in your conjec-

* See footnote page 105.

ture, that I am a member of the University of Cambridge, where I shall take my degree of A.M. this term, but were Reasoning, Eloquence or Virtue the objects of my search, Granta is not their metropolis, nor is the place of her Situation an 'El Dorado' far less an Utopia, the Intellects of her children are as stagnant as her Cam, and their pursuits limited to the Church, – not of Christ, but of the nearest Benefice. – As to my reading, I believe I may aver without hyperbole, it has been tolerably extensive in the historical department, so that few nations exist or have existed with whose records I am not in some degree acquainted from Herodotus down to Gibbon. – Of the Classics I know about as much as most Schoolboys after a Discipline of thirteen years, of the *Law* of the *Land* as much as enables me to keep 'within the Statute' (to use the Poacher's vocabulary) I did study 'the Spirit of Laws' and the Law of Nations, but when I saw the latter violated every month, I gave up my attempts at so useless an accomplishment. Of Geography – I have seen more land on maps than I should wish to traverse on foot, of Mathematics enough to give me the headache without clearing the part affected, of Philosophy Astronomy and Metaphysicks, more than I can comprehend, and of Common Sense, so little, that I mean to leave a Byronian prize at each of our 'Alma Matres' [sic] for the first Discovery, though I rather fear that of the Longitude will precede it. – I once thought myself a Philosopher and talked nonsense with great Decorum, I defied pain and preached up equanimity, for some time this did very well, for no one was in *pain* for me but my Friends, and none lost their patience but my hearers, at last a fall from my horse convinced me, bodily suffering was an Evil, and the worst of an argument overset my maxims and my temper at the same moment, so I quitted Zeno for Aristippus, and conceive that Pleasure constitutes the 'ro kayor'. In Morality I prefer Confucius to the ten Commandments, and Socrates to St. Paul (though the two latter agree in their opinion of marriage) in Religion, I favour the Catholic Emancipation but do not acknowledge the Pope, and I have refused to take the

Sacrament because I do not think eating Bread or drinking wine from the hand of an earthly vicar, will make me an Inheritor of heaven. – I hold virtue in general, or the virtues severally, to be only in the Disposition, each *a feeling* not a principle. – I believe Truth the prime attribute of the Deity, and Death an eternal Sleep, at least of the Body. – You have here a brief compendium of the Sentiments of the *wicked* George Ld. B. – and till I get a new suit you will perceive I am badly cloathed.

Another Christian correspondent was Francis Hodgson who did finish up in the bosom of the Church long before he reached Abraham's. The relationship between him and Byron was always a warm one, as we shall see later, and he was one of those to whom Byron wrote most fondly on the eve of his first travels abroad: 'I am like Adam the first convict sentenced to transportation, but I have no Eve, and have eaten no apple but what was sour as a crab and thus ends my first chapter.'

One of the wise courses followed by Thomas Moore in his biography – an example followed by few others – was to publish almost in full ' "a memorandum-book", as he called it, the account, as I find it hastily and promiscuously scribbled out, of all the books in various departments of knowledge, which he [Byron] had already perused . . .' The list is prodigious and indeed incredible as a reckoning of what Byron had actually read at such an age. But he had started early and went on reading all his life. He scarcely ever wrote to his mother without an entreaty to her about looking after his books. He did absorb a large quantity of the feast which would have been indigestible in its entirety. It is worth looking back at Moore's memorandum:

a list of *History* books, his favourite topic, cover eighteen different countries, all the well-known ones and a legion not so well known: *Biography*, covers all the British poets; *Law*, from Paley to Bolingbroke, 'Hobbes I detest'; *Geography*; *Poetry*; all the British classics as before detailed with most of the living poets – some *French* in the original, of which the Cid is

my favourite – Little Italian – *Greek* and *Latin* without number: *Eloquence*, from Demosthenes to the British Parliament
of 1742: *Divinity*, . . . 'I abhor all books of religion, though I
reverence and love my God, without the blasphemous
notions of sectaries or beliefs in their absurd and damnable
heresies, mysteries, and Thirty-Nine Articles': *Miscellanies*,
Spectator, Rambler, World etc. Novels 'by the thousand' . . .
'All the books here enumerated [it was in fact much larger]
I have taken down from memory . . . Since I left Harrow, I
have become idle and conceited, from scribbling rhyme and
making love to women.'

The idleness was far from profound. Byron had written that on
the night of 30 November 1807 – and then went on reading.
   It might be misleading to pick out favourites from such a list;
yet one exception must be made. On the flyleaf of Owen
Ruffhead's *The Life of Alexander Pope*, one of his Cambridge pos-
sessions, he scrawled:

Of Pope's pithy conciseness of style Swift – no diffuse writer
himself – has so emphatically said –

> For Pope can in one couplet fix
> More sense than I can do in six

The biographer suggested that Pope had written his book 'to
bring mankind to look upon this life with comfort and pleasure'. Byron underscored the word 'mankind', and wrote in the
margin: 'A malignant race with Christianity in their mouths
and Molochism in their hearts.' Here, I believe, is the first traceable reference in which Byron relates his suspicions about religion to his hatred of all the blood and tears of war, and it is
instructive indeed that the relationship should have been
prompted by Pope. 'Molochism' was a word which Byron had
invented; it is curious that it has not gained more currency considering how the thing has been so evidently in existence from
that day to this. Milton wrote frequently about Moloch, and so
occasionally did Coleridge. Byron knew better than any of his

111

predecessors what a world-wide phenomenon warmaking and all its apparatus could be.

Byron's devotion to Pope was a love he learnt at his mother's knee and never ceased to cherish thereafter. Here was his truest, bosom companion throughout his whole life, and he never wavered in his readiness to acknowledge the debt. 'As a child', he himself wrote, 'I first read Pope's Homer with a rapture which no subsequent work could ever afford, and children are not the worst judges of their own language.' To be forced to read Homer in Greek could be a punishment even for children eager to learn; Pope came as the liberator. But this was only the first of his boons; even as a child Byron could begin to detect the different quality of instruction which Pope was seeking to impart, a testament of a quite different order from anything he had heard dispensed, with fire and brimstone, from Calvinist pulpits. The time would come when he would rush to Pope's defence as 'the most *perfect* of our poets, and the purest of our moralists'. No strain is needed to suggest that here was one of the sources where Byron learnt his politics. 'The two books he loved best throughout his life', wrote Professor G. Wilson Knight*, 'were, without any question, the Old Testament and the works of Pope.' Byron, in later years, made a mocking note of the fact that Pope had had the misfortune to be 'edited only by priests'. He fell into the hands of his enemies or, say, Warburton, 'who was a polemical person and as fit to edit Poetry as Pope to preach in Gloucester Cathedral.' But Byron was refreshed by the strong

---

* Professor G. Wilson Knight has made the fullest examination of Byron's kinship with Pope in his 1954 volume *The Poetry of Pope* and in his earlier volume of essays (1939) *The Burning Oracle*, which also includes, in one essay, a magnificent piece of Byronic rhetoric about Byron himself. The title of that volume was taken from Byron's *Sardanapalus*; it was one of my own first introductions to the subject, and for sheer exultation in Byronic glory and excitement Knight is still hard to beat. He has, of course, written several other better known and more controversial books on the subject, in particular, the trilogy: *Lord Byron: Christian Virtues, Lord Byron's Marriage* and *Byron and Shakespeare*. None of these is to be missed or dismissed, even when a principal part of his argument may not be accepted. With him still the burning oracle never loses the power and lustre to be found in that original essay.

strand of scepticism in Pope, which Pope, in turn, had acquired from *his* master. The young Alexander Pope pored over the essays of Montaigne as the young Byron pored over Pope's poetry and marked passage after passage which came to shape his sceptical creed: 'This is', he wrote inside the back cover of his Charles Cotton edition, '(in my opinion) the very best Book for information of Manners, that has been writ. The author says nothing but what everyone feels at the Heart. Whoever deny it, are not more Wise than Montaigne, but less honest.' Montaigne would insist, or rather cunningly insinuate, that to accept the nature of the visible world as it is is so much wiser than to seek to make it conform to some scriptural or ecclesiastical edict. 'Our religion,' said Montaigne again, now invoking Lucretius to his aid, 'is intended to extirpate Vices; whereas it skreens, nourishes and incites them.' Byron could fold to his bosom those same passions and recapture the old Montaigneite, Popeian hatred of oppression and dream of peace:

> O stretch thy Reign, fair Peace!
> > from Shore to Shore,
> Till Conquest cease, and Slavery be
> > no more;
> Till the freed *Indians* in their
> > native Groves
> Reap their own Fruits, and woo their
> > Sable Loves.

By what genius was it that Pope compressed the Indian spectacle throughout the ages into that magnificent passage? Byron must have approved.

It is not hard to picture also the Byron of Cambridge or Southwell or Newstead adopting as part of his liberation such a passage as this from the *Essay on Man*:

> But still this world (so fitted for the knave)
> Contents us not. A better shall we have?
> A kingdom of the Just then let it be:
> But first consider how those Just agree.

113

> The good must merit God's peculiar care;
> But who, but God, can tell us who they are?
> One thinks on Calvin Heav'n's own spirit fell;
> Another deems him instrument of hell;
> If Calvin feel Heav'n's blessing, or its rod,
> This cries there is, and that, there is no God.
> What shocks one part will edify the rest,
> Nor with one system can they all be blest.
> The very best will variously incline,
> And what rewards your Virtue, punish mine.

The little Queen Anne man, as Byron later so lovingly called him, could raise the human argument to the heights, to make himself the 'poet of a thousand years'; he could expose the wickedness of war and tyranny as none had done before, and he could, in the next breath, endear himself in lesser matters. A century before Byron himself, Pope was protesting with brilliant vehemence and clarity against the way so-called Christian country-lovers could torture animals on or off the hunting field.

It was the Byronic grand tour, and the avalanche of poetry unloosed by it, which created his fame and his legend. No doubt is possible about the potency of the event and the aftermath. Not much dispute is needed about the various new sources of his inspiration. No other English poet was ever able to make such an entry on the international stage, commanding at once an audience across national frontiers. Although the breed is always youthful, few other young poets have been able to accumulate such an array of kaleidoscopic impressions. They can still dazzle the observer to this day; yet even this matchless parade of word and deed leaves something of Byron's essence still lacking.

He set sail from Falmouth in June 1809, and one of his last acts was to send a loving, excited, touching letter to his mother: 'the world is all before me'; he told her too how he had chosen one of his servants: 'I like him, because like myself he seems to be a friendless animal.' He wrote to his bosom friend Citoyen

Charles Skinner Mathews – the nickname was obviously bestowed in deference to his revolutionary sympathies – and explained or boasted how he had scoured the port for sexual excitement and found fulfilment in a phrase of Petronius: 'Plen. and opta bit – coit', which being interpreted meant 'complete intercourse to one's heart's desire'. He wrote to his parson friends with overflowing gaiety:

> Still to laugh by far the best is,
> Then laugh on – and do now
> Laugh at all things
> Great and small things.

He wrote again from Lisbon and reported on the delights of the Moorish palace on the heights of Cintra where the author of *Vathek* had lived; he had some knowledge of and sympathy for 'the great Beckford'. He eagerly reported – 'must observe that the village of Cintra in Estramadura is the most beautiful perhaps in the world'. And he called at a nearby convent and surveyed their large library, and 'the proud monks asked me if the *English* had any books in their country.' He passed through Cadiz, and learnt to make it rhyme with ladies. He saw something of the devastation left by the war, a glimpse such as Goya himself had immortalized, but not, as yet for him, the dominant theme: 'Spain is all in arms, and the French have everything to do over again, the barbarities on both sides are shocking. I passed some French prisoners on the road from Badajoz to Seville, and saw a spy who was condemned to be shot. . .' This was his first sight of what war meant, but soon he had another to report to his mother. 'You have heard of the battle near Madrid, and in England they call it a victory! two hundred officers and 5000 men killed, all English . . .'* He

---

* The best account of what Byron saw on his journey through Portugal and Spain – apart from Byron's own – is contained in Gordon Kent Thomas's *Lord Byron's Iberian Pilgrimage*. He mentions the local tradition about the Portuguese hotel where Byron made his first plans for *Childe Harold*, and even more revealing, his own estimates of the part played by this tour in starting *Don Juan*. The imprint of the war upon his mind is properly recognized.

needed no excuse to discuss such high matters with his mother, but he well knew she had other practical concerns too . . . 'if I wed I will bring you home a sultana with half a score cities for a dowry, and reconcile you to an Ottoman daughter-in-law with a bushel of pearls not larger than ostrich eggs or smaller than walnuts.' Then he sailed on to Malta, and met a real-life heroine, at least for the few weeks while the passion lasted. He found his way to the court of Ali the Lion, Ali Pasha in Albania, the half-model for countless Byronic heroes or villains. The scene was for Byron himself the high peak of the whole tour. Nothing else as yet surpassed the magnificence of their reception, even though the French Ambassador sneered at these 'soi-disants mylords, . . . these fops at the feet of a savage for their bread and butter'. Here, too, at Ioannina in Albania, on 31 October 1809 – according to his own account – he started work on the first canto of *Childe Harold*. He was stirred afresh by the spectacle of Mount Parnassus with a flight of eagles circling round its summit. Yet it was another bird which left its mark: 'The last bird I ever fired at was an eaglet, on the shore of the Gulf of Lepanto, near Vostizza. It was only wounded, and I tried to save it – the eye was so bright. But it pined and died in a few days; and I never did since, and never will, attempt the death of another bird.'

He went to Greece on his first visit, and pleaded

> Maid of Athens, ere we part
> Give, oh, give back my heart.

The Maid in question was twelve at the time; the relationship was platonic. He had the chance to meditate on the ruins of the Acropolis, and the imperialist spoilers of the place, ancient and modern; time, too, to enlist Lucretius in his debates on the immortality of his soul.

He went to Smyrna and Constantinople and crossed the 'broad Hellespont' and never ceased to boast of the feat: 'This morning [3 May 1810] I *swam* from *Sestos* to *Abydos*, the immediate distance is not above a mile but the current renders it hazardous, so much so, that I doubt whether Leander's conjugal powers must not have been exhausted in his passage to Paradise . . .' Constantinople gripped his imagination and cured any home sickness:

> I will trouble you no more at present except to state that all climates and nations are equally interesting to me; that mankind are everywhere despicable in different absurdities; that the farther I proceed from your country the less I regret leaving it, and the only advantage you have over the rest of mankind is the sea, that divides you from your foes; your other superiorities are merely imaginary. I would be a citizen of the world . . .

What other poet of his age would speak in such terms, at the height of the war which came to dominate his imagination more than that of most others of his generation? He was the more ready to do so, since the news reaching him from home could make him bitterly ashamed. He learnt how English soldiers were being let loose upon the English enemy: 'Have the military murdered any more mechanics?' He could never extract a direct answer to these questions, and at last, after nearly two years of adventures, some meticulously and magnificently recorded by himself and his companions and some still the subject of furious controversy, he returned with a touch of trepidation to his home country. If he was in truth the mad, melancholy spirit portrayed both by his own hand and by others', he never showed signs of being subdued for long. He was persuaded of the wisdom of the way he himself had learnt. 'I am convinced,' he told his mother, 'of the advantages of looking at mankind instead of reading about them, and of the bitter effects of staying at home with all the narrow prejudices of an Islander, that I think there should be a law amongst us to set our young men abroad for a term among the few allies our wars have left us.' And all the while, of course, despite the disavowals, he had been reading and writing and reading again. He never stopped, and he was always ready to experiment with new ways of writing. 'I trust to find my library in tolerable order' was almost his last message to his mother before she died.

And (on 28 June 1811) just on the eve of his return, he could write:

> I am coming back with little prospect of pleasure at home and with a body a little shaken by one or two smart fevers, but a spirit I hope yet unbroken. My affairs, it seems, are considerably involved, and much business must be done with lawyers, colliers, farmers, and creditors. Now this to a man who hates bustle as he hates a bishop, is a serious concern.

One of the great formative periods of Byron's life – one of the great fighting periods, and with him the two can never be separated – was the six months following his return from the grand tour. It is in his moments of resilience against odds that he rises to his true height, and usually these were masked from his contemporaries. Not for years later, for generations later, could the full record of those months be pieced together. Apart from shorter pieces and squibs, he had brought back with him two lengthy poems – some eight hundred lines of *Hints from Horace*, a new satire shaped on the *English Bards* model, and two cantos of an original work, whatever else it was, *Childe Harold*. Byron himself thought it would be safer to proceed with the satire; he was diffident about both. And perhaps his greatest good fortune was that, quite peremptorily, the first proposed publisher turned it down. William Miller of Albemarle Street, one of the booksellers from whom Byron, the bookworm, bought so avidly, turned it down on political and religious grounds in general and, in particular, because of the few verses which assailed Lord Elgin, the purchaser of the Parthenon marbles, and one of Miller's authors. Byron appreciated Miller's case and looked with a more favourable eye on his own work which could stir such enmity. 'It is in men as in soils,' wrote Swift, quoted by Thomas Moore, 'where sometimes there is a vein of gold which the owner knows not of.' And it does appear that the young Lord Byron, not usually arraigned for his bashfulness, was genuinely doubtful, even alarmed, about *Childe Harold*.

Partly, no doubt, he was still smarting from Brougham's lash; partly he knew how much more his previous reputation was at stake; partly he was a better self-critic than most people then or thereafter would allow. Byron was nervous in making literary judgements, yet all those nerves could leave him when he faced a political judgement or a political challenge or the two together.

Soon, and for a few weeks, these initial disputations with printers and booksellers were brutally interrupted. First, even before he had returned to Newstead, he had news of his mother's death: 'I heard *one* day of her illness, the next of her death . . . now feel the truth of Mr Gray's observation "that we can only have one mother".' And there was no pretence or hypocrisy in his mourning, and he was especially outraged by some scurrilous newspaper which behind his back and hers had attacked them both. 'I will have no stain on the Memory of my Mother, with a very large portion of foibles and irritability, she was without a Vice (and in these days that is much) the laws of my country shall do her and me justice in the first instance, but if they were deficient, the laws of modern Honour should decide, cost what it may, gold or blood, I will pursue to the last the cowardly calumniator of an absent man and a defenceless woman . . . .' This was his note to his lawyer, two days after her death.

Two days later again, he wrote from Newstead to another of his Cambridge companions, Scrope Beardmore Davies: 'Some curse hangs over me and mine. My mother lies a corpse in this house; one of my best friends is drowned in a ditch.' Charles Skinner Mathews wrote his last letter to Byron on Friday, on the Saturday he was drowned in the Cam: 'In ability who was like Mathews? How did we all shrink before him?' Hobhouse, he knew, admired and loved him even more, and Byron wrote to offer comfort. 'I have neither hopes nor fears beyond the Grave, yet if there is within us a "spark of Celestial fire" M has already "mingled with the Gods" . . . I can neither receive or administer Consolation . . . I have tried reading and boxing, and swimming and writing, and rising early and sitting late, and water and wine with a number of ineffectual remedies.' He even gave some mordant orders for his own departure. 'The body of Lord B to be buried in the vault of the garden of Newstead, without any ceremony or burial service whatever, or any inscription, save his name and age. His dog not to be moved from the said vault.'

But full-scale dejection seldom gripped him for long. He could laugh at trials, sometimes almost, as he would admit, with a hint of hysteria, and some companion could touch his playfulness, even at the most awkward moments, Scrope Davies or his sister Augusta, for a start. He hardly knew her yet, but he could already touch the chord which stirred her:

> I hear you have been increasing His Majesty's subjects, which in these times of War and tribulation is really patriotic notwithstanding Malthus tells us that were it not for Battle, Murder and Sudden death, we should be overstocked, I think we have latterly had a redundance of these national benefits, and therefore I give you all credit for your matronly behaviour . . . I should be glad to see you here (as I think you have never seen the place) . . . By the by, *I* shall marry if I can find any thing inclined to barter money for rank, within six months; after which I shall return to my friends the Turks . . .

He was soon pressing Augusta to join him at Newstead; she could awaken his light-hearted, light-headed responses, even by correspondence:

> I don't know what Scrope Davies meant by telling you I liked Children, I abominate the sight of them so much that I have always had the greatest respect for the character of *Herod*. – But as my house here is large enough for us all, we should go on very well, & I need not tell you that I long to see *you*. . . . I have little to add that you do not already know, and being quite alone, have no great variety of incident to gossip with, I am but rarely pestered with visitors, & the few I have I get rid of as soon as possible. – I will now take leave of you in the Jargon of 1794. 'Health & *Fraternity*!'

And again:

> . . . As to a Lady B. – when I discover one rich enough to suit
> me & foolish enough to have me, I will give her leave to
> make me miserable if she can. – Money is the magnet, as to
> Women, one is as well as another, the older the better, we
> have then a chance of getting her to Heaven. – So, your
> Spouse does not like brats better than myself; now those
> who beget them have no right to find fault, but *I* may rail
> with great propriety. – My 'Satire!' – I am glad it made you
> laugh for Somebody told me in Greece that you was angry, &
> I was sorry, as you were perhaps the only person whom I did
> *not* want to *make angry*. – But how you will make *me laugh* I
> don't know, for it is a vastly *serious* subject to me I assure you,
> therefore take care, or I shall hitch *you* into the next Edition
> to make up our family party. – Nothing so fretful, so despic-
> able as a Scribbler, see what *I* am, & what a parcel of Scoun-
> drels I have brought about my ears, & what language I have
> been obliged to treat them with to deal with them in their
> own way; – all this comes of Authorship, but now I am in
> for it, & shall be at war with Grubstreet, till I find some bet-
> ter amusement . . . .

One major part of his activities was concerned with his
publishing ventures, and the advice and admonitions he
received, either direct from John Murray or from his friend and
intermediary, Robert Charles Dallas. Soon after he had his first
chance of seeing *Childe Harold* in manuscript, Murray had
responded with tentative sympathetic objections and suggestions. Some expressions concerning Spain and Portugal,
Murray wrote, 'do not harmonize with the general feeling',
might interfere with the popularity of the poem: 'I hope your
Lordship's goodness will induce you to obviate them, and, with
them, perhaps, some religious feelings which may deprive me
of some customers among the Orthodox.' Byron, even the
young Byron untutored in the ways of lily-livered, censorious
publishers, was on the alert at once. Already his politics merged
with his religious views, and comforting the Orthodox was not
one of his intentions in life:

The time seems to be past when (as Dr Johnson said) a man was certain to 'hear the truth from his Bookseller', for you have paid me so many compliments, that, if I was not the veriest scribbler on Earth, I should feel affronted. – As I accept your compliments, it is but fair I should give equal or greater credit to your objections, the more so as I believe them to be well founded. – With regard to the political & metaphysical parts, I am afraid I can alter nothing, but I have high authority for my Errors in that point, for even the *Æneid* was a *political* poem & written for a *political* purpose, and as to my unlucky opinions on Subjects of more importance, I am too sincere in them for recantation. – On Spanish affairs I have said what I saw, & every day confirms me in that notion of the result formed on the Spot, & I rather think honest John Bull is beginning to come round again to that Sobriety which Massena's retreat had begun to reel from its Centre, the usual consequence of *un*usual success. – So you perceive I cannot alter the Sentiments, but if there are any alterations in the structure of the versification you would wish to be made, I will tag rhymes, & turn Stanzas, as much as you please. – As for the *Orthodox*, let us hope they will buy on purpose to abuse, you will forgive the one if they will do the other. – You are aware that anything from my pen must expect no quarter on many accounts, & as the present publication is of a Nature very different from the former, we must not be sanguine . . .

And then two weeks later: 'You hinted to me that you wished some alterations to be made. If they have nothing to do with politics or religion, I will make them with great readiness.'

And never for long would these arguments about publishing and politics escape from his persistent argument about religion. With one of his religious friends, Francis Hodgson, the argument seemed to be especially close, and throughout the whole period of his absence Byron had sustained between them his tone of intimate raillery:

[I] hope you will find me an altered personage, I do not

mean in body but in manner, for I begin to find out that nothing but virtue will do in this damned world. I am tolerably sick of vice which I have tried in its agreeable varieties, and mean on my return to cut all my dissolute acquaintance, leave off wine and 'carnal company', and betake myself to politics and Decorum . . .

But this was no more than a passing moment.

. . . I have really no friends in the world, though all my old school companions are gone forth into the world, and walk about in monstrous disguises, in the garb of Guardsmen, lawyers, parsons, fine gentlemen, and such other masquerade dresses. – So I have shaken hands and cut with all these busy people, none of whom write to me, indeed I asked it not, and here I am a poor traveller and heathenish philosopher, who hath perambulated the greatest part of the Levant, and seen a great quantity of very improveable land and sea, and after all am no better than when I set out, Lord help me . . .

Soon after his return he discovered how serious Hodgson's intentions were. 'So you are going (going indeed) into orders. Make a dash before you are a deacon.' Several others joined the correspodence or the argument which must have dominated so many nights at Newstead. 'I will have nothing to do with your immortality; we are miserable enough in this life, without the absurdity of speculating upon another. If men are to live, why die at all? And if they die, why disturb the sweet and sound sleep that "knows no waking" . . .' Letter after letter showed how with what intelligence and delicacy Byron could conduct the debate with such an adversary:

As to revealed religion, Christ came to save men; but a good Pagan will go to heaven, and a bad Nazarene to hell; 'Argal' (I argue like the gravedigger) why are not all men Christians? or why are any? If mankind may be saved who never heard or dreamt, at Timbuctoo, Otaheite, Terra Incognita, etc., of Galilee and its Prophet, Christianity is of no avail, if they cannot be saved without, why are not all orthodox? It is a little hard to send a man preaching to Judaea, and leave the rest of the world – Negers and what not – *dark* as their complexions, without a ray of light for so many years to lead them on high; and who will believe that God will damn men for not knowing what they were never taught? I hope I am sincere; I was so at least on a bed of sickness in a far distant country, when I had neither friend, nor comforter, nor hope, to sustain me. I looked to death as a relief from pain, without a wish for an after-life, but a confidence that the God who punishes in this existence had left that last asylum for the weary.

(Whom the Gods love die young)

I am no Platonist, I am nothing at all; but I would sooner be a Paulician, Manichean, Spinozist, Gentile, Pyrrhonian, Zoroastrian, than one of the seventy-two villainous sects who are tearing each other to pieces for the love of the Lord and hatred of each other. Talk of Galileeism? Show me the effects – are you better, wiser, kinder by your precepts? I will bring you ten Mussulmans shall shame you in all goodwill towards men, prayer to God, and duty to their neighbours. And is there a Talapoin, or a Bonze, who is not superior to a fox-hunting curate? But I will say no more on this endless theme; let me live, well if possible, and die without pain. The rest is with God, who assuredly, had He *come* or *sent*, would have made Himself manifest to nations, and intelligible to all.

I shall rejoice to see you. My present intention is to accept Scrope Davies's invitation; and then, if you accept mine, we shall meet *here* and *there.* Did you know poor Matthews? I shall miss him much at Cambridge.

And again:

I thank you for your song, or, rather your two songs – your new song on love, and your *old song* on *religion.* I admire the *first* sincerely, and in turn call upon you to *admire* the following on Anacreon Moore's new operatic farce, or farcical opera – call it which you will:–

> Good plays are scarce,
> So Moore writes farce;
>   Is fame like his so brittle?
> We knew before
> That 'Little's' Moore,
>   But now *'tis Moore* that's *Little.*

I won't dispute with you on the arcana of your new calling; they are bagatelles, like the King of Poland's rosary. One remark and I have done: the basis of your religion is *injustice*; the *Son of God*, the *pure*, the *immaculate*, the *innocent*, is sacrificed for the *guilty.* This proves *His* heroism; but no more does away with *man's* guilt than a schoolboy's volunteering to be flogged for another would exculpate the dunce from negligence, or preserve him from the rod. You degrade the Creator, in the first place, by making Him a begetter of children; and in the next you convert Him into a tyrant over an immaculate and injured Being, who is sent into existence to suffer death for the benefit of some millions of scoundrels, who, after all, seem as likely to be damned as ever. As to miracles, I agree with Hume that it is more probable men should *lie* or be *deceived*, than that things out of the course of nature should so happen. Mahomet wrought miracles, Brothers the prophet had *proselytes*, and so would Breslau the conjurer, had he lived in the time of Tiberius.

Besides, I trust that God is not a *Jew*, but the God of all mankind; and, as you allow that a virtuous Gentile may be saved, you do away the necessity of being a Jew or a Christian.

I do not believe in any revealed religion, because no religion is revealed; and if it pleases the Church to damn me for not allowing a *nonentity*, I throw myself on the mercy of the *'Great First Cause, least understood,'* who must do what is most proper; though I conceive He never made anything to be tortured in another life, whatever it may in this. I will

125

neither read *pro* nor *con.* God would have made His will known without books, considering how very few could read them when Jesus of Nazareth lived, had it been His pleasure to ratify any peculiar mode of worship. As to your immortality, if people are to live, why die? And our carcases, which are to rise again, are they worth raising? I hope, if mine is, that I shall have a better *pair of legs* than I have moved on these two-and-twenty years, or I shall be sadly behind in the squeeze into Paradise. Did you ever read 'Malthus on Population?' If he be right, war and pestilence are our best friends, to save us from being eaten alive, in this 'best of all possible worlds'.

I will write, read, and think no more; indeed, I do not wish to shock your prejudices by saying all I do think. Let us make the most of life, and leave dreams to Emanuel Swedenborg.

Now to dreams of another genius – poesies. I like your song much; but I will say no more, for fear you should think I wanted to coax you into approbation of my past, present, or future acrostics. I shall not be at Cambridge before the middle of October; but, when I go, I should certes like to see you there before you are dubbed a deacon. Write to me, and I will rejoin.

Months later – on 4 December, to be precise – he was still arguing with Hodgson on the same themes and had obviously been arguing with himself in the meantime: 'I have read Watson to Gibbon. He proves nothing, so I am where I was, verging towards Spinoza; and yet it is a gloomy Creed, and I want a better, but there is something Pagan in me that I cannot shake off. In short, I deny nothing, but doubt everything.'

Throughout that autumn and winter of 1811 Byron, it might be thought, had plenty to restrain him from political diversions, apart even from the work on his own poems and the perpetual debate with his assortment of would-be religious advisers. On one of his visits to London he attended a momentous dinner party with three fellow poets, each at the time much more famous than himself: Thomas Campbell, Samuel Rogers, and

Thomas Moore. 'Among the impressions which this meeting left upon me', wrote Moore, 'what I chiefly remarked was the nobleness of his air, his beauty, the gentleness of his voice and manners, and – what was naturally not the least attraction – his marked kindness to myself.' The immediate and unbreakable friendship formed between the two was most honourable to them both. About three years before Byron had been blithely and gratuitously assailing the Moore he had never known in *English Bards*; the ending of the quarrel was executed on Byron's part with an exquisite punctiliousness, and Moore never forgot. 'Such did I find Lord Byron, on my first experience of him; and such, – so open and manly-minded – did I find him to the last.'

Back at Newstead, other novelties competed for his attention.

> Lucietta my dear,
> That fairest of faces!
> Is made up of kisses;
> But, in love, oft the case is
> Even stranger than this is
> There's another, that's slyer
> Who touches me higher, –
> A Witch, an intriguer
> Whose manner and figure
> Now piques me, excites me,
> Torments and delights me –

Lucy was one of the servant maids at Newstead at whom Byron made passes; Susan Vaughan was the witch and obviously something more serious – 'a very pretty Cambrian girl of whom I grew foolishly fond', as he told Hobhouse.

Newstead itself had plenty to offer; but Byron would not immolate himself behind its monastic walls. He was stirred by the events which he could see in the neighbouring villages; more shaken by the spectacle of human crime and cruelty before his eyes than most of the miseries he had seen in his travels. He gave his first inkling of it in a letter to Hobhouse in Dublin: 'I presume ye papers have told of ye Riots in Notts, breaking of frames and heads, and out-manoeuvring the military?' He had followed these events – the so-called Luddite revolt of the Nottinghamshire weavers – with rising interest and anger. He toured the neighbouring villages and saw for himself: one of his guides was the Revd John Becher, the same who had advised the suppression of his first poems. For some days in the middle of the month striking weavers thrown out of their jobs sought an organized response to the call of their leader, General Lud. The breaking of machinery and the entering of homes when the frames were installed,was followed by scenes described as riots until the soldiers were called in. Between the first counter-assault and 9 December, 900 cavalry and 1000 infantry were sent to Nottingham and early in the New Year, these forces were increased by two additional regiments. Byron saw at first hand both the action of the frame makers and the furious, ill-considered response. He attended at least one of the meetings of magistrates at Nottingham County Hall, and voiced his opposition to the projected counter measures. No doubt he was aware of the strong terms in which his friend John Becher had written to the Home Office (on 11 February 1812) stressing the seriousness of the crisis, but also suggesting a remedy:

> It would materially conduce to settle the minds of the workmen if they learned that Parliament was not unmindful of their distress . . . Since the late depreciation of wages is the first that has occurred within the memory of man in the lace and stocking manufactures of this county the poor have been less prepared than those in other districts for the indigent situation to which they are so unexpectedly reduced, and may therefore have been incited to the perpetration of more flagrant excesses than would otherwise have prevailed.

John Becher was no agitator; he merely reported what he saw, and in the years that followed he took upon himself more of the usual characteristics of a country parson upholding the Tory cause. The response from the Home Office revealed the scale of the government's panic. A Bill was suddenly prepared for introduction into Parliament to make frame-breaking a capital offence. On 25 February Byron wrote to Lord Holland, the reigning monarch of the great Whig household, who happened also to be one of the recorders in Nottingham, and one whom Byron could also approach afresh through the good offices of his two new friends, Samuel Rogers and Thomas Moore:

With my best thanks I have the honour to return the Notts letter to your Lordship. – I have read it with attention, but do not think I shall venture to avail myself of its contents, as my view of the question differs in some measure from Mr Coldham's. – I hope I do not wrong him, but *his* objections to ye. bill appear to me to be founded on certain apprehensions that he & his coadjutors might be mistaken for the *'original advisers'* (to quote him) of the measure. – For my own part, I consider the manufacturers as a much injured body of men sacrificed to ye. views of certain individuals who have enriched themselves by those practices which have deprived the frame workers of employment. – For instance; – by the adoption of a certain kind of frame 1 man performs ye. work of 7 – 6 are thus thrown out of business. – But it is to be observed that ye. work thus done is far inferior in quality, hardly marketable at home, & hurried over with a view to exportation. – Surely, my Lord, however we may rejoice in any improvement in ye. arts which may be beneficial to mankind; we must not allow mankind to be sacrificed to improvements in Mechanism. The maintenance & well doing of ye. industrious poor is an object of greater consequence to ye. community than ye. enrichment of a few monopolists by any improvement in ye. implements of trade, which deprives ye workman of his bread, & renders ye. labourer 'unworthy of his hire.' – My own motive for opposing ye. bill is founded on it's palpable injustice, & it's certain inefficacy. – I have seen the state of these miserable men, & it is a disgrace to a civilized country. – Their excesses may be condemned, but cannot be subject of wonder. – The effect of ye. present bill would be to drive them into actual rebellion. – The few words I shall venture to offer on Thursday will be founded upon these opinions formed from my own observations on ye. spot. – By previous enquiry I am convinced these men would have been restored to employment & ye. county to tranquillity. – It is perhaps not yet too late & is surely worth the trial. It can never be too late to employ force in such circumstances. – I believe your Lordship does not coincide with me entirely on this subject, & most cheerfully & sincerely shall I submit to your superior judgment & experience, & take some other line of argument against ye. bill, or be silent altogether, should you deem it more adviseable. – Condemning, as every one must condemn the conduct of these wretches, I believe in ye. existence of grievances which call rather for pity than punishment. – I have ye honour to be with great respect, my Lord, yr. Lordship's

most obedt. & obliged Servt
Byron

P.S. – I am a little apprehensive that your Lordship will think me too lenient towards these men, & *half a framebreaker myself.*

He had also been writing or re-writing during these months of mounting tension the most direct and explicit of any political poem he had so far penned. Sections of the first cantos of *Childe Harold* he certainly considered political, as he told Murray, and he had trouble enough in protecting them from censorious anxieties; but he knew, none better surely, that *The Curse of Minerva* carried the argument much further. Ostensibly, from the manner in which the poem was published three years later, it was started at the Capuchin Convent in Athens on 17 March 1811, and the soft, opening lines gave little indication of what was to come:

> Slow sinks, more lovely ere his race be run
> Along Morea's hills the setting sun,
> Not as in Northern climes obscurely bright,
> But one unclouded blaze of living light;

But Minerva, the goddess of wisdom, war, and all the liberal arts, or to adopt her Greek name, Athena, the protectress of Athens, had a terrible curse to unloose on all those who had despoiled her, both the ancient conquerors and the wretched money-grubbers of modern times.

'Mortal!' ('twas thus she spake) 'that blush of shame
Proclaims thee Briton, once a noble name;
First of the mighty, foremost of the free,
Now honoured *less* by all, and *least* by me:
Chief of thy foes shall Pallas still be found –
Seek'st thou the cause of loathing? – look around.
Lo! here, despite of war and wasting fire,
I saw successive tyrannies expire:
'Scap'd from the ravage of the Turk and Goth,
Thy country sends a spoiler worse than both.
Survey this vacant, violated fane;
Recount the relics torn that yet remain:
These Cecrops placed, *this* Pericles adorn'd,
That Adrian rear'd when drooping Science mourn'd.
What more I owe let Gratitude attest –
Know Alaric and Elgin did the rest.
That all may learn from whence the plunderer came
The insulted wall sustains his hated name:
For Elgin's fame thus grateful Pallas pleads,
Below, his name; above, behold his deeds!
Be ever hail'd with equal honour here
The Gothic monarch and the pictish peer:
Arms gave the first his right, the last had none,
But basely stole what less barbarians won.
So when the Lion quits his fell repast
Next prowls the Wolf, the filthy Jackall last:
Flesh, limbs and blood the former make their own,
The last poor brute securely gnaws the bone.
Yet still the Gods are just, and crimes are crost:
See here what Elgin won, and what he lost!
Another name with *his* pollutes my shrine:
Behold where Dian's beams disdain to shine!
Some retribution still might Pallas claim,
When Venus half aveng'd Minerva's shame.'

The curse on Elgin himself and the associated guilt which it shed on his native land have naturally attracted attention. But *The Curse of Minerva* had a different, more comprehensive, target. It was Byron's first combined onslaught – the first in English literature – on the inextricable evils: war and all the kindred horrors, empire- and money-making. Byron could never see them apart for long and here they were all assembled together: England, Britannia, Albion imposing her barbarian will on the lesser breeds, from the defenceless Danes to the Indians, to the enemy at home, the frame-makers of his newly-adopted Southwell and Nottingham:

'So let him [Elgin] stand through ages yet unborn,
Fix'd statue on the pedestal of Scorn;
Though not for him alone revenge shall wait,
But fits thy country for her coming fate:
Hers were the deeds that taught her lawless son
To do what oft Britannia's self had done.
Look to the Baltic – blazing from afar,
Your old ally yet mourns perfidious war:
Not to such deeds did Pallas lend her aid,
Or break the compact which herself had made;
Far from such councils, from the faithless field
She fled – but left behind her Gorgon shield:
A fatal gift that turn'd your friends to stone,
And left lost Albion hated and alone.

'Look to the East, where Ganges' swarthy race
Shall shake your tyrant empire to its base;
Lo, there Rebellion rears her ghastly head,
And glares the Nemesis of native dead;
Till Indus rolls a deep purpureal flood,
And claims his long arrear of northern blood.
So may ye perish! Pallas when she gave
Your free-born rights, forbade ye to enslave.

'Look on your Spain, she clasps the hand she hates,
But coldly clasps, and thrusts you from her gates.

132

Bear witness, bright Barossa! thou canst tell
Whose were the sons that bravely fought and fell.
But Lusitania, kind and dear ally,
Can spare a few to fight, and sometimes fly.
Oh glorious field! by Famine fiercely won,
The Gaul retires for once, and all is done!
But when did Pallas teach that one retreat
Retriev'd three long Olympiads of defeat?

'Look last at home, ye love not to look there
On the grim smile of comfortless despair:
Your city saddens, loud though revel howls,
Here Famine faints, and yonder Rapine prowls:
See all alike of more or less bereft,
No misers tremble when there's nothing left.
"Blest paper credit", who shall dare to sing?
It clogs like lead Corruption's weary wing:
Yet Pallas pluck'd each Premier by the ear,
Who gods and men alike disdain'd to hear;
But one, repentant o'er a bankrupt state,
On Pallas calls, but calls, alas! too late:
Then raves for (Stanhope), to that Mentor bends,
Though he and Pallas never yet were friends:
Him Senates hear whom never yet they heard,
Contemptuous once, and now no less absurd:
So once of yore, each reasonable frog
Swore faith and fealty to his sovereign "log".
Thus hail'd your rulers their Patrician clod,
As Egypt chose an Onion for a God.

'Now fare ye well, enjoy your little hour,
Go grasp the shadow of your vanish'd power;
Gloss o'er the failure of each fondest scheme,
Your strength a name, your bloated wealth a dream:
Gone is that Gold, the marvel of mankind,
And Pirates barter all that's left behind.
No more the hirelings, purchas'd near and far,
Crowd to the ranks of mercenary war.

The idle merchant on the useless quay,
Droops o'er the bales no bark may bear away;
Or back returning sees rejected stores
Rot piecemeal on his own encumber'd shores:
The starv'd mechanic breaks his rusting loom,
And desperate mans him 'gainst the common doom.
Then in the Senate of your sinking state,
Show me the man whose counsels may have weight.
Vain is each voice where tones could once command,
E'en factions cease to charm a factious land;
Yet jarring sects convulse a sister isle,
And light with maddening hands the mutual pile.

For Byron, the hated English Ministers were the aggressors, the pitiless war makers who would as soon and more expeditiously unloose savage reprisals against their own people as any foreign enemies. It would indeed have been an embarrassment if *The Curse of Minerva* had been published in November 1811, when the troops were ransacking workers' homes around Newstead and just a few weeks before an English Prime Minister was assassinated – to the sound of much rejoicing in neighbouring working-class homes – in the Palace of Westminster itself. But it was there, inside him. *The Curse of Minerva* is not considered one of Byron's greatest poems; indeed some later friendly critics have pronounced it dull and flat, but he had an affection for it himself, and it was the first occasion when he chose an enemy fully worthy of his steel: not the wretched Elgin but the barbarity of British imperialism.

FOUR

London

If the papers lie not (which they generally do) . . .
Detached Thoughts, 1821

The Byron who woke one morning to find himself famous was the creator of a single volume: *Childe Harold's Pilgrimage: A Romaunt.* He was twenty-four years old, and the publication date was Saturday, 10 March, 1812. He had delivered his maiden speech in the House of Lords barely ten days before, and it might be thought that the conjunction of these two events added to the sensation. But, according to his own testimony, the opposite was the case: the one blotted out the other. His speech was reported in the newspapers only in a greatly abbreviated or bowdlerized form, and even those who heard it were not quite so overwhelmed as he was himself. Neither the House of Lords nor the House of Commons yields readily to those who would take it by storm; each, in its varying posture, prefers to be flattered and wooed. Accents which seem like thunderclaps inside those Gothic walls may produce not even an echo outside. Oratory and literature seldom find themselves on easy terms, although the orators may be the last to make the discovery. The young Byron had a lovely voice, a long-standing ambition to display his powers of declamation and, most important of all, a blazing message to deliver. *Childe Harold* brought a quite different kind of fame.

A good case can be made for the claim that the speech was greater than the poem. It came hot from the furnace of riot and near-revolution in Nottingham. Although Byron had recapitulated it until he was word perfect, it was not by any reckoning a piece of contrived eloquence: more, a burst of controlled

135

passion. The young Byron was outraged by what he had seen, and what he reported, and the wretched remedies, even worse than the disease, which the Ministers in power were proposing. Even read today, the indictment still scorches. True, as John Drinkwater described in his account of the scene in the Lords, 'a certain air of unsuccess' hangs about the affair.

> And yet the speech itself was, in its kind, nothing less than magnificent. In the House Byron was, no doubt, betrayed into the fatal diffidence that makes many men do no justice to themselves on public occasions; unsure of himself before an audience, we can hear his tone, a little shrill, a little defensive, a little arrogant, wholly out of keeping with the things that he was saying. But when he was preparing his speech he was, clearly, exalted by a real passion to a very high rhetorical pitch. Read aloud now, the irony, the indignation and the tenderness of the address come stinging into life on a forgotten cause. The arrangement is admirable, and the exposition sparkles with point and energy. One is tempted to quote extracts, but the speech must be read as a whole, or its remarkable momentum is missed.*

* Prompted by this most discerning judgement in Drinkwater's *The Pilgrim of Eternity*, it seems appropriate to print the whole speech in an appendix [see Appendix I], especially since the forgotten cause of how parts of England trembled on the edge of revolt, provoked by pitiable distress, may not seem quite so untopical as it did when Drinkwater wrote his book in 1924. Moreover, Byron himself had a particular interest in the speech after it had been bowdlerized in the newspaper reports of the time. Years later (in 1824), just before his death, a pamphlet containing all his parliamentary speeches was prepared by himself for publication and published by Rodwell & Martin of New Bond Street.

It may be noted here that Drinkwater's judgement, and my own, about the quality of Byron's speech are fiercely and lavishly contested by the most recent commentator on the subject, Malcolm Kelsall in his *Byron's Politics*. In his dismemberment of the speech, he seeks to illustrate Byron's lack of sincerity and resolution, his general ineffectualness. I disagree so profoundly with almost every conclusion Professor Kelsall reaches that no profitable argument between us is possible. However, on the framebreaker affair, he makes the charge that Byron was guilty of intensifying

Moreover, his determination to speak out was matched by the interested appeals for the whole matter to be suppressed. One chief apologist for the Government's case in the House of Commons had been the aspiring Mr William Lamb (later Lord Melbourne); his plea had a touch of real sophistication:

> As to the disputes between masters and their handworkers, do not think it right to inquire into them as causes of the riots – such inquiry only tends to inflame the minds of the working-men, who generally conclude that they have rights which are infringed upon by the masters, and that they are justifiable in retaliating violence on them for the infringement of those supposed rights.*

---

* *The Luddites and other Essays* (Katanka 1971). It is sad to record that the most up-to-date book on the Luddites, *Land of Content: The Luddite Revolt of 1812* by Robert Reid, while offering the results of considerable research on other aspects of the subject, contains no more than a few cursory and misleading references to Byron. The book does show what a brutal affair the suppression sanctified by Parliament truly was, and Byron would have appreciated the revelations given here of the unsuspected role played by one of the chief political figures of the time – the up-and-coming, on-the-make Whig lawyer, Henry Brougham, who was supposed to be defending some of the Luddite leaders in court, and who did nothing of the kind.

---

his anger as he went along: 'There is one language for Holland, another for a Senate Philippic and a third for a more popular readership.' Indeed, there was such a shift of emphasis, and why not? The twenty-year-old Byron cannot be convicted of anything but common sense in furthering the cause of his adoption, if he addressed his patron, his fellow peers and the outside public in somewhat different language. Indeed again, at other stages in the argument, Malcolm Kelsall will berate Byron for using in the Lords language which the people outside might not understand. When he does adapt his language to the people outside he is accused of descending to 'a mere popularist jingle'. The safest rule with Professor Kelsall is to recognize that with him Byron, young and old, can do nothing right or honourable. The reader of his early pages should be warned that a little later 'The Isles of Greece' verses are to be mocked as well-nigh meaningless; so we may still prefer to share John Drinkwater's view about the magnificence and the downright honesty of the frame-worker speech.

It was hard to know which angered Byron the more: the outrages themselves or the excuses such as these which he heard
from the Ministers or their supporters. He wrote a poem especially for the occasion, which he sent for anonymous publication
in the *Morning Chronicle* in March.

'An Ode to the Framers of the Frame Bill'

Oh well done Lord E[ldo]n! and better Lord R[yde]r!
Britannia must prosper with councils like yours;
HAWKESBURY, HARROWBY, help you to guide her,
Whose remedy only must *kill* ere it cures:
Those villains, the Weavers, are all grown refractory,
Asking some succour for Charity's sake –
So hang them in clusters round each Manufactory,
That will at once put an end to *mistake*.

The rascals, perhaps, may betake them to robbing,
The dogs to be sure have got nothing to eat –
So if we can hang them for breaking a bobbin,
'Twill save all the Government's money and meat:
Men are more easily made than machinery –
Stockings fetch better prices than lives –
Gibbets on Sherwood will *heighten* the scenery,
Showing how Commerce, *how* Liberty thrives!

Justice is now in pursuit of the wretches,
Grenadiers, Volunteers, Bow-street Police,
Twenty-two Regiments, a score of Jack Ketches,
Three of the Quorum and two of the Peace;
Some Lords, to be sure, would have summoned the Judges,
To take their opinion, but that they ne'er shall,
For LIVERPOOL such a concession begrudges,
So now they're condemned by *no Judges* at all.

Some folks for certain have thought it was shocking,
When Famine appeals, and when Poverty groans,
That life should be valued at less than a stocking,
And breaking of frames lead to breaking of bones.

138

If it should prove so, I trust, by this token,
(And who will refuse to partake in the hope?)
That the frames of the fools may be first to be *broken*,
Who, when asked for a *remedy*, sent down a *rope*.

And then a few days later, since his blood was up, he sent another anonymous protest about the conduct of the Prince Regent at a famous Carlton House dinner party; the prince was said to have made his young daughter weep by the abuse heaped on his former friends among the Whig leaders.

'Lines to a Lady Weeping'

Weep, daughter of a royal line,
    A Sire's disgrace, a realm's decay;
Ah, happy! if each tear of thine
    Could wash a father's fault away!

Weep – for thy tears are Virtue's tears –
    Auspicious to these suffering isles;
And be each drop in future years
    Repaid thee by thy people's smiles!

Meantime, Byron himself had no doubt about the supposed rights of the persecuted men and women to whose aid he had come, though he may have been aware that not all his friends and backers, Lord Holland for one, might exactly share his feelings. Before publication, he despatched a copy of *Childe Harold* to his leader pleading forgiveness for all 'my other buffooneries' – a reference perhaps to some feeble lines about Lord Holland which he had included in *English Bards*.

How was it that *Childe Harold* swept all before it, even the rival reputation of its author which seemed to be blossoming in another sphere? Byron's own nervousness about the project did not diminish as the day of publication came nearer. His one sure conviction was that he must fight to preserve the parts of the poem which might cause most offence; otherwise his pride of authorship was quite open to challenge. Some of his newly-acquired friends were highly dubious. Samuel Rogers was sent some printed sheets before publication day: 'This,' he said, 'in spite of all its beauty, will never please the public: they will dislike the querulous repining tone that pervades it, and the dissolute character of the hero.' Walter Scott's first verdict was scarcely more favourable:

> It is I think a very clever poem but gives no good symptom of the writer's heart or morals . . . . Vice ought to be a little more modest and it must require at least equal to the noble lords other powers to claim sympathy gravely for the ennui arising from being tired of his wassailers and his paramours. There is a monstrous deal of conceit in it too for it is informing the inferior part of the world that their little old-fashioned scruples and limitations are not worthy of his regard . . . .

Scott himself, the most popular writer of the day, would not have risked such a solecism. Oddly, for the very first indication of the excitement with which *Childe Harold* was received, we may turn to the famous report, almost as famous as the poem itself, of that unlikely literary critic, the sixty-year-old Duchess of Devonshire:

> The subject of conversation, of curiosity, of enthusiasm almost, one might say, of the moment is not Spain or Portugal, Warriors or Patriots, but Lord Byron! . . . . This poem is on every table and himself courted, visited, flattered, and praised wherever he appears. He has a pale, sickly, but handsome countenance, a bad figure, animated and amusing conversation, and, in short, he is really the topic almost of every conversation – the men jealous of him, the women of each other.*

* Two delightful volumes are indispensable (if not exhaustive; how could they be?) in quoting the contemporary and subsequent literary comment on Byron's works as they appeared: First, *Byron: The Critical Heritage*, edited by Andrew Rutherford. Professor Rutherford has also written his own *Byron: A Critical Study*, a volume which, for my taste, puts much too much emphasis on the aristocratic Byron. But since his later, incomparable

Such was the London of 1812, and clearly the young Byron had struck a mood quite different from anything he himself had calculated. Yet it is worth noting too that right from the start different brands of critics did recognize some of the themes which he himself had been at pains to stress. The *Quarterly Review*, the highest authority among the Tories, made the accusation that Harold, the hero, was if not a 'craven, at least a mortal enemy to all martial exertions . . . When we read the preceding sarcasms on the "bravo's trade", we are induced to ask, not without some anxiety and alarm, whether such are indeed the opinions which a British peer entertains of a British army.' And there was worse to come. Were not the opening stanzas of the second canto designed as a deeper challenge still to religion itself, to the question of life and death which should still be kept within its religious preserves: 'The common courtesy of society', continued the *Quarterly*, 'has we think, very justly proscribed the intensive introduction of such topics as these into conversation; and as no reader probably will open *Childe Harold* with the view of inquiring into the religious tenets of the author . . . we cannot but disapprove, in point of taste, these protracted meditations.' And on this double score the Whigs were hardly less observant and censorious than the Tories. Francis Jeffrey in the *Edinburgh Review* could not withhold his praise for 'a volume of very considerable power, spirit and originality' or, indeed, for 'a tone of self-willed independence and originality about the whole composition – a certain plain manliness and strength of manner. . . .' But he could not omit the indictment:

Lord Byron speaks with the most unbounded contempt of the Portuguese – with despondence of Spain – [England's treasured allies at the time, be it noted] and in a very slighting and sarcastic manner of wars, and victories, and military heroes in general. Neither are his religious opinions

---

Critical Heritage, all is forgiven. Second, is *Byron in England: His Fame and Afterfame* by Samuel C. Chew, published by Murray in 1924 – another treasure to be set beside John Drinkwater's.

more orthodox, we apprehend, than his politics; for he not only speaks without any respect of priests, and creeds, and dogmas of all descriptions, but doubts very freely of the immortality of the soul and other points as fundamental.

These are some of the ideas which Byron vastly amplified in later years; it is useful to be reminded how prominently they figured in his mind, whatever various attributions of theme and interest were ascribed to him by others. Byron wrote, be it not forgotten, at a moment when London was celebrating victories in what Wordsworth called 'the most righteous cause in which, since the opposition of the Greek Republic to the Persian invader at Thermopylae and Marathon, sword was ever drawn'. Byron knew how Wordsworth, Scott and a host of other poetical propagandists could summon men to battle. These are not the most frequently quoted words from *Childe Harold*, but they presented the theme which he would never betray or abandon.

> By Heaven! it is a splendid sight to see
> (For one who hath no friend, no brother there)
> Their rival scarfs of mix'd embroidery,
> Their various arms that glitter in the air!
> What gallant war-hounds rouse them from their lair,
> And gnash their fangs, loud yelling for the prey!
> All join the chase, but few the triumph share;
> The Grave shall bear the chiefest prize away,
> And Havoc scarce for joy can number their array.
>
> Three hosts combine to offer sacrifice;
> Three tongues prefer strange orisons on high;
> Three gaudy standards flout the pale blue skies;
> The shouts are France, Spain, Albion, Victory!
> The foe, the victim, and the fond ally
> That fights for all, but ever fights in vain,
> Are met – as if at home they could not die –
> To feed the crow on Talavera's plain,
> And fertilize the field that each pretends to gain.

There shall they rot – Ambition's honour'd fools!
Yes, Honour decks the turf that wraps their clay!
Vain Sophistry! in these behold the tools,
The broken tools, that tyrants cast away
By Myriads, when they dare to pave their way
With human hearts – to what? – a dream alone.
Can despots compass aught that hails their sway?
Or call with truth one span of earth their own,
Save that wherein at last they crumble bone by bone?

Oh, Albuera! glorious field of grief!
As o'er thy plain the Pilgrim prick'd his steed,
Who could foresee thee, in a space so brief,
A scene where mingling foes should boast and bleed!
Peace to the perish'd! may the warrior's meed
And tears of triumph their reward prolong!
Till others fall where other chieftains lead
Thy name shall circle round the gaping throng,
And shine in worthless lays, the theme of transient song!

Enough of Battle's minions! let them play
Their game of lives, and barter breath for fame:
Fame that will scarce reanimate their clay,
Though thousands fall to deck some single name.
In sooth 'twere sad to thwart their noble aim
Who strike, blest hirelings! for their country's good,
And die, that living might have prov'd her shame;
Perish'd, perchance, in some domestic feud,
Or in a narrower sphere wild Rapine's path pursu'd.

Full swiftly Harold wends his lonely way
Where proud Sevilla triumphs unsubdued:
Yet is she free – the spoiler's wish'd-for prey!
Soon, soon shall Conquest's fiery foot intrude,
Blackening her lovely domes with traces rude.
Inevitable hour! 'Gainst fate to strive
Where Desolation plants her famish'd brood
Is vain, or Ilion, Tyre might yet survive,
And Virtue vanquish all, and Murder cease to thrive.

But all unconscious of the coming doom,
The feast, the song, the revel here abounds;
Strange modes of merriment the hours consume,
Nor bleed these patriots with their country's wounds:
Not here War's clarion, but Love's rebeck sounds;
Here Folly still his votaries enthralls;
And young-eyed Lewdness walks her midnight rounds:
Girt with the silent crimes of Capitals,
Still to the last kind Vice clings to the tott'ring walls

Not so the rustic – with his trembling mate
He lurks, nor casts his heavy eye afar,
Lest he should view his vineyard desolate,
Blasted below the dun hot breath of war.
No more beneath soft Eve's consenting star
Fandango twirls his jocund castanet:
Ah, monarchs! could ye taste the mirth ye mar,
Not in the toils of Glory would ye fret;
The hoarse dull drum would sleep, and Man be happy yet!

In one political mood, *Childe Harold* would pour scorn on 'Ambition's honoured fools', the wantonness of war and all its horror. In another the poem would summon free men to action:

Hereditary bondsmen! know ye not
Who would be free themselves must strike the blow?
By their right arms the conquest must be wrought.

Clearly Byron's pointed, direct assaults on State and Church – and as often as he could achieve it, on both together at the same time – was not the combination which entranced the Duchesses and their daughters. Quite other ingredients made the whole dish so appetizing and original. But it is also worth noting that his politics – even at the height of the war with Napoleon – were no fatal bar in some of the circles where he suddenly found himself so notorious and so eagerly pursued. The sister of the above-mentioned Duchess of Devonshire had once canvassed the constituents of Westminster on behalf of Charles James Fox, with her kisses. Lady Oxford, who soon had her eye on him, was noted, apart from other gifts, for the way in which she would mix a genuine strand of radicalism with her Whiggery; Horne Tooke, the old Westminster radical, charged with high treason in 1794, had been one of her political tutors. Neither Lady Melbourne nor her daughter-in-law, Lady Caroline Lamb – the publication of *Childe Harold* was responsible for these notable introductions – were principally renowned for their politics, but each in their varying degrees had received their political tuition in the environs of Holland House where the memory of Charles James Fox was still properly revered and where the curious links with Napoleon's Paris were sustained all through the war. Byron could easily shock some of his new associates with expressions of his politics. Neither Lord Holland nor Lady Caroline's husband had any sympathy with Nottingham frame-breakers but the mood at Holland House, nonetheless, was one of principled Foxite opposition to the worst excesses of the war, and suddenly the young little-known Byron had stepped forward to express these ideas and ideals in a quite unexpected manner.

What followed the publication of *Childe Harold* is usually and excusably told in terms of how London society, led by Lady Caroline, swooned before him. The scene became all the more irresistible since Byron takes up the story – for twentieth-century readers at least – in his letters to Lady Melbourne, the one person apart from himself who, almost certainly, knew the full truth of what happened in all his tempestuous, world-famous affairs of the next four years. Their minds, their hearts, their pulses, their passions beat as one, and in reporting every twist and turn in his romantic fortunes to her Byron developed his own matchless, ultra-modern prose style. 'If Byron conquered Lady Melbourne', wrote J. D. Symon, 'she in turn conquered him.' Writing of Lady Melbourne, he himself concurred:

I write with most pleasure – and her answers, so sensible, so tactique – I never met with half her talent. If she had been a few years younger, what a fool she would have made of me, had she thought it worth her while – and I should have lost a valuable and most agreeable *friend*. Mem: A mistress never

145

is nor can be a friend. While you agree you are lovers; and
when it is over, anything but friends.

Of course, with her he never boasted; that would have been
intolerable. He was mostly laughing, conspiring, even occasionally resorting to his Swiftian posture of inverted hypocrisy.
He knew for sure she would never betray him, and so the world
was granted this incomparable treasure: a more uninhibited
exchange of sentiment and revelation than anything he could
achieve even with his growing body of other correspondents.
J. D. Symon puts the point accurately; 'She was a sharer, perhaps the sole sharer, in the central mystery of the poet's life:
"Why don't you go off with me?" he said at one critical
moment; "I am sure our elopement would have greater effect –
cause a greater sensation as our orators say – than any event of
the kind – since Eve ran away with the apple." '

But the world, the London, of 1812, had to judge the scene
without the benefit of these intimate insights. And since the
young Byron saw his own country from the vantage point of a
continent at war, some foreign observers have captured the
mood better than our own. André Maurois wrote:

The French Revolution, and then Bonaparte, had given
birth in thousands of young Europeans to glorious hopes
which Napoleon had betrayed. In England especially, the
sentiment of the vanity of life was dominant in a society
sickened of pleasures by laxity of morals, of martial ambition by long-drawn-out wars, of political ambition by the
continuance of a Tory government made invincible by danger. The poets, in their impotence or timidity, had not
voiced this secret revulsion. Childe Harold was the first to
echo the tragic scepticism of a sickened generation. Art had
at last come into step with life. At last, a young Englishman,
akin to those who read him, had discovered the Europe of
1812 as revolutions and war had left it. For a people severed
from all continental life by ten years of blockade, the story
of a journey in Albania amongst the Suliotes was more
amazing than a voyage to the Indies or the South Sea

Islands . . . It was a poem of the sea; and the Viking breed, so long held off from the Ocean by the blockade, could catch in it the salt tang of sea spray which they were beginning to miss.

And perhaps André Maurois understood something about us even better than our pulsating Viking blood: how Byron took the whole nation in every class by storm by writing about the forbidden subject of sex as if it was one fit for mockery.*

The story of his love affairs is not the subject of this book; I am concerned with the persistence he showed in returning, refreshed, to his chosen political path. However, some features and oddities or eccentricities are worth noting. He did sweep Lady Caroline off her feet, although clearly she was most ready to be swept – 'I have always thought you the cleverest most agreeable, absurd amiable perplexing, dangerous fascinating little being that lives now or ought to have lived 2000 years ago – I won't talk to you of beauty. I am no judge but our *beauties* cease to be when near you, and therefore you have either some or something better.' After that, not much remained to be said – although Byron, the bookworm, did bring her a new book every day. Partly he wanted to hold in check what discomfited him so much, the spectacle of her dancing. But without that daily literary ration, would she ever have written *Glenarvon*? (The books he chose to discuss with his various women are a revelation in themselves, particularly since it refutes the suggestion that he so detested bluestockings.)

Meantime, even while he embarked upon the engaging task

---

* I was encouraged to turn back to André Maurois' *Byron*, first published in France in February 1930, by Arnold Bennett's review in the *Evening Standard*. The review and the book offer something, even though the two together got some important matters shamefully wrong. Byron, Bennett still insisted, was a sexual debauchee on a truly Napoleonic scale; he was nothing of the sort. But what Bennett did understand was the particular qualification which this biographer brought to his assignment: '. . . Maurois is French, and the French have comprehended, what has never been comprehended in Britain, that sex can be very funny at times.'

of Lady Caroline's education, he did find time also for another considerable appearance in the House of Lords on a most reputable theme. On 11 April, on the Catholic Claims Bill, he worthily backed the old Foxite principle of religious toleration and taunted the Tory Minister with the charge that their policies would be well received in Paris: 'It is on the basis of your tyranny Napoleon hopes to build his own.' The case was elaborated with more than a touch of the panache which had characterized his maiden speech. All his listeners, he said, were advocates of 'church and state', but not 'a state of exclusion and despotism' which refused to the Catholics 'all temporal blessings whatsoever'. And he recalled the observation of 'the great Lord Peterborough', a leading Whig of Queen Anne's day, who had said he was for 'a parliamentary king and a parliamentary constitution but not for a parliamentary God and a parliamentary religion'. Then Byron concluded: 'The interval of a century has not weakened the force of the remark. It is indeed time that we should leave off . . . these Lilliputian sophistries whether our "eggs are broken at the broad or narrow end".' To rebuke Tory intolerance with a Swiftian flourish showed just how the deed should be done.

Another, and a much more elusive, affair was launched in that same *Childe Harold* year with Lady Oxford; it lasted indeed, although most biographers (not Doris Langley Moore) overlook the fact, twice as long as the much more meticulously chronicled housetop-proclaimed one with Lady Caroline; and how much more suitable she truly was. Lady Oxford, at forty

> resembled a landscape by Claude Lorrain, with a setting sun, her beauties enhanced by the knowledge that they were shedding their last dying beams, which threw a radiance around. A woman is only grateful for her *first* and *last* conquest. The first of poor dear Lady Oxford's was achieved before I entered on this world of care; but the last, I do flatter myself, was reserved for me, and a *bonne bouche* it was.

He spent some of the most idyllic months of his life, recovering

from Caroline, in the Lucretian retreat at Eywood in Hereford-
shire, with Lord Oxford, nicknamed Potiphar, complaisance
itself. But with Lucretius and Lady Oxford and the country
house where his old idol, Alexander Pope, was properly honoured, how could he ever be enticed back to London? For a
while (according to a report which reached Sir Walter Scott via
Thomas Moore) Byron kept in his Albany rooms a portrait of
Lady Caroline hanging on one side of the chimneypiece and a
portrait of Lady Oxford on the other. Sir Walter wondered
whether William Lamb might not resent it, but expected no
protest from 'a poor Nincompoop, such as Lord Oxford'.

It is fascinating to see how the Byronic wit and humour, his
unique mixing of the two qualities into one, had developed so
soon: Lady Melbourne brought the gift to its full splendid development before anyone else. Thomas Moore was starting to
achieve with him some of the same results; Scrope Davies and a
few others could stir overflowing effervescence; and with some
other natural allies he established good relations, if not quite on
the same uninhibited footing. Taking Thomas Moore with him,
one bright May morning in 1813, he went to pay his respects to
Leigh Hunt, recently incarcerated in Cold Baths Field Prison,
for the most estimable offence of having insulted the Prince
Regent in the columns of his *Examiner* more directly even than
Byron had dared to do. At first, Moore and Byron were a little
chagrined to find some other visitors; the author of *Childe Harold*
could still be genuinely shy. But a good friendship was formed;
Byron called again with some bundles of books, and after a few
months happily reported a new friendship consolidated:

> To-day responded to La Baronne de Staël Holstein, and sent
> to Leigh Hunt (an acquisition to my acquaintance – through
> Moore – of last summer) a copy of the two Turkish tales.
> Hunt is an extraordinary character, and not exactly of the
> present age. He reminds me more of the Pym and Hampden
> times – much talent, great independence of spirit, and an
> austere, yet not repulsive, aspect. If he goes on *qualis ab*
> *incepto*, I know few men who will deserve more praise or
> obtain it. I must go and see him again; – the rapid succession

of adventure, since last summer, added to some serious uneasiness and business, have interrupted our acquaintance; but he is a man worth knowing; and 'though, for his own sake, I wish him out of prison, I like to study character in such situations. He has been unshaken, and will continue so. I don't think him deeply versed in life; – he is the bigot of virtue (not religion), and enamoured of the beauty of that 'empty name', as the last breath of Brutus pronounced, and every day proves it. He is, perhaps, a little opinionated, as all men who are the *centre* of *circles*, wide or narrow – the Sir Oracles, in whose name two or three are gathered together – must be, and as even Johnson was; but, withal, a valuable man, and less vain than success and even the consciousness of preferring 'the right to the expedient' might excuse.

He did also make one last effort to participate in what he came to scorn as 'parliamentary mummeries'. He presented a petition on behalf of the old parliamentary reformer, Major Cartwright, paying graceful tribute to the man himself: 'one whose long life has been spent in one unceasing struggle for the liberty of the subject against that undue influence, which has increased, is increasing and ought to be diminished . . .' He recalled the scene without much exhilaration, – apart from lamenting Lady Oxford's absence:

> I presented Cartwright's last year; and Stanhope and I stood against the whole House, and mouthed it valiantly – and had some fun and a little abuse for our opposition. But 'I am not i' th' vein' for this business. Now, had * * [Lady Oxford] been here, she would have *made* me do it. *There* is a woman, who, amid all her fascination, always urged a man to usefulness or glory. Had she remained, she had been my tutelar genius. ***
>
> Baldwin is very importunate – but, poor fellow, 'I can't get out, I can't get out – said the starling.' Ah, I am as bad as that dog Sterne, who preferred whining over 'a dead ass to relieving a living mother' – villain – hypocrite – slave –

sycophant! but *I* am no better. Here I cannot stimulate myself to a speech for the sake of these unfortunates, and three words and half a smile of * * [Lady Oxford] had she been here to urge it (and urge it she infallibly would – at least, she always pressed me on senatorial duties, and particularly in the cause of weakness) would have made me an advocate, if not an orator. Curse on Rochefoucault for being always right! In him a lie were virtue, – or, at least, a comfort to his readers . . .

I shall soon be six-and-twenty [22 January 1814]. Is there any thing in the future that can possibly console us for not being always *twenty-five*?

> 'Oh Gioventu!
> Oh Primavera! gioventu dell' anno.
> Oh Gioventu! primavera della vita'.

How he could console himself, what he could talk about at first hand, whether at Holland House or Cold Baths prison, was the scene of the broken, bleeding, war-torn continent whose presence and problems he understood better than most of his contemporaries. He had seen it with his own eyes and did not forget.

Childe Harold was such a swift, stupendous success that multitudes have accused him – many in his lifetime and many more since – of being seduced by it. Was he not content to relapse into a vicious literary self-indulgence to match the orgies of his private life? Did he not really repeat, for a period of three years or more, the easy formula which produced the guaranteed response? Some of the famous sequels were dashed off in a few weeks or even a few days: did any of them add anything of enduring significance to the themes of *Childe Harold*? All of them presented the self-same Byronic hero in much the same pose. The list of those famous titles seems to clinch the case and sometimes Byron himself, in some confessional letter to one of his correspondents, would help to clinch it too. *The Giaour* (published 5 June 1813), *The Bride of Abydos* (published 2 December 1813), *The Corsair* (published 1 February 1814), *Lara* (published

6 August 1814), *The Siege of Corinth* (published 7 February 1816) and *Parisina* (published 7 February 1816) – all these famous pieces in the Byronic canon, best-sellers in their time, could be wiped out altogether without much loss to his reputation as poet or politician; but this admission, echoing some of the crudest charges against his poetry, may give a false impression too. Despite the haste with which Byron wrote some of these pieces, he also took great pains with a few of them, to revise and rewrite, notably *The Giaour*. Each of them, whatever the other distractions offered, had a political purpose in mind; each would display in the end the one virtue of resistance to the fates which would count against a thousand crimes. Each carried somewhere the Byronic trade mark of protest against war and tyranny.

> Clime of the unforgotten brave! –
> Whose land from plain to mountain-cave
> Was Freedom's home or Glory's grave –
> Shrine of the mighty! can it be,
> That this is all remains of thee?
> Approach thou craven crouching slave –
> Say, is not this Thermopylae?
> These waters blue that round you lave
> Oh servile offspring of the free –
> Pronounce what sea, what shore is this?
> The gulf, the rock of Salamis!
> These scenes – their story not unknown –
> Arise, and make again your own;
> Snatch from the ashes of your sires
> The embers of their former fires,
> And he who in the strife expires
> Will add to theirs a name of fear,
> That Tyranny shall quake to hear,
> And leave his sons a hope, a fame,
> They too will rather die than shame;
> For Freedom's battle once begun,
> Bequeathed by bleeding Sire to Son,
> Though baffled oft is ever won.

Those lines came from the unpronounceable hero of *The Giaour*, and the scene was set amid the desolation of the Morea where, as Byron insisted in his advertisement, 'the cruelty exercised on all sides was unparalleled even in the annals of the faithful' – and by the faithful, for sure, he did not mean only the Mussulman terror. The heroes and the heroines did have marked features of their own when observers, or critics, took the trouble to notice. What was clear and consistent, if still somewhat negative or defensive, was the deepening political commitment – the claim can be made for *Lara*, written in the spring of 1814 and published in August. For some, *Lara* became the favourite of the tales, for Leigh Hunt for example, precisely because the politics were more explicit, an open justification of revolt against the established powers. But the poem had also been hailed as the one which seeks most ambitiously to present a portrait. Byron and Lady Byron talked to each other on these lines. He allegedly said to her of *Lara*: 'There's more of me in that than any of them', and she said to him that it had a stronger mysterious effect than any of them. And the cause of this effect must have been the stunning portrait of the hero which makes its appearance in canto XVII (and, indeed, continues in cantos XVIII and XIX).

> In him inexplicably mix'd appeared
> Much to be loved and hated, sought and feared;
> Opinion varying o'er his hidden lot,
> In praise or railing ne'er his name forgot;
> His silence formed a theme for others' prate –
> They guess'd – they gazed – they fain would know his fate.
> What had he been? what was he, thus unknown,
> Who walked their world, his lineage only known?
> A hater of his kind? yet some would say,
> With them he could seem gay amidst the gay;
> But own'd, that smile if oft observed and near,
> Waned in its mirth and withered to a sneer;
> That smile might reach his lip, but passed not by,
> None e'er could trace its laughter to his eye:

Yet there was softness too in his regard,
At times, a heart as not by nature hard,
But once perceiv'd, his spirit seem'd to chide
Such weakness, as unworthy of its pride,
And steel'd itself, as scorning to redeem
One doubt from others' half withheld esteem;
In self-inflicted penance of a breast
Which tenderness might once have wrung from rest;
In vigilance of grief that would compel
The soul to hate for having lov'd too well.

There was in him a vital scorn of all:
As if the worst had fall'n which could befall
He stood a stranger in this breathing world,
An erring spirit from another hurled;

'Here Byron has said the final word about himself' – if true, it would indeed make this an unforgettable self-portrait. It is not quite that, but the claim, backed by Lady Byron's comments, leaves disturbing afterthoughts.*

These were also the years when Byron was engaged in the most notorious of his love affairs, at least those which were supposed to have shaped his destiny – the alleged incest with his sister Augusta, the rare delightful essay in platonism with Lady

---

* The claim is made and the verses set out in a well-known volume called: *Byron and the Need of Fatality* by Charles du Bos, first published in France in 1931 and first published in England by Putnam in 1932. For all its brilliance and persuasive power – the author calls the *Lara* extract 'the most magnificent eruption that ever burst from the heart of the Byronic volcano' – the book is one of the most bitter libels against Byron ever published. *Astarte*, the sensational volume privately published in 1907 in which the accusations of incest were presented more specifically, is swallowed whole and the Lady Byron case is presented with fresh venomous additions such as the allocation to Lady Melbourne of the role of villainess-in-chief. However, some were introduced by this book to the *Lara* portrait; T.S. Eliot called it a masterpiece of self-analysis. So it is; but it is still only a profile of Byron and only his enemies would see it as a full portrait.

Frances Webster, and the fatal marriage with and separation from Annabella Milbanke. Of course these affairs influenced intimately and profoundly what he wrote, however diverse may be the interpretations placed upon them. What may be more surprising is the way his political interest was woven into all his work, despite all distractions. One batch of these poems was gathered together under the title *Hebrew Melodies*. Since they contained some of his best known – and one or two of the loveliest – of his lyrics, the political content has been largely overlooked. Another great batch took the form of squibs, epigrams, translations from Martial, and a dozen other different disguises, published or unpublished, to match the topical twist of the moment, and a few of these started to tackle the greatest political themes of his age: the Revolution, the Napoleonic conquest, and the counter-revolution.

Byron's own *Ode to Napoleon Buonaparte* was published anonymously at an awkward moment in Napoleonic history – on 16 April 1814, just after he had surrendered at Fontainebleau and was to be despatched to Elba. Byron would not join the rejoicing crowds in the London streets. He did not stir from his own rooms for three days after the abdication. 'At this present writing,' he wrote to Moore, 'Louis the Gouty is wheeling in triumph into Piccadilly, in all the pomp and rabblement of Royalty. I had an offer of seats to see them pass; but, as I have seen a Sultan going to mosque and been at *his* reception of an ambassador, the most Christian King "hath no attractions for me".' He wrote to his publisher at the same time: 'You know I am a Jacobin, and could not wear white nor see the installation of Louis the Gouty . . .' But he could not bear also the scene which he envisaged in Paris: 'I can't help thinking my little Pagod will play them some trick still', he had written when he first heard the news, and then a day later: 'Ah, my poor little Pagod, Napoleon has walked off his pedestal. He has abdicated, they say. This would draw molten brass from the eyes of Zatarail. What! "Kiss the ground before young Malcolm's feet, and then be baited by the rabble's curse!" I cannot bear such a crouching catastrophe.' Then, taking his epigraph from Gibbon – 'By this shameful abdication, he protracted his life a few years,

in a very ambiguous state, between an Emperor and an Exile' –
he unloosed a terrible, mounting invective:

> And Earth have spilt her blood for him,
> Who thus can hoard his own?
> And Monarchs bowed the trembling limb,
> And thanked him for a throne

Byron's bitterness was a sign of how liberal England – Charles
James Fox's England – had refused to share the emotions of the
war against France.

A bare few months (September 1813) before, he had been
writing (to Thomas Moore, as it happens): 'What say you to
Buonaparte. I back him against the field barring Catalepsy and
the Elements. Nay, I almost wish him success against all
countries but this, – were it only to shake the Morning Post. . . .'
Or a few months later (on 4 November) to Lady Melbourne:
'Buonaparte has lost all his allies but me and the King of
Wirtemberg. . . .' He might have been expected to have some
sympathy for Mme. de Staël who had been in London throughout that previous summer, upholding her principled opposition
to Napoleonic tyrannies. But Byron said her politics had 'sadly
changed. She is for the Lord of Israel and the Lord of Liverpool –
a vile antithesis of a Methodist and a Tory – and talks of nothing
but devotion and the Ministry . . .' Maybe his temper was not
improved when she started to lecture him about his love affairs
– 'that I had used Caroline barbarously – that I had no feeling,
and was totally *insensitive* to *la belle passion*, – and had been all
my life. I am very glad to hear it, but did not know it before.' But
perhaps he did listen to her after all. Byron's April 1814 invective against Napoleon had a Staëlite tinge to it, as some other
erstwhile Bonapartist apologists were forced to acknowledge.

At the very least he would have been wiser to have waited,
and when the news came of the escape from Elba, he took it
with a splendid grace, celebrating with Thomas Moore:

> I can forgive the rogue for utterly falsifying every line of
> mine Ode – which I take to be the last and uttermost stretch

of human magnanimity. Do you remember the story of a certain abbé, who wrote a Treatise on the Swedish Constitution, and proved it indissoluble and eternal? Just as he had corrected the last sheet, news came that Gustavus III had destroyed this immortal government. 'Sir,' quoth the abbé, 'the King of Sweden may overthrow the *constitution*, but not *my book*!!' I think *of* the abbé, but not *with* him.

Making every allowance for talent and the most consummate daring, there is, after all, a good deal in luck or destiny. He might have been stopped by our frigates – or wrecked in the Gulf of Lyons, which is particularly tempestuous – or – a thousand things. But he is certainly Fortune's favourite, and

> Once fairly set out on his party of pleasure,
> Taking towns at his liking and crowns at his leisure,
> From Elba to Lyons and Paris he goes,
> Making *balls for* the ladies, and *bows to* his foes.

You must have seen the account of his driving into the middle of the royal army, and the immediate effect of his pretty speeches. And now, if he don't drub the allies, there is 'no purchase in money.' If he can take France by himself, the devil's in't if he don't repulse the invaders, when backed by those celebrated sworders – those boys of the blade, the Imperial Guard, and the old and new army. It is impossible not to be dazzled and overwhelmed by his character and career. Nothing ever so disappointed me as his abdication, and nothing could have reconciled me to him but some such revival as his recent exploit; though no one could anticipate such a complete and brilliant renovation.

Or the lines he wrote when Napoleon was waiting on the *Bellerophon* for despatch to St Helena:

> Farewell to the Land, where the gloom of my Glory
> Arose and o'ershadowed the earth with her name –
> She abandons me now, – but the page of her story,
> The brightest or blackest, is filled with my fame.

I have warred with a world which vanquished me only
When the meteor of Conquest allured me too far;
I have coped with the nations which dread me thus lonely,
The last single Captive to millions in war!

Farewell to thee, France! – when thy diadem crowned me,
I made thee the gem and the wonder of earth, –
But thy weakness decrees I should leave as I found thee,
Decayed in thy glory, and sunk in thy worth.
Oh! for the veteran hearts that were wasted
In strife with the storm, when their battles were won –
Then the Eagle, whose gaze in that moment was blasted,
Had still soared with eyes fixed on victory's sun!

Farewell to thee, France! – but when Liberty rallies
Once more in thy regions, remember me then –
The violet still grows in the depth of thy valleys;
Though withered, thy tears will unfold it again –
Yet, yet, I may baffle the hosts that surround us,
And yet may thy heart leap awake to my voice –
There are links which must break in the chain that has
    bound us,
Then turn thee and call on the Chief of thy choice!

Hebrew Melodies were not designed to challenge the spirit
of the age in the same direct way. Francis Hodgson, still on
the crusading warpath in the hope of winning so spectacular a
convert, expressed his dismay that most of them had 'no connection' with religion. Lady Caroline Lamb, in a less elevated
ecclesiastical tone, dismissed them as trash: 'I who read his
loftier lay with transport will not admire his flaws and nonsense.' Thomas Moore protested too, but maybe he had a twinge
of professional jealousy. Normally he kept all other emotions
well in control beneath his good nature, but here surely Byron
must have known he was trespassing on Moore's own preserves with the assistance of his sub-standard musician, Isaac
Nathan: 'Was there ever anything so bad as the Hebrew
Melodies? Some of the words are of course good, tho' not so
good as might have been expected – but the Music! Oh Lord God

of Israel! What stuff it is. . . .' Maybe most surprising of all was the reticence of Annabella Milbanke, who copied out most of them with pious discrimination.

Professor Wilson Knight gave to one of his Byron books the incongruous title *Lord Byron: The Christian Virtues*. Is this where he got them – from Annabella? For she did argue with Byron about religion, about Christianity, more directly than anyone else. She was destined to suffer more from his Calvinistic upbringing than anybody, or at least that was her own eventual conclusion. On 8 October 1812, when she was still rejecting Byron's first approach via Lady Melbourne, she completed her 'Character of Lord Byron' which she had set aside a few months before:

> The passions have been his guide from childhood, and have exercised a tyrannical power over his very superior intellect. Yet amongst his dispositions are many which deserve to be associated with Christian principles – his love of goodness in its chastest form, and his abhorrence of all that degrades human nature, prove the uncorrupted purity of his moral sense. . . . There is a chivalrous generosity in his ideas of love and friendship, and selfishness is totally absent from his character. In secret he is the zealous friend of all the human feelings; but from the strangest perversion that pride ever created, he endeavours to disguise the best points of his character . . . so that his mind is continually making the most sudden transitions – from good to evil – from evil to good. He is inclined to open his heart unreservedly to those whom he believes *good* . . . even without the preparation of much acquaintance. He is extremely humble towards persons whose character he respects, and to them he would probably confess his errors. . . .

When the wooing again became serious between them, the religious debate was resumed and Byron did not complain. He loved arguing about the Bible, and Annabella held her own in this field better than most. The affair or non-affair with Lady Frances had intervened, and this of course had been reported to

Lady Melbourne, not at all in the same vein he was becoming accustomed to use about her niece. Whoever his correspondent might be and even in his reports on love affairs, he was always finding himself provoked into some fresh political attack on the Government – as in his letter to Lady Melbourne in September 1813:

W[ebster] don't want sense nor good nature but both are occasionally obscured by his suspicions & absurdities of all descriptions – he is passionately fond of having his wife admired – & at the same time jealous to jaundice of every thing & every body – I have hit upon the medium of praising her to him perpetually behind her back – & never looking at her before his face – as for her I believe she is disposed to be very faithful – & I don't think any one now here is inclined to put her to the test. – . . . Ld. Petersham is coming here in a day or two – who will certainly flirt furiously with Ly. F[rances] – & I shall have some comic Iagoism with our little Othello – I should have no chance with his Desdemona myself – but a more lively & better dressed & formed personage might in an innocent way – for I really believe the girl is a very good well disposed wife & will do very well if she lives & he himself don't tease her into some dislike of her lawful owner. – I passed through Hatfield the night of your *ball* – suppose we had jostled at a turnpike! – At Bugden I blundered on a Bishop – the Bishop put me in mind of ye Government – the Government of the Governed – & the governed of their *indifference* towards their governors which you must have remarked as to all *parties* – these reflections expectorated as follows – you know I *never* send you my scribblings & when you read these you will wish I never may. –

Tis said – *Indifference* marks the present time
Then hear the reason – though 'tis told in rhyme –
A King who *can't* – a Prince of Wales who *don't* –
Patriots who *shan't* – Ministers who *won't* –
What matters who are *in* or *out* of place
The *Mad* – the *Bad* – the *Useless* – or the *Base*?

That same week, five days later, he wrote to Annabella on the half-forbidden topic which he was, however, always eager to discuss:

I now come to a subject of your enquiry which you must have perceived I always hitherto avoided – an awful one 'Religion' – I was bred in Scotland among Calvinists in the first part of my life – which gave me a dislike to that persuasion – since that period I have visited the most bigotted & credulous of countries – Spain – Greece – Turkey – as a spectacle the Catholic is more fascinating than the Greek or ye. Moslem – but the *last* is the only believer who practices the precepts of his Prophet to the last chapter of his creed. – My opinions are quite undecided – I may say so sincerely – since when given over at Patras in 1810 – I rejected & ejected three Priest-loads of spiritual consolation by threatening to turn Mussulman if they did not leave me in quiet – I was in great pain & looked upon death as in that respect a relief – without much regret of the past – & few speculations on the future – indeed so indifferent was I to my *bodily* situation – that though I was without any attendant but a young Frenchman as ill as myself – two barbarous Arn[a]outs – and a deaf & desperate Greek Quack – and my English servant (a man now with me) within 2 days journey – I would not allow the last to be sent for – worth all the rest as he would have been in attendance at such a time because – I really don't know why – unless it was an indifference to which I am certainly not subject when in good health. – I believe doubtless in God – & should be happy to be convinced of much more – if I do not at present place implicit faith on tradition & revelation of any human creed I hope it is not from a want of reverence for the Creator but the created – & when I see a man publishing a pamphlet to prove that Mr *Pitt* is risen from the dead (as was done a week ago) perfectly positive in the truth of his assertion – I must be permitted to doubt more miracles equally well attested – but the *moral* of Christianity is perfectly beautiful – & the very sublime of Virtue – yet even there we find some of its finer precepts in earlier axioms of the Greeks. – particularly 'do unto others as you would they should do unto you.' – the forgiveness of injuries – & more which I do not remember. . . .

Well before the actual wedding, by the way, Byron sent Annabella a mammoth reading list. He started with a long line of historians, Italian, Spanish and the rest. She 'would know without his telling her who are the best "modern historians" – and Gibbon is well worth a hundred perusals'. Geography was another field where he made his recommendations, and the classics: 'I have a Tacitus with Latin on one page and Italian on the other. . . .' Novels, essayists, a volume of Machiavelli – 'but I shall only bore you with my *shoulds* and suggestions'. He knew very well he would do nothing of the kind; none of her predecessors had ever complained on this score. He could entrance her with the argument: 'I should regret any *sceptical bigotry* as equally pernicious with the most credulous intolerance. Of the Scriptures themselves I have ever been a reader and admirer as compositions particularly the *Arab-Job* – and parts of Isaiah – and the Song of Deborah.' Annabella might be excused, if she looked up Deborah first, if she did not know it already. He was always willing, with her as with others, not to be too assertive in his scepticism, but a little while later, he would need to make sure that his concessions to orthodoxy did not deceive: 'I philosophise as well as I can – and wish it over one way or the other without many glimpses at the future – why I came here – I know not – where I shall go it is useless to enquire – in the midst of myriads of the living and the dead worlds – stars – systems – infinity – why should I be anxious about an atom?' Byron practised no deception with her or anyone else about his beliefs. He was too genuinely curious, too naturally hostile to any form of pretence in such matters, too practised in stating his case to all and sundry, parsons, mother-confessors, fellow-book addicts and lovers. He was a born educator and self-educator. Even on his honeymoon – the treaclemoon, as he later called it – he could find consolations in the Seaham library, and even in his recommended guides to English literature, even to Annabella, he was more inclined to commit sins of omission than to make the list too long. He knew Shakespeare almost as he knew the Bible, and he preferred Cleopatra to Eve – she 'strikes me as the epitome of her sex, – fond, lively, sad, tender, teasing, humble, haughty, beautiful, the devil! – coquettish to the last, as well with the "asp" as with Anthony.' Truly poor Annabella had some competition.

They continued their religious debate through the whole period of their marriage, and since they were both such experts it must have formed one of their most agreeable diversions from topics which might set their teeth on edge. Several of the *Hebrew Melodies* were copied out by Annabella herself, and since her political sense was also strong we must suppose that she understood what he was saying and how violent was the mounting protest in his breast. *The Vision of Belshazzar*, for example, was more even than another frontal attack on one of his favourite targets, the Prince Regent. Most other Monarchs were there with him in the dock, even if the English king deserved a special contempt. 'Lament that ever thou hadst birth – Unfit to govern, live, or die.' The words which, as he put it in *Don Juan*, 'shook Belshazzar in his Hall/And took his kingdom from him' were the *Rights of Man*. And how could she transcribe without a shudder, how coolly can we read today, the mighty climax to which he raised his *Hebrew Melodies*, leaving no sense of religious repose behind.*

'All is Vanity, Saith the Preacher'

Fame, wisdom, love, and power were mine,
    And health and youth possessed me;
My goblets blushed from every vine,
    And lovely forms caressed me;
I sunned my heart in beauty's eyes,
    And felt my soul grow tender;
All earth can give, or mortal prize,
    Was mine of regal splendour.

* The extracts from *Hebrew Melodies* are taken, like the other poems, from the McGann *The Complete Poetical Works*, Volume III. But it is worth noting furthermore, as McGann does himself, the excellent single volume,

I strive to number o'er what days
　　Remembrance can discover,
Which all that life or earth displays
　　Would lure me to live over.
There rose no day, there rolled no hour
　　Of pleasure unembittered;
And not a trapping decked my power
　　That galled not while it glittered.

The serpent of the field, by art
　　And spells, is won from harming;
But that which coils around the heart,
　　Oh! who hath power of charming?
It will not list to wisdom's lore,
　　Nor music's voice can lure it;
But there it stings for evermore
　　The soul that must endure it.

Goethe once remarked that Byron should have lived to exe-
cute his vocation – to dramatize the Old Testament. But that is
what he had done, continuing with *Hebrew Melodies* and starting
much earlier. The more closely he looked, the more sceptical he
became about the religion of his ancestors. The task called for
the wisdom of Solomon and the patience of Job, but it was typical of Byron to remark that neither of these sacred figures could
be seen to retain, under scrutiny, the qualities attributed to
them. He more and more saw the injustice and horror of the
world around him, and how much it might be necessary to
extirpate the ghost stories of his Calvinistic childhood. 'Trust
Byron', was the family motto in which he took pride and
which, excusably, might arouse fury in the breast of, say, Lady
Caroline. But, there were some great matters in which he *could*

Byron's Hebrew Melodies by Thomas L. Ashton. Byron, and even more a few
of Byron's friends, had some fierce quarrels with Isaac Nathan who wrote
the music and organized the collaboration. Byron claimed to have made
the compilation, 'partly from Job etc. and partly my own imagination . . .
It is odd that this should fall to my lot, who have been abused as "an
infidel". Augusta says "they will call me a Jew next." '

be trusted. For him, political consistency was a virtue to be guarded, and he applied his considerable intelligence to the task.

> As for me, by the blessing of indifference, I have simplified my politics into an utter detestation of all existing governments; and, as it is the shortest and most agreeable and summary feeling imaginable, the first moment of an universal republic would convert me into an advocate for single and uncontradicted despotism. The fact is, riches are power, and poverty is slavery all over the earth, and one sort of establishment is no better, nor worse, for a *people* than another. I shall adhere to my party, because it would not be honourable to act otherwise; but, as to *opinions*, I don't think politics *worth* an *opinion*. *Conduct* is another thing: – if you begin with a party, go on with them. I have no consistency, except in politics; and *that* probably arises from my indifference on the subject altogether.

Or, more simply, and despite the affected disinterest, as he said a few days later, nothing would make him 'Torify his nature'. Here was not the sole cause of his banishment from England, at the height of his fame, but it was one of them.

FIVE

Geneva

I was sick of the Salons long before I left England.
Letter, 17 February 1823

A bare twelve months intervenes between the publication of
Hebrew Melodies, many of them happily transcribed by Annabella, and the first batch of poems despatched to his publisher
from the continent, with the labour or delight of transcription
having been taken over by Claire Clairmont or Mary Shelley.
This was the year of his matrimonial crisis and fiasco; the birth
of his child; a personal financial crisis involving, most horrific
of all, the sale of his books; and his departure from England,
amid ignominy and insult. It was also the year in which, by his
own standards, he showed himself least prolific in writing poetry. Apart from the other distractions, he could draw no comfort
from the political scene which many of his contemporaries,
poets no less than politicians, must have found quite satisfactory. He certainly could not join with any relish the junketings
offered by London society at the time.

'Politics!', he exclaimed and underlined in a postscript to
Leigh Hunt – 'The barking of the wardogs for their carrion has
sickened me of them for the present.' And then a few weeks
later, to Thomas Moore: 'But I am sick at heart of politics and
slaughters; and the luck which Providence is pleased to lavish
on Lord XX [Castlereagh] is only proof of the little value the
gods set upon prosperity, when they permit such ––s as he and
that drunken corporal, old Blucher, to bully their betters.' Some
of these expressions of disgust with the world around him
found their way into *The Siege of Corinth* and *Parisina* which
Annabella was still transcribing, but Byron himself was

166

dissatisfied with the patchwork effect. He was giving much of his time in these months to his duties of management at the Drury Lane Theatre, but he was not encouraged to try to turn playwright when he saw what failures others might contrive. Nor was he tempted to return to the House of Lords, despite a compliment from Leigh Hunt about his capacities as an aspiring orator: ' – if you knew what a hopeless and lethargic den of dullness and drawling our hospital is – during a debate – and what a mass of corruption in its patients – you would wonder – not that – I very seldom speak – but that I ever attempted it – feeling – and I trust I do – independently.' He was for sure, in January 1816, more independent than ever. 'However,' he continued to Hunt

> when a proper spirit is manifested 'without doors' I will endeavour not to be idle within – do you think such a time is coming? Methinks there are gleams of it – my forefathers were on the other side of the question in Charles's days – and the fruit of it was the title and the loss of an enormous property – If the old struggle comes on – I shall use the one and shall never regain the other – but – no matter – there are things even in this world – better than either. . . .

It was natural that he should show this side of his political temperament to Leigh Hunt. If the old struggle came on, the modern representative of the Byron family would now be on the other side. As if to clinch the judgement, he deeply mourned, as a serious blow to all true reformers, the death of Samuel Whitbread, who had served with him on the Drury Lane management. However, it was much more for his politics that Byron hailed him as 'a great and good man'. He also gladly responded at this time to an appeal from the *Examiner*, to contribute to a fund for Mrs Elizabeth Margarot, widow of Maurice Margarot, member of the Corresponding Society transported to Botany Bay.

Just occasionally, throughout the early months of 1816 when the wrangle with Lady Byron's lawyers or parents was rising to its climax, Byron would try to break through the barriers, to find consolation, too, by a renewal of his political engagements. February 26th was such a day. He wrote one elaborate letter to Leigh Hunt, thanking him for a prefatory note to his poem as 'a public compliment and a private kindness'. He wrote another to Lady Byron: 'Dearest Pip – I wish you would make it up – for I am dreadfully sick of all this – and I cannot foresee any good that may come of it . . . I am terribly tired of the stately style of our letters and obliged to take refuge in that which I was used to.' And then a third, to James Perry, the editor of the *Morning Chronicle*: 'If you *dare* publish the enclosed . . . print it as a translation from some recent *French poetry* – but *keep* my *secret*. . . .' Perry did, and adopting Byron's own suggestion, attributed the 'Ode (From the French)' to Chateaubriand, a man most infamous in Byron's eyes for the way he had turned his coat against Napoleon on the very day the Allies had entered Paris. Few would have been likely to be deceived by the Chateaubriand attribution, but the joke at his expense was the more delicious since the wavering allegiance to Napoleon was much more that of his disappointed revolutionary following, the Jacobins or near-Jacobins who found it hard to stomach his Royalist diversions.

> Who, of all the despots banded,
>   With that youthful chief competed?
>   Who could boast o'er France defeated,
> Till lone tyranny commanded?
> Till, goaded by ambition's sting,
> The Hero sunk into the King?
> Then he fell; So perish all,
> Who would men by man enthral.

Chateaubriand, in all his guises or disguises, would never have written in those terms nor could most other observers have imagined that this was the moment to reassert the demand for 'equal rights and laws/Hearts and hands in one great cause'. But that was the true Byronic spirit, much more typical than some affected melancholy or defeatism:

O'er glories gone the invaders march,
Weeps Triumph o'er each levelled arch –
But let Freedom rejoice,
With her heart in her voice;
But, her hand on her sword,
Doubly shall she be adored;
France hath twice too well been taught
The 'moral lesson' dearly bought –
Her Safety sits not on a throne,
With CAPET or NAPOLEON!
But in equal rights and laws,
Hearts and hands in one great cause –
Freedom, such as God hath given
Unto all beneath his heaven,
With their breath, and from their birth,
Though Guilt would sweep it from the earth;
With a fierce and lavish hand
Scattering nations' wealth like sand;
Pouring nations' blood like water,
In imperial seas of slaughter!

But the heart and the mind,
And the voice of mankind,
Shall arise in communion –
And who shall resist that proud union?
The time is passed when swords subdu'd –
Man may die – the soul's renew'd:
Even in this low world of care
Freedom ne'er shall want an heir;
Millions breathe but to inherit
Her for ever bounding spirit –
When once more her hosts assemble,
Tyrants shall believe and tremble –
Smile they at this idle threat?
Crimson tears will follow yet.

Sometime during this very same week he tried his hand at a
new form for him, a short story, a prose satire, called 'The Tale of

Calil'. Most of the signs seems to suggest that it was aimed at a follower of Napoleon's whose betrayal was even smoother, cooler and more offensive in his eyes than Chateaubriand's. For a good political reason, maybe, the story was never published at the time; indeed it lay undisturbed in some alcove in the Murray office in Albemarle Street until 1985. The target was Prince Talleyrand, whom the newly restored Louis XVIII had been ready to adopt as his chief Minister. Byron was outraged, and immediately incorporated his fury in a memorandum which mounted a tremendous attack on

> This man, the renegade of all religions, the betrayer of every trust; the traitor to every government; the Arch-Apostle of all apostacy; Ex-Bishop, Ex-royalist, Ex-citizen, Ex-republican, Ex-minister, Ex-prince, whose name every honest lip quivers to pronounce; the very thought of whom is a pollution from which the imagination struggles to escape – this living record of all that public treason, private treachery, and moral infamy can accumulate in the person of one degraded being – is the organ of the regenerated Government of France.

Neither this memorandum nor 'The Tale of Calil' written a few months later was published at the time, and yet Byron did not normally show much respect for the prevailing popular moods. A likely guess is that he felt he should not attract too much gratuitous political enmity on the top of all the rest he had brought down upon his unbowed shoulders. And part of his detestation of Talleyrand derived from his lingering half-hero-worship of Napoleon. It was not a good moment for parading all his natural recklessness.

Just at this time, even amid the turmoil of his preparations for departure from England, he wrote a few poems or fragments which did see the light of day, some of them being published much against his will. Sometime in these March days he was starting his affair with Claire Clairmont (or she was starting hers with him), and maybe she was the inspirer of the stanzas received at Murray's office on 28 March, later called 'Stanzas for Music':

> There be none of Beauty's daughters
> With a magic like thee;
> And like music on the waters
> Is thy sweet voice to me:

Claire certainly, according to every testimony, had a lovely voice, with whatever vices or disadvantages it may have been accompanied. She pursued Byron; he never called it love, although, if the 'Stanzas to Music' were indeed written for her, she had some reason for being deceived. If he had been embarked upon a great new affair with her, might it not be more probable that he would have kept the verses to show her later? Maybe the lovely lyric was written at some other time altogether, for some other nightingale.

Two other poems, supposedly of a much more incriminating nature, were written in the last weeks of March, but were not intended by him for publication, at least at that time. One, 'Fare Thee Well!', was written on the day after the preliminary separation agreement between Byron and Lady Byron was signed, and might truly be taken as a genuine last-minute effort on his part to repair the damage. He sent the poem first to her, and waited in vain for a response. A few days later he composed 'A Sketch from Private Life', a much more savage affair, directing much of the responsibility for the separation on Mary Jane Clermont, one of Lady Byron's advisers-cum-servants. These two documents fell into the hands of Henry Brougham who was supposed to be acting as mediator between the parties, but who in fact backed Lady Byron throughout. Brougham concerted his tactics with John Scott, editor of the *Champion*, and in the issue of 14 April the two poems were published, accompanied by a blistering general attack on Byron's revolutionary politics; his 'Ode (From the French)', hardly less than his matrimonial troubles, had caused the deepest offence. John Scott, like Byron himself, came from Aberdeen; he had a touch of John Knox in his nature combined with a more modern streak about the way in which sensations could sell newspapers; his idea of patriotism at that hour was comprised in Wordsworth's 'Thanksgiving Ode', happily reprinted in his columns with no qualms from him about the bloody sanctifications which it contained.* The whole brew, brilliantly mixed, set a standard for the rest of the newspapers. Only two of them, James Perry's Whiggish *Morning Chronicle* and Leigh Hunt's *Examiner*, refused to join the hunt. 'In England', wrote the French historian Taine, 'the press does the duty of the police', and the occasion he had in mind was Byron's expulsion with full dishonour from his native land in April 1816.

This was also the occasion which provoked Macaulay to write his famous lament: 'We know of no spectacle so ridiculous as the British public in one of its periodical fits of morality.' He understood well how much Byron had been forced to endure, and his verdict is all the more convincing since his general view of Byron's character and achievement was deeply, inexcusably, hostile. But nothing should detract from the insight he showed at this particular moment:

> The obloquy which Byron had to endure was such as might well have shaken a more constant mind. The newspapers were filled with lampoons. The theatres shook with execrations. He was excluded from circles where he had lately been the observed of all the observers. All those creeping things that riot in the decay of nobler natures hastened to their repast; and they were right; they did after their kind. It is not every day that the savage envy of aspiring dunces is gratified by the agonies of such a spirit, and the degradation of such a name.

To this depiction of the scene – Macaulay at his graphic best – it is difficult to believe that any addition should be made. And yet

---

* John Scott's role is most recently described in *Regency Editor* by Patrick O'Leary. He had a great quarrel with Haydon (according to Haydon) about the morality of publishing such material: 'If you do you will be guilty of great dishonour: it will make the paper sell, said Scott, I replied it is a private business and no business of yours – I saw it was no use. Scott left me, I saw he was rankling and longing to be at Byron.' The best full discussion of the 'Fare Thee Well' poems affair is contained in Doris Langley Moore's account, in *The Late Lord Byron*.

it was true also, and needs to be underlined, that some foreign observers could feel an even deeper sense of outrage. One of these was George Brandes* who could write about Byron's departure from England in even more memorable terms:

> this was a period when ecclesiastical authority and narrow-minded social conservatism, both in a tottering condition, were endeavouring to uphold each other. Taking a bird's-eye view of the psychological history of Europe during the first two decades of the century, it actually seems to us as if the whole edifice of hypocrisy, the foundations of which were laid in the writings of the French emigrés, which rose steadily in those of the German Romanticists, and towered to a giddy height during the French Reaction, now suddenly fell on the head of one man.

If the one man was truly the self-regarding poseur sometimes portrayed, this was the moment when he might have strutted on the stage to some effect, and the full reflection might have been seen in his poetry. Max Beerbohm drew (some sixty years later) an unforgettable caricature about Byron leaving England: it is the picture of the coxcomb fully conscious of his trials. But Macaulay's impressions drawn from the Holland House atmosphere of the time or Brandes's picture drawn from the continental impressions have a much truer validity. He did write some moving poems to Augusta, and he kept a diary for her benefit too. But more remarkable was the determination he showed in turning to other themes, mostly political themes or rather, political-cum-religious themes. The two could never be kept separate in his mind for long.

The last piece which he was provoked to write on English soil were lines written at the Dover grave of his fellow Whiggish poet, Charles Churchill; he hailed 'The Glory and the

---

* George Brandes, a Danish literary critic, wrote his survey of European literature in 1901; it appeared under the title *Main Currents in Nineteenth Century Literature*. He wrote at a time when the hostility towards Byron in his native land was still strong, and wrote in terms which still scorch today.

Nothing of a Name'. Churchill had sometimes had to endure political abuse, but nothing on the same scale. Then he made the crossing, on the night of 25 April, and took early steps to ensure that Augusta and Hobhouse and a few others should know of his progress to his destination, Geneva. Byron was an observant traveller or, rather, observant when he could tear himself away from his books. He read and rubber-necked and reported by turns, and his account of the journey was by no means that of one perpetually aggrieved.* The melancholy, satanic Byron seldom intruded into his diary entries or letters; to Hobhouse, he wrote:

> . . . Our route by the Rhine has been beautiful – & much sur-passing my expectation – though very much answering in it's outlines to my previous conceptions. – The Plain at Waterloo is a fine one – but not much after Marathon & Troy – Cheronea – & Platea. – Perhaps there is something of prejudice in this – but I detest the cause & the victors – & the victory – including Blucher & the Bourbons. – . . . We have seen all the sights – churches & so forth – & at Coblentz crossed the Rhine – and scrambled up the fortress of Ehrenbreitstein now a ruin – we also saw on the road the sepulchres – & monuments of Generals Marceau & Hoche & went up to examine them – they are simple & striking – but now much neglected if not to say defaced by the change of times & this cursed after-crop of rectilignes & legitimacy. – At Manheim we crossed the Rhine & keep on this side to avoid the French segment of Territory at Strasburg – as we have not French passports – & no desire to view a degraded country – & oppressed people. . . . pray remember me to all the remembering – & not less to the superb Murray – who is now enjoying inglorious ease at his green table – & wishing for somebody to keep him in hot water. – Wishing you all prosperity – I am ever . . .

---

* Jerome McGann, in a review of the 1816–1817 volume of letters in the *Times Literary Supplement*, pointed out, with all his authority, that this vol-ume displays a tension rarely evident in his correspondence, and that this streak persisted even after his arrival on the continent.

And again:

> . . . I do not like boring you with descriptions of what I hope you will see – and shall only say that all my expectations have been gratified – & there are things – not inferior to what we have seen elsewhere – & one or two superior – such as Mont Blanc – & the Rhine.

But the view was never allowed to interfere with the books. Just having arrived in Geneva in the early days of June, he could not refrain from despatching a special note to another old friend, Pryce Gordon, who had done him a peculiar favour when they met in Brussels: 'I cannot tell you what a treat your gift of Casti has been to me. I have almost got him by heart. I had read his "Animali Parlanti", but I think these "Novelle" much better. I long to go to Venice to see the manners so admirably described.' This was the first particular mention of Venice by Byron in any context. Casti was to play a notable part in his story, but for the moment his journey and his thoughts took a different turn. And then, at the end of June came two letters, one to Hobhouse and the other to Murray, with some momentous revelations and suppressions:

> . . . I have taken a very pretty villa in a vineyard – with the Alps behind – & Mt Jura and the Lake before – it is called Diodati – from the name of the Proprietor – who is a descendant of the critical & illustrissimi Diodati – and has an agreeable house which he lets at a reasonable rate per season or annum as suits the lessee – . . . Tell Murray I have a 3d Canto of Childe Harold finished – it is the longest of the three – it being one hundred & eleven Stanzas – I shall send it by the first plausible conveyance. – At the present writing I am on my way on a water-tour round the Lake Leman – and am thus far proceeded in a pretty open boat which I bought & navigate – it is an English one & was brought lately from Bordeaux – I am on shore for the Night . . . Tomorrow we go to Meillerei – & Clarens – & Vevey – with Rousseau in hand – to see his scenery – according to his

delineation in his Heloise now before me. – The views have hitherto been very fine – but I should conceive less so than those of the remainder of the lake. – All your letters (that is *two*) have arrived – thanks & greetings. – what – & who – the devil is 'Glenarvon'. I know nothing – nor ever heard of such a person.

To Murray:

Dear Sir – I am thus far (kept by stress of weather) on my way back to Diodati (near Geneva) from a voyage in my boat round the lake – & I enclose you a sprig of *Gibbon's Acacia* & some rose leaves from his garden – which with part of his house I have just seen – you will find honourable mention in his life made of this 'Acacia' when he walked out on the night of concluding his history. – The garden – & *summer house* where he composed are neglected – & the last utterly decayed – but they still show it as his 'Cabinet' & seem perfectly aware of his memory. – My route – through Flanders – & by the Rhine to Switzerland was all I expected & more. – I have traversed all Rousseau's ground – with the Heloise before me – & am struck to a degree with the force & accuracy of his descriptions – & the beauty of their reality: – Meillerie – Clarens – & Vevey – & the Chateau de Chillon are places of which I shall say little – because all I could say must fall short of the impressions they stamp. – Three days ago – we were most nearly wrecked in a Squall off Meillerie – & driven to shore – I ran no risk being so near the rocks and a good swimmer – but our party were wet – & incommoded a good deal: – the wind was strong enough to blow down some trees as we found at landing – however all is righted & right – & we are thus far on return. – Dr Polidori is not here – but at Diodati – left behind in hospital with a sprained ancle acquired in tumbling from a wall – he can't jump. – I shall be glad to hear you are well – & have received for me certain helms & swords sent from Waterloo – which I rode over with pain & pleasure. – I have finished a third Canto of Childe Harold (consisting of one hundred & seventeen stanzas (longer than either of the two former) – & in some parts –

it may be – better – but of course on that *I* cannot determine.
– I shall send it by the first safe-looking opportunity.

Glenarvon was a reminder that the London of his past was not quite dead and buried; it was the title of a book by Lady Caroline Lamb.* But Byron had quite different distractions. The visit to Chillon stirred him to celebrate the famous sixteenth-century prisoner, François Bonivard – 'Eternal spirit of the chainless mind!' – and then to tell the whole fable and how Bonivard made friends with his fellow inmates, the spiders and the mice.

> And I, the monarch of each race
> Had power to kill –, yet, strange to tell!
> In quiet we had learn'd to dwell,
> Nor slew I of my subjects one
> What sovereign hath so little done?

This last couplet was too strong for monarchical Tory stomachs in Murray's office, and it was cut, much to Byron's annoyance.
He wrote another sonnet on 'the love of mighty minds':

> Rousseau – Voltaire – our Gibbon – and de Stael –
> Leman! these names are worthy of thy shore.

These names, with a few others of almost equal glory, he started to weave into something more ambitious than he had ever attempted before; something prompted by what he had freshly seen on blood-soaked battlefields, but something inspired too by the publicists, the philosophers, the propagandists who had prepared the way for 1789: altogether, a great, continuous, revolutionary anthem. And he had with him a new companion in his trials and triumphs. Along with Claire to the shores of Geneva had come Shelley and Mary Shelley. Claire and Mary – they were each eighteen years old – offered youth and

---

* The best, recent comment on *Glenarvon* I have read appeared in the *Byron Journal* for 1981 by Malcolm Kelsall. He refers too to the others who have written on the subject, but comments himself chiefly on the Irish background to the whole story. Lady Caroline had deeper political tastes than is often supposed, and Byron had helped to incite them.

excitement and loveliness and immediate assistance with manuscripts. Byron himself was only twenty-eight, Shelley was twenty-three. He had sent Byron a copy of his *Queen Mab* three years before, but they had never met. The friendship, intellectual and emotional, was to prove historic, and some part of the impact was immediate. Each was naturally shy and unready to offer full friendship all at once. But neither had ever met anyone else from whom each could learn so much and so ardently and with whom, in particular, they could share their particular brands of learning. As they made that first expedition on the lake, Byron and Shelley started talking to one another about the books they loved, and they never stopped.* They had the same Promethean sense of adventure, a common fury as they clashed with the combined power of Church and State. Byron spoke for both of them:

> Thy Godlike crime was to be kind,
> To render with thy precepts less
> The sum of human wretchedness,
> And strengthen Man with his own mind;

* For many of us the introduction to this relationship was John Buxton's *Byron and Shelley* published in 1968. It remains a delight and treasure of the first order. Nearly ten years later appeared Charles E. Robinson's *Shelley and Byron: The Snake and Eagle Wreathed in Fight*. John Beer, reviewing this volume in the *Times Literary Supplement*, asked why such an excellent theme had not been tackled often before. Almost any book on Byron must constantly return to the same relationship which greatly developed at their later meetings. Charles Robinson in his fascinating account of the suddenness of Shelley's impact – his 'dosing' of Byron with Wordsworth, as Byron jocularly protested, for example – seems to me to make the impact all too sudden. The way in which Byron could translate immediate sensations and experiences so swiftly was a phenomenon; but several of the ideas to which he gave expression in his travels round Lake Geneva came, I would have thought, much more from the sources he himself cited – Rousseau in particular – rather than from Wordsworth and Shelley combined. The other volume on this topic which no one should miss is Richard Holmes's *Shelley: The Pursuit*. He stresses Shelley's diffidence in Byron's presence even when he was giving some account of the near-transcendental visions which he had seen. However, more on this matter will follow later.

The sympathy between the two was so swift and sure that it was Shelley, a few weeks later, who offered the first safe-looking opportunity for getting the manuscript of *Childe Harold* Canto III back to London. Shelley thought he was empowered to correct the proofs. But Murray and Gifford moved at once to check the Shelley influence and indeed to excise all the political notes, many of them with a strong radical content, which Byron despatched at the same time. Some of these do add a special sharpness, although of course the poem itself retained its stupendous force. Byron knew it was something much more powerful than he had ever attempted before, 'the best which I have ever written'. 'The two key figures', writes McGann, 'are of course Napoleon and Rousseau, and it is part of the brilliance of the poem that Byron treated both with such pitiless sympathy.' True, indeed, and yet it may also be insisted that Rousseau displaces Napoleon. The famous, terrible war scenes in which 'Rider and horse, – friend, foe – in one red burial blent' make way, not as was sometimes over-emphasized to Words-worthian scenes of mountain tops and loftiest peaks which Shelley had allegedly sought to instil, but rather to an ecstatic acceptance of the new doctrine which Rousseau had described first and foremost and in a language which, however translated, had set the world alight.

> . . . Conquerors and Kings,
> Founders of sects and systems, to whom add
> Sophists, Bards, Statesmen, all unquiet things
> Which stir too strongly the soul's secret springs,
> And are themselves the fools to those they fool;
> Envied, yet how unenviable! what stings
> Are theirs! One breast laid open were a school
> Which would unteach mankind the lust to shine or rule . . .

All too eagerly in the ensuing years – and even more so in this century – the greatness and originality of Rousseau were dismissed or denied. A highly select trio of near-contemporary critics, Hazlitt, Stendhal and Heine, all reared on *La Nouvelle Héloïse* themselves, would repudiate any such slur. But the pre-eminence which Byron accords to Rousseau is in a sense all the more remarkable since he gave it first. A sly insinuation has sometimes been added that Byron had somehow been tempted to undervalue him and his influence because of his lowly birth and plebeian manners and inept lovemaking. Instead, Byron understood the Rousseau of *La Nouvelle Héloïse* – he recalled page after page to Shelley – and he also understood in every fibre of his being the other Rousseau, the herald of the Revolution. The verses in which he did it have never lost their brightness and their power. He taught his world – our world –

> To look on One, whose dust was once all fire,
> A native of the land where I respire
> The clear air for a while – a passing guest,
> Where he became a being, – whose desire
> Was to be glorious; 'twas a foolish quest,
> The which to gain and keep, he sacrificed all rest.

> Here the self-torturing sophist, wild Rousseau,
> The apostle of affliction, he who threw
> Enchantment over passion, and from woe
> Wrung overwhelming eloquence, first drew
> The breath which made him wretched; yet he knew
> How to make madness beautiful, and cast
> O'er erring deeds and thoughts, a heavenly hue
> Of words, like sunbeams, dazzling as they past
> The eyes, which o'er them shed tears feelingly and fast.

> His love was passion's essence – as a tree
> On fire by lightning; with ethereal flame
> Kindled he was, and blasted; for to be
> Thus, and enamoured, were in him the same.
> But his was not the love of living dame,
> Nor of the dead who rise upon our dreams,
> But of ideal beauty, which became
> In him existence, and o'erflowing teems
> Along his burning page, distempered though it seems.

This breathed itself to life in Julie, *this*
Invested her with all that's wild and sweet;
This hallowed, too, the memorable kiss
Which every morn his fevered lip would greet,
From hers, ...

It was, for the devotees of *La Nouvelle Héloïse*, the most famous kiss in history; but with Byron, as with all others truly touched by the Romantic ardour, it marked the beginnings of a political faith too.

For then he was inspired, and from him came,
As from the Pythian's mystic cave of yore,
Those oracles which set the world in flame,
Nor ceased to burn till kingdoms were no more:
Did he not this for France? which lay before
Bowed to the inborn tyranny of years?
Broken and trembling, to the yoke she bore,
Till by the voice of him and his compeers,
Roused up to too much wrath which follows o'ergrown fears?

And what if the result of the first turmoil was not what the revolutionaries had prophesied, not the unclouded dawn? But at once comes the true Byronic refusal to accept defeat.

They made themselves a fearful monument!
The wreck of old opinions – things which grew
Breathed from the birth of time: the veil they rent,
And what behind it lay, all earth shall view.
But good with ill they also overthrew,
Leaving but ruins, wherewith to rebuild
Upon the same foundation, and renew
Dungeons and thrones, which the same hour re-fill'd,
As heretofore, because ambition was self-will'd.

But this will not endure, not be endured!
Mankind have felt their strength, and made it felt.
They might have used it better, but, allured
By their new vigour, sternly have they dealt

On one another; pity ceased to melt
With her once natural charities. But they,
Who in oppression's darkness caved had dwelt,
They were not eagles, nourish'd with the day;
What marvel then, at times, if they mistook their prey?

This was Byron, be it not forgotten, rejecting the doctrine that the misdeeds of the Revolution should condemn the Revolution itself.

No question is necessary about the strength and depth of Shelley's influence on this lakeside journey, and several of the passages suppressed by the Albemarle censors reinforce this fact even though Shelley's name does not appear on them. But Byron wrote in plain prose, stressing that it was not a matter merely of undivided passion, of 'a sense of the existence of loving in its most extended and sublime capacity, and of our own participation of its good, of its glory: it is the great principle of the universe, which is there more condensed, but not less manifested; and which, though knowing ourselves a part, we lose our individuality, and mingle in the beauty of the whole.' Would he have ever written that, and the verses which accompanied it, without Shelley at his side? Yet once again it should be insisted; Rousseau's direct influence must never be underrated. A few verses earlier – in the censored notes – Byron had written of the single kiss for which Rousseau would make his walk every morning: 'Rousseau's description of his feelings on this occasion may be considered as the most passionate, yet not impure description and expression of love that ever kindled into words; which after all must be felt, from their very force, to be inadequate to the delineation: a painting can give no sufficient idea of the ocean.' Even without Shelley, Rousseau had overwhelmed him, more so than any other poet of the age, and he alone among them had felt the power of Rousseau's presence in his native habitations and surroundings. And it was he who was introducing Rousseau to Shelley and not the other way round. Moreover, another Byronic explosion was the product of his practical nature, coupled maybe by the promptings of another of his lakeside heroes who never found a place in Shelley's Valhalla, Gibbon.

The hills are covered with vineyards, and interspersed with some small but beautiful woods; one of these was named the 'Bosquet de Julie', and it is remarkable that, though long ago cut down by the brutal selfishness of the monks of St Bernard (to whom the land appertained), that the ground might be inclosed into a vineyard for the miserable drones of an execrable superstition, the inhabitants of Clarens still point out the spot where its trees stood, calling it by the name which consecrated and survived them.

Rousseau has not been particularly fortunate in the preservation of the 'local habitations' he has given to 'airy nothings'. The Prior of Great St Bernard has cut down some of his woods for the sake of a few casks of wine, and Buonaparte has levelled part of the rocks of Meillerie in improving the road to the Simplon. The road is an excellent one, but I cannot quite agree with a remark which I heard made, that 'La route vaut mieux que les souvenirs.'

And what of those other names which stirred them, the equal almost of 'Clarens! sweet Clarens, birth-place of deep love!': Gibbon, the part prompter surely of his damnation of the St Bernard monks for their vandalism, Voltaire, and Madame de Staël herself. No one could say that it was some harsh sectarian creed which he espoused, rather a synthesis drawn from what the old century bequeathed and what the new one heralded:

> Lausanne! and Ferney! ye have been the abodes
> Of names which unto you bequeath'd a name;
> Mortals, who sought and found, by dangerous roads,
> A path to perpetuity of fame:
> They were gigantic minds, and their steep aim,
> Was, Titan-like, on daring doubts to pile
> Thoughts which should call down thunder, and the flame
> Of Heaven, again assail'd, if Heaven the while
> On man and man's research could deign do more than smile.

The one was fire and fickleness, a child,
Most mutable in wishes, but in mind,
A wit as various, – gay, grave, sage, or wild, –
Historian, bard, philosopher, combined;
He multiplied himself among mankind,
The Proteus of their talents: But his own
Breathed most in ridicule, – which, as the wind,
Blew where it listed, laying all things prone, –
Now to o'erthrow a fool, and now to shake a throne.

The other, deep and slow, exhausting thought,
And hiving wisdom with each studious year,
In meditation dwelt, with learning wrought,
And shaped his weapon with an edge severe,
Sapping a solemn creed with solemn sneer;
The lord of irony, – that master-spell,
Which stung his foes to wrath, which grew from fear,
And doom'd him to the zealot's ready Hell,
Which answers to all doubts so eloquently well.

They *were* gigantic minds, and Byron, with his spacious vision in this third canto, made himself of their number.

One other name – the fourth in his Genevan sonnet – did not make her appearance in Canto III, although some of her writings were preparing the way for the next developments in his life. Considering the honour he paid to these gigantic minds, it is not so easy to realize why *Childe Harold* was still considered such an egotistical affair. Maybe that effect was produced by the last, most moving lines to his daughter: 'My voice shall with the future visions blend/And reach into thy heart.' Or possibly again, the misapprehension was due to the few verses which preceded it, 'I stood and stand alone, – remembered or forgot', verses which appeared to revive the theme, the pageant of his bleeding heart. But the true message is utterly different. Indeed, it is hard to believe that Hazlitt in particular could ever have read these verses and not seen some resemblance to his own predicament and his own reconquest of his central faith.

I have not loved the world, nor the world me;
I have not flattered its rank breath, nor bow'd
To its idolatries a patient knee, –
Nor coin'd my cheek to smiles, – nor cried aloud
In worship of an echo; in the crowd
They could not deem me one of such; I stood
Among them, but not of them; in a shroud
Of thoughts which were not their thoughts, and still could,
Had I not filed my mind, which thus itself subdued.

I have not loved the world, nor the world me, –
But let us part fair foes; I do believe,
Though I have found them not, that there may be
Words which are things, – hopes which will not deceive,
And virtues which are merciful, nor weave
Snares for the failing: I would also deem
O'er others' griefs that some sincerely grieve;
That two, or one, are almost what they seem, –
That goodness is no name, and happiness no dream.

The phrase about words and things rings through Hazlitt's prose as it does through Byron's poetry. A little later, the insight started to appear: but how could he have read these last verses without an understanding that they were allies in the same cause against the same enemies?

Byron's visits to Madame de Staël at Coppet made a notable contribution to his later education.* Of course he had met her frequently before in London at the height of his and her fame. He honoured her for her independence, and he was well aware, thanks to his reading, what a powerful woman she was. She in turn treated him with real kindness and even offered to try to reopen the way to a reconciliation with Lady Byron, but Byron himself knew the obstacles were mounting not receding. He

---

* A good account of Byron's relations with Madame de Staël is given by Ernest Giddey, Professor of English and Vice-Rector at Lausanne University, in the volume, *Lord Byron and His Contemporaries*, delivered at the Sixth International Byron Seminar. Madame de Staël was one of those who introduced him to Italy and he would never disguise that debt.

had the chance to read on the spot Benjamin Constant's *Adolphe* – 'it is a work', he wrote at the time, 'which leaves an unpleasant impression but very consistent with the consequences of not being in love – which is perhaps as disagreeable as anything – except being so. . . .' One suggestion retailed via Lady Blessington's gossip (and therefore to be treated with reserve) is that he asked her whether she was the heroine 'which rendered her famous'. He is also alleged to have told her that her two volumes *Delphine* and *Corinne* were 'very dangerous productions to be put into the hands of young women', and again, that *Adolphe* should be given to every reader of *Corinne* as an antidote. Such impertinences could bring her response: 'She came down upon me like an avalanche, whenever I told her my amiable truths, sweeping everything before her, with that eloquence that always overwhelmed but never convinced.' No doubt that was the recollection of the efforts of her spoken eloquence, but the same quality infused her writing. The Byron of 1816 and the years which followed was more impressed by *Corinne* than by *Adolphe*. And so were multitudes of his generation, much more so than the cynical readers of modern times.

Canto III might invite criticism even from his friends; Hobhouse said it was much too full of 'mysteries and metaphysics', and doubtless he would have protested even more strongly if he had known that Byron had been provoked to embark on his own version of a Goethean, Faustian melodrama. But included in the batch of poems which Shelley brought back with him to London on 16 August, was one which fitted not at all into any of these categories and which, unfortunately, for reasons not easy to unravel, attracted little critical attention at the time. Much of the contemporary interest in the work seemed to be directed to the quite false claim that Byron had been guilty of plagiarizing a Thomas Campbell poem called 'The Last Man' published a year before. Thomas Campbell made the accusation himself. Then later, with more justice, an association between Byron's poem and Mary Shelley's novel was suggested. But the poem itself, 'Darkness', read with the context of 1816 in control, tells much more of Byron's politics, his own particular mixture of politics and religion; for, first and most importantly, readers may look here in vain for the Byronic hero. He has disappeared altogether from the scene and does not survive the holocaust to tell the tale. Most other stories of the last man describe, most implausibly, how he lived to philosophize another day. Byron will admit no such sentimental conclusion. The only last hero, if there is one, is his dog: a fresh and casual acknowledgment of his thesis that in his paradise the animals would not be permitted to be made helpless victims of their sadistic masters. More important: what are the causes of the world-wide, immeasurable catastrophe? The assault is directed, without any diversions whatever, against the makers of wars and those who offer the altars and trumpets of religion to excuse what they achieve, the ultimate desolation. It is hard to imagine any poem on so great a theme to which may be better applied the prime Keatsian virtue of disinterestedness, the determination to say what he thought, without any egotistical intrusion, sublime or otherwise.

Of course, one part of the interest of reading 'Darkness' today derives from the fact that it describes what might happen more graphically than the modern nuclear scientists have been able to do: but Byron cannot be blamed for that. He describes how human beings and the institutions they contrive to cover their hypocrisies and bolster their pride produce the universal catastrophe.

> I had a dream, which was not all a dream.
> The bright sun was extinguish'd, and the stars
> Did wander darkling in the eternal space,
> Rayless, and pathless, and the icy earth
> Swung blind and blackening in the moonless air;
> Morn came, and went – and came, and brought no day,
> And men forgot their passions in the dread
> Of this their desolation; and all hearts
> Were chill'd into a selfish prayer for light:
> And they did live by watchfires – and the thrones,
> The palaces of crowned kings – the huts,

The habitations of all things which dwell,
Were burnt for beacons; cities were consumed,
And men were gathered round their blazing homes
To look once more into each other's face;
Happy were those who dwelt within the eye
Of the volcanos, and their mountain-torch:
A fearful hope was all the world contain'd;
Forests were set on fire – but hour by hour
They fell and faded – and the crackling trunks
Extinguish'd with a crash – and all was black.
The brows of men by the despairing light
Wore an unearthly aspect, as by fits
The flashes fell upon them; some lay down
And hid their eyes and wept; and some did rest
Their chins upon their clenched hands, and smiled;
And others hurried to and fro, and fed
Their funeral piles with fuel, and looked up
With mad disquietude on the dull sky,
The pall of a past world; and then again
With curses cast them down upon the dust,
And gnash'd their teeth and howl'd: the wild birds shriek'd,
And, terrified, did flutter on the ground,
And flap their useless wings; the wildest brutes
Came tame and tremulous; and vipers crawl'd
And twined themselves among the multitude,
Hissing, but stingless – they were slain for food:
And War, which for a moment was no more,
Did glut himself again; – a meal was bought
With blood, and each sate sullenly apart
Gorging himself in gloom: no love was left;
All earth was but one thought – and that was death,
Immediate and inglorious; and the pang
Of famine fed upon all entrails – men
Died, and their bones were tombless as their flesh;
The meagre by the meagre were devoured,
Even dogs assail'd their masters, all save one,
And he was faithful to a corse, and kept

The birds and beasts and famish'd men at bay,
Till hunger clung them, or the dropping dead
Lured their lank jaws; himself sought out no food,
But with a piteous and perpetual moan
And a quick desolate cry, licking the hand
Which answered not with a caress – he died.
The crowd was famish'd by degrees; but two
Of an enormous city did survive,
And they were enemies; they met beside
The dying embers of an altar-place
Where had been heap'd a mass of holy things
For an unholy usage; they raked up,
And shivering scraped with their cold skeleton hands
The feeble ashes, and their feeble breath
Blew for a little life, and made a flame
Which was a mockery; then they lifted up
Their eyes as it grew lighter, and beheld
Each other's aspects – saw, and shriek'd, and died –
Even of their mutual hideousness they died,
Unknowing who he was upon whose brow
Famine had written Fiend. The world was void,
The populous and the powerful – was a lump,
Seasonless, herbless, treeless, manless, lifeless –
A lump of death – a chaos of hard clay.
The rivers, lakes, and ocean all stood still,
And nothing stirred within their silent depths;
Ships sailorless lay rotting on the sea,
And their masts fell down piecemeal; as they dropp'd
They slept on the abyss without a surge –
The waves were dead; the tides were in their grave,
The moon their mistress had expired before;
The winds were withered in the stagnant air,
And the clouds perish'd; Darkness had no need
Of aid from them – She was the universe.

It is a warning, not a poem of despair. Yet no one took much notice. I sometimes conclude that when Byron discovered how little the world would heed his direct descriptions of the wickedness and futility of war he turned to other means of speaking to his age. And, fortunately for the gaiety of nations, this change of mood coincided with his arrival in Venice.

Sometimes Byron, the philosopher-moralist, was mocked, by a long line of experts in subsequent generations, but of course by his contemporaries too. Perhaps the fashion was set by Goethe, and where he paved the way a whole flock of Pharisees and parasites rushed to follow. In the household of Johann Wolfgang von Goethe in Weimar much honour was accorded to the young Byron, some of it arising from the rapture with which his writings were received by Goethe's daughter-in-law, but the great man himself could show genuine enthusiasm too. However, a strain of patronage was evident in his judgement of Byron, as of many other of his contemporaries. For all the qualities he was ready to attribute to Byron, he could not resist the comment – 'The moment he reflects, he is a child' – a truly damning verdict, the more one ponders on it; enough to ensure that Byron should never be allowed to intrude for long on to the high altitudes which Goethe had made his own. If Byron was not an adult philosopher-poet, treating the greatest subjects, then much of what he wrote was pretentious drivel – for example, the dramatic poem, as he called it, *Manfred* which he started to write but failed to complete amid his Alpine tours. Inevitably comparisons were drawn between *Manfred* and Goethe's *Faust* which Byron had read three years before, if only in a bad translation in one of Madame de Staël's books. Byron, with all justice on his side, repudiated any question of plagiarism, and it is not recorded whether the charge of childishness ever reached his ears: almost certainly not, for Byron would surely have mounted his reply in a legitimate burst of Byronic invective. For *Manfred*, whatever else it was – maybe Byron did tackle it even better later, as we shall see – was a serious poem on a tremendous theme, as declared by Manfred in his opening speech, when he challenges some of the central doctrines of religion, Christian and some others:

Sorrow is knowledge: they who know the most
Must mourn the deepest o'er the fatal truth,
The Tree of Knowledge is not that of life.*

Byron did have his periods of deep dejection. At the end of a long letter to Thomas Moore, written from Verona, he included this lament: 'My day is over – what then? – I have had it.' But Venice was still to come, and the darkness would be broken.

---

* When Nietzsche transcribed those lines he called them 'immortal': for they stated the terrible fact that man might bleed to death through the truth that he recognizes. When Bertrand Russell transcribed the Nietzsche transcription, he did not dissent: this, from the greatest philosopher of our century, who sought to revive some of the classical and sceptical themes of eighteenth-century philosophy at its peak, might be thought a sufficient answer to Goethe, and the riposte is further illustrated by the fact that Bertrand Russell, in his *A Short History of Western Philosophy*, published in 1945, devoted a whole chapter to Byron, and only a few subsidiary sentences to Goethe. The verdict is made the more valid by the evidence contained in the same chapter that Russell was no Byron-worshipper. But he did see and recognize how widely and deeply the Byronic influence had penetrated, even amongst those who sought to disown him. 'Close thy *Byron*: open thy *Goethe*,' Thomas Carlyle had said in a sentence almost as famous as Goethe's reference to his childishness. 'But', says Russell, 'Byron was in his blood, whereas Goethe remained an aspiration.'

One possible explanation of the apparent contradictions in Goethe's verdict arises possibly from the Foot thesis which I offer with not too strong a philosophical assurance. In so many famous households of the time, the women understood Byron better than the men: Goethe's daughter-in-law better than Goethe himself; Lady Melbourne better than her husband; Jane Welsh Carlyle better than Carlyle; Mary Shelley (marginally) better than Shelley; Fanny Brawne better than John Keats; Macaulay's half-sister Margaret better than Macaulay. His much-misunderstood mother who instilled his first notions of political principle had understood him better than all the parsons recruited for his instruction, and his sister Augusta could laugh with him more readily than anyone else until his last beloved Teresa started to do the same. I had thought at one stage, when I read in *Don Juan* of 'Adam's fall and Eve's slip', that I might be able to add the name of an even more eminent woman to my list. But no: Eve, as I fear we shall have to learn later in the proper place, played a role of the direst and dirtiest nature in the politics of Paradise.

She, alas, was *not* one of the mother figures on whose bosom Byron would choose to relax.

In more modern times, the list in his favour among the women has continued. Where would the academic men be without the library doors unlocked by Elizabeth Boyd, the two rich, previously-buried golden treasure houses thrown open to us by Iris Origo and Doris Langley Moore and the single drop of pure silver devised by Elma Dangerfield, in her description of the Geneva expedition? And again, one of the very best introductions to Byron's poetry – prompted by Doris Langley Moore's guidance – is *Bright Darkness* by Anne Fleming; a beautifully produced and constructed book by a true Byron lover. 'The only way to understand the phenomenon of Byron's fame', she says, 'is to read the poetry.' No Byronist, old or new, like myself, who turns to this volume will be disappointed.

SIX

Venice I

I have also been in love these three months.

7 March 1817

Like most visitors to Venice throughout the centuries, Byron had his own vision of the city in advance, and then, for him as for most others, *La Serenissima* excelled all anticipations. He was not content to mark the wonders all around him; he was soon weaving the new experiences with the old and preparing for action. He made the city his own, encouraged others, especially some of his English compatriots, to see it with new eyes, and, by some alchemy unknown to the magicians, the history, the loveliness, the politics, the spirit of the place and the people were transmuted into new forms of expression, a fresh Promethean display of defiance. In present-day Venice, the Byronic landmarks can be found round every vista: so much has his view been superimposed on what was there before. But part of the miracle was due to the speed and the assurance with which he could adapt new ideas and new forms to suit his own individual purposes.

He wrote to Thomas Moore within a few days of his arrival in what became later one of the most often-quoted of his letters:

It has always been (next to the East) the greenest island of my imagination. It has not disappointed me; though its evident decay would perhaps, have that effect upon others. But I have been familiar with ruins too long to dislike desolation. Besides, I have fallen in love, which, next to falling into the canal (which would be no use, as I can swim) is the best or worst thing I could do.

193

Then he described Marianna Segati, the wife of the draper who lived in the Frezzeria, just off the Piazza San Marco, the street where the courtesans were alleged to congregate right from the times of his most famous precursor in this field, Sir Thomas de Coryate. 'She has the voice of a lute – and the song of a seraph (though not quite so sacred) besides a long postscript of graces – virtues and accomplishments – enough to furnish out a new Chapter of Solomon's Song. – But her great merit is finding out mine. – There is nothing so amiable as discernment.' And this, amazing to relate, was written within a couple of weeks of his arrival. He started too, just to test his brain power, to learn Armenian. He wrote also to Augusta: 'I go every morning to the Armenian Convent (of *friars not nuns* my child)', adding happily, 'The lady [Marianna] has luckily for me been less obdurate than the language.' To all his correspondents, already in the first few weeks after his arrival his spirit seemed to be rising: 'I like Venice and its marine melancholy', he wrote to Hobhouse, – 'and rather wish to *have seen* Rome than to *see* it.' And then again to Augusta: 'I remember a methodist preacher who on perceiving a profane grin on the faces of part of his congregation – exclaimed "no *hopes* for *them* as *laughs*" and thus it is – with us – we laugh too much for hopes – and so even let them go – I am sick of sorrow – & must even content myself as well as I can – so here goes – I won't be woeful again if I can help it.'

Venice was never green, whatever other colour she might adopt or simulate, among all the reds and blues and purples captured by all the painters, including Turner, whom Byron introduced to the city. He was always a stickler for accuracy in these matters. For the rest, it was the place of his dreams, offering neither lofty unrelieved alpine tragedy nor mere frivolous escapism, but the bitter-sweet mixture which for him was nearer the truth. On Christmas Eve, 1816 – six weeks after he had arrived in Venice – he wrote a letter a thousand words long to Thomas Moore in which all these sudden contrasting emotions were combined.* The whole must be read for the full,

* Soon after returning from a Byronic seminar in Venice in September, 1986, I heard Professor J. Drummond Bone speak on this letter and expound its elaborate appeal in a manner which impressed all who heard

unbowdlerized Byron, yet these extracts do suffice to show how he was already grafting his Venetian experience on to some earlier themes:

> . . . Oh, by the way, I forgot, when I wrote from Verona, to tell you that at Milan I met with a countryman of yours – a Colonel [Fitzgerald], a very excellent, good-natured fellow, who knows and shows all about Milan, and is, as it were, a native there. He is particularly civil to strangers, and this is his history, – at least, an episode of it.
>
> Six-and-twenty years ago, Col. [Fitzgerald], then an ensign, being in Italy, fell in love with the Marchesa [Castiglione], and she with him. The lady must be, at least, twenty years his senior. The war broke out; he returned to England, to serve – not his country, for that's Ireland – but England, which is a different thing; and *she* – heaven knows what she did. In the year 1814, the first annunciation of the Definitive Treaty of Peace (and tyranny) was developed to the astonished Milanese by the arrival of Col. [Fitzgerald], who, flinging himself full length at the feet of Mad. [Castiglione], murmured forth, in half-forgotten Irish Italian, eternal vows of indelible constancy. The lady screamed, and exclaimed, 'Who are you?' The Colonel cried, 'What! don't you know me? I am so and so,' etc., etc., etc.; till, at length, the Marchesa, mounting from reminiscence to reminiscence through the lovers of the intermediate twenty-five years, arrived at last at the recollection of her *povero* sub-lieutenant. She then said, 'Was there ever such virtue?' (that was her very word) and, being now a widow, gave him apartments in her palace, reinstated him in all the rights of wrong, and held him up to the admiring world as a miracle of incontinent fidelity, and the unshaken Abdiel of absence. . . .
>
> . . . The day after to-morrow (to-morrow being Christmas-day) the Carnival begins. I dine with the Countess

---

it. I went home to read it again that night. It is truly a masterpiece, although several other letters, especially from Venice, qualify for that title.

Albrizzi and a party, and go to the opera. On that day the Phenix, (not the Insurance Office, but) the theatre of that name, opens: I have got me a box there for the season, for two reasons, one of which is, that the music is remarkably good. The Contessa Albrizzi, of whom I have made mention, is the De Staël of Venice; not young, but a very learned, unaffected, good-natured woman; very polite to strangers, and, I believe not at all dissolute, as most of the women are. She has written very well on the works of Canova, and also a volume of Characters, besides other printed matter. She is of Corfu, but married a dead Venetian – that is, dead since he married.

My flame (my 'Donna' whom I spoke of in my former epistle, my Marianna) is still my Marianna, and I her – what she pleases. She is by far the prettiest woman I have seen here, and the most loveable I have met with any where – as well as one of the most singular. I believe I told you the rise and progress of our *liaison* in my former letter. Lest that should not have reached you, I will merely repeat, that she is a Venetian, two-and-twenty years old, married to a merchant well to do in the world, and that she has great black oriental eyes, and all the qualities which her eyes promise. Whether being in love with her has steeled me or not, I do not know; but I have not seen many other women who seem pretty. The nobility, in particular, are a sad-looking race – the gentry rather better. And now what art *thou* doing?

> What are you doing now,
>   Oh Thomas Moore?
> What are you doing now,
>   Oh Thomas Moore?
> Sighing or suing now,
> Rhyming or wooing now,
> Billing or cooing now,
>   Which, Thomas Moore?

Are you not near the Luddites? By the Lord! if there's a row, but I'll be among ye! How go on the weavers – the breakers of frames – the Lutherans of politics – the reformers?

> As the Liberty lads o'er the sea
> Bought their freedom, and cheaply, with blood,
>> So we, boys, we
>> Will *die* fighting, or *live* free,
> And down with all kings but King Ludd!
>
> When the web that we weave is complete,
> And the shuttle exchanged for the sword,
>> We will fling the winding-sheet
>> O'er the despot at our feet,
> And dye it deep in the gore he has pour'd.
>
> Though black as his heart its hue,
> Since his veins are corrupted to mud,
>> Yet this is the dew
>> Which the tree shall renew
> Of Liberty, planted by Ludd!

There's an amiable *chanson* for you – all impromptu. I have written it principally to shock your neighbour ** [Hodgson?], who is all clergy and loyalty – mirth and innocence – milk and water.

> But the Carnival's coming,
>> Oh Thomas Moore,
> The Carnival's coming,
>> Oh Thomas Moore,
>
> Masking and humming,
> Fifing and drumming,
> Guitarring and strumming,
>> Oh Thomas Moore.

. . . When does your Poem of Poems come out? I hear that the E[dinburgh] R[eview] has cut up Coleridge's Christabel, and declared against me for praising it. I praised it, firstly,

197

because I thought well of it; secondly, because Coleridge was in great distress, and after doing what little I could for him in essentials, I thought that the public avowal of my good opinion might help him further, at least with the booksellers. I am very sorry that J[effrey] has attacked him, because, poor fellow, it will hurt him in mind and pocket. As for me, he's welcome – I shall never think less of J[effrey] for any thing he may say against me or mine in future.

I suppose Murray has sent you, or will send (for I do not know whether they are out or no) the poems, or poesies, of mine, of last summer. By the mass! they're sublime – 'Ganion Coheriza' – gainsay who dares!

Sometimes Byron's Venetian years are described as if the carnival and its accompaniments dominated his life. But it was never like that, even in the early days when he was tasting every new delight with his customary catholicity. He could never cut loose from the tug of politics, and even in those first months when he was writing little poetry, he was deeply concerned about what was happening in Albemarle Street to the poems Shelley had taken back the previous autumn. He naturally rejoiced when Thomas Moore called Canto III 'magnificent', but he still wondered, genuinely, what others might say: 'It is', he replied to Moore, on 28 January

a fine indistinct piece of poetical desolation, and my favourite. I was half mad during the time of its composition, between metaphysics, mountains, lakes, love unextinguishable, thoughts unutterable, and the nightmare of my own delinquencies. I should, many a good day, have blown my brains out, but for the recollection that it would have given pleasure to my mother-in-law; and, even *then*, if I could have been certain to haunt her – but I won't dwell upon these trifling family matters. Venice is in the *estro* of her carnival, and I have been up these last two nights at the ridotto and the opera, and all that kind of thing. . . .'

But he had no doubts about the poem's strong political content. He was constantly reaffirming his anxieties. Had Murray published it properly, he asked Kinnaird. 'I shall not pardon him – I suspect him as a Tory.' He wrote to Augusta in the same sense: 'If Murray has mutilated the MS with his Toryism', he would not be forgiven.

Venice so suited Byron's temperament in those months that he was reluctant to depart on the projected journey to Rome with Hobhouse and inhibited in his writing – or least inhibited by his own reckless standards – in how he should finish the ambitious *Manfred: A Dramatic Poem* which he had brought with him unfinished from Geneva. Shelley had advised him to rewrite the last Act, and Byron was ready to adopt his advice. But his self-criticisms were usually more telling than those which came from elsewhere. He was a poor critic of his fellow poets but a good one of himself. He finished the rewriting in April and sent it off to London with some diffidence, accompanied by none of the warnings against the mutilation of his manuscripts which *Childe Harold* Canto III had seemed to make so necessary and which were later to become persistent and explicit. Byron was never guilty of the plagiarism of Goethe with which he was often charged; he claimed that he had never read Goethe's *Faust*, and he was never at any time given to lies or hypocrisy. But maybe he did feel that *Manfred* was too much modelled on established patterns or ancient themes, just at the moment when the Italian sun and the Venetian sky were casting their rays across a whole new world. Byron had studied the works of, say, Abate Giambattista Casti more closely than those of Johann Wolfgang von Goethe. He had picked his way through a French translation of *Faust* in a book of Madame de Staël's, but he could be excused if he showed more real enthusiasm for Casti, and if it had not been for this reprehensible preference, would we have ever had *Don Juan*? Goethe, by the way, to do him credit, was also, before Byron, a devotee of Casti, even if he never allowed this taste to demean his own writing. He had the delight which, alas, Byron never shared of hearing the Abbé, 'who gave me great pleasure by reading his unpublished *Novelle Galanti*. His clear and natural style of recitation brought his witty, if very risqué stories to life.' The *Novelle* had been first published in 1790 and thereafter were frequently republished before finding their way on to the Papal Index. His *Animal Parlanti*, published first in Paris in 1802 and republished in London that same year, had been banned in France by Napoleon, just about the time when Casti died in 1803: a notable double censorship which would have appealed to Byron, if he had ever known about it. Murray despatched a new translation, by the English poet William Stewart Rose, to Byron in 1816, and Byron, as we have seen, had mentioned how 'I have almost got him by heart'. It is strange that no other similarly illuminating references to Casti appear in Byron's vast correspondence, but one explanation may be that he was similarly getting quite a number of other Italian poets by heart. He had learnt to speak some Italian before he had ever set foot on Italian soil, and, thereafter, made himself proficient in every requirement including Venetian slang; he learnt to swear 'by the body of Diana'. He steeped himself in the great Italian classics, from Dante and Petrarch onwards and downwards, learning some of his Italian Risorgimento ideals from the one and pausing to rebuke the stern Platonism of the other. He unearthed another classical favourite in the fifteenth-century Luigi Pulci, whom he learnt to translate brilliantly and literally with the same touch and whose taste for lascivious diversions he happily paraded to justify his own similar lapses or predilections.* The exact sequence in which these new bosom friendships were made is not possible or necessary to establish.

He did at last depart on his journey to Rome on 17 April, but apart even from the carnival and the other carousals, he had

---

* The fullest and best account of the Italian influence on Byron's writing is supplied in Peter Vassallo's: *Byron: The Italian Literary Influence*, a wonderful book which combines unfailing judgement with a series of original discoveries; in particular, the discovery of the scale of Giambattista Casti's influence. It is both impossible and unnecessary to contest the main Vassallo thesis that Casti played a major role in shaping the new Italian Byron: impossible in the face of his book's detailed comparisons between verses of the two poets on similar themes, and unnecessary in the sense that the author is not seeking to establish any foolish charge of plagiarism.

plenty of other pursuits to make those first Venetian months most memorable. He wrote his famous lyric, to cure him from the night before, an echo from Aberdeen: 'So we'll go no more a-roving/So late into the night.' His visits to the Armenian Convent were no pose or sinecure: he gladly undertook on behalf of what he considered 'the priesthood of an oppressed and a noble nation' a translation of several chapters of their Bible and assistance in the compilation of an Armenian grammar; this last, it seems, was withheld from publication for fear that its anti-Turkish comments might arouse antagonism – or, maybe, they did understand all too well how unorthodox was the verdict he passed on that memory of the real Paradise:

> If the Scriptures are rightly understood, it was in Armenia that Paradise was placed – Armenia, which has paid as dearly as the descendants of Adam for that fleeting participation of its soil in the happiness of him who was created from its dust. It was in Armenia that the flood first abated, and the dove alighted. But with the disappearance of Paradise itself may be dated almost the unhappiness of the country; for though long a powerful kingdom, it was scarcely ever an independent one, and the satraps of Persia and the pachas of Turkey have alike desolated the region where God created man in his own image.

Back in St Mark's Square, he found time to mark and mock the manner in which the Austrian authorities directed their affairs and insulted the Venetians, as he recounted to his correspondents in Albemarle Street:

> I missed seeing the new Patriarch's procession to St Mark's the other day (owing to my indisposition) with six hundred and fifty priests in his rear – a 'goodly army'. – The admirable government of Vienna in its edict from thence – authorizing his installation – prescribed as part of the pageant – a 'Coach & four horses' to show how very very 'German to the matter' this was – you have only to suppose our Parliament commanding the Archbishop of Canterbury to

proceed from Hyde Park Corner to St Paul's Cathedral in the Lord Mayor's Barge – or the Margate Hoy. – There is but St Marc's place in all Venice – broad enough for a carriage to move – & it is paved with large smooth flagstones – so that the Chariot & horses of Elijah himself would be puzzled to manoeuvre upon it – those of Pharaoh might do better – for the Canals & particularly the Grand Canal are sufficiently capacious & extensive for his whole host. – of course no coach could be attempted – but the Venetians who are very naive as well as arch – were much amused with the ordinance.

And he found time too, like any other tourist, to clamber up the staircase of the Doge's Palace:

I am aware of what you say of Otway – and am a very great admirer of his – all except of that maudlin bitch of chaste lewdness & blubbering curiosity Belvidera – whom I utterly despise, abhor, & detest – but the story of Marino Falieri – is different & I think so much finer – that I wish Otway had taken it instead; – the head conspiring against the body – for refusal of redress for a real injury; – jealousy, treason – with the more fixed and inveterate passions (mixed with policy) of an old or elderly man – the Devil himself could not have a finer subject – & he is your only tragic dramatist. – When Voltaire was asked why no woman has ever written even a tolerable tragedy? 'Ah (said the Patriarch) the composition of a tragedy requires *testicles'*. – If this be true Lord knows what Joanna Baillie does – I suppose she borrows them. There is still, in the Doge's palace the black veil painted over Falieri's picture & the staircase whereon he was first crowned Doge, & subsequently decapitated. – This was the thing that most struck my imagination in Venice – more than the Rialto, which I visited for the sake of Shylock – and more too than Schiller's *'Armenian'* – a novel which took a great hold of me when a boy – it is also called the 'Ghost Seer' – & I never walked down St Mark's by moonlight without thinking of it & – 'at nine o'clock he died!' – But I

hate things *all fiction* & therefore the *Merchant* & *Othello* –
have no great associations to me – but *Pierre* has – there
should always be some foundation of fact for the most airy
fabric – and pure invention is but the talent of a liar. . . . You
talk of 'marriage' – ever since my own funeral – the word
makes me giddy – & throws me into a cold sweat – pray
don't repeat it. – Tell me that Walter Scott is better – I would
not have him ill for the world – I suppose it was by sympathy that I had my fever at the same time. – I joy in the success of your Quarterly – but I must still stick by the *Edinburgh*
– Jeffrey has done so by me I must say through everything –
& this is more than I deserved from him. – I have more than
once acknowledged to you by letter the 'Article' (& Articles)
say that you have received the said letters – as I do not otherwise know what letters arrive. Both reviews came – but
nothing more. M[aturin]'s play & the extract not yet come. –
There have been two Articles in the Venice papers one a
review of C. Lamb's 'Glenarvon' (whom may it please the
beneficient Giver of all Good to damn in the next world! as
she has damned herself in this) with the account of her
scratching attempt at *Canicide* (at Lady Heathcote's) – and
the other a review of C[hilde] Har[ol]d in which it proclaims me the most rebellious & contumacious Admirer of
Buonaparte – now surviving in Europe; – both these articles
are translations from the literary Gazette of German Jena.

Reluctantly still, but warning his friends that he would soon
be back in Venice, 'which is my head, or rather my heart-quar-
ters', he set out for the Holy City in a not quite holy mood. He
had been reading Voltaire, quite a good preparation, but as
usual he preserved his own independent judgement. Sometimes the saints could make him a sinner, and the infidels could
almost restore a primitive faith:

I do not know what to believe – or what to disbelieve –
which is the devil – to have no religion at all – all sense &
senses are against it – but all belief & much evidence is for it
– it is walking in the dark over a rabbit warren – or a garden

203

with steel traps and spring guns. – for my part I have such a detestation of *some* of the articles of faith – that I would not subscribe to them – if I were as sure as St Peter *after* the Cock crew. – The most consistent infidel was the Prussian Frederick – because during all the disasters of the 7 years' war – he was as full of his materialism as when in quiet at Potsdam – & like his friend La Metrie who died 'denying G-d & the physicians.'

Byron's journey to Rome and back was spectacular, memorable and brief. He left Venice on April 17th and was restored to his Marianna on May 28th. The natural supposition, encouraged by his own comment at the time, was that she was the chief enticement, but there were other elements at work in his nature too. Secular, many-coloured, republican, liberating, revolutionary Venice suited his temperament better than monumental Rome, even if he was one of the first, the first Englishman at least, to recognize the modern kinship between so many Italian cities.

He travelled via Bologna, 'celebrated for the production of Popes, Cardinals, painters and sausages'; Ferrara, which prompted him to lament the imprisonment of fellow poet Tasso; Perugia, which offered the shortest route; Firenze, where apart from the Venus of Canova and de Medicis, tombs of Machiavelli, Michael Angelo, and Alfieri were 'all I care to see here'. He hastened on, reading and writing, finding the time not only for *The Lament of Tasso* but to complete *Manfred* too. He himself was pleased with it – ' "these be good rhymes" – as Pope's papa said to him – when he was a boy.' And so they were. But the remains of *Manfred* were more like an awkward duty discharged. Rome itself did not disappoint. 'The Niobe of nations!' as he later called her; 'there she stands, childless and crownless', and there he was inspired to write some of his lines which have matched the sight of 'She who was named Eternal'. Yet he was delighted – 'as I would be with a bandbox – that it is a fine thing to see – finer than Greece . . . I have been riding my saddle horses every day – and been to Albano – its lakes – and to the top of the Alban mount – and to Frascati – Aricia – etc. etc. . . . As a

whole – ancient and *modern* – it beats Greece – Constantinople –
everything – at least that I have ever seen.' Thus, for Byron, the
excitement was genuine and irrepressible; he was so seldom
the world-weary observer hinted at in some of his own asides.
But he did not make Rome his own, and indeed never troubled
to return. He took to his heart or head no Roman heroes. He
dedicated one poem to the sixteenth-century rebel Rienzi; he
might have seemed a natural subject. But Venice had already
filled his mind and imagination with other preoccupations of
much greater subtlety. Neither the Forum nor St Peter's
spurred him as did the decapitated Marino or Verrocchio's
statue near the Janipolo, and the tearful Niobe was not his idea
of a heroine.

It is notable also, as always with Byron, to take account of
what he was reading and how he might be distracted even from
fresh sights all around him. Gibbon, as we know, was already
more than a favourite; he was woven into his mind. He had just
received too, from John Murray, his new ration of Walter Scott,
his anonymous 'Tales of My Landlord', as Byron called it: 'I
have read with pleasure – and perfectly understand now why
my sister and aunt are so very positive in the very erroneous
impression that they must have been written by me.' He had
time for good humour, but time too for an unrestrained explosion of anger against not so much his own enemies back at
home but those who recommended that the literary oponents of
Church and State might suffer the same penalties as more overt
revolutionaries. It is good to see that the sins of Robert Southey
were not forgotten by Byron, even when he was being guided
among the treasures of St Peter's:

> Southey's Wat Tyler is rather awkward – but the Goddess
> Nemesis has done well – he is – I will not say what – but I
> wish he was something else – I hate all intolerance – but
> most the intolerance of Apostacy – & the wretched vehe-
> mence with which a miserable creature who has contra-
> dicted himself – lies to his own heart – & endeavours to
> establish his sincerity by proving himself a rascal – *not* for
> changing his opinions – but for persecuting those who are of

less malleable matter – it is no disgrace to Mr Southey to have written Wat Tyler – & afterwards to have written his birthday or Victory Odes (I speak only of their *politics*) but it is something for which I have no words for this man to have endeavoured to bring to the stake (for such would he do) men who think as he thought – & for no reason but because they think so still, when he has found it convenient to think otherwise. – Opinions are made to be changed – or how is truth to be got at? we don't arrive at it by standing on one leg? or on the first day of our setting out – but though we may jostle one another on the way that is no reason why we should strike or trample – *elbowing's* enough. – I am all for moderation which profession of faith I beg leave to conclude by wishing Mr Southey damned – not as a poet – but as a politician. There is a place in Michael Angelo's last judgment in the Sistine Chapel which would just suit him – and may the like await him in that of our Lord and (*not his*) Saviour Jesus Christ – Amen!

Back in Venice – or in the Villa Foscarini on the bank of the Brenta River at La Mira, a village some seven miles outside and an excellent retreat for writing – he was able to put some other matters in an easier perspective, even his guilty anxieties for Augusta, if such they were. He wrote her in June:

I repeat to you again and again – that it would be much better at once to explain your mysteries – than to go on with this absurd obscure hinting mode of writing. – What do you mean? – what is there known? or can be known? which *you & I* do not know much better? & what concealment can you have from me? *I* never shrank – & it was on your account principally that I gave way at all – for I thought they would endeavour to drag you into it – although they had no business with anything previous to my marriage with that infernal fiend – whose destruction I shall yet see. – Do you suppose that I will rest – while any of their branch is unwithered?do you suppose that I will turn aside till they are trodden under foot? – do you suppose that I can breathe

206

till they are uprooted? – Do you believe that time will alter
them or me? – that I have suffered in vain – that I have been
disgraced in vain – that I am reconciled to the sting of the
scorpion – & the venom of the serpent? which stung me in
my slumber? – If I did not believe – that Time & Nemesis – &
circumstances would requite me for the delay – I would ere
this have righted myself. – But 'let them look to their
bond' . . .*

Venice was offering, apart even from Marianna and her successors, a new rhythm, a new meter, a new humour, a new leap
in common consciousness with his Italian friends, much of it
adapted from Casti; but even while he acquired these cadences,
he was making a fresh political departure. Canto IV was his
most mature political poem. His own excitement mounted as
he felt what he was achieving. 'I have been working up my
impressions into a 4th Canto of C.H.', he wrote to Murray
on July 1st '. . . I have no idea yet of the possible length or
calibre. . . .' And then he gave the first taste:

> I stood in Venice on the 'Bridge of Sighs'
> . . . There – there is a brick of your new Babel . . .

And then again, on 9 July: 'I have done 56 stanzas of Canto 4th
. . . so down with your ducats.' And then again on 15 July: 'I
have finished (that is written – the file comes afterwards)
ninety & eight stanzas.' And then again, on 15 July: 'the stanzas
of Canto 4th have jumped to 104 – & such stanzas! by St
Anthony! (who has a church by my elbow and I like to be
neighbourly) some of them are the right thing.' And then again,
in September, while he waited for proofs: 'I look upon C.H. as
my best.' And while he waited he showed his kinship with
other authors. All hints that he truly felt the profession to be

* Jerome McGann picked out this passage in his review in the *Times Literary Supplement* of Marchand Volume V. It was one of the first signs of
Byron's relief from the tensions he had brought with him in exile and
underlined how he had agreed to the separation reluctantly and only
because of his concern to keep his sister out of the proceedings.

below his lordly pretensions – emotions sometimes fostered by his own self-mockery – were refuted by individual instances . . . 'I would never prevent or oppose the publication of *any* book in *any* language, – on my own private account.' He was refusing to play the censor to an Italian edition of Lady Caroline's *Glenarvon*. And then, more portentously, as he argued with his publishers about financial rewards, he compared his own output with that of his contemporaries and some of our classics – particularly Pope: '. . . and I was really astonished (I ought not to have been so) and mortified – at the ineffable distance in point of sense – harmony – effect – and even *Imagination* Passion – & *Invention*, between the little Queen Anne's Man – & us of the lower Empire.' Yet he could not suppress a bursting pride, no pinchbeck vanity, about what he was writing. 'My own sentiments on Venice, etc., Such as they are . . .' he wrote to a new friend, Richard Hoppner, the English Consul, who had sent him some of his own verses. Venice in all her modern glory was all around him; she would be allotted the leading role. But much more consciously than ever before he had prepared a political testament, of which Venice was only a part.

Almost every direct reference to Venice, from the very first mention of the Bridge of Sighs, carries within it a joyousness, an exuberance, which was much more truly Byronic than any affected melancholy: 'The revel of the earth, the masque of Italy.' Yet this was the Venice of the Napoleonic surrender, of the first years of ignominy under Austrian occupation. Defeat and incipient decay were there on every hand; the suffocation should have been unbearable. Another observer of the Napoleonic surrender, as impressionable and astute as Byron, who had witnessed precisely the same Venetian scene just two years before was Henri Beyle, alias Stendhal. By quite independent processes of perception and thought, he had reached the same conclusion: that Venice retained its resilience, its individuality, its carnival spirit, its place as the happiest plot of earth beneath the Holy Alliance heavens. Stendhal thought this mood – indeed, the spirit of Venice itself – was best expressed in Rossini's opera, *The Italian Girl in Algiers*, from its carnival gaiety in the middle to the fervent outpourings of Italian patriotism at the end: 'Remember your Fatherland, and fearlessly fulfil your duty; behold, in every corner of Italy the rebirth of examples of daring and valour.' To hear that sung, as it first was sung in the San Benedetto Theatre on 22 May 1813, or, better still, later at the Fenice, was to overhear the Italian debate beneath the Austrian whips and guns. Stendhal's own acceptance of this mood, his readiness to forget his old Napoleonic allegiance, was doubtless due to the fact that he spent the Hundred Days (or many of them) in the arms of his mistress, Angela Pietragina, in Venice. He emerged on the day after Waterloo to drink his coffee and drown his dishonour at Florian's. Venice recovered quicker than any other city which had endured comparable afflictions. Byron sensed the same rejuvenation. Stendhal said of him: 'He attributed his own transformation to his residence in Venice.' Doubtless he had no absolutely firm foundation for the claim, particularly since the only occasion on which they met was in Milan several months before Byron had ever set foot in the place. But it was true that the wary English Lord he had met in Milan bore little enough resemblance to the Byron of a few years later. And it was true, as Stendhal claimed with more authority than any other traveller of the time: 'Venice is a world apart, whose existence is unsuspected by the rest of sad Europe.' This was the Venice of Burati, of Goldoni, of Casti, above all, of Rossini. Byron had made the same discovery.

As usual, he owed much of his direct inspiration to books; even his world-notorious vision of the prison and the palace from the Bridge of Sighs, or rather the bridge overlooking it, was derived from Mary Ann Radcliffe's *Mysteries of Udolpho* which had appeared a few years before and which Byron had happily plundered rather than plagiarized. His true Venetian allegiance was much older:

> I loved her from my boyhood – she to me
> Was as a fairy city of the heart.

He readily acknowledged his tutors, Otway, Radcliffe (yes, she was there), Schiller, Shakespeare. England, above all other lands, should have remembered her Venetian alliances, and yet an English delegate – the hated Castlereagh – had signed in May 1814 the Treaty of Paris which assigned Venice back to Austria. Byron hated the Austrian subjugation, paraded in the place he called 'still the finest square in Europe'. Venice, the true Venice, had once made Emperors and Popes bend the knee, yet now 'An Emperor trampled where an Emperor knelt.' Byron believed the days of glorious freedom could come again.

> . . . the Ocean queen should not
> Abandon Ocean's children; in the fall
> Of Venice think of thine, despite thy watery wall.

Byron's historical sense mingled with his own patriotism, and he was always invoking past memories to guide future action:

> Immortal waves that saw Lepanto's fight!
> For ye are names no time nor tyranny can blight.

England and Venice had so often found themselves ranged against the same enemy. Would not Venice offer him sanctuary 'Should I leave behind/The inviolate island of the sage and free'? He had not sought exile; he had one real dream of immortality:

> . . . I twine
> My hopes of being remembered in my line
> With my land's language.

Venice was not some hostile shore, to feed his bitterness, but rather a new home to enlarge his love of freedom. He chose Venice as his place of refuge from all the Italian cities, and came to know her and her history as no Englishman had done before, and to repay his debt in a quite unexpected coinage. He set about learning the politics of Venice, the politics of Italy, and for Byron politics meant action, not philosophy.

One part of the new canto, and it would have been enough by itself for its greatness, was his hymn to Italian unity, the first bugle-call – from an Englishman, at least – for the Italian

Risorgimento.* He recruited the Italian poets, ancient and modern, to the crusade, starting with Dante

> He arose
> To raise a language, and his land reclaim
> From the dull yoke of her barbaric foes . . .

and happily placed nearby his own version of a contemporary sonnet by Vincenzo da Filicaia.†

> Italia! oh Italia! thou who hast
> The fatal gift of beauty, which became
> A funeral dower of present woes and past,
> On thy sweet brow is sorrow plough'd by shame,
> And annals graved in characters of flame.
> Oh God! that thou wert in thy nakedness
> Less lovely or more powerful, and could'st claim
> Thy right, and awe the robbers back, who press
> To shed thy blood, and drink the tears of thy distress;

---

* All of us are indebted here again to Peter Vassallo's book (see page 200). He has a passage in which he relates Byron's awakening interest in Italy and more especially in Rome to Madame de Staël's *Corinne in Italy*. The important claim is overwhelmingly established, but I believe it comes with a further fascinating inference: some parts of Byron's Roman comments were in this sense derivative. All the more so was Venice shaped in his own image.

† 'He (Byron)', wrote Professor G.M. Trevelyan in the introduction to his *English Songs of Italian Freedom*, an anthology published in 1914, 'was the first Englishman who saw, in those dark days, that the Italians had a cause and a purpose of their own.' Professor Trevelyan was no uncritical admirer of Byron; he was inclined to adopt the strictures of his uncle, Lord Macaulay. So this tribute is all the more impressive. However, when I quoted this sentence at a Byron Seminar in Venice, in September 1986, it was kindly and courteously pointed out to me by Professor Gordon Thomas, of Brigham Young University, that Wordsworth had written in this sense earlier – in his pamphlet about the Convention of Cintra, and in some correspondence at the time. All honour to Wordsworth – and Gordon Thomas. However, I must repeat the claim that Byron was the first Englishman to speak in this sense in a way which fired the crusade.

> Then might'st thou more appal; or, less desired,
> Be homely and be peaceful, undeplored
> For thy destructive charms; then, still untired,
> Would not be seen the armed torrents pour'd
> Down the deep Alps; nor would the hostile horde
> Of many-nation'd spoilers from the Po
> Quaff blood and water; nor the stranger's sword
> Be thy sad weapon of defence, and so,
> Victor or vanquish'd, thou the slave of friend or foe.

Here Byron introduced a slight variation. The Italian poet had talked of the French spoilers; Byron made them many-nationed. Whatever he did, both the censors and the Austrian police went in pursuit of Canto IV. Where, we wonder, were all those confiscated copies concealed at the time: are they still secluded in unplundered libraries or even monastic cells, like the suppressed Greek and Roman texts which once heralded the Renaissance? Indeed Byron could even rally the Church to his aid, in such a life and death struggle.

>   Italy!
> Time, which hath wrong'd thee with ten thousand rents
> Of thine imperial garment, shall deny,
> And hath denied, to every other sky,
> Spirits which soar from ruin: – thy decay
> Is still impregnate with divinity . . .

Possibly these last lines might be thought too quiescent, too recoiling. Byron would never leave matters in that posture for long.

> Yet, Italy! through every other land
> Thy wrongs should ring, and shall, from side to side;
> Mother of Arts! as once of arms; thy hand
> Was then our guardian, and is still our guide;
> Parent of our Religion! whom the wide
> Nations have knelt to for the keys of heaven!
> Europe, repentant of her parricide,

Shall yet redeem thee, and, all backward driven,
Roll the barbarian tide, and sue to be forgiven.

The timing and the scale of Byron's message combined to illustrate how acute his political understanding could be. He had learnt to speak this language of freedom in Venice in a single year and without the journey to Rome he could hardly have spoken with such assurance for the whole new country of his adoption. He put out of his reckoning the popular fallacies about the Italian people peddled by English arrogance: he knew better. 'It has been somewhere said by Alfieri that the human plant grows more robust [in Italy] than in any other land and even the atrocious crimes committed there are a proof of it.' And then he made a new proclamation with all the power at his command:

that man must be wilfully blind, or ignorantly heedless, who is not struck with the extraordinary capacity of this people, or, if such a word be admissible, their *capabilities*, the facility of their acquisitions, the rapidity of their conceptions, the fire of their genius, their sense of beauty, and amidst all the disadvantages of repeated revolutions, the desolation of battles and the despair of ages, their still unquenched 'longing after immortality', – the immortality of independence.

If Byron's beloved Italy was to be summoned to revolutionary action, if England was to tread the same path, as he believed to be most probable, the mechanisms of revolution must be taken apart, the theory must be unravelled. If Byron had been such a child in these great matters, as Goethe had supposed, he would hardly have chosen to pose again the most awkward, unresolved dilemmas left by the French experience. He hated the bloodshed he had seen all around him. He had never sought to disguise these dreadful scenes in a romantic glow. Yet to fight for freedom would mean more killings, and where would they end, and would they win the victories which suffering men and women cried out for? Byron set out on these mighty explorations, and it was surely his own conviction that he was conducting them without cant or pretence of any kind which made him feel that Canto IV was, to date, his masterpiece. He cast an observant eye on our own English revolution, the one that had succeeded:

> The sagest of usurpers, Cromwell; he
> Too swept off senates while he hew'd the throne
> Down to a block – immortal rebel! See
> What crimes it costs to be a moment free
> And famous through all ages!

No one had written about Cromwell in those terms for generations; he was still the butt of Royalist caricature. And Byron whose ancestors had fought on the wrong side at Naseby or Worcester had acquired from somewhere the knowledge which enabled him to describe in such a few indelible strokes the lineaments of a real revolutionary figure. He had learnt the meaning of Cromwell's day, 3 September, his double day of victory and death, the day of the storm which had swept across England. Cromwell had been the victim of Nemesis – and Byron remarked playfully, 'she is my particular belief and acquaintance – and I won't blaspheme against her for anybody.' True and excusable, but Byron's interest was not confined to some inexorable, inexplicable working of the fates. He wanted to explore what happened to the self-appointed, self-willed leaders.

> The men of iron; and the world have rear'd
> Cities from out their sepulchres: men bred
> In imitation of the things they fear'd,
> And fought and conquered, and the same course steer'd
> At apish distance . . .

Sometimes the performance of mankind's rescuers demanded scrutiny and reproof, but Byron could feel in his bones the long agony of the oppressed.

What from this barren being do we reap?
Our senses narrow, and our reason frail,
Life short, and truth a gem which loves the deep,
And all things weigh'd in custom's falsest scale;
Opinion an omnipotence, – whose veil
Mantles the earth with darkness, until right
And wrong are accidents, and men grow pale
Lest their own judgments should become too bright,
And their free thoughts be crimes, and earth have too
  much light.

And thus they plod in sluggish misery,
Rotting from sire to son, and age to age,
Proud of their trampled nature, and so die,
Bequeathing their hereditary rage
To the new race of inborn slaves, who wage
War for their chains, and rather than be free,
Bleed gladiator-like, and still engage
Within the same arena where they see
Their fellows fall before, like leaves of the same tree.

I speak not of men's creeds – they rest between
Man and his Maker – but of things allowed,
Averr'd, and known, – and daily, hourly seen –
The yoke that is upon us doubly bowed,
And the intent of tyranny avowed,
The edict of Earth's rulers, who are grown
The apes of him who humbled once the proud,
And shook them from their slumbers on the throne;
Too glorious, were this all his mighty arm had done.

That was Byron returning to the Napoleon whose presence or
shadow he and his generation could never escape for long. Was
Napoleon a true child and champion of the Revolution? Why
had he betrayed the great cause? *Can tyrants but by tyrants
conquered be?* Could there not come some escape from the cycle
of killing and horror? And then followed the mighty lines
which compressed the tragedy into what for Byron was the
most baffling of all challenges. He would never accept the

justice of man's expulsion from the Garden of Eden, and now his generation was confronted by a political apocalypse no less unjust.

> But France got drunk with blood to vomit crime,
> And fatal have her Saturnalia been
> To Freedom's cause, in every age and clime;
> Because the deadly days which we have seen,
> And vile Ambition, that built up between
> Man and his hopes an adamantine wall,
> And the base pageant last upon the scene,
> Are grown the pretext for the eternal thrall
> Which nips life's tree, and dooms man's worst – his second fall.

Thus Byron denounced the betrayal of the Revolution and the bloodletting which was its sign and symbol. No one could make the charge that he had looked for phrases of palliation or excuse. Yet he gave at once his historic answer, words often wrenched from their context. Let it never be forgotten: the moment he chose to deliver the new revolutionary defiance, the very hour of defeat.

> Yet, Freedom! yet thy banner, torn, but flying,
> Streams like the thunder-storm *against* the wind;
> Thy trumpet voice, though broken now and dying,
> The loudest still the tempest leaves behind;
> Thy tree hath lost its blossoms, and the rind,
> Chopp'd by the axe, looks rough and little worth,
> But the sap lasts, – and still the seed we find
> Sown deep, even in the bosom of the North;
> So shall a better spring less bitter fruit bring forth.

Childe Harold, Byron himself, revisits again and again that moment of defeat and defiance. He can turn to a love story and tell it with a new freshness, how the purple Midnight veiled that mystic meeting, in a cave, a Venetian one, I'll bet, shaped out for the greeting of an enamoured Goddess. But for how long?

Of its own beauty is the mind diseased,
And fevers into false creation: – where,
Where are the forms the sculptor's soul hath seized?
In him alone. Can Nature shew so fair?
Where are the charms and virtues which we dare
Conceive in boyhood and pursue as men,
The unreach'd Paradise of our despair,
. . .

Few – none – find what they love or could have loved
Though accident, blind contact, and the strong
Necessity of loving, have removed
Antipathies – but to recur, ere long,
Envenomed with irrevocable wrong;
And Circumstance, that unspiritual god
And miscreator, makes and helps along
Our coming evils with a crutch-like rod,
Whose touch turns Hope to dust, – the dust we all have trod.

Our life is a false nature – 'tis not in
The harmony of things, – this hard decree,
This uneradicable taint of sin,
This boundless upas, this all-blasting tree,
Whose root is earth, whose leaves and branches be
The skies which rain their plagues on me like dew –
Disease, death, bondage – all the woes we see –
And worse, the woes we see not – which throb through
The immedicable soul, with heart-aches ever new.

Here was a cry of fury about man's fate to match the political
desperation of a few moments before. But once again came a
quick riposte.

Yet let us ponder boldly – 'tis a base
Abandonment of reason to resign
Our right of thought – our last and only place
Of refuge; this, at least, shall still be mine:
Though from our birth the faculty divine

217

Is chain'd and tortured – cabin'd, cribb'd, confined,
And bred in darkness, lest the truth should shine
Too brightly on the unprepared mind,
The beam pours in, for time and skill will couch the blind.

Yes, again and again and still we need not find the repetition tiring, against all those massed against him and his cause, 'learning to lie with silence':

But I have lived, and have not lived in vain:
My mind may lose its force, my blood its fire,
And my frame perish even in conquering pain,
But there is that within me which shall tire
Torture and Time, and breathe when I expire;
. . .

And here the buzz of eager nations ran,
In murmured pity, or loud-roared applause,
As man was slaughtered by his fellow man.
And wherefore slaughtered? wherefore, but because
Such were the bloody Circus' genial laws,
And the imperial pleasure. . . .

Childe Harold has bent his knee to no earthly or heavenly force; he acknowledges no master but the very power of thought instilled by some decree within him. He does turn to another scene, the dark-heaving Ocean, boundless, endless and sublime, the image of Eternity, and what better one has ever been offered?

Thou glorious mirror, where the Almighty's form
Glasses itself in tempests; in all time,
Calm or convuls'd – in breeze, or gale, or storm,
Icing the pole, or in the torrid clime
Dark-heaving; – boundless, endless, and sublime –
The image of Eternity – the throne
Of the invisible; even from out thy slime
The monsters of the deep are made; each zone
Obeys thee; thou goest forth, dread, fathomless, alone.

218

On 7 January 1818 Hobhouse made the note in his diary: 'passed the evening with B, who put the last hand to his *Childe Harold'*. Next morning he left for England with the manuscript. And Venice was already working her will upon Byron in a quite novel fashion.

SEVEN

Venice II

It is called *Don Juan*, and is meant to be a little
quietly facetious upon everything.

19 September 1818

On 27 January 1818, Byron wrote to Murray: 'I sent you Beppo –
some weeks agone – you had best publish it alone – it has politics and ferocity. . . .' He was anxious how it might be received,
by his publisher and the public, but he himself was pleased and
proud. Did he know how closely he had touched perfection?

He had drawn on many models, Casti, Berni, and Boiardo
and Pulci among the Italians and John Hookham Frere, an
English contemporary who had adopted and adapted the
Italian *ottava rima* before him: to all of these he was happy to
acknowledge his debt, although perhaps a slight reticence
appeared in mentioning Casti, to whom the debt was greatest.
The story he had heard from the husband of his Italian mistress
Marianna; he could put most Venetian encounters to good use.
All of it, all the ninety-nine stanzas, had been swiftly written in
the previous September. The whole is a miracle of lightness,
softness, high spirits, the immaculate Venice of Rossini in all its
pristine glory. The seductions of the carnival were portrayed as
never before – at least for an English audience. But where were
the self-vaunted politics? *Beppo* soon acquired a reputation for
something quite different by 'the language, that soft bastard
Latin, which melts like kisses from a female mouth'. True, there
were some English politics which were done with no more
than a flick of a wrist: even so, Byron thought Murray & Co.
might tamper with them.

'England! with all thy faults I love thee still.'
  I said at Calais, and have not forgot it;
I like to speak and lucubrate my fill;
  I like the government (but that is not it);
I like the freedom of the press and quill;
  I like the Habeas Corpus (when we've got it);
I like a parliamentary debate,
Particularly when 'tis not too late;

I like the taxes, when they're not too many;
  I like a seacoal fire, when not too dear;
I like a beef-steak, too, as well as any;
  Have no objection to a pot of beer;
I like the weather, when it is not rainy,
  That is, I like two months of every year.
And so God save the Regent, Church, and King!
Which means that I like all and every thing.

Our standing army, and disbanded seamen,
  Poor's rate, Reform, my own, the nation's debt,
Our little riots just to show we are free men,
  Our trifling bankruptcies in the Gazette,
Our cloudy climate, and our chilly women,
  All these I can forgive, and those forget,
And greatly venerate our recent glories,
And wish they were not owing to the Tories.

Maybe, in another sense, Byron regarded *the whole poem* – the way, the only way, it should be read – as political, for he was setting in contrast Italian (or even Moslem) methods of love-making and matchmaking with English hypocrisy, with the woman taking command, if not at will, at least with a flaunting power. Two months later he was still insisting: 'As for Beppo I will not alter or suppress a syllable for any man's pleasure but my own.' This was a different tone from any he had ever used before, at least in private among his coterie of special friends, about his own writing. The new self-confidence was to be decisive for the whole history of English literature. *Beppo* deserves the credit.

221

Sometimes *Beppo* is associated – curiously it may seem to modern tastes or judgements – with the period in Byron's Venetian life when he is supposed to have plunged almost irrecoverably and with the most debilitating effects even on his physical appearance, into a life of dissipation, sometimes with one mistress or sometimes with several. True enough, *Beppo* was written in a couple of days or nights, according to such reliable observers as Hobhouse, at the very time when these rumours about his sexual feats were starting to reach the outside world. So *Beppo* may help to sustain a quite different thesis: that the days or nights of dissipation were more the exception than the rule and that he was applying his mind with his usual zest to the exciting world around him and the books on his table. *Beppo*, for sure, was not the product of a melancholy, downcast spirit but much more that of one who had sensed a new vitality in Venice itself, among the Italians whose capabilities he extolled in that memorable introduction to Canto IV. The Venice of Goldoni, of Casti, Burati, and many more of the same gifts, had been, just a few decades before, the happiest city in Europe. So much of that spirit, like the carnival itself, had survived the fall of the Republic and the Napoleonic betrayal. He could not help telling his correspondents back home how ravishing was the spectacle: 'The view of the Rialto – of the piazza – and the Chaunt of Tasso (though less frequent than of old) are to me worth all the cities on earth – save Rome and Athens.' And as the weeks passed, Venice could displace even these from their pre-eminence. Venice, past, present and future, had captivated him and he could turn with ease from one aspect to another. He had taken a Palazzo on the Grand Canal for what looked, for him, like an epoch ahead.

> For my own part, after going down to Florence & Rome last year, I returned to Venice where I have since remained – & may probably continue to remain for some years – being partial to the people the language & the habits of life; – there are few English here – & those mostly birds of passage, – excepting one or two who are domesticated like myself. – I have the Palazzo Mocenigo on the Canal' Grande for three

years to come – & a pretty Villa in the Euganean hills for the Summer for nearly the same term. – While I remain in the city itself – I keep my horses on an Island with a good beach, about half a mile from the town, so that I get a gallup of some miles along the shore of the Adriatic daily – the Stables belong to the Fortress – but are let on fair terms. – I was always very partial to Venice – and it has not hitherto disappointed me – but I am not sure that the English in general would like it – I am sure that I should not, if *they* did – but by the benevolence of God – they prefer Florence & Naples – and do not infest us greatly here. – In other respects it is very agreeable for Gentlemen of desultory habits – women – wine – and wassail being all extremely fair & reasonable – theatres etc. good – & Society (after a time –) as pleasant as anywhere else (at least to my mind) if you will live with them in their own way – which is different of course from the Ultramontane in some degree. – The Climate is Italian & that's enough – and the Gondolas etc. etc. & habits of the place make it like a romance – for it is by no means even now the most regular & correct *moral* city in the universe. – Young and old – pretty & ugly – high and low – are employed in the laudable practice of Lovemaking – and though most Beauty is found amongst the middling & lower classes – this of course only renders their amatory habits more universally diffused. – I shall be very glad to hear from or of you when you are so disposed – & with my best regards to Lady Frances – believe me . . .

Venice could also strike deeper chords and he tried his hand at a full-scale ode on the city's political subjugation.

> O Venice! Venice! When thy marble walls
> Are level with the waters, there shall be
> A cry of nations o'er thy sunken halls,
> A loud lament along the sweeping sea!
> If I, a northern wanderer, weep for thee
> What should thy sons do?

He pictured the moment of defeat:

> And even the Lion all subdued appears
> And the harsh sound of the barbarian drum,
> With dull and daily dissonance, repeats
> The echo of thy Tyrant's voice . . .

Yet even these words could not dispel

> . . . the busy hum
> Of cheerful creatures, whose most sinful deeds
> Were but the overflowing of the heart,
> And flow of too much happiness . . .

Mostly the Ode was a lament for the lost Republic and a protest against the barbaric principles to be imposed in its place:

> Ye men, who pour out your blood for kings as water,
> What have they given your children in return?
> A heritage of servitude and woes
> A blindfold bondage, where your hire is blows . . .

At the end the Ode envisaged Venice cowering beneath the 'senseless sceptre of monarchy', and freedom driven into exile across the Atlantic. But the whole did not suit his mood. And the same may be said, less assuredly, about another brilliant exploration, which he attempted at the same time. *Mazeppa* was prompted by his recent reading of Voltaire's *History of Charles XII*. At first glance, this might look like an easy reversion to the 'Harrys and Larrys, Pilgrims and Pirates' which he himself claimed to have abjured. On the contrary, *Mazeppa* has several fresher features: the attack on the Puritan king who led his soldiers to slaughter, and the breathtaking rhythm of Mazeppa's race. Still, the conclusion was not clear – to modern critics, and maybe to Byron himself. *Beppo*, in his own judgement which mattered more than anyone else's, offered a new and much more exciting world. In the weeks when the potential menace from the censors in Albemarle Street threatened both *Childe Harold* and *Beppo*, he was contemplating a counter-attack all his own. On July 3rd he started work on the first intimations of *Don*

Juan. A few weeks passed before he was ready to tell Thomas Moore how the new poem was meant to be 'a little quietly facetious upon everything' and how yet it might be 'too free for these very modest times'.

One spur to the writing of *Don Juan*, and one not usually associated with his Venetian revels, had been the arrival sometime in the previous autumn of a copy of Coleridge's *Biographia Literaria*.* He had turned to it at once, and in particular to the passages in which Coleridge had criticized the committee of the Drury Lane Theatre for having staged a play called *Bertram* by Maturin, a comment which Byron characterized as 'not very grateful nor graceful on the part of the worthy auto-biographer'. since the piece had been chosen in preference to a submission of his own. Byron had always been ready to assist Coleridge with publishers or by other means; he was the one among the Lakers whose talents he was least tempted to deride. But the tone of this latest product of the Christian counter-revolution stirred within him a combined anger and contempt: 'Mr Coleridge', he wrote at the time

* The discoveries or revelations about the influence of Coleridge's *Biographia Literaria* on *Don Juan* are contained in Volume V of Jerome McGann's *The Complete Poetical Works*. An excellent review in the *Times Literary Supplement* for 23 January 1987 by Neil Barry – making amends perhaps for the criticisms in the same journal of Volume I – underlined how important these passages were: 'To have pointed out hitherto unsuspected connections between two of the *magna opera* of the Romantic period, when so much criticism and commentary has already been lavished on them, is no mean achievement.' True, and it may also be said that Jerome McGann has achieved the very considerable feat of adding here to the information and original judgement which he himself had already offered in his *Don Juan in Context* published in 1976. The more even such an expert as he examines the evidence, the more all-pervasive and the more radical Byron's politics become. As with *Don Juan* itself, the best advice is to read the whole of McGann's *Don Juan in Context*: otherwise some truly Byronic touches may be overlooked, such as his summons of Milton to Byron's aid: 'One is probably safe in assuming that Milton would not have approved – would probably have disavowed his wayward offspring. But then fathers from at least the time of Jahweh have always fallen out with those children most fashioned in their own image and likeness.'

may console himself with the 'fervour – the almost religious fervour' of his and Wordsworth's disciples as he calls it – if he means that as any proof of their merits – I will find him as much 'fervour' in behalf of Richard Brothers and Joanna Southcotte – as ever gathered over his pages or round his fireside. He is a shabby fellow – and I wash my hands, of, and after him.

That had been Byron's immediate response to Murray when the offending volume first found its way on to his bedside table. But as the months passed, the effect cut deeper. The spectacle of Byron grappling with the transcendental agonies of the *Biographia Literaria* at the very time when he was transferring his affections from Marianna Segati to Margarita Cogni is not the one that was noticed in the reports which found their way back to London. But it was no small part of the truth. Both the particular idea of Don Juan as a potential hero and the more general notion of the need for a counter-assault on the continent-wide Tory reaction were prompted by this same volume. Not much honour was accorded by his contemporaries to Coleridge as the great Tory prophet, and his *Biographia Literaria* was not even republished in his lifetime. But perhaps Byron sensed what later critics came to define: that Coleridge was the most formidable and persistent intellectual influence on the Tory side. Anyhow, Byron determined to retaliate with all his might and all his wit. He had his own way of doing it, but no doubt he was fortified to discover that, in this particular contest, he was not alone. The *Edinburgh Review* was one of the journals despatched to him regularly from Albemarle Street. It is inconceivable that he would have missed the issue of August 1817, which dealt manfully with the same pious, nauseating peroration. The article was anonymous, but the writer was William Hazlitt who had indeed been the target of Coleridge's most blistering attack, as one who had written 'with a malignity so avowedly and exclusively personal as is, I believe, unprecedented even in the present contempt of all humanity that disgraces and endangers the liberty of the press'. Byron stepped between these two bruising antagonists. He knew the one but not the other, but he could hardly fail to have approved the manner in which the *Edinburgh Review* strove to close the debate:

> This is the true history of our reformed Antijacobin poets; the life of one whom is here recorded. The cant of Morality, like the cant of Methodism, comes in most naturally to close the scene: and as the regenerated sinner keeps alive his old raptures and new-acquired horrors, by anticipating endless ecstasies or endless tortures in another world; so, our disappointed demagogue keeps up that 'pleasurable poetic fervour' which has been the cordial and the bane of his existence, by indulging his maudlin egotism and his mawkish spleen in fulsome eulogies of his own virtues, and nauseous abuse of his contemporaries – in making excuses for doing nothing himself, and assigning bad motives for what others have done. – Till he can do something better, we would rather hear no more of him.

Every discoverer of Venice wants to parade his knowledge to newcomers; it is part of the city's secret that she seems to be unveiling her charms individually to each newly arrived suitor. And Byron had a special right to insist on his sense of proprietorship. No Englishman had ever come to know the place as he did: mostly, before he changed the fashion, Rome, Florence and several other Italian cities figured higher on the list of the growing numbers of English visitors. Byron quickly concluded that the city of his adoption could be recruited to serve his causes or that Venice had much to teach him about the way that practical cause should be served. And within a few days of starting on *Don Juan* he had the chance of sharing his exhilaration with one whom he already knew to be, not so much a kindred political spirit, although there were already great political themes on which their minds did converge, but a true fellow poet on whom he could test his own ideas, his rhythms, his genius – not that Byron yet applied that term to himself. Wordsworth needed Coleridge; Pope needed Swift; Byron needed Shelley. And Shelley arrived at three o'clock on the afternoon of 23 August 1818 at the Palazzo Mocenigo, and returned there late that evening, having ridden with Byron on the Lido, and did not leave until the early hours.

One topic between them was not concerned at all with poetry and politics. Shelley had been corresponding for weeks with Byron in the interests of his daughter Allegra and her mother Claire. Allegra had arrived in Venice a few weeks before in the guardianship of Elise, a servant from the Shelley household. Shelley brought Claire with him and pretended that he had left her at Padua. No mention was made of Claire's presence; that would have ruptured all proceedings. However, such was the relationship between them, such the instant eagerness to examine and refresh each other's minds, that the argument banished all other affections and intrusions.

Shelley wrote a poem about that argument of such beauty and power, of such intricate construction that it is obviously a sacrilege to wrench passages from it; his *Julian and Maddalo* must be read as a whole. However, he also wrote, a few months later, a letter to his friend Thomas Peacock back in England, in which he furiously attacked some of Byron's ideas and some of his misdemeanours: a letter, we must note, not written in the heat of some controversy, but a considered, elaborate verdict. Such is mankind's (and womankind's) taste for gossip that the sexual titillations have acquired a much greater notoriety than the poem which indeed was not published in Shelley's lifetime. Shelley himself can bear none of the responsibility for this disproportionate sense of values. What Byron would have thought of the Peacock letter is hard to estimate; at the very least it would have impaired their intimacy then and thereafter. But Byron could not have complained about the poem – unless he had also been apprised how some modern critics have interpreted it.

> Concerning God, freewill, and destiny
> Of all that earth has been, or yet may be;
> All that vain men imagine or believe,
> Or hope can paint or suffering may achieve,
> We descanted . . .

228

Indeed, they discussed these religious themes, and their political implications, and how their common objectives of a world freed from such hideous strife and suffering as they saw all around them might be achieved: how mankind might move to accomplish the Revolution. Byron, Count Maddalo, was introduced in the Preface, and was ever a fairer portrait drawn?

> Count Maddalo is a Venetian nobleman of ancient family and of great fortune, who, without mixing much in the society of his countrymen, resides chiefly at his magnificent palace in that city. He is a person of the most consummate genius, and capable, if he would direct his energies to such an end, of becoming the redeemer of his degraded country. But it is his weakness to be proud: he derives, from a comparison of his own extraordinary mind with the dwarfish intellects that surround him, an intense apprehension of the nothingness of human life. His passions and his powers are incomparably greater than those of other men; and, instead of the latter having been employed in curbing the former, they have mutually lent each other strength. His ambition preys upon itself, for want of objects which it can consider worthy of exertion. I say that Maddalo is proud, because I can find no other word to express the concentered and impatient feelings which consume him; but it is on his own hopes and affections only that he seems to trample, for in social life no human being can be more gentle, patient, and unassuming than Maddalo. He is cheerful, frank, and witty. His more serious conversation is a sort of intoxication; men are held by it as by a spell. He has travelled much; and there is an inexpressible charm in his relation of his adventures in different countries.

It is necessary to contrast the striking features portrayed here, and beautifully reproduced in the verses which followed – some of Shelley's greatest, provoked after a period of frustration by his reunion with Byron – with the deformed, desperate creature drawn in the Peacock letter. We may note that the poem is based on first-hand, first-sight information acquired by Shelley himself through his call at the Palazzo Mocenigo, whereas some at least of the items in the letter derive from hearsay or second thoughts. We may note too that some of the sections of *Childe Harold* Canto IV which Shelley found so objectionable were supposedly derived from Byron's experience in the Venetian brothels. These are extraordinary deductions which would not seem plausible to the modern reader. Some other reasons are required to explain Shelley's outburst. But let us study the letter:

I entirely agree with what you [Peacock] say about Childe Harold. The spirit in which it is written is, if insane, the most wicked and mischievous insanity that ever was given forth. It is a kind of obstinate and selfwilled folly in which he hardens himself. I remonstrated with him in vain on the tone of mind from which such a view of things alone arises. For its real root is very different from its apparent one, and nothing can be less sublime than the true source of these expressions of contempt and desperation. The fact is, that first, the Italian women are perhaps the most contemptible of all who exist under the moon; the most ignorant, the most disgusting, the most bigotted, the most filthy. Countesses smell so of garlick that an ordinary Englishman cannot approach them. Well, L[ord] B[yron] is familiar with the lowest sort of these women, the people his gondolieri pick up in the streets. He allows fathers and mothers to bargain with him for their daughters, and though this is common enough in Italy, yet for an Englishman to encourage such sickening vice is a melancholy thing. He associates with wretches who seem almost to have lost the gait and phisiognomy of man, and who do not scruple to avow practices which are not only not named but I believe seldom even conceived in England. He says he disapproves, but he endures. He is not yet an Italian and is heartily and deeply discontented with himself, and contemplating in the distorted mirror of his own thoughts, the nature and the destiny of man, what can he behold but objects of contempt and despair? But that he is a great poet, I think the address to

230

Ocean proves [in *Childe Harold* IV]. And he has a certain degree of candour while you talk to him but unfortunately it does not outlast your departure. You may think how unwillingly I have left my little favourite [Allegra cancelled] Alba in a situation where she might fall again under his authority. But I have employed arguments entreaties every thing in vain, and when these fail you know I have no longer any right. No, I do not doubt, and for his sake I ought to hope that his present career must end up soon by some violent circumstance which must reduce our situation with respect to Alba into its antient tie.

Canto IV was a considerable departure from the mood which Shelley himself had helped to induce in Canto III, and Shelley had every right to argue with Byron about it – as he did in the poem. But for most readers surely, old and new, Canto IV did mark an advance in Byron's political thinking, as Canto III had advanced so much on his previous writing; he was struggling to face the dilemmas posed in Canto III, to discover the truthful answers, to expose the reasons why deep strands of scepticism were woven into his politics as they had been almost since childhood, and into his religious faith. When Shelley mapped out the path to a new Paradise Byron could never forget how our ancestors had, amid flaming injustice, been thrown out of the old one. No one, least of all those who wished to make a new revolution, could forget how the great revolution of their time had been, not betrayed – Byron rarely resorted to that simple or simplistic charge – but diverted into quite unforeseen, unwelcome channels. He could not forget, no compassionate citizen of his world could forget, how the revolution and those who inherited its legacy had resorted, been driven inexorably maybe, to bloody methods themselves. Was this hideous cycle always to be repeated? He did not indict the men who had inspired the revolution, like Rousseau, or the men who had ruled in Paris, or Napoleon, the child or champion of the revolution, whichever he might be. He knew the roles they had all played, and how stupendous was the drama, an event in history to equal or surpass what had been enacted in Greece or Rome.

But now, as Byron saw more clearly than any other observer among the poets, the last act was witnessing the continent-wide repression of the victorious Legitimist powers, the Holy Alliance. Or, maybe, could not the final tragedy be averted, by massive human endeavour, at the eleventh hour or even later? Byron constantly probed these great questions; Canto IV was full of them. To suggest, as Shelley did in the letter, that this plunge into insanity was somehow derived, or even affected by his personal delinquencies, his Venetian night life, by some traits in his character, was both an absurdity and an insult. It was a measure perhaps of what transcendental flights, unleashed from all reality, Shelley could contrive.

So what was Byron's crime in Shelley's eyes and, even more, in the eyes of his followers? The implication was that by his melancholy, by his posturing, by his Venetian diversions, by his refusal to follow the mountainous Utopian road marked out for him by Shelley, he had been guilty not of a betrayal – even in his Peacock letter he did not use that bitter word – but of a weakening in his revolutionary impulse, a surrender to the fates. What he saw in the distorted mirror of his own thoughts, as Shelley called them, instilled a brand of defeatism.

That surely is what the Shelley attack does mean; but it was monstrously false. Defeat was something Byron would never accept, either from God or man or woman. Defiance was his final stand, whatever the odds. Some of his most famous passages, in Canto IV in particular, express this mood immortally. Shelley himself adopted the most famous of them when he turned to portray his Prometheus:

> Yet, Freedom! yet thy banner, torn, but flying,
> Streams like the thunderstorm *against* the wind.

Rarely would Byron yield to despair. Of course he knew, as well as Shelley, how deep could be the chasms in which the human spirit might be imprisoned or broken. Indeed, he could not agree, as Shelley asserted in the poem, that the chains which 'our spirit bind' are 'brittle perchance as straw'. Byron did not believe that real chains were fashioned of such materials. But

232

always, almost always, in his poetry and his life, in the next moment the spark of defiance would be rekindled. More and more, as his art matured, he contemplated not the distorted mirror of his own thoughts, but the real world around him, a world which he found unjust by every human (or animal) test which could be applied. The road to Utopia was blocked: only fools or fanatics would pretend that it could be easily reopened. But the war against human degradation would continue relentlessly, all the better conducted, if the follies of the past were not repeated, if the nature of the enemy was properly gauged, if the blood-soaked courses which man had pursued could be proscribed. More and more, Byron was affected by the blood he had seen flowing through the centuries, across the Europe of his day. Perhaps this is why, after visiting the Colosseum, he pictured – who else would have done it? – the suffering of the bull, to match the blessed blood sacrifices approved by Abel, the favoured son of Adam. Byron had much more practical experience of the world than most of his fellow poets, including Shelley. He knew the Italians among whom he was living much better than any other English visitor. He had studied the politics of the Italians from the first day he set foot on Italian soil, indeed much earlier. Even his beloved Casti, whom he had by heart and whom he treasured for his lascivious wit, was also bitterly anti-war in his satire, so much so that both the Pope and Napoleon found it necessary to censor his books. It was something more than a single contrast between the two when, as John Buxton has written, 'Shelley could see only the present degradation of Italy; Byron hoped for her future freedom.'*

* John Buxton's invaluable volume on *Byron and Shelley* has been cited before. He concludes his chapter on the Venetian reunion: 'Talking together that day in Venice each brought out what was best and most characteristic in the other, and, so, fired with an intense excitement of writing poetry, they set out there and then on the chief work of their lives.' Charles Robinson's *Shelley and Byron*, also cited before, is a more elaborate and ambitious comparison of the place of the two poets in our literature, and may be read with a rising excitement and fury. For sometimes he pillories Byron as a political innocent or defeatist, at least compared with Shelley, when the facts, I would say, point to the opposite conclusion.

Don Juan was born in Venice, and the birth-mark remained gloriously indelible. Without his Venetian experience, without the protection Venice offered for his pride, it is hard to believe that his Donny Johnny, as he was quickly christened, could ever have survived so tempestuous an infancy. Like Venetian adventurers before him, with their symbol, the lion and the book, his poem traversed the known world, but always looked for a Venetian homecoming. Other great poets had been driven from their native lands, condemned to an outlawry much harsher than his, but none had fallen from such an early pinnacle of acclaim, and then found their masterpiece mocked as the main barrier which would keep them debarred from decent society. At that moment, Byron needed the support of a different tradition: Venice and Italy supplied it, and he never forgot the debt. In a suppressed Dedication to the poem, he still proclaimed:

> Italy!
> Thy late reviving Roman soul desponds
> Beneath the lie this state-thing breathed o'er thee
> Thy clanking chain, and Erin's yet green wounds,
> Have voices.

This particularly diminutively named, contemptuously dismissed 'state-thing' was Robert Southey, Poet Laureate, one who like so many others, had started out as a friend of the French Revolution, and then turned Tory: Southey, in Byron's eyes and those of many others, could, despite the severe competition, be accorded the title of Epic Renegade; not only had he changed his colours in return for reward from the Tory Ministers; he had led the cry against those who held to their old convictions. True, Byron had his own special grudge to repay: 'The Son of a Bitch', he wrote to Hobhouse (on 11 November 1818), 'on his return from Switzerland two years ago – said that Shelley and I "had formed a League of Incest and practised our precepts with etc." – he lied like a rascal. . . .' But Southey's earlier offences had been directed against others much less able to defend themselves than Byron. So Byron generously enlarged his attack to embrace all the apostate poets, all the Lakers in and

out of place. He now included even Coleridge of whom he had
sometimes spoken more kindly:

> And Coleridge, too, has lately taken wing,
> But like a hawk encumbered with his hood
> Explaining Metaphysics to the nation –
> I wish he would explain his Explanation.

Wordsworth was assailed more directly and effectively,
through comparison with his hero, Milton: Milton had 'closed
the *tyrant-hater* he begun'.

> Think'st thou, could he, the blind Old Man, arise
>   Like Samuel from the grave, to freeze once more
> The blood of monarchs with his prophecies,
>   Or be alive again – again all hoar
> With time and trials, and those helpless eyes
>   And heartless daughters, worn, and pale, and poor,
> Would *he* adore a sultan? *he* obey
> The intellectual eunuch Castlereagh?

These last two lines had originally been inscribed thus:

> Would *he* subside into a hackney Laureate
> A scribbling, self-sold, soul-hired scorned Iscariot?

This particular insult was forgone on the grounds that Iscariot
was a poor rhyme for Laureate – maybe he also thought he was
overdoing it. The politicians, 'Cobbling at manacles for all mankind', Castlereagh at their head, needed to be treated even more
roughly than the poets. Moreover, Southey had been given a
blow more contemptuous than that dealt to any other:

> Gasping on deck, because you soar too high, Bob,
> And fall for lack of moisture, quite a-dry, Bob!

This was said to be the gibe which provoked so much con-
sternation back among Murray's advisers, since, in Regency

slang, 'a dry Bob' meant coition without emission. But the whole Dedication, more even than the single phrase, was the likely cause of the offence, and when, after considerable exchanges between Albemarle Street and the Palazzo Mocenigo, it was agreed that the poem itself must be published anonymously, Byron agreed to dropping the Dedication: 'I won't attack the dog in the dark – such things are for scoundrels and renegades like himself.' But much graver issues were soon at stake. The poem itself, just the first canto, had arrived, and the assembled friends and experts had not yet had time actually to read it. On 29 December, Hobhouse wrote to say that 'your humble advisers' would soon meet to decide what 'final counsel' they might presume to offer. His publisher would be no obstacle, as Byron had been seeming to fear: 'You shall hear all in a day or two. Murray, I believe, would publish a Fanny Hill or an Age of Reason of yours – The Hitch will not come thence – so be tranquil . . .'* The hitch did come a few days later – in a three-thousand-word letter despatched on 5 January – from Hobhouse himself, with Scrope Davies at his side to give him moral support. After a paragraph of apologies for daring to act as they did, he explained how he and Scrope had read the poem, each exclaiming to the other at various points: *it will be impossible to publish this*. Murray came in at one point 'incontinently' mentioning that he would like to have the date of publication for advertising purposes, only to be told that such a moment might never occur. During the next two days, the judgements of Douglas Kinnaird and of Mr Hookham Frere, were also invited. Some particular passages, those which touched his own domestic affairs, were said to cause particular offence, but the trouble was, in Mr Frere's expert judgement:

the whole turn of the poem – from the flings at religion – and from the slashing right and left at other worthy writers

* *Byron's Bulldog: The letters of John Cam Hobhouse to Lord Byron*, edited by Peter W. Graham. Peter Graham has also written, most originally and instructively, on 'The Venetian Climate of *Don Juan*' in *The Byron Journal*, 1987.

of the day. . . . Next, the immoral turn of the whole and the rakish air of the half real hero will injure your reputation both as a man and a poet . . . I recollect you used to object to Tom Moore his luxuriousness and to me my use of gross words, yet your scenes are one continued painting of what is most sensual . . . Now it will be impossible for any lady to allow Don Juan to be seen on her table . . . But do not do it – all the idle stories about your Venetian life will be more than confirmed . . . I am not preaching to you of the deeds themselves but merely of the inexpediency of even appearing to make a boast of them. Our English world will not stand that.

But this was just the start: 'Almost all I have said about indecency will apply to the sneers at religion . . . The parody on the commandments though one of the best things in the poem is surely inadmissable. I can hardly think you meant it to stand.' As for Southey, some of those lines could only be published, if Byron intended to return home and face a duel. But altogether: 'I know not how any amputation will save it: more particularly as the objectionable parts are in point of wit and humour and poetry the very best beyond all doubt of the whole poem. This consideration, therefore, makes me sum up with strenuously advising a total suppression of Don Juan.'

Hobhouse himself was engaged at that moment in his first election at Westminster, and maybe this added to his anxieties. But Byron had readily agreed in advance not to cause any embarrassment about the exact timing of publication, and Hobhouse, to do him credit, was genuinely concerned about the fate of his friend, and he recruited every available kindred spirit to assist in his remonstrances. 'Tom Moore read it in my room the other day and perfectly coincided with us about the impossibility of entire publication . . . The more I read and think on the subject, the more I am convinced on the utter necessity of suppression . . .' That was not some craven publisher taking precautions to protect his own good name or even his other authors. It was his dearest political friend acutely aware of the latest mood in Regency London and confronted, as he believed, with a work which was only fit for the cesspit or the flames.

Byron's magnificent answer came promptly, with the accompanying threat that he had another canto almost ready.

> With regard to the Poeshie – I will have no 'cutting & slashing' as Perry calls it – you may omit the stanzas on Castlereagh – indeed it is better – & the two *'Bobs'* at the end of the 3d. stanza of the dedication – which will leave 'high' & 'dry' good rhymes without any *double* (or Single) Entendre' – but no more – I appeal – not 'to Philip fasting' but to Alexander drunk – I appeal to Murray at his ledger – to the people – in short, Don Juan shall be an entire horse or none. – If the objection be to the indecency, the Age which applauds the 'Bath Guide' & Little's poems – & reads Fielding & Smollett still – may bear with that; – if to the poetry – I will take my chance. – I will not give way to all the Cant of Christendom. . . .

However, the matter could not quite be resolved thus. Momentarily Byron acquiesced in non-publication, 'but I am a scribbler fond of his bantling', and no doubt his confidence in the printed word was such that once produced, without any real emasculation, its future would be assured. Meantime he upbraided the censors in turn. To Murray:

> If they had told me the poetry was bad – I would have acquiesced – but they say the contrary – and others talk to me about morality – the first time I ever heard the word from anybody who was not a rascal that used it for a purpose – I maintain that it is the most moral of poems – but if people won't discover the moral that is their fault not mine.

To Kinnaird:

> Your opinion & that of the others is I dare say quite right – & that there will be a war of Criticism & Methodism in consequence – but 'I have supped full of horrors' and it must be a 'dismal treatise' that will make my 'fell of hair stir & move' nowadays. – The poem has merit you all say – very well –

leave the rest to the chances. . . . Don't answer me with any more damned preachments from Hobhouse – about public opinion – I never flattered that & I never will – & when the public leaves off reading what I write – the booksellers will tell us – & then I shall respect it more than ever I did yet – though I would not change a word to regain it even then – unless it had my own approbation. – Do you or anybody else suppose that I am to be lectured out of some thousand pounds more or less? Sunburn me if I submit to it – & I wonder at you & Scrope – though not at Hobhouse – for acquiescing in such nonsense.

And again to Murray:

The Second Canto of Don Juan was sent on Saturday last by post in 4 packets – two of 4 – & two of three sheets each – containing in all two hundred & seventeen stanzas octave measure. – But I will permit no curtailments except those mentioned about Castlereagh & the two *'Bobs'* in the introduction. – You sha'n't make *Canticles* of my Cantos. The poem will please if it is lively – if it is stupid it will fail – but I will have none of your damned cutting & slashing. – If you please you may publish *anonymously* [;] it will perhaps be better; – but I will battle my way against them all – like a Porcupine. – So you and Mr Foscolo etc. want me to undertake what you call a 'great work' an Epic poem I suppose or some such pyramid. – I'll try no such thing – I hate tasks – and then 'seven or eight years!' God send us all well this day three months – let alone years – if one's years can't be better employed than in sweating poesy – a man had better be a ditcher. – And works too! – is Childe Harold nothing? you have so many *'divine'* poems, is it nothing to have written a *Human* one? without any of your worn out machinery. – Why – man – I could have spun the thought of the four cantos of that poem into twenty – had I wanted to book-make – & it's passion into as many modern tragedies – since you want *length* you shall have enough of *Juan* for I'll make 50 cantos.

239

And since the story has been told mostly through Hobhouse's eyes, let us conclude with his communication to Byron on 27 April.

> The lord's will be done – You are resolved that the pomes shall be printed; and printed the pomes shall be; aye, and published too. The first sheet has gone through my hands and has been transmitted to you for final approbation. The marginals are mine: and humbly I beseech you to consider them attentively, as you may depend upon it that my hook shall not be a desperate one and shall only be employed where your luxuriance is absolutely too rich. I think I have marked but three in the first sheet, including the *dry bob* and a line about a piss-bucket, and also god-damn. That I should ever have lived to see you come to this! On my stars and garters! Since I have such ill luck from the one I wish I was hanged in the other – However I shall delay dangling at the bed post until I see the Don fairly before the world and then I will lay my death at your door and leave myself to be wept by the Reformers and avenged by the Eclectic Review.

And this last presumably was supposed to allay Byron's temper; but not at all.

> Mr Hobhouse is at it again about indelicacy – there is no *indelicacy* – if he wants that let him read Swift – his great idol – but his imagination must be a dunghill with a viper's nest in the middle – to engender such a supposition about this poem. For my part I think you are all crazed – What does he mean about 'God damn' – there is 'damn', to be sure – but no 'G-d' whatever.

Hobhouse addressed directly was treated slightly more leniently, now that he was past the Rubicon. 'Neither you nor Murray say aught of *Canto Second* – from whence I infer *your* disapprobation – and *his fear* to have *any opinions at all* till he knows what the Public think.'

What all these wretched commotions had achieved was a full

suppression of the anti-Southey Dedication – leaving him to be exterminated another day – a few unauthorized bowdlerizations of verses which Hobhouse & Co. thought too hot to print at any price, and the pretence of anonymity. One reader who would certainly have read the Dedication with understanding and relish was William Hazlitt. He was the only man, despite some considerable contenders in the competition, who could write a prose invective against Southey to equal Byron's poem. He was one of the victims whom Southey would gladly have consigned to Botany Bay. So on this, as on so many other political topics of the greatest significance, Byron and Hazlitt had a common interest and common enemies, but by some miserable intervention of fate they were always finding themselves at cross purposes. If Hazlitt had been allowed to read the Dedication, it is hard to believe he would not have offered a glowing and magnanimous response. Instead, they were goaded near to a new quarrel. For the same censors who suppressed the Dedication achieved also a much less noted and notable excision of another piece which Byron proposed to be published along with the first two cantos of *Don Juan* – a reply by Byron to an attack on him by Hazlitt on the tender subject of Napoleon Bonaparte.

Byron said that Hazlitt, in one of his recent lectures in the Surrey Institution, had accused him of 'having lauded Buonaparte to the skies in the hour of his success, and then peevishly wreaking my disappointment on the god of my idolatry'. Byron was deeply aggrieved by such a charge, as well he might be. He was accused, as he said, of 'the basest of crimes, viz. "praising publicly the same man whom I wished to deprecate in his adversity" '. His reply was threefold: one, he had never in fact written of Napoleon, except since his decline; second, that what he had written about Napoleon in Canto III of *Childe Harold* had been described as a proper delineation, 'the man himself', and third, that he had written more in his praise in 1818 and thereafter than in 1814, when he had written first. The answers were not printed, Hobhouse having persuaded him that Hazlitt was '*beneath* notice – besides this shows an eagerness to reply to every paltry criticism'. However, the point was not so paltry.

Byron could excuse himself on the ground that prior to his *Ode to Napoleon* written in April 1814, he had written nothing directly about the Colossus who bestrode his world as he bestrode Hazlitt's. But the Ode had been published at a moment of excruciating delicacy in Napoleon's career – and Hazlitt's and Byron's. A few months earlier, or indeed a few months later, Byron would not have written in those terms, deeply derogatory, if not utterly damning. A few years later, in his notes for *Childe Harold*, he had described Bonaparte as 'a man who with all his vices and his faults never yet found any adversary with a tithe of his talents (as far as the expression can apply to a conqueror) or his good intentions, his clemency, or his fortitude'. That was not quite the tone of the Ode; those appeasing words might not have been enough to soften Hazlitt's animosities on this subject altogether, but they might have helped.

As it was, although unknown to Byron it seems, Hazlitt wrote in the spring of 1818, another lengthier comment on Byron's Napoleonic relationships which might have provoked an even more furious response. Hazlitt's essay appeared anonymously in the *Yellow Dwarf* on 2 May 1818. It was a full-scale review of the fourth canto of *Childe Harold*, much of it expressing disappointment, but some of it picking for the highest commendation some special passages of high political content. However, it is hard not to believe that this gnawing argument about Hazlitt's hero, Napoleon, remained the major source of their dissensions:

> His Lordship does not understand the Apollo Belvidere or the Venus de Medicis, any more than Bonaparte. He cants about the one and against the other, and in doing the last, cuts his own throat. We are not without hopes that his friend Mr Hobhouse will set this matter right in his 'Historical Illustrations'; and shew that, however it may suit his Noble Friend's poetical cross-purposes, politically and practically speaking, a house divided against itself cannot stand. He first, in his disdain of modern times, finds nothing to compare with the grandeur of antiquity but Bonaparte; and

then 'as 'twere in spite of scorn,' goes on to disdain this idol, which he had himself gratuitously set up, in a strain of effeminate and rancorous abuse worthy of Mr Words-worth's pastoral, place-hunting Muse. Suppose what is here said of 'the child and champion of Jacobinism' to be true, are there not venal tongues and venal pens enough to echo it, without his Lordship's joining in the cry? Will 'the High Legitimates, the Holy Band' be displeased with these cap-tious efforts to level the object of their hate to the groveling standard of royalty? Is there not a division of labour even on Mount Parnassus? The other writers of prose and verse, who enter the Temple of Fame by Mr Murray's door in Albemarle-street, have their cues. Mr Southey, for instance, never sings or says, or dreams of singing or saying, that the Prince Regent is not so great a man as Julius Caesar. Why then should Lord Byron force the comparison between the modern and the ancient hero? It is because the slaves of power mind the cause they have to serve, because their own interest is concerned; but the friends of liberty always sacri-fice their cause, which is *only* the cause of humanity, to their own spleen, vanity, and self-opinion. The league between tyrants and slaves is a chain of adamant; the bond between poets and the people is a rope of sand. Is this a truth, or is it not? If it is not, let Lord Byron write no more on this subject, which is beyond his height and his depth. Let him not tram-ple on the mighty or the fallen! Bonaparte is not Beppo.

Hazlitt in the grip of one of his superlative invectives could be as unrelenting as Byron. If they had ever met and talked, one feels, how moving and mighty the reconciliation could have been, how fruitful for the great causes which they shared. Hazlitt could acknowledge that mood. In that same essay, in May 1818: 'We give this judgement against our wills; and shall be happy should we live to see it reversed by another genera-tion. All our prejudices are in favour of the Noble Poet, and against his maligners.' And as the world prepared to receive *Don Juan*, the maligners were mobilizing as never before; even his bosom friends were in a high state of alarm; even his publisher was ready to desert. After *Beppo*, Murray called for 'another lively tale'. He had got somewhat more.

The best way to read *Don Juan* is to read it, not stopping, from beginning to end, all seventeen cantos.* Only thus can the full force of the poem, the mixture of tragic and comic genius, be appreciated. Few people in his lifetime, not even Byron himself, were enabled to read it in this fashion; but this is the surest way to measure its real greatness. Only thus can it be seen as Professor McGann described it: 'a conscious attempt to explain critically the meaning of the entire period in Europe stretching from 1789 to 1823'. Here was the epic which Shelley had urged him to write, the culminating achievement which made him the poet of the Revolution, and which has preserved for him that reputation in the ensuing two centuries. How much of the end of the journey he could foresee when he set out upon it in Venice in the summer of 1818, how much he described at each stage in his progress, these are obviously matters of debate or guesswork, and the moments when he renewed his revolutionary vision are as exciting in themselves as the time when he set out alone, or almost alone, against the wind.

* The advice to read *Don Juan* thus, I got from a Macmillan Casebook Series, edited by John Jump on *Childe Harold's Pilgrimage* and *Don Juan*, which contained an essay by Swinburne. 'His magnificent masterpiece', he wrote, and he was by no test always complimentary about Byron, 'will not bear dissection or distraction. The merit of *Don Juan* does not lie in any part, but in the whole. There is in that great poem an especial and exquisite balance and sustenance of alternate tones which cannot be expressed or explained by the utmost ingenuity of selection.' Later, for reasons which seem inexplicable, Swinburne joined the ranks of Byron's detractors, but he stiffly repudiated the attack from another detractor, Thackeray, who was fool enough to say that Byron *'never* wrote from his heart'. On one single point, replied Swinburne, 'the imputation is insupportable and unjust. He wrote from his heart when he wrote of politics . . .'

Anyhow, my particular thanks are due to Jump, Swinburne and Macmillan's together. Incited by that passage I took a copy of *Don Juan* into hospital one week, and read it all and recovered. The copy I read was the Riverside Edition, edited by Leslie Marchand, and it remains a favourite, although there are several others, the most notable and priceless and indispensable being Volume V of Professor McGann's *The Complete Poetical*

The 'cursed puritanical committee' which assembled in Murray's room, composed of as unlikely a bunch of penitent sinners as could be found anywhere in Regency London, had been shocked, although they could hardly admit as much, by one principal feature of the extraordinary production, the manner in which wit, playfulness, literary criticism, indecency, religion, poetry and politics were all served up in the same splendid dish. One ingredient could never be separated from the others; so if there was to be any effective suppression it would have to be applied to the whole affair. Hobhouse had been right about that from the start. Apart from any direct Dedications or newly designed Ten Commandments, how could one deal with a poem which tackled serious subjects thus:

> 'Tis a sad thing, I cannot choose but say,
>   And all the fault of that indecent sun,
> Who cannot leave alone our helpless clay,
>   But will keep baking, broiling, burning on,
> That howsoever people fast and pray
>   The flesh is frail, and so the soul undone:
> What men call gallantry, and gods adultery,
> Is much more common where the climate's sultry.

Or thus:

> 'Tis said that Xerxes offer'd a reward
>   To those who could invent him a new pleasure;
> Methinks, the requisition's rather hard,
>   And must have cost his majesty a treasure:
> For my part, I'm a moderate-minded bard,
>   Fond of a little love (which I call leisure);
> I care not for new pleasures, as the old
> Are quite enough for me, so they but hold.

Works (see also note page 225). Before Oxford and McGann together produced that work of art in 1986, the field had been worthily held by Truman Guy Steffan's elaborate four-volume *Don Juan*, the edition which first proved how carefully Byron had written and re-written his masterpiece.

Or thus:

> But sweeter still than this, than these, than all,
>   Is first and passionate love – it stands alone,
> Like Adam's recollection of his fall:
>   The tree of knowledge has been pluck'd – all's known –
> And life yields nothing further to recall
>   Worthy of this ambrosial sin, so shown,
> No doubt in fable, as the unforgiven
> Fire which Prometheus filch'd for us from heaven.

Or thus:

> This is the patent-age of new inventions
>   For killing bodies, and for saving souls,
> All propagated with the best intentions;
>   Sir Humphrey Davy's lantern, by which coals
> Are safely mined for in the mode he mentions,
>   Timbuctoo travels, voyages to the Poles,
> Are ways to benefit mankind, as true,
> Perhaps as shooting them at Waterloo.

But further flagrant breaches of the rule must be forbidden – except to remark that Canto II, considered by many contemporary readers as no less offensive, contained one of the loveliest love poems in the language. And it should not be forgotten that the idyllic picture of young love described there did not succeed in winning any reprieve for *Don Juan* on its first appearance. Hobhouse's fears were fully justified by the outburst which greeted the large quarto volume presented to the world, without the author's name, without John Murray's name, with only his printer Thomas Davidson's imprint, on 15 July 1819. 'I have had my own way – in spite of everybody and am satisfied,' wrote Byron when the news was conveyed to him. *Blackwood's* which led the attack was not at all lacking in followers. 'A more thorough and intense infusion of genius and vice – power and profligacy' there had never been. 'Impiously railing against his God – madly and meanly disloyal to his sovereign and his country – and brutally outraging all the best feelings of family honour, affection and confidence . . . it appears . . . as if this miserable man . . . were resolved to show us that he is no longer a human being, even in his frailties; – but a cool unconcerned fiend.'*

* This quotation, and one of the fullest accounts of the reaction to *Don Juan* at every stage and indeed the rest of Byron's writings, is given in one of the very best books about him, *Byron in England: His Fame and After-Fame* by Samuel C. Chew, already referred to on page 141. He cites not only the well-established magazines, giving their verdicts, but the host of others who followed the example: 'From 1816 till his death pamphleteers followed Byron as jackals trail after a wounded lion.' Since 1924 the attention directed to *Don Juan* has, of course, vastly increased. And it required the poet's eye of W.H. Auden to make the calculation that Don Juan himself was involved in only five seductions, and could not be regarded always as the aggressor or initiator even in these. Auden's essays appear in *The Dyer's Hand and Other Essays*. The number of seductions was scrupulously reduced to four, on a recount, when the essay was reprinted, along with many other excellent ones, in *Twentieth Century Interpretations of Don Juan*, edited by E. E. Bostetter.

EIGHT

Venice–Ravenna I

One must not be particular, but take rebellion
when it lies in the way.

5 January 1821

He was no less resilient in the moment after publication: a
harder test. Henry James derisively remarked that 'Byron was
always defying something, and if a slab had been put wherever
this performance came off, these commemorative tablets
would be in many parts of Europe as thick as milestones.'* He
happened to be referring in that particular gibe to Byron's boast-
ing about his feats as a swimmer, but the moment when, even
amid the comforts and diversions of the Palazzo Mocenigo, he
withstood the blows about his head on the first publication of
Don Juan deserves some recognition.

The immediate source of irritation, and how galling it must
have been, was that he got no news at all. Authors often need to
attune themselves to this chronic habit of secrecy among publishers, but Byron's circumstances were exceptional. On 1
August 1819 he wrote to Murray:

> . . . as you write the day after publication – it can hardly be
> decided what opinion will predominate. – You seem in a
> fright – and doubtless with cause. – Come what may – I
> never will flatter the Million's canting in any shape – cir-
> cumstances may or may not have placed me at times in a sit-
> uation to lead the public opinion – but the public opinion –
> never led nor ever shall lead me, – I will not sit on 'a
> degraded throne' so pray put Messrs Southey – or Sotheby –

* This remark appears in Henry James's *Italian Hours*; see also pages 279
and 280.

or Tom Moore – or Horace Twiss upon it – they will all of them be transported with their coronation.

On 9 August he felt entitled to remonstrate: 'Of Don Juan I hear nothing further from *you* – you chicken-hearted, silver paper Stationer you?' Such reports as he had heard, roundabout, did not seem fierce. So he persisted to Murray:

> I will write a preface that *shall* exculpate *you* and Hobhouse etc. *completely* . . . At the same time I will cut you all up (and *you* in particular) like Gourds. You have no more soul than the Count de *Caylus* (who assured his friends on his death-bed – that he had none, and that *he* must know better than they – whether he had one or no) and no more blood than a Water-Melon – And I see there have been asterisks – and what Perry used to call *'damned* cutting and slashing'.

As the days passed he almost despaired. To Hobhouse on 23 August: 'Why don't you write, pray do – never mind *Don Juan* – let him tumble – and let me too – like Jack and Gill.' And then, slightly more seriously to Murray on the same day: 'Continue to keep the anonymous about Juan – it helps us to fight against overwhelming numbers'. Or then again, a day later: 'Keep the *anonymous* in every case – it helps what fun there may be – but if the matter grows serious about *Don Juan* and you feel *yourself* in a scrape – or *me* either – *own that I am the author.*' It is hard to believe that any real doubts existed anywhere, but there were legal implications. Even in September he was still bewailing to Kinnaird: 'Of the Don himself I hear nothing.' On 12 August he still felt himself suffering from the wounds inflicted by Murray in his publication day message of 23 July, and along with his protest, he felt it necessary to defend before his English audience the case for the mixture of comedy and tragedy which Italian readers might find not so unfamiliar:

> You are right – Gifford is right – Crabbe is right – Hobhouse is right – you are all right – and I am all wrong – but do pray let me have that pleasure. – Cut me up root and branch –

quarter me in the Quarterly – send round my 'disjecti
membra poetae' like those of the Levite's Concubine – make
– if you will – a spectacle to men and angels – but don't ask
me to alter for I can't – I am obstinate and lazy – and there's
the truth. – But nevertheless – I will answer your friend C.V.
who objects to the quick succession of fun and gravity – as if
in that case the gravity did not (in intention at least)
heighten the fun. – His metaphor is that 'we are never
scorched and drenched at the same time!' – Blessings on his
experience! – Ask him these questions about 'scorching and
drenching'. Did he never play at Cricket or walk a mile in
hot weather? – did he never spill a dish of tea over his testicles in handing the cup to his charmer to the great shame of
his nankeen breeches? – did he never swim in the sea at
Noonday with the Sun in his eyes and on his head – which
all the foam of ocean could not cool? did he never draw his
foot out of a tub of too hot water damning his eyes and his
valet's? did he never inject for a Gonorrhea? – or make
water through an ulcerated Urethra? – was he ever in a turkish bath – that marble paradise of sherbet and sodomy? –
was he ever in a cauldron of boiling oil like St John? – or in
the sulphureous waves of hell? (where he ought to be for his
'scorching and drenching at the same time') did he never
tumble into a river or lake fishing – and sit in his wet
cloathes in the boat – or on the bank afterwards 'scorched
and drenched' like a true sportsman? – 'Oh for breath to
utter' – but make him my compliments – he is a clever fellow for all that – a very clever fellow.

The same letter continued with a response to the frightened
inquiries from London:

You ask me for the plan of Donny Johnny – I *have* no plan – I
had no plan – but I had or have materials – though if like
Tony Lumpkin – I am 'to be snubbed so when I am in spirits'
the poem will be naught – and the poet turn serious again. –
If it don't take I will leave it off where it is with all due
respect to the Public – but if continued it must be in my own

way – you might as well make Hamlet (or Diggory) 'act mad' in a strait waistcoat – as trammel my buffoonery – if I am to be a buffoon – their gestures and my thoughts would only be pitiably absurd – and ludicrously constrained. – Why Man the Soul of such writing is it's licence? – at least the *liberty* of that *licence* if one likes – *not* that one should abuse it – it is like trial by Jury and Peerage – and the Habeas Corpus – a very fine thing – but chiefly in the *reversion* – because no one wishes to be tried for the mere pleasure of proving his possession of the privilege.

Apart even from the publication of *Don Juan*, the summer and the autumn of 1819 saw some tumultuous events in Byron's own life, in the England he had left behind, in the Italy of his adoption. 1819 was the darkest year which Europe had known since the peace treaties were signed in 1815, and Byron was aware of what was happening in the outside world, even if he had his own special forms of distraction. He recounted to his friends back home how he had escaped from the embraces of his more flamboyant mistresses, and had pursued or been pursued by (with him, at least in his own estimation the two processes always ran concurrently) the Contessa Teresa Guiccioli. Within a few days the enticement had been consummated; within a week or two, he was involved in his 'last attachment'; within a few months he was even momentarily turning his back on Venice, pursuing her to her home in Ravenna, ready en route or on the way back to endure the rigours of continental travel. He hated these moves; they interfered with his writing and reading. The affair with Teresa became the most satisfactory of his life and the best documented. He told his side of the story, at first with a little self-mockery, with some less than gallant references to her, but soon his love letters to her, most of them in Italian, poured forth the truth. She told her story, years later, it is true, but the love for Byron was still overflowing. Most intelligent observers at the time could see what a wonderful match it was for both of them, and the most notable and best informed of these was Pietro

Gamba, the sixteen-year-old adoring brother of his nineteen-year-old sister.*

Second only to Venice, Ravenna became both the head-quarters and the heartquarters of his Italian inspiration, and it may be more apt to emphasize how much of his Venetian experience he brought with him and how one was always enfolded in the other. He might have no settled long-term plan for Donny Johnny but he was already contemplating the next round of adventures for his hero. Several other even more direct Venetian themes were competing for his attention. He wrote one of his first love letters to Teresa in her copy of Madame de Staël's *Corinne*. He himself had been quite ready to adopt *Corinne* as his guide to 'the glory and welfare of Italy', to Venice especially where the city is presented in a loving, if melancholy light. Madame de Staël at Coppet had offered to help seek a mediation with Lady Byron. Her truly greatest gift to Byron was the way she placed Teresa's hand in his and fostered their common devotion to the Italian cause. How much the world owes to her for this act alone, and how delighted he must have been to discover that his new love shared this literary enthusiasm: 'It is a favourite book of yours – and the writer was a friend of mine.' Some of the lyrics he wrote then were obviously directed to her,

* The great book on the affair, a truly splendid biographical study on its own, is of course *The Last Attachment* by Iris Origo, first published (by Jonathan Cape and John Murray) in 1949 and reprinted by John Murray, with a new introduction, in 1971. Considering the never-ceasing world-wide interest in Byron and his love life it is indeed extraordinary that the rich Italian materials which came into Iris Origo's hands had never been explored before. Perhaps Providence felt a debt was due to the forever-maligned Byron. So the discoveries were reserved for a woman whose sympathy could be worthy of Teresa's. On her deathbed (in Italy, in 1873) Teresa wrote: 'The more Byron is known, the better he will be loved.' It is also worth recording how, in her introduction to her own book, Iris Origo selected for special mention John Drinkwater's verdict: Byron spoke of Teresa as 'a woman of more quality and character than history has commonly realized . . . He talked at times as if this was not so, but then he talked at times as if everything was not so that was . . . He had, on the whole, a more genuine and lasting respect for her than he had for any other woman in his life.'

including the *Stanzas to the Po*:

> River! that rollest by the ancient walls
> Where dwells the Lady of my Love . . .

No one is quite sure to this day where those ancient walls were, but once he had arrived in Ravenna and was safely lodged in a house so near her home, he acted directly on her promptings and was happy to admit it. He carried with him his copy of Dante's *Inferno* and wrote on the flyleaf the inscription: 'This edition . . . I placed with my own hands upon the tomb of Dante, in this City, at the hour of four in the afternoon, June 12, 1819. Having thus brought the thoughts of Alighieri once more in contact with his ashes, I shall regard this work, not with higher veneration, but with greater affection as something like *"a copy from the author"*.' Byron's original Dedication to *The Prophecy of Dante* was dated 21 June:

> So sweet a language from so fair a mouth
> Ah! to what effort would it not persuade?

So sweet a Dedication might have been expected to introduce Dante and his Beatrice. Instead, he himself claimed that the poem's primary aim had been to foreshadow the 'liberty and resurrection of Italy', and, even if some other themes are woven into it, the aim was brilliantly achieved. *The Prophecy* not only recites the history of Italy from Dante's time onwards; it has a taste of what was to come later. 'The Italians, with a pardonable rationality, are particularly jealous of all that is left them as a nation – their literature.' He wrote of that literature in a manner which wooed by the same arts Teresa and the conspirators starting to organize their resistance to Austrian barbarism. He had his own kinship with a poet driven into exile, but the whole prophecy was a general call to action:

> Hast thou not bled? and hast thou still to bleed,
> Italia? Ah! to me such things, foreshown
> With dim sepulchral light, bid me forget

In thine irreparable wrongs my own;
We can have but one country, and even yet
　　Thou'rt mine – my bones shall be within thy breast,
　　My soul within thy language, which once set
With our old Roman sway in the wide West;
　　But I will make another tongue arise
　　As lofty and more sweet, in which exprest
The hero's ardour, or the lover's sighs,
　　Shall find alike such sounds for every theme
　　That every word, as brilliant as thy skies,
Shall realize a poet's proudest dream,
　　And make thee Europe's nightingale of song;
　　So that all present speech to thine shall seem
The note of meaner birds, and every tongue
　　Confess its barbarism when compared with thine.

The refrain was, as he said, much more directed to his new
Italian comrades:

Yes! thou, so beautiful, shalt feel the sword,
　　Thou, Italy! so fair that Paradise,
　　Revived in thee, blooms forth to man restored:
Ah! must the sons of Adam lose it twice?
　　Thou, Italy! whose ever golden fields,
　　Plough'd by the sunbeams solely, would suffice
For the world's granary; thou, whose sky heaven gilds
　　With brighter stars, and robes with deeper blue;
　　Thou, in whose pleasant places Summer builds
Her palace, in whose cradle Empire grew,
　　And form'd the Eternal City's ornaments
　　From spoils of kings whom freemen overthrew;

The cry came even stronger than in the last canto of *Childe
Harold*:

Oh! my own beauteous land! so long laid low,
　　So long the grave of thy own children's hopes,

When there is but required a single blow
To break the chain, yet – yet the Avenger stops,
   And Doubt and Discord step 'twixt thine and thee,
   And join their strength to that which with thee copes;
What is there wanting then to set thee free,
   And show thy beauty in its fullest light?
   To make the Alps impassable; and we,
Her sons, may do this with *one* deed – Unite!

Many are poets but without the name,
   For what is poesy but to create
   From overfeeling good or ill; and aim
At an external life beyond our fate,
   And be the Prometheus of new men . . .

Sometimes Byron, in his hours of dejection, would dismiss the writer's art, the poet's art, as a secondary profession, and too often his mockeries have been taken at their first estimate. At Dante's tomb, in the Ravenna which had given him refuge, the inspiration was of a quite different order:

The genius of my country shall arise,
   A Cedar towering o'er the Wilderness,
Lovely in all its branches to all eyes,
   Fragrant as fair, and recognized afar,
   Wafting its native incense through the skies.
Sovereigns shall pause amidst their sport of war,
   Wean'd for an hour from blood, to turn and gaze
   On canvas or on stone; and they who mar
All beauty upon earth, compell'd to praise,
   Shall feel the power of that which they destroy;
   And Art's mistaken gratitude shall raise
To tyrants who but take her for a toy
   Emblems and monuments, and prostitute
   Her charms to pontiffs proud, who but employ
The man of genius as the meanest brute
   To bear a burthen, and to serve a need,
   To sell his labours, and his soul to boot:

255

Who toils for nations may be poor indeed
   But free; who sweats for monarchs is no more
   Than the gilt chamberlain, who, clothed and fee'd,
Stands sleek and slavish, bowing at his door.
   Oh, Power that rulest and inspirest! how
   Is it that they on earth, whose earthly power
Is likest thine in heaven in outward show,
   Least like to thee in attributes divine,
   Tread on the universal necks that bow,
And then assure us that their rights are thine?

   An exile, saddest of all prisoners,
   Who has the whole world for a dungeon strong,
Seas, mountains, and the horizon's verge for bars,
   Which shut him from the sole small spot of earth
   Where – whatsoe'er his fate – he still were hers,
His country's, and might die where he had birth –
   Florence! when this lone spirit shall return
   To kindred spirits, thou wilt feel my worth,
And seek to honour with an empty urn
   The ashes thou shalt ne'er obtain – Alas!
   'What have I done to thee, my people?' Stern
Are all thy dealings, but in this they pass
   The limits of man's common malice, for
   All that a citizen could be I was;
Raised by thy will, all thine in peace or war,
   And for this thou hast warr'd with me.

Some readers of *The Prophecy of Dante* have posed the question, as about so many other of his poems, greater or lesser ones, whether he did not here freshly reveal the unresolved dilemma in his own mind: was his predominant interest political, in this instance stirred by his involvement in the movement of Italian liberation, or was he not always obsessed much more with his own exile, and the universal sense of man's exile from truth or a tolerable existence? These mighty issues and a multitude of kindred ones, can be argued for ever, and Byron's poetry can be

flawed through its failure to resolve them. However, if the discussion here seems to sway back and forth, an effective arbiter
can be introduced in the shape of the Papal authorities in
Ravenna or later in the Grand Duchy of Tuscany. They continued to pursue and suppress *The Prophecy* wherever they could get
their hands on it; it was 'most decidedly not written in the spirit
of our Government, or any of the Italian Government, as in it,
Lord Byron makes Dante advocate democracy and the independence of Italy for the salvation and good of the country'. The
police reports were exaggerating. Byron was not advocating
'democracy', but for the rest the fact that the police went to such
lengths, over such a period, may suggest that the political content of the poem was not quite so obscure as modern critics still
insist.

Sometime during that summer, despite his deepening Italian
interests, both emotional and political, he embarked on two
other literary projects which might have been thought sufficiently absorbing to exclude much else. He dashed off some
memoirs, mostly dealing with matters before he had left London, and when Thomas Moore arrived in Venice for a four-day
visit he 'put my life (in M.S.) into his hands – (not for publication)'. He wanted to defend himself, but it is hard to believe that
he was not also prompted by a sheer creative urge. He had a gift
for prose along with the poetry, and he could take a real aesthetic delight in exercising it. And he could hardly stop himself
from pouring out new stanzas of *Don Juan*. He made one outburst to Douglas Kinnaird, to whom he seemingly spoke more
freely than the others:

As to 'Don Juan' – confess – confess – you dog – and be can-
did – that it is the sublime of *that there* sort of writing – it may
be bawdy – but is it not good English? it may be profligate –
but is it not *life*, is it not *the thing*? – Could any man have written it – who has not lived in the world? – and tooled in a
post-chaise? in a hackney coach? in a Gondola? against a
wall? in a court carriage? in a vis a vis? – on a table? – and
under it? – I have written about a hundred stanzas of a third
Canto – but it is damned modest – the outcry has frightened

me. – I had such projects for the Don – but the *Cant* is so much stronger than *Cunt* – now a days, – that the benefit of experience in a man who had well weighed the worth of both monosyllables – must be lost to despairing posterity.

And to Hoppner:

> . . . he [Murray] told me the sale had not been great – 1200 out of 1500 quarto I believe (which is nothing after selling 13000 of the Corsair in one day) but that the 'best Judges &c.' had said it was very fine and clever and particularly good English & poetry and all those consolatory things which are not however worth a single copy to a bookseller – and as to the author – of course I am in a damned passion at the bad taste of the times – and swear there is nothing like posterity – who of course must know more of the matter than their Grandfathers. – There has been an eleventh commandment to the women not to read it – and what is still more extraordinary they seem not to have broken it. – But that can be of little import to them poor things – for the reading or non-reading a book – will never keep down a single petticoat . . .

Moreover, as the weeks passed, *Don Juan* threatened to involve him in a new complication. Murray's semi-anonymous quarto edition had been pirated by some radical publishers, notably William Hone who had himself been tried for blasphemy a few years before, and Murray wanted to apply for an injunction to protect the copyright. Byron was alarmed lest he should suffer the same fate as Shelley over his *Queen Mab*; he had been deprived of the guardianship of his daughter, once the publication had been pronounced *indecent* and *blasphemous*. Moreover, and with some justice, he had little faith in the courts:

> Murray it seems wishes to try a question of copyright of Don Juan – and bring *in my* name – I would rather pay him back the money; – as he will be sure to lose – the Chancellor would decide against him as he decided on Wat Tyler – as the cry is at present up with that fool Carlile and his trash in such a manner – that they would re-crucify Christ himself if

258

he re-appeared in his old humble accoutrements – and had only his word for his credentials.

As it happened, the fear proved groundless; Murray won the case. But assaults from other quarters mounted to a new intensity. *Blackwood's* in August unloosed an horrific and comprehensive attack on his life and character. He was deeply hurt, and felt constrained to produce an elaborate reply which however was not published until after his death. These conditions might not seem conducive to easy writing, especially as he felt constrained to keep the next sections 'very decent – but *dull* – damned dull.'

Cantos III and IV, written originally as one long single canto, were started on 17 September and finished on 30 November, 1819. Considering that these 240-odd verses were devised while discouragement came from every quarter, while fresh torrents of abuse arrived with every despatch of the magazines, while there were constantly renewed freezing admonitions from his friends, while he himself was afflicted by one of his rare moods of doubt about his own discovery of his best *métier*, the achievement becomes an act of combined courage and persistence unmatched hitherto even by Byron himself. The richness, the variety, the unification of extremes equals, at least, anything that had gone before. What could surpass the love scenes in Canto II? Indeed, to quote Professor Grierson, there is nothing like that

> in English poetry except some of the songs of Burns and the complex, vibrant passion, sensual and spiritual, of Donne's songs and elegies. And considering the descriptive element alone – to use the English language so simply and naturally to produce an effect so vivid, vivid to every sense, and not the eye alone, for one hears the splash of the waves, one feels the cool, strong air of the salt sea-wind, the wet hard sand beneath one's feet, the glow of the sky in the inner chambers of the soul . . .'*

* The verses referred to by Professor Grierson and his references are made in his *The Background of English Literature*, published in 1934.

And how to descend from these heights without bathos or offence? Cantos III and IV, the immediate product of the Venetian aftermath, touched moments of greatness, not excelling Haidee's lovemaking, but still to be imprinted forever on the mind, and mostly the political mind, it must be added, of his own generation, and how many since? The most famous of all, the great song of liberty,

> The Isles of Greece, the Isles of Greece!
> Where burning Sappho loved and sung . . .

captivated an audience at once, and has never seemed to lose its brightness and force and summons to resistance. It ended, incongruously, it might seem for a moment, with a return to the more familiar legendary Byronic figure, described thus by one biographer, and a good one, 'here Byron gave symbolical and almost prophetic expression to the brooding and solitary genius that ended his life.'*

> Place me on Sunium's marbled steep,
>   Where nothing, save the waves and I,
> May hear our mutual murmurs sweep;
>   There, swan-like, let me sing and die:
> A land of slaves shall ne'er be mine –
> Dash down yon cup of Samian wine!

But was his genius ever truly so solitary, at least in these later years? The hero of *Don Juan*, with his myriad moods and manifestations, was much more a man concerned with the tumults in the world all around him than the hero of *Childe Harold*. He never lost the capacity to use 'The words which shook Belshazzar in his hall/And took his kingdom from him . . .'. And the mood could always change, as if lit up by lightning. His homecomings had a perennial curiosity.

* This comes from J. D. Symon's book. See page 88.

Arriving at the summit of a hill
    Which overlook's the white walls of his home,
He stopp'd. – What singular emotions fill
    Their bosoms who have been induced to roam!
With fluttering doubts if all be well or ill –
    With love for many, and with fears for some;
All feelings which o'erleap the years long lost,
And bring our hearts back to their starting post.

The approach of home to husbands and to sires,
    After long travelling by land or water,
Most naturally some small doubt inspires –
    A female family's a serious matter;
(None trusts the sex more, or so much admires –
    But they hate flattery, so I never flatter;)
Wives in their husbands' absences grow subtler,
And daughters sometimes run off with the butler.

And always, or almost always he found it impossible to escape
the political pressures, the ravages of war which he saw all
around him, even in his rides through the pine forests of
Ravenna with Teresa at his side:

I canter by the spot each afternoon
    Where perish'd in his fame the hero-boy,
Who lived too long for men, but died too soon
    For human vanity, the young De Foix!
A broken pillar, not uncouthly hewn,
    But which neglect is hastening to destroy,
Records Ravenna's carnage on its face,
While weeds and ordure rankle round the base.

I pass each day where Dante's bones are laid:
    A little cupola, more neat than solemn,
Protects his dust, but reverence here is paid
    To the bard's tomb, and not the warrior's column:
The time must come, when both alike decay'd,
    The chieftain's trophy, and the poet's volume,
Will sink where lie the songs and wars of earth,
Before Pelides' death, or Homer's birth.

With human blood that column was cemented,
  With human filth that column is defiled,
As if the peasant's coarse contempt were vented
  To show his loathing of the spot he soil'd;
Thus is the trophy used, and thus lamented
  Should ever be those blood-hounds, from whose wild
Instinct of gore and glory earth has known
Those sufferings Dante saw in hell alone.

With *Don Juan*, although few people realized it except Byron himself, and he only in his most lonely moments, he had stepped into a new world. His political association became something much more real, an immediate throbbing commitment to the Italian cause. He was deeply anxious about what might be the fate of his Italian friends, Teresa's family among the foremost of course, but many others besides. And it is instructive to remember that Professor Grierson fixed the moment precisely when he crossed the frontier between thought and action. Words are things, wrote Byron in the same Canto III as he had done in *The Prophecy of Dante*, and, says Grierson:

His political activity began with his departure from Venice for Ravenna; and he was prepared to go to all lengths had not the Italians recoiled. The expedition to Greece was not the outcome of a sudden impulse to escape from idleness and ennui. It was a second chapter in the history of his endeavour to serve the cause of emancipation with his sword as well as his pen. Milton and Swift are the only other Englishmen of Letters whose writings have been not only literary works but deeds. The former exercised but little influence on the actual course of events, but a careful study of his last poems in relation to the political pamphlets and *De Doctrina* will show that they were more to their author than works of art alone. They were great political acts; declarations by the poet intended to be trumpet-calls to action, a vindication of freedom conceived as obedience to reason and reason only, addressed to the English people and the

Christian world, and if they failed to find such hearing as he desired, yet before *Paradise Lost* had been published Milton's name had a European reputation, 'and the only inducement of several foreigners that came over into England was chiefly to see Oliver Protector and Mr John Milton'. Swift was a pamphleteer, but his pamphlets ended a European war and shook the government of Ireland, and it was not the satire alone which did so but the personality, the fearless pride and strength of the man who launched them. And Byron's voice rang through Europe . . . .

It was the new voice, trained in Venice and Ravenna, which Europe was to hear.

NINE

Venice–Ravenna II

There is not an Italian who loathes them more
than I do.

16 February 1821

While his Italian associations, emotional and political, the two
intertwining, deepened into a new experience, the news from
England – throughout most of that autumn of 1819 – brought
evidence of new tensions of a more convulsive, revolutionary
character. Byron himself did not hesitate to use the actual word
'revolution' in some of his inquiries, although he could hardly
be expected to sense from afar what were the true changes
taking place, among the performers or on the political stage
itself. He was always fascinated to hear any items of news he
could extract from his correspondents, but the full account was
not likely to be supplied from Murray's mostly Tory coterie.
Exiles are inclined still to see the political scene in their own
countries, as it was at the time of their departure. 1819 and 1820
were very different from 1815 and 1816, in the Age of Waterloo
and Peterloo.

Sometimes a few of the old Whig leaders, sustaining the
truest strand in the Charles James Fox tradition, would
understand the strength and the justice of popular protest, even
when the bulk of the party would huddle into protective
conclaves or even actual coalitions with the ascendant Tory
administrations. Sometimes the cravenness of the Whigs, in the
moments of crisis for their class, would provoke contemptuous
protest from their allies or near-allies on the fringe, from men
who had staked out a position of independence thanks directly
to Whig timidity. Among these were men like Samuel
Whitbread or Francis Burdett whom Byron had long adopted as

his political heroes, since the time of the Luddite riots or earlier. Hobhouse, like Byron, found these leaders to be the most attractive figures on the political stage, and soon after his return to England in 1819, he attached his fortunes to theirs, to those of Sir Francis Burdett in particular, the Member for Westminster since 1807.

However, the new ferment called for new guidance, new leadership and new leaders, and an assembly of aspirants offered their services, especially those who had shown some awareness of how the printing press could play a new role in political life. One of these was William Cobbett, a man of genius in the use of his pen but gifted too in his knowledge of the new phenomenon of popular politics. A second was Richard Carlile, a pamphleteer and printer combined – as they had often to be in those times – who kept an earlier radical tradition alive by printing the works of Thomas Paine; he had not the journalistic genius of the others but his indomitable spirit made good any deficiencies. A third was Henry Hunt, a gentleman farmer by trade without any skill as a writer who could nonetheless excel all his rivals on the platform, and who had the political insight to recognize what powerful popular forces were at work in the England of his time. Henry Hunt was by no means always on good terms with his fellow leaders of the people; rather, he always seemed to be scrutinizing their methods of operation with suspicion and jealousy. It was Robert Southey who nick-named him 'Orator Hunt', and we can only regret that Byron did not know the origin of the sneer. Hunt somehow embodied best the rising anger of a people denied the most elementary rights, and yet, at the very same moment, had the revolutionary intelligence to forswear the resort to violence – which is just what the Government and its *agents provocateurs* wanted. Not that anyone in those times, not even Hunt, used the word 'democracy'. He called it the struggle for parliamentary reform, universal suffrage, the ballot. His followers raised the cry 'Hunt and Liberty', thus adapting the phrase from 'Wilkes and Liberty'; Hunt understood better than his famous forbear what it meant. He had earned his position as a leader in some notable clashes with the authorities, even before he stepped to the very centre of the stage, to play a foremost role in a key scene in English revolutionary history, the Peterloo massacre of 16 August 1819, when the panic-stricken Manchester magistrates incited the yeomanry to run amok, killing eleven innocent demonstrators and maiming many more. Only Hunt's presence of mind and his notorious white hat warded off a worse disaster. No one, not even the leading politicians in that 'dungeon Parliament' nor the judges who dispatched him to his 'Ilchester Bastile', as he called it, nor even Byron we must add, in a misguided remonstrance from faraway Ravenna, could rob him of the dignity which he displayed at that hour. Andrew Marvell's comment might apply:

> He nothing common did or mean
> Upon that memorable scene.

However, Henry Hunt's real role was not seen in that light at the time – except maybe by himself. Years passed before something like the truth of his part could be unravelled, and one excuse for this injustice to his reputation may be that in the aftermath of Peterloo it was legitimate for personal feelings and accomplishments to be submerged. Sir Francis Burdett, for example, read the report of the massacre and sat down at once to write a letter to his electors of Westminster to express his

> shame, grief and indignation . . . What, kill men unarmed, unresisting: and gracious God, women too! disfigured, maimed, cut down, and trampled on by Dragoons. Is this England? This a Christian land? . . . Will the gentlemen of England support or wink at such proceedings? They have a great stake in their country; they hold great estates, and they are bound in duty and in honour to consider them as retaining fees on the part of their country, for upholding its rights and liberties; surely they will at length awake and find they have duties to perform. They can never stand tamely by as lookers-on whilst bloody Neros rip open their mother's womb; they must join the general voice, loudly demanding justice and redress . . . .

No one could doubt the strength of Sir Francis' appeal, including Lord Sidmouth at the Home Office. The printer was summoned to the Home Office and Sir Francis was charged, convicted and sentenced to Newgate for having published a malicious and seditious libel. Henry Hunt a few months later was sentenced to two years' imprisonment.

How soon Byron read a report about Peterloo, how soon he could have been expected to appreciate what had really happened, is not at all clear even now; indeed the misrepresentation of Henry Hunt's role started in the early months after the event, and was hardly rectified for generations. Byron's own first reactions were concealed in some hints or half-hints in his correspondence. No evidence exists that he ever read the substantial report in *The Times* or the Burdett letter. If he had, taking account of his admiration for Burdett personally, and of the Burdett political creed as stated in the letter, he would surely have responded more eagerly. As it was, the hints came, the very first to Kinnaird on 19 August: 'Do you think there will be a row? Civil war or anything in that line?' Or to Hobhouse on the 20th: 'Philosophy would be in vain – let us try action. – In England I see and read of reform 'and there never were such troublesome times especially for *Constables*' . . . There is much of Hunt and Harrison and Sir Charles (Linsey) Wolseley – but we hear nothing of you and Burdett.' And then to Augusta on 15 October:

If there is to be a scene in England to which all seems approaching – by the violence of the political parties – you will probably see me in England in the next spring but I have not decided yet the part I ought to take. They say in Italy that 'Che nasce Patrizio innora Patrizio' and I am not democrat enough to like a tyranny of blackguards – such fellows as Bristol Hunt – are a choice of evils with Castlereagh – except that a Gentleman scoundrel is always preferable to a vulgar one. To me it appears that you are on the eve of a revolution which won't be made with rose water however. If so I will be one. As Liston says, 'I love a row.'

And then again, to Kinnaird, on 26 October, a more considered view:

You may write somewhat oftener – Mr Galignani's messenger gives the outline of your public affairs – but I see no results – you have no man yet – (always excepting Burdett – & you & H[obhouse] and the Gentlemanly leaven of your two-penny loaf of rebellion) don't forget however my charge of horse – and commission for the Midland Counties and by the holies! You shall have your account in decimals. – Love to Hobby – but why leave the Whigs?

Why leave the Whigs? Some of them at least had been good allies at the time of his own departure. And then again to Murray, on 8 November: 'What folly is this of Carlile's trial – why let him have the honours of a martyr? it will only advertise the books in question.'

Over that winter of 1820 Byron became momentarily estranged from some of his natural political associates in England, Hobhouse among the foremost, who was elected as a Member for Westminster in the closing weeks of the year of Peterloo. Apart even from the political implications, he should have shown more of his natural personal sensitivity in recognizing how significant was this series of events in the career of his friend. Moreover, considering how much affinity he felt with Burdett's politics, how much he was inclined to look to Burdett as a leader, he might have been expected to be complimenting Hobhouse on his discernment in starting his political career under such excellent auspices. The explanation seems to be that he was much more absorbed in the developing Italian political situation which threatened to break out into actual fighting, with his newfound friends the Gambas actually involved, and that his estimate of English politics remained congealed at an earlier stage when the Whig leaders were mostly resisting the Tories. When, soon after his election, Hobhouse was transferred from the House to Newgate, Byron greeted the event from afar with his bantering but still brutal:

> Wherefore do you hate the Whigs
> My boy Hobbie O
> Because I would reform the den
> As Member for the Mobby O.

However, at this point, Hobhouse, like Burdett, knew what he was talking about and was deeply hurt by Byron's quite unexpected assault, and he replied with a reference to a quotation from *A Midsummer Night's Dream* which must have touched Byron's heart:

> Is all the counsel that we two have shared,
> The sisters' vows, the hours that we have spent
> When we have chid the hasty-footed time
> For parting us – O, is all forgot
> All schooldays friendships; childhood innocence.

The offending verses had never been intended for publication; they were no more than a piece of 'buffooneries' between them such as they had often exchanged and Murray had no business to publish it. Moreover, as Byron acknowledged when the two men next met, he had truly been ignorant of the precise political situation in England when he wrote it. But again, in April of that year, when the dust might have been expected to have settled and when Byron's verdict might have been taken as a more comprehensive one, he expressed his view in a manner which seemed to cut a deeper gulf between Hobhouse's new-found radicalism and his own unreconstructed Whiggery.

> By yesterday's post I had yrs. of the 31st. Ulto. – The papers told me that you had got *out*, and got *in*, I am truly glad of both events – though I could have wished the one had had no connection with the other. – I beg your pardon for confounding you with Hunt and Cobbett – but I thought that the Manchester business had effected a reconciliation – at least you all (bating Cobbett) attended one meeting, soon after it – but I am glad to hear you have nothing to do with those scoundrels – I can understand and enter into the feelings of Mirabeau and La Fayette – but I have no sympathy with Robespierre – and Marat – whom I look upon as in no respect worse than those two English ruffians – if they once had the power. – You will hardly suppose that I should deny to you – what I said to another – I *did* use such an expression

on the subject of Bristol Hunt – and I repeat it – I do not think the man who would overthrow all laws – should have the benefit of any, he who plays the Tyler or Cade might find the Walworth or Iden – he who enacts the Clodius – the Milo – and what is there in Bristol Hunt and Cobbett – *so* honest as the former – or *more* patriotic than the latter? – 'Arcades Ambo' blackguards both. – Why our classical education alone – should teach us to trample on such unredeemed dirt as the *dis*honest bluntness – the ignorant brutality, the unblushing baseness of these two miscreants; – and all who believe in them. – I think I have neither been an illiberal man nor an unsteady man upon politics – but I think also that if the Manchester Yeomanry had cut down *Hunt only* – they would have done their duty – as it was – they committed *murder* both in what they did – and what they did *not* do, – in butchering the weak instead of *piercing* the wicked, in assailing the seduced instead of the seducer – in punishing the poor starving populace, instead of that pampered and dinnered blackguard who is only less contemptible than his predecessor *Orator Henley* because he is more mischievous. – What I say thus – I say as publicly as you please – if to praise such fellows be the price of popularity – I spit upon it, as I would in their faces. –

Upon reform you have long known my opinion – but *radical* is a new word since my time – it was not in the political vocabulary in 1816 – when I left England – and I don't know what it means – is it uprooting? – As to yourself it is not in the power of political events to change my sentiments – I am rejoiced to see you in parliament because I am sure you will make a splendid figure in it, and have fought hard to arrive there – and I esteem and admire Burdett as you know – but with these and half a dozen more exceptions – I protest, not against *reform* – but my most thorough contempt and abhorrence – of all that I have seen, heard, or heard of the persons calling themselves *reformers*, *radicals*, and such other names, – I should look upon being free with such men, as much the same as being in bonds with felons. – I am no enemy to liberty however, and you will be glad to hear that there is some chance of it in Italy. . . .

Here was the Byron of 1820, expressing in private correspondence and ready to assert in public, as he particularly mentioned, views which would have found favour, say, with the Holland House of 1814, with the Whigs whom he had no wish to leave or desert. And sometimes these assertions, although never in fact publicly proclaimed, are accepted as his final judgement on the political choices at stake. But no such conclusion is justified. Byron's political view was always being propelled forward by his own reading of the events he saw around him, by the spectacle of the human cruelties he saw inflicted, or the resistance to such encroaching horrors. He found himself responding to these events in his poetry and in his actions. And the years 1820 and 1821 were no exception to this rule; indeed, in one sense, they marked a new start in his appreciation of what was happening to his world. Italy, the beloved country of his adoption, trembled on the verge of a real revolution, one in which men and women would risk their lives and all Europe was threatened by counter-revolution, by the Holy Alliance. Byron understood better than any other man of his time what victory for the Holy Alliance would mean across the whole continent, and he was resolved more than ever to wield more mightily all the weapons at his disposal.

He had been absorbing Italian politics – listening and talking – ever since he first set foot on the land, at Milan in 1816. He was ready to play his part, and not merely as a sympathetic spectator, in 'a push against those rascally Austrians who have desolated Lombardy, and threaten the rest of this bel paese'. A few days before, in a letter to Murray, he had been even more specific:

> . . . for I shall think it by far the most interesting spectacle and moment in existence – to see the Italians send the Barbarians of all nations back to their own dens. – I have lived long enough among them – to feel more for them as a nation than for any other people in existence – but they

want Union – and they want principle – and I doubt their success – however they will try probably – and if they do – it will be a good cause – no Italian can hate an Austrian more than I do – unless it be the English – the Austrians seem to me the most obnoxious race under the Sky. – But I doubt – if anything be done – it won't be so quietly as in Spain; – to be sure Revolutions are not to be made with Rose-water – where there are foreigners as Masters. . . .

And then a few days later an unforgettable English–Italian contrast:

We are on the verge of a *row* here – last night they have over-written all the city walls – with 'up with the Republic ['] & ['] death to the Pope &c. &c,' this would be nothing in London where the walls are privileged – & where when Somebody went to Chancellor Thurlow to tell him as an alarming sign that he had seen 'Death to the king' on <Hyde> the park wall – old Thurlow asked him if he had ever seen 'C – t' chalked on the same place, to which the alarmist responding in the affirmative – Thurlow resumed '& so have I for these last 30 years and yet it never made my p--k stand.' – But here it is a different thing[;] they are not used to such fierce political inscriptions – and the police is all on the alert, and the Cardinal glares pale through all his purple.

He had sense enough to distinguish between what he read and what he could see with his own eyes: 'I can't pretend to foresee what will happen among you Englishers at this distance – but I vaticinate a *row* in Italy – & in which case I don't know that I won't have a finger in it. – I dislike the Austrians and think the Italians infamously oppressed . . . .'

It was pardonable for him to consider the Italian repression more strict and serious than what he knew of England. There he had to contend with his own publishers and the supposed opinion on grounds of taste; in Italy itself almost all his Italian poems, with Canto IV of *Childe Harold* at the head of the list, were suppressed. His brave Italian translator Leoni lamented:

272

You are probably not unaware that my version of the 4th Canto of Childe Harold has been confiscated everywhere; and I myself have been obliged to suffer vexations both ridiculous and absurd in spite of the fact that some verses were excluded by the censor. But as prohibition usually increases curiosity, so that ode [poem] on Italy is more sought after than ever, and I am thinking of having it reprinted in England without excluding anything. – Wretched condition of this nation of mine! if one can call a nation a land so debased by fortune, by men and by its very own self.

Byron had every excuse for insisting that his Pulci translation should not be bowdlerized by some prim, reactionary censor. In the shadow of the great Dante, Luigi Pulci had been dismissed by even such an authority as John Milton as both ludicrous and scurrilous. But Byron had learnt better; Pulci had taken his place, and a most eminent and honoured one, among the Italian poets whom he had studied most carefully since his arrival in Venice. He had no false modesty about the value he set on his extremely effective translation of *Morgante Maggiori* and he insisted with all the emphasis at his command, *'I won't have a line omitted.'* Partly this was a proper estimate of the trouble and skill he had lavished on his wonderful discovery, and partly he wanted him as a shield: 'Pulci must answer for his own irreligion', which meant that Byron would gladly answer for it too. He also tried his hand, although not quite so successfully, at some direct Dante translations. Here he had the assistance of many leading Ravennese who had 'all the finer passages of Dante at the finger ends', and especially, of course, of Teresa herself who could almost repeat any part of the *Divine Comedy*. For all these excellent reasons, he absorbed the same air as Dante. 'I was never tired of my rides in the pine-forest: it breathes of the *Decameron*; it is poetical ground. Francesca lived, and Dante was exiled and died at Ravenna. There is something inspiring in such an air.'* However, for all Teresa's tuition and

---

* These quotations appear in Thomas Medwin's *Conversations of Lord Byron*, 1824, a source which has always to be treated with suspicion, since several

Dante's embraces, it was much more to Pulci or politics that he would naturally turn. Even in the midst of the passion which kept him from other pursuits, he wrote, in a few months, his first full-scale drama.

The idea of writing about Marino Faliero, the Doge of Venice executed and disgraced for high treason, had occurred to Byron ever since he first saw the decapitated corpse on the Giant's stairway in the Doge's Palace on his first arrival in Venice, or maybe the first prompting could be traced back even further to his reading of Thomas Otway's *Venice Preserved*. However, the Doge in that portrait was a very different one from the hero whose true history Byron claimed to have disinterred, with much careful labour, from the records. So when he settled down actually to write, in the spring of 1820, the theme had been maturing in his mind for four years, a longer period of preparation than he usually allowed, and the moment when he chose to write was significant too. Venice, Bologna, Ravenna, everywhere where he moved, was alive with conspiracies and rumours of revolution. The chief conspirators, apart even from the Doge, Israel Bertuccio and Philip Catendaro could be seen everywhere he went,

> – not numerous nor yet too few
> For their great purpose; they have arms, and means,
> And hearts, and hopes, and faith, and patient courage . . .

They were real heroes who stayed steadfast to the end, never staining their cause of just rebellion against a tyranny which deserved to be overthrown. The Doge himself had not quite the same plain case to present; he had sworn a special ducal oath of allegiance to the state against which he conspired. Yet the reader's sympathies are overwhelmingly retained on his side. No wavering develops even when one of his fellow patricians, in a brilliant scene, wheedles the fatal confession about the plot

---

of his supposedly verbatim reports can be disproved by other evidence. However, these quotations also appear in Frederick L. Beaty's *Byron and the Story of Francesca De Rimini*, the best piece on the subject.

from the weakest nerved or most compassionate of the plotters.
Even so and at every turn and extremity, the Doge dominates
the scene – and the future:

> This gives us to eternity – we'll meet it
> As men whose triumph is not in success
> But who can make their own minds all in all,
> Equal to every fortune.

The situation of the Doge has been likened to Byron's own at
the time: a patrician leader cut off from, and cast out by, his fellow patricians, one who despises the mob even while he is
tempted or impelled to act with it, the Whig aristocrat incapable
of joining the blackguards with all his heart and intelligence.
And the Venice of Marino Faliero did bear many likenesses to
the Venice conquered and betrayed by the French, by Napoleon,
by the Austrians:

> Yes, the hours
> Are silently engendering of the day,
> When she, who built 'gainst Attila a bulwark,
> Shall yield, and bloodlessly and basely yield
> Unto a bastard Attila, without
> Shedding so much blood in her last defence
> As these old veins, oft drain'd in shielding her,
> Shall pour in sacrifice. – She shall be bought
> And sold, and be an appanage to those
> Who shall despise her! – She shall stoop to be
> A province for an empire, petty town
> in lieu of capital, with slaves for senates,
> Beggars for nobles, pandars for a people!

Time and again, throughout the play, it is the effective
resistance to the tyrants which mounts the tension:

> They cannot quench the memory of those
> Who would have hurled them from their guilty thrones,
> And such examples will find heirs, though distant.

That surely is the inescapable, reiterated moral which survives even the Doge's final curse on his city:

> Gehenna of the waters! Thou sea Sodom!
> Thus I devote thee to the infernal Gods!
> Thee and thy serpent seed!

And even then the climax is not quite touched:

> Strike as I would
> Have struck those tyrants! Strike deep as my curse
> And the People still murmur,
> Then they have murder'd him who would have freed us.

It is hard to imagine after this how it could be occasionally argued that the main subject matter was something different, namely the political situation in England, with its revolutionary potentialities, and Byron's ambivalent attitude towards it. If so (to pose no more than one insoluble question), who do Israel Bertuccio or Philip Catendaro, who went valiantly to their deaths for their revolutionary cause, represent; who are their English counterparts? There are none in Byron's eyes. But he knew them well in the Italian roles, and if he *was* the Doge of Venice, he knew well enough which side he was on, without any doubts on his political intelligence being cast by modern professors. He could not have cursed the Gehenna of the waters, the degradation of Venice, if any reconciliation was to be contemplated with those who suppressed the revolution and sought to heap such eternal infamy on his name. The only resort left to him was the appeal to posterity, the hope that in some future age, some Byron might come to the rescue of his reputation.

Moreover, it must be noted – but not, I agree, as a conclusive argument – that Byron always claimed to be writing historical plays, not political ones. By this, I presume he meant that he was trying to elucidate what truly happened in historical situations – what was the real motivation of the men and women involved – rather than describing, consciously or unconsciously, a modern analogy. No doubt he did sometimes stray into these fields, and none should wish that he had refrained. But he was also truly interested in the discovery of what actually had happened. In his Preface to *Marino Faliero* he included the charming sentence: 'I know no justification at any distance of time for calumniating an historical character; surely truth belongs to the dead, and to the unfortunate.' Without Byron, the name of Marino Faliero might still have stood as a synonym of treachery in the highest place. The picture of Byron pacing through the streets of Venice in search of truth, to add a necessary stroke to his leading character as he ransacked the archives, is not so familiar, but there it is in his own account:

> The black veil which is painted over the place of Marino Faliero amongst the doges, and the Giant's Staircase where he was crowned, and discrowned, and decapitated, struck forcibly upon my imagination, as did his fiery character and strange story. I went in 1819 in search of his tomb more than once to the church San Giovanni e San Paolo, and as I was standing before the monument of another family, a priest came up to me and said, 'I can show you finer monuments than that.' I told him that I was in search of that of the Faliero family, and particularly of the Doge Marino's. 'Oh,' said he, 'I will show it you;' and conducting me to the outside, pointed out a sarcophagus in the wall with an illegible inscription. He said that it had been in a convent adjoining, but was removed after the French came, and placed in its present situation; that he had seen the tomb opened at its removal; there were still some bones remaining, but no positive vestige of the decapitation.

One cannot help wondering also whether he discussed with the priest in the church the delicate matter of Marino's faith, often a question in dispute among the most eminent of the Doge's followers and a further reason for Byron's affection for the city. Marino had explained his suspicion that one cause of the way his fellow patricians had turned upon him was traceable to the treatment he had meted out to some priest who dared advise him of his duty. And when his wife Angiolina had appealed to his Christian instincts, he had made a most memorable reply:

Angiolina:	Heaven bids us to forgive our enemies.
Doge:	Doth Heaven forgive her own?
	Is Satan saved
	From wrath eternal?

Whatever may have been lacking in *Marino Faliero* as a drama, he was entitled to protest in his letters home: 'all I have done is meant to be purely Venetian.' And then again: 'It is full of republicanism – so will find no favour in Albemarle Street.' And the Doge himself was a true Venetian, one worthy to stand beside such a man as Paolo Sarpi, ready, if need be, in the interests of Venice, to defy the Pope of Rome, or even higher religious authorities.

TEN

Venice–Ravenna III

Who is the hero of Paradise Lost? Why Satan.

12 May 1821

Throughout most of his stay in Ravenna – it lasted for nearly three years – the Venetian influence took pride of place in his writing, merging at first with other Italian themes and then with the wider political ideas which came to dominate his mind. The evidence is there in his letters and his poetry. But some observers have judged the Ravenna years in quite different terms; his interest in the Italian politics is dismissed as at best amateurish and at worst dilettante. Indeed, most curiously, it is claimed that his activities and his output confirm the charges about his self-absorption, his grotesque egotism. A most notable critic in this field is Henry James, the same who had derided the Byronic landmarks of defiance. He presented, in the volume quoted before, a not easily forgettable description of Byron in Ravenna:

> If Dante's tomb is not Dantesque, so neither is Byron's house Byronic, being a homely, shabby, two-storied dwelling, directly on the street, with as little as possible of isolation and mystery. In Byron's time it was an inn, and it is a rather curious reflection that 'Cain' and the 'Vision of Judgement' should have been written at an hotel. The fact supplies a commanding precedent for self-abstraction to tourists at once sentimental and literary. I must declare that my acquaintance with Ravenna considerably increased my esteem for Byron and helped to renew my faith in the sincerity of his inspiration. A man so much *de son temps* as the

279

author of the above-named and other pieces can have spent two long years in this stagnant city only by the help of taking a great deal of disinterested pleasure in his own genius . . . .

This may sound, at first hearing, more like James himself; but he persists:

He had indeed a notable pastime – the various churches are adorned with monuments of ancestral Guicciolis – but it is none the less obvious that Ravenna, fifty years ago, would have been an intolerably dull residence for a foreigner of distinction unequipped with intellectual resources. The hour one spends with Byron's memory there is almost compassionate. After all, one says to oneself as one turns away from the grandiloquent little slab in front of his house and looks down the deadly provincial vista of the empty, sunny street, the author of so many superb stanzas asked less from the world than he gave it.

However, during this period when he took such a disinterested and, we must suppose, disproportionate pleasure in his own genius, he wrote (apart from the two pieces already mentioned, *Cain* and *The Vision of Judgement*, and apart from many lesser works) three other major poems and plays; Canto V of *Don Juan*; the three plays, *Marino Faliero*, *The Two Foscari* and *Sardanapalus*; and a long prose argument about poetry in general and Pope in particular.* It could be claimed that the period was as productive as any in his whole life, especially since he had a revolution and a love affair on his hands at the same time.†

* See Appendix II.
† The manner in which the myth is perpetuated may be illustrated by a sentence from a review by Bevis Hillier of Volume VIII of Marchand's edition of the Letters in the *Sunday Times*: 'The three main poems Byron managed to write in this year of dabbling in revolutions – "Sardanapalus", "Cain" and "The Vision of Judgment" seem to confirm that he mistook his poetic vocation. It is the ephemeral satire of the "Vision", aimed at the Poet Laureate, Southey, and not the grand historical designs of the other two that has weathered best.'

A brief selection from his host of comments, in the autumn of 1820 and the first months of 1821, may indicate the hopes and fears he had for his Italian friends and the Italian cause. Often his views are expressed with wit or mordancy but this should not permit the deduction that he must be convicted of flippancy too:

August 31: Depend upon it there will be savage work if once they begin here – the French Courage proceeds from vanity – the German from phlegm – the Turkish from fanaticism & opium – the Spanish from pride – the English from coolness – the Dutch from obstinacy – the Russian from insensibility – but the *Italian from anger* – so you'll see that they will spare nothing.

September 7: My last letters will have taught you to expect an explosion here – it was primed & loaded – but they hesitated to fire the train. – One of the Cities shirked from the league. – I cannot write more at large – for a thousand reasons. – Our *'puir hill folk'* offered to strike – and to raise the first banner. – But Bologna paused – and now 'tis Autumn and the season half over – 'Oh Jerusalem! Jerusalem! ['] the Huns are on the Po – but if once they pass it on their march to Naples – all Italy will rise behind them – the Dogs – the Wolves – may they perish like the Host of Sennacherib! – If you want to publish the Prophecy of Dante – you never will have a better time.

And that last is what the Austrian censors thought too. In October, he offered his support to the Neapolitan conspirators:

An Englishman, a friend to liberty, having understood that the Neapolitans permit even foreigners to contribute to the good cause, is desirous that they should do him the honour of accepting a thousand louis, which he takes the liberty of offering. Having already, not long since, been an ocular witness of the despotism of the Barbarians in the States occupied by them in Italy, he sees, with the enthusiasm natural to a cultivated man, the [glorious] determination of the Neapolitans to assert their well-won independence. As a member of the English House of Peers, he would be a traitor to the principles which placed the reigning family of England on the throne, if he were not grateful for the noble lesson so lately given both to people and to kings. The offer which he desires to make is small in itself, as must always be that presented from an individual to a nation; but he trusts that it will not be the last they will receive from his countrymen. His distance from the frontier, and the feeling of his personal incapacity to contribute efficaciously to the service of the nation, prevents him from proposing himself as worthy of the lowest commission, for which experience and talent might be requisite. But if, as a mere volunteer, his presence were not a burden to whomsoever he might serve under, he would repair to whatever place the Neapolitan Government might point out, there to obey the orders and participate in the dangers of his commanding officer, without any other motive than that of sharing the destiny of a brave nation, defending itself against the self-called Holy Alliance, which but combines the vice of hypocrisy with despotism.

And here, incidentally, was Byron's first challenge to the so-called Holy Alliance; he understood the menace to freedom across Europe as soon as anybody. And this too, to Lady Byron, in October, about his daughter:

Pray let her be taught Italian, – I hope by the time she is twenty that Italy will be free and regenerated – Alas! at what a price of blood & butchery – must it be so – but anything is better than those Barbarians at the gate – if you had seen their infamous tyranny – their ignorant atrocity in Lombardy – & wherever they set their hoofs; – it would make even your temperate blood boil. – Imagine the effect it must have upon these 'children of the Sun'. – Their passage of the Po will be followed by confiscations and arrests and insurrection – besides the Neapolitan war. – The Suspicion of the government here is extreme – even of Strangers – (most of whom have retired) they sent an order the other day to *disarm my Servants* (who by the way *did not* carry arms) imagine what must be the state of things when a solitary stranger puts them upon such precautions? – I answered them that they might make what regulations they chose for such servants as were Papal – but they should not disarm *me* – unless by actual force – in a country where they 'shoot a man a week' like Bob Acres 'in the Country'. – They said no more – but there is a general espionage – they seem to dread my influence on the younger men with whom they conceive me to be popular. – This is what they give out themselves. – They are mistaken however – I never was personally popular anywhere – and in Italy popularity at present is limited to *Opera Singers* and will continue to be so – till there is a renewed Rome . . . .

This to Kinnaird, a few days later:

My motives are the almost immediate explosion which must take place in Italy in the impending event of the passage of the Po by the Barbarians now in great force on that river – and the fall further of the English funds in consequence – as your Tory Scoundrels will right or wrong take part in any foreign war . . .

To Kinnaird again:

The affairs of this part of Italy are simplifying – the liberals have delayed till it [is] too late for them to do anything to [the] purpose – If the Scoundrels of Troppau [Troppau was, of course, where the Holy Alliance leaders were meeting] decide on a Massacre (as is probable) the Barbarians will march in by one frontier and the Neapolitans by the other. – They have *both asked* permission of his Holiness – so to do – which is equivalent to asking a man's permission to give him a kick on the a-se – if he grants it, it is a sign that he can't return it. – The worst of all is that this devoted country will become for the six thousandth time since God made man in his own image – the seat of war. – I recollect Spain in

1809 – and the Morea & parts of Greece in 1810–1811 – when Veli Pacha was on his way to combat the Russians – (the Turkish armies make their *own country* like an enemy's on the march) and a small [sketch?] also of my own County of Nottingham under the Luddites when we were burning the Frames – and sometimes the Manufactories – so that I have a tolerable idea of what may ensue. Here all is suspicion and terrorism – bullying – arming – and disarming – the Priests scared – the people gloomy – and the Merchants buying up corn to supply the armies. – I am so pleased with the last piece of Italic patriotism – that I have underlined it for your remark – it is just as if our Hampshire farmers should prepare magazines for any two Continental Scoundrels who could land and fight it out in New forest.

And to Murray:

Of the state of things here – it would be difficult & not very prudent to speak at large – the Huns opening all letters – I wonder if they can read them when they have opened them? – if so they may see in my most legible hand – that I think them damned Scoundrels and Barbarians – their Emperor a fool – & themselves more fools than he – all of which they may send to Vienna – for anything I care. – They have got themselves masters of the Papal police and are bullying away, – but some day or other they will pay for all. – It may not be very soon – because these unhappy Italians have no union, nor consistency among themselves, but I suppose that Providence will get tired of them at last – & that God is not an Austrian.

Of course he had his own interest, and why not? To Murray again: 'You are losing (like a Goose) the best time for publishing the Dante and the Tragedy – *now* is the moment for Italian subjects.'

With the New Year, the commotions around him and his responses cut deeper. North and South, the Italy whose thrust for unity and independence he had forecast and fostered, did show signs of real advance, although Byron, the realist, never underrated the perils:

January 5. Weather cold – carriage open, and inhabitants somewhat savage – rather treacherous and highly inflamed by politics. Fine fellows, though, – good materials for a nation. Out of chaos God made a world, and out of high passions comes a people. . . .

. . .

I wonder what figure these Italians will make in a regular row. I sometimes think that, like the Irishman's gun (somebody had sold him a crooked one), they will only do for 'shooting round a corner;' at least, this sort of shooting has been the late tenor of their exploits. And yet, there are materials in this people, and a noble energy, if well directed. But who is to direct them? No matter. Out of such times heroes spring. Difficulties are the hot-beds of high spirits, and Freedom the mother of the few virtues incident to human nature.

A forecast of Garibaldi?

January 9: At eight went out – heard some news. They say the King of Naples has declared, by couriers from Florence, to the *Powers* (as they call now those wretches with crowns) that his Constitution was compulsive, &c., &c., and that the Austrian barbarians are placed again on *war* pay, and will march. Let them – 'they come like sacrifices in their trim', the hounds of hell! Let it still be a hope to see their bones piled like those of the human dogs at Morat, in Switzerland, which I have seen.

Heard some music. At nine the usual visitors – news, *war*, or rumours of war. Consulted with P. G., &c., &c. They mean to *insurrect* here, and are to honour me with a call thereupon. I shall not fall back; though I don't think them in force or heart sufficient to make much of it. But, *onward*! it is now the time to act, and what signifies *self*, if a single spark of that which would be worthy of the past can be bequeathed unquenchedly to the future? It is not one man, nor a million, but the *spirit* of liberty which must be spread. The waves which dash upon the shore are, one by one, broken, but yet the *ocean* conquers, nevertheless. It overwhelms the

285

Armada, it wears the rock, and, if the *Neptunians* are to be believed, it has not only destroyed, but made a world. In like manner, whatever the sacrifice of individuals, the great cause will gather strength, sweep down what is rugged, and fertilize (for *sea-weed* is *manure*) what is cultivable. And so, the mere selfish calculation ought never to be made on such occasions; and, at present, it shall not be computed by me. I was never a good arithmetician of chances, and shall not commence now.

Was this just an idle rhetorical prophecy? Not to the young Mazzini who read and marked it.

> *January 13*: Dined – news come – the *Powers* mean to war with the peoples. The intelligence seems positive – let it be so – they will be beaten in the end. The king-times are fast finishing. There will be blood shed like water, and tears like mist; but the peoples will conquer in the end. I shall not live to see it but I foresee it.
>
> . . .
>
> If the Neapolitans have but a single Massaniello amongst them, they will beat the bloody butchers of the crown and sabre. Holland, in worse circumstances, beat the Spains and Philips; America beat the English; Greece beat Xerxes; and France beat Europe, till she took a tyrant; South America beats her old vultures out of their nest; and, if these men are but firm in themselves, there is nothing to shake them from without.

These were included in his New Year notes, of which Mazzini became a devoted, inspired reader. 'What is Poetry? – The feeling of a Former world and Future.' And this, said the same Mazzini, is 'the best definition I know'. The best definition at least for men of action, and so Mazzini counted him: 'Never did he desert the cause of the peoples; never was he false to human sympathies.' They led to some of the most moving words Byron ever wrote, words which for all their usage have retained their resonance ever since:

February 18: Today I have had no communication with my Carbonari cronies; but, in the mean time, my lower apartments are full of their bayonets, fusils, cartridges, and what not. I suppose that they consider me as a depot, to be sacrificed, in case of accidents. It is no great matter, supposing that Italy could be liberated, who or what is sacrificed. It is a grand object – the very *poetry* of politics. Only think – a free Italy!!!

When he was once asked whether he was the author of a new play on Jerusalem, he replied: how could he be, never having been there? He had never been to Nineveh, but the scene of his new tragedy, *Sardanapalus*, had all the fading splendour of Venice and her empire for a background, and must be accepted as another Venetian play. He said he had been reading about his Assyrian emperor since he was twelve years old, and no doubt that was true, but the precise moment when he chose to write about him was naturally significant. The hated Holy Alliance of Kings – the Alliance which he did more than anyone else to make hated – was preparing to unloose war on the peoples and, more especially, on his own newly-adopted Italian comrades-in-arms. Moreover, Sardanapalus was a more complex character than any other of his heroic creations, and his character developed in the play; the charge that Marino Faliero did not was one of the many criticisms levelled against Byron's dramatic skills. Sardanapalus, both the play and the man, may be the subject of diverse interpretations. Once seen in his full light, with all the shades and shadows and the burning oracle in place, and one must look afresh on Byron in Ravenna, on the eve of what he thought might be terrible events: the renewal in a more pitiless form of the war which had already left such a trail of senseless devastation and human misery.

At first hearing, *Sardanapalus* might seem to be a play about the weakling king, the lover of ease and dissipation, unfit to rule, who merely invites by the appeasement of his rebellious subjects the destruction of himself, his house, his imperial authority. But this would hardly be sufficient material for a tragedy; more a morality play for monarchs of the same kind

into which some sought to convert Marino Faliero, making
him the victim of his follies, not his virtues. Yet, even more than
in Marino's case, the sympathies of the reader are enlisted on
the side of Sardanapalus against all his enemies amid all his
afflictions, even when he enunciates scandalous doctrines.
Even in the early scenes, when the indulgence is at its height or
lowest depth – 'Eat, drink, and love: the rest's not worth a fillip'
– he establishes his dignity and his argument, whether he is
confronting the criticisms of his loyal Salemenes or his beloved
Myrrha. How convincingly he argues to each, and how the
argument contains much more than a momentary validity:

> Oh, thou wouldst have me doubtless set up edicts –
> 'Obey the king – contribute to his treasure –
> Recruit his phalanx – spill your blood at bidding –
> Fall down and worship, or get up and toil.'
> Or thus – 'Sardanapalus on this spot
> Slew fifty thousand of his enemies.
> These are their sepulchres, and this his trophy.'
> I leave such things to conquerors; . . .
> I feel a thousand mortal things about me
> But nothing godlike, – unless it may be
> The thing which you condemn, a disposition
> To love and to be merciful, to pardon
> The follies of my species, and (that's human)
> To be indulgent to my own.

Or again:

> If I must shed blood, it shall be by force.
> Till now, no drop from an Assyrian vein
> Hath flowed for me, nor hath the smallest coin
> Of Nineveh's vast treasures e'er been lavished
> On objects which could cost her sons a tear:
> If then they hate me, 'tis because I hate not:
> If they rebel, 'tis because I oppress not.
> Oh, men! ye must be ruled with scythes, not sceptres,
> And mowed down like the grass, else all we reap
> Is rank abundance, and a rotten harvest

Of discontents infecting the fair soil,
Making a desert of fertility.

Could these claims be improved? Yes they could indeed when
he elaborates to Myrrha: 'Why, child, I loathe all war, and war-
riors.' Even she would have it that kings should sometimes be
better feared than loved.

Myrrha:	I speak of civil popular love, *self*-love,
	Which means that men are kept in awe and law,
	Yet not oppressed – at least they must not think so,
	Or, if they think so, deem it necessary,
	To ward off worse oppression, their own passions.
	A King of feasts, and flowers, and wine, and revel,
	And love, and mirth, was never King of Glory.
Sardanapalus:	Glory! what's that?
Myrrha:	Ask of the Gods thy fathers.
Sardanapalus:	They cannot answer; when the priests speak for them,
	'Tis for some small addition to the temple.
Myrrha:	Look to the annals of thine Empire's founders.
Sardanapalus:	They are so blotted o'er with blood, I cannot.
	But what wouldst have? the Empire *has been* founded.
	I cannot go on multiplying empires.

Myrrha has touched them, Sardanapalus and Byron, on one of
their sorest scars: their suspicion of the priests, their special
detestation of the use of church bells to summon men and
women to bloody battles. Sardanapalus brands Beleses, the
soothsayer, as the most contemptible of the conspirators.

Keep thy smooth words and juggling homilies
For those who know thee not.

If the play was ever intended as a judgement on Sardanapalus rather than his assailants, what becomes of these invectives against the holy men who send others to their death, and who remain the immovable targets of his wrath to the end? No one ever knew better: 'With new kings rise new altars.'

At one stage indeed, still in the early Acts, Sardanapalus develops his full humanist doctrine, the kind which Montaigne might have enunciated, and clearly it is not intended to be satire; they talk of the stars:

Beleses: Monarch! respect them.
Sardanapalus: Oh! for that – I love them;
                  I love to watch them in the deep blue vault,
                  And to compare them with my Myrrha's eyes;
                  I love to see their rays redoubled in
                  The tremulous silver of Euphrates' wave,
                  As the light breeze of midnight crisps the broad
                  And rolling water, sighing through the sedges
                  Which fringe its banks: but whether they may be
                  Gods, as some say, or the abodes of Gods,
                  As others hold, or simply lamps of night,
                  Worlds – or the lights of Worlds – I know nor care not.
                  There's something sweet in my uncertainty
                  I would not change for your Chaldean lore . . .
                  That there are worse things betwixt earth and heaven
                  Than him who ruleth many and slays none;
                  And, hating not himself, yet loves his fellows
                  Enough to spare even those who would not spare him
                  Were they once masters – but that's doubtful. Satraps!
                  Your swords and persons are at liberty
                  To use them as ye will – but from this hour
                  I have no call for either.

But what happens, it may still be insisted, in the crisis? Is it not the case that 'the king of peace' is overthrown and destroyed, that he who sought 'but to be loved, not worshipped', is trampled down by those who know what force means and how it must be allowed to rule? And what does Sardanapalus mean – what does Byron mean – by the holocaust in which emperor and empire are all consumed, standing thus as a warning to all ensuing times? Is it meant to mean no more than that kings should keep their subjects in their menial place, not tempt them with touches of magnanimity which can in turn only encourage insolence and rebellion: that the old war drums should be allowed, and encouraged, to resound and claim fresh victims as they did before? The play and the moral have been read thus; if so, it is hard to imagine Byron bothering to write it, the more so since he, through Sardanapalus, gives warning at the end against such monstrous misinterpretation.

> So much for monuments that have forgotten
> Their very record.

If the destruction of the Assyrian empire meant no more than this, why should Byron, the war-hater, have stopped to take notice?

The real answer must be offered in quite different terms. Sardanapalus, the weakling, shows that he is fully capable of brave deeds: his hatred of pain, his scepticism, his love of peace have nothing to do with cowardice. He will not yield to sudden acts of vengeance; he will not savage the herald who brings him evil news – 'My life's last act shall not be one of wrath' – he will not revert to the old, evil Assyrian tradition.

> I would not so purchase
> The empire of Eternity. Hence – hence –
> Old Hunter of the earliest brutes! and ye,
> Who hunted fellow-creatures as if brutes!
> Once bloody mortals – and now bloodier idols,
> If your priests lie not! And thou, ghastly Beldame!
> Dripping with dusky gore, and trampling on
> The carcasses of Inde – away! away! . . .

291

> I am content: and, trusting in my cause,
> Think we may yet be victors and return
> To peace – the only victory I covet.
> To me war is no glory – conquest no
> Renown. To be forced thus to uphold my right
> Sits heavier on my heart than all the wrongs
> These men would bow me down with. Never, never
> Can I forget this night, even should I live
> To add it to the memory of others.
> I thought to have made mine inoffensive rule
> An era of sweet peace 'midst bloody annals,
> A green spot amidst desert centuries,
> On which the Future would turn back and smile,
> And cultivate, or sigh when it could not
> Recall Sardanapalus' golden reign.
> I thought to have made my realm a paradise,
> And every moon an epoch of new pleasures.
> I took the rabble's shouts for love – the breath
> Of friends for truth – the lips of woman for
> My only guerdon – so they are, my Myrrha;
> Kiss me. Now let them take my realm and life!
> They shall have both, but never *thee*!

Just before the end too he speaks to his Myrrha, his Teresa, when she talks of despair, in a language to which Byron had often resorted at the moments of last extremity:

> No: not despair precisely: when we know
> All that can come, and how to meet it, our
> Resources, if firm, may merit a more noble
> Word than this to give it utterance.

It is impossible to believe that Byron ever believed that the fate of Sardanapalus or Myrrha was a just one, especially when one recalls their dramatic opponents. 'The light to lesson ages' was a magnificent flame of Byronic defiance – if not enough to touch the heart of Henry James.

He turned, too, after only a brief interval, from the works of man to the works of God; never having been able to draw too sharp a distinction between the two. If he was not truly so familiar with Sardanapalus in his boyhood, the claim was certainly true of his next chosen hero. As he felt his full powers as a poet, he wanted to settle his scores with his old Calvinistic God, although the censure could be applied equally to all other Christian faiths where the expulsion from Eden, the fall of man, the branding of Cain, were accepted as worthy traditions for the human race to accept and honour. Byron examined the facts honestly, as he so often did, and found them shameful and shocking and insulting to his reason and his humanity. Above all, the persistence of cruelty and torture, the way men and women were ready to flay one another, and the animals too, might not this evil tradition owe something to the burning sacrifices which we had been taught to bow down before and adore? It was daring enough to adopt Marino Faliero, the decapitated traitor, as his Venetian hero, or the effeminate Sardanapalus to mock martial Assyria; but the idea of choosing Cain, the first murderer, to confound the Christians can still stun the imagination.

Every effort has been made from the day of its publication ever afterwards or even before, to rob the author of *Cain*, in one form or degree or another, of his honesty, his daring, his directness, his undying topicality. His own Preface, by the way, written on the day after he had finished the original draft, and before he could measure the avalanche about to engulf him, is worth studying. He could often explain better – and more wittily – what he was up to than any of his commentators. If anyone objected to his interpretation of the Bible story, he replied 'with Bishop Watson upon similar occasions, when the Fathers were quoted to him as Moderator in the Schools of Cambridge, "Behold the Book" – holding up the Scripture'. As for some accusations against him,

the reader will please to bear in mind (what few choose to recollect), that there is no allusion to a future state in any of the books of Moses nor indeed in the Old Testament (– any such allusion would therefore be an anachronism). For a reason for this extraordinary omission he may consult Warburton's *Divine Legation;* whether satisfactory or not, no better has yet been assigned. I have therefore supposed it new to Cain, without, I hope any perversion of Holy Writ. With regard to the language of Lucifer, it was difficult for me to make him talk like a clergyman upon the same subjects; but I have done what I could to restrain him within the bounds of spiritual politeness. If he disclaims having tempted Eve in the shape of the serpent, it is only because the book of Genesis has not the most distant allusion to anything of the kind, but merely to the Serpent in his Serpentine capacity.

And at this point ignorant modern readers should be reminded that the epigraph for the whole work is taken from that same sacred book: 'Now the Serpent was more subtil than any beast of the field which the Lord God had made.' According to the record, the Serpent was responsible for most of the subsequent trouble; but who was responsible for the Serpent and his much-vaunted subtlety?

Like *Don Juan, Cain* should be read in its one tremendous sweep.* Yet a few passages do epitomize what came to be the creed of the revolutionaries throughout the ages; the spirit of men who reject the decrees of the God who 'loves blood':

* The most complete edition of Cain is Truman Guy Steffan's *Lord Byron's Cain,* from which these extracts are taken: the whole affair, the whole stupendous outburst, text and criticism, is matchlessly presented. However, like most Byron addicts, I must add three other volumes which helped introduce me to the subject: First, John D. Jump's *Byron* which contains, apart from much other excellent comment, biographical and critical, a special, near-perfect chapter on *Cain.* Second, another volume edited by John D. Jump, *Byron: A Symposium,* produced at the time of the 150th anniversary of his death, in 1975. It contains some of the very best essays on him – notably Gilbert Phelps's 'The Byronic Byron', Francis Berry's 'The Poet of Childe Harold' (showing again how the poets write the best prose), and Anne Barton's piece on the political plays – not overlooking John Jump's own contributions.

It is proper to mention here too Edward E. Bostetters' essay 'Byron and the Politics of Paradise' which he contributed to the PMLA (Publications

Lucifer: Souls who dare use their immortality,
          Souls who dare look the omnipotent tyrant in
          His everlasting face and tell him that
          His evil is not good!
          . . .

Lucifer: I tempt none,
          Save with the truth. Was not the tree, the tree
          Of knowledge? And was not the tree of life
          Still fruitful? Did *I* bid her pluck them not?
          Did *I* plant things prohibited within
          The reach of beings innocent, and curious
          By their own inocence? I would have made ye
          Gods; and ev'n He who thrust ye forth, so thrust ye
          Because 'ye should not eat the fruits of life
          And become gods as we.' Were those his words?
Cain: They were, as I have heard from those who
             heard them
          In thunder.
Lucifer: Then who was the demon? He
          Who would not let ye live, or he who would
          Have made ye live forever in the joy
          And pow'r of knowledge?
Cain: Would they had snatched both
          The fruits, or neither!

---

of the Modern Language Association of America) in 1960. The whole is excellent but especially the conclusion in which the political implications are stressed:

> Byron's general intent was undoubtedly, to borrow a metaphor from I. A. Richards, 'to infect his pages with such a virulent culture of doubt' that all unthinking acceptance of dogma would wither in the minds of his readers. And that he clearly intended the play to be an attack on the social and political as well as the religious implications of the dogma is evident from the letter which in November 1822 he wrote to Kinnaird in respect to the uproar over Cain. 'As to myself I shall not be deterred by any outcry; your present public hate me, but they shall not interrupt the march of my mind nor prevent me from telling those who are attempting to trample on all thought, that their thrones shall yet be rocked to their foundations.'

Lucifer: One is yours already;
The other may be still.
Cain: How so?
Lucifer: By being
Yourselves in your resistance. Nothing can
Quench the mind if the mind will be itself
And centre of surrounding things; 'tis made
To sway.
. . .

Cain: But why *war*?
Lucifer: You have forgotten the denunciation
Which drove your race from Eden: war with all
     things
And death to all things and disease to most things
And pangs and bitterness. These were the fruits
Of the forbidden tree.
Cain: But animals –
Did they too eat of it, that they must die?
Lucifer: Your Maker told ye, they were made for you
As you for him. You would not have their doom
Superior to your own? Had Adam not
Fall'n, all had stood.
Cain: Alas, the hopeless wretches!
They too must share my sire's fate like his sons,
Like them too without having shared the apple. . . .
. . .

Lucifer: I have a victor, true, but no superior.
Homage he has from all, but none from me.
I battle it against him, as I battled
In highest heav'n. Through all eternity
And the unfathomable gulfs of Hades
And the interminable realms of space
And the infinity of endless ages,
All, all, will I dispute. And world by world
And star by star and universe by universe
Shall tremble in the balance, till the great
Conflict shall cease, if ever it shall cease,
Which it ne'er shall, till he or I be quenched.

And what can quench our immortality
Or mutual and irrevocable hate?
He as a conqueror will call the conquered
Evil, but what will be the good he gives?
Were I the victor, his works would be deemed
The only evil ones. And you, ye new
And scarce-born mortals, what have been his gifts
To you already, in your little world?

Cain: But few and some of those but bitter.

Lucifer: Back
With me then to thine earth and try the rest
Of his celestial boons to you and yours.

. . .

One good gift has the fatal apple giv'n –
Your reason; let it not be over-swayed
By tyrannous threats to force you into faith
'Gainst all external sense and inward feelings.
Think and endure and form an inner world
In your own bosom, where the outward fails.
So shall you nearer be the spiritual
Nature, and war triumphant with your own.

One of his own most delightful comments on the new production was sent to Thomas Moore – he could never take too
seriously Moore's pretensions to piety.

> Cain [he wrote] comes back and kills Abel in a fit of dissatis
> faction, partly with the politics of Paradise which had
> driven them all out of it, and partly because (as it is written
> in Genesis) Abel's sacrifice was the more acceptable to the
> Deity. I trust that the Rhapsody has arrived – it is in three
> acts, and entitled 'A Mystery', according to the former Chris
> tian custom, and in honour of what it will probably remain
> to the reader.

But of course Byron must have known better than anyone that
the mystery would not be mildly received. He knew how sharp
and bold was the defiance, and the effect was instantaneous. 'In

European literature, which in 1821 lay stifling in the clutches of orthodoxy,' wrote George Brandes, 'there was a perfect revolution when *Cain* appeared, like a herald of revolt. . . .' It is hard to believe that the date of *Cain*'s impact could be fixed so exactly, although 1821 had for liberal, revolutionary Europe a greater significance than for secluded, reactionary England. It was the year when the first post-1815 rebellions were crushed. Byron understood what was happening and Brandes expressed that Europe-wide comprehension:

> Byron revolves in his mind the Bible legend: Adam has been tamed; Eve has been cowed; Abel is a gentle, submissive boy; Cain is young humanity – pondering, questioning, desiring, demanding. . . . This mark of Cain is the mark of humanity – the sign of suffering and immortality. Byron's drama represents the struggle between suffering, searching, striving humanity and that God of hosts, of lightnings, and of storms, whose weakened army are forced to let go a world which is writhing itself free from his embrace.'*

1821, not quite so potently as 1848 but still on an historic scale, was a year of revolutionary uprising and defeat. Byron was an observer, almost a participant, and when the Italian rising was broken, he expressed a twinge of disgust that the resistance had not been stronger and better organized. But this did not mean that he had abandoned the cause. The repression was severe; Byron knew as well as anybody, and must have heard of the fate of so many of his friends. He had been with Hobhouse in 1816, and Hobhouse contrasted those times with what he saw four years later:

---

* George Brandes's *Main Currents in Nineteenth Century Literature* (first published in 1901) can best be read, like *Don Juan*, as a whole; but his *Byron: The Revolutionary Spirit* provides him with his magnificent peroration: the spectacle, as Francis Berry put it, of 'not merely Byron the liberal but Byron the liberator'. Brandes, wrote Sir George Otto Trevelyan, no mean judge, 'has a great, manly, and, to my mind, almost unerring judgement of poetry. . . . I rather take, more than most people, the continental view of Byron.'

I passed through Milan in 1822. All my friends of the Liberal Party had disappeared. Where is Di Breme? 'He is happy in having died; he has seen none of these things' was the reply. And Silvio Pellico? 'In an Hungarian dungeon'. Bosier: too? 'In prison'. De Tracy? 'Also in confinement'. Confalonieri? 'Reprieved on the scaffold; but whether dead or in prison now, no one knows'. Count Luigi Porro? 'In exile'. He had been executed in effigy a few days before my arrival. Such were the bitter fruits of that unhappy attempt to shake off the Austrian yoke in 1821.*

Sardanapalus: A Tragedy, The Two Foscari: A Tragedy, and *Cain: A Mystery* were published in the same volume on 19 December 1821, each taking shelter behind the other, as it were. But nothing could submerge *Cain* altogether, as Hobhouse and several others had wished. It was, and remained, a call to arms, as Byron had designed. *The Two Foscari* was something much milder altogether, undertaken as a play which could be performed, perhaps, when Byron still had reason to believe that *Marino* had not been the failure sometimes supposed. It was most memorable for the lovely outburst about Venice:

> My beautiful, my own
> My only Venice, – *this is breath!*
> Thy breeze
> Thine Adrian sea-breeze, how it fans my face!
> The very winds feel native to my veins
> And cool them into calmness.

But it should also have been no less memorable for a dazzling prose invective against Robert Southey contained in an Appendix, in which Byron set out his views on what was stirring in England. If this, his own addition at the time, had not so frequently been suppressed or overlooked by subsequent publishers, much confusion might have been averted. The idea that any of his plays was designed as a defence of the old order was a

* Hobhouse included this recollection in his book on Italy: *Italy from 1816 to 1860* by Lord Broughton (John Murray 1861).

misapprehension both of his mood and his intention. He did not relish the coming revolution, but was convinced it *would* come if English statesmen and politicians did not show themselves the friends of liberty, making the cause their own instead of leaving it to be usurped by others. In the days of Charles James Fox that was a good Whig doctrine: but who was deserting it? If the Whigs left, he would have to leave the Whigs:

> Another charge made, I am told, in the 'Literary Gazette' is, that I wrote the notes to 'Queen Mab;' a work which I never saw till some time after its publication, and which I recollect showing to Mr Sotheby as a poem of great power and imagination. I never wrote a line of the notes, nor ever saw them except in their published form. No one knows better than their real author, that his opinions and mine differ materially upon the metaphysical portion of that work; though in common with all who are not blinded by baseness and bigotry, I highly admire the poetry of that and his other publications.
>
> Mr Southey, too, in his pious preface to a poem whose blasphemy is as harmless as the sedition of Wat Tyler, because it is equally absurd with that sincere production, calls upon the 'legislature to look to it,' as the toleration of such writings led to the French Revolution: *not* such writings as Wat Tyler, but as those of the 'Satanic School.' This is not true, and Mr Southey knows it to be not true. Every French writer of any freedom was persecuted; Voltaire and Rousseau were exiles, Marmontel and Diderot were sent to the Bastille, and a perpetual war was waged with the whole class by the existing despotism. In the next place, the French Revolution was *not* occasioned by any writings whatsoever, but must have occurred had no such writers ever existed. It is the fashion to attribute everything to the French revolution, and the French revolution to everything but its real cause. That cause is obvious – the government exacted too much, and the people could neither *give* nor *bear more*. Without this, the Encyclopedists

300

might have written their fingers off without the occurrence of a single alteration. And the *English* revolution – (the first, I mean) – what was it occasioned by? The *puritans* were surely as pious and moral as Wesley or his biographer? Acts – acts on the part of government, and *not* writings against them, have caused the past convulsions, and are tending to the future.

I look upon such as inevitable, though no revolutionist: I wish to see the English constitution restored and not destroyed. Born an aristocrat, and naturally one by temper, with the greater part of my present property in the funds, what have *I* to gain by a revolution? Perhaps I have more to lose in every way than Mr Southey, with all his places and presents for panygyrics and abuse into the bargain. But that a revolution is inevitable, I repeat . . .

These passages, apart from their intrinsic value as a guide to what Byron truly thought about these not inconsiderable questions, have a heightened interest because they must have been written just at, or soon after, the time when Shelley had come to Ravenna on a ten-day visit. At once their old fellowship had been renewed; great arguments were pursued deep into the night; and one outcome, apart from this first public defence of Shelley contained in the *Foscari* Appendix, was an arrangement for future collaborations. Byron agreed to move from Ravenna, as Teresa had been urging, since she was no longer allowed to live there. Shelley offered his services in helping the move to Pisa, and Byron eagerly responded to the proposition that he should join with a few others to start a new journal of their own. Shelley broke the news excitedly to Leigh Hunt back in Hampstead. Hunt, and his brother John, naturally shared the excitement. The precious volume with the three plays and the often-suppressed Appendix looked as if it might become one of large significance in the literature of the times: a common publishing venture undertaken by Byron and Shelley, with Hunt offering his by no means insignificant contribution. Indeed, when Leigh Hunt replied, he talked of a triumvirate: 'What! are there not three of us? And ought we not to have as much strength and variety as possible? We will divide the world between us, like the Triumvirate, and you shall be the sleeping partner, if you will; only it shall be with a Cleopatra, and your dreams shall be worth the giving of kingdoms.'

Three other commentators on that 1821 volume deserve a special notice. One was Lord Macaulay who, as we shall see, probably did more than any other great critic to confirm the portrait of the satanic Byron. Neither Sardanapalus nor even Myrrha could help to soften his strictures – he saw Sardanapalus 'more coarsely drawn than any character we can remember', and Myrrha not even being significant enough to find a place in his gallery of Byron's 'women who, like his men, are all of one breed'. Macaulay professed himself baffled how such rampant, unrestrained egotism could exert such charm and did not refrain from the prophecy that 'a few more years will destroy whatever remains of that magical potency which once belonged to the name of Byron.'*

A second commentator was Richard Carlile who wrote his appreciation in Dorchester gaol. His most immaculate hero was the author of *Queen Mab* and no one would ever be allowed to displace him, but Byron, by the publication of *Cain*, had given 'a never-fading respectability to the school of Paine, or the Satanic School as Robert Southey calls it'. Carlile's newspaper, *The Republican*, published from gaol only survived a few issues in the early months of 1822, but he was happy to note what discomfiture it had caused Royal reviewers and Royalty itself.

Another oddity in Byronic criticism of that same volume may be seen in the elaborate and absorbing essay which appeared in the *Edinburgh Review* for 1822. The author has usually been assumed to be Francis Jeffrey, Lord Jeffrey, the guiding spirit of the *Edinburgh Review* and all it stood for in the Whig world, and neither he nor his biographer nor other critics have attempted to question the attribution. However, Hazlitt had thought at one stage that he had been engaged to review the book, and frequent occasions occur when Jeffrey adapted or incorporated

---

* The main Macaulay judgement appears in his essay 'Moore's Life', published in 1830.

considerable passages from his authors in his own essays. 'My Sardanapalus is to be in', Hazlitt wrote just after he had seen Jeffrey in Edinburgh. What happened thereafter has never been unravelled. Here, in the review itself, some passages could certainly not, with any decency, ever have been written by Hazlitt; for *Cain*, we are told, should never have been published:

> It will give great scandal and offence to pious persons in general . . . here the *whole argument* – and a very elaborate and specious argument it is – is directed against the goodness and the power of the Deity, and against the reasonableness of religion in general; and there is no answer so much as attempted to the offensive doctrines that are so strenuously articulated. The Devil and his pupil have the field entirely to themselves. . . .

Hazlitt could never have framed these sentences; they come fittingly enough from Jeffrey's Edinburgh pulpit. Indeed, later in the piece, the thunderous damnation rises to a tone rarely exceeded from any contemporary quarter. Jeffrey was a powerful master of invective when he wanted to be, and here he acted from a sense of overpowering duty. He did believe that Byron, unknowingly perhaps, was doing the Devil's work, and doing it with a seductive skill which no one else could rival.

However, at several other points in the same review, a very different note is struck; it does appear that two hands are at work. A reader is almost startled, even at this late date, to see Byron's assault on Robert Southey extracted from the Appendix and offered to the reader with much commendation both for its style and its content. Hazlitt would have applauded, even if it was not his hand which did the deed. And stranger still, with the writer apologizing for his inconsistency, is the careful, perceptive, laudatory, almost loving analysis of *Sardanapalus*, which on this occasion is differentiated from the rest of Byron's dramatic writing, and accorded a much higher place. Sardanapalus himself 'enjoys life and triumphs in death; and whether in prosperous or adverse circumstances, his soul smiles out superior to evil'. But, of course, 'the chief charm and vivifying angel of the piece is Myrrha . . . a beautiful, heroic, devoted and ethereal being – in love with the generous and infatuated monarch – ashamed of loving a barbarian – and using all her influence over him to ennoble as well as to adorn his existence, *and* to arm him against the terrors of its close. Her voluptuousness is that of the heart – her heroism of the affections.'

Hazlitt was reading *Sardanapalus* at the very hour when he was at the height of his affair with his Sarah, and he affected to see a likeness between her and Myrrha. 'Myrrha is most like S.W., only I am not like Sardanapalus,' he wrote while he still thought he was to be the reviewer. It is hard to believe that he did not contribute the paragraphs in the review about *Sardanapalus*, and pleasant to reflect how Myrrha and Teresa and his Sarah, maybe, started to reform his ideas of Byron.* For, as he kept thinking of his Sarah, while separated from her in his Berwick inn, on his way back from Scotland, he could hear the wind sigh through the lattice, and keep repeating to himself over and over again (a very rare choice indeed for him) two lines of Byron's tragedy:

> So shalt thou find me ever at thy side
> Here and hereafter, if the last may be . . .

* A surmise about Hazlitt having written the review was contained in some passages which appeared in his grandson's book, the *Hazlitt Memoirs*. However, the suggestion that he wrote the whole of it is impossible. The joint product seems much more probable. Evidence may also be adduced from an enemy, John Wilson of *Blackwood's*. He noted that Jeffrey 'in a moment of silliness permitted Hazlitt to help his reviews. Every paragraph, he wrote, that 'Billy dipped his ugly paw in' was detectable.

ELEVEN

Pisa

I really cannot know whether I am or am not
the Genius you are pleased to call me, but I am
very willing to put up with the mistake, if it be
one.

Letter to Isaac Disraeli, 10 June 1822

At Ravenna he felt his poetic power, his power to move the world, rising to a new pitch; then came a blow which could have been mortal. Teresa wrung from him a promise not to continue with *Don Juan*. The laughing, loving reproofs with which he at first concealed his anxieties in his reports to Murray and Company cannot alter the hard fact: here once again the epic was in danger of destruction. Hobhouse and Murray and Gifford and the rest of Christendom, not excluding those practised protectors of the nation's morals Thomas Moore and Scrope Davies, had recruited a quite unexpectedly powerful ally. To appeal to Byron's lover was a resort which might not have occurred to the strictly male coterie in Albemarle Street, but of course this is precisely the remedy which Lady Melbourne or Lady Oxford, say, would have confidently recommended. (One of the incidental reasons why the Whigs held him was those Whig women; they were so much more persuasive and desirable than the Tories, as his disciple Disraeli was later to testify.) Without their aid, the remedy was applied. In his love affairs, Byron would readily confess that he was often likely to alight on the nearest perch, but he also wished to claim that on philosophical or political questions, he was much more deliberate and discriminating. Who could suppose that, on the real question of *Don Juan's* propriety and place in his life, he was swayed by her arguments?

The first news of Teresa's successful proscription was conveyed to Albemarle Street playfully enough. To Hobhouse he wrote:

> I have also agreed to a request of Madame Guiccioli's *not* to continue that poem further. – She had read the French translation and thinks it a detestable production. – This will not seem strange even in Italian morality – because women all over the world always retain their Free masonry – and as that consists in the illusion of the Sentiment – which constitutes their sole empire – (all owing to Chivalry – & the Goths – the Greeks knew better) all works which refer to the *comedy* of the passions – & laugh at Sentimentalism – of course are proscribed by the whole *Sect*. – I never knew a woman who did not admire Rousseau – and hate Gil Blas & de Grammont and the like – for the same reason. – And I never met with a woman English or foreign who did not do as much by D.J. – As I am docile – I have yielded and promised to confine myself to the 'high flying of Buttons' (you remember Pope's phrase) for the time to come. – You will be very glad of this – as an earlier opponent of that poem's publication.

Partly he must have been touched by her tender insistence; and partly he had his hands and mind full with other literary engagements; he was just finishing *Sardanapalus* and starting *Cain*, and while he waited for the reaction to these and earlier pieces, he found no difficulty, through the high summer and autumn of 1821, in filling in his time with some less portentous exertions; trifles by his standard. He wrote *The Blues* in August, 'The Irish Avatar' and *The Vision of Judgement* in September, and started *Heaven and Earth* in September. Apart from the 'Avatar', included in a letter to Moore and published in Paris at the time, none of these, for differing reasons, was to be speedily published. They could have provided a suitable trilogy to succeed the *Cain-Sardanapalus-Foscari* volume. So we can still pause to be amazed by both the bulk and the variety of the Ravenna output. Even with *Don Juan* assigned to his fate, his literary interest was overwhelmingly political. Indeed almost every letter he wrote in these, his last months in Ravenna, testify to his concern about the persecution of his friends, by the intrigues of the Austrian Government – 'the most infamous in history'. Thanks to his associations both with Teresa's family and many of his other Carbonari friends, he was regarded by the police and the priests as 'a Chief of the Coalheavers'. He was proud of the title, and quite unwilling, as he was sometimes slanderously accused, to treat lightly 'the general desolation of families' which he could see all around him. He hated moving, and for purposes of work Ravenna suited him ('I don't see anyone . . . I live with my books and my horses,' he assured a slightly sceptical Teresa). But he persuaded her to move from Ravenna with the promise that he would soon follow, and took the wise precaution of putting Allegra into the convent in nearby Bagno Cavallo. Amid all the political commotions, it was a safe and excusable choice.

However, in the midst of these disturbances – emotional and political – on 8 August 1821 Cantos III, IV and V of *Don Juan* were published in London, and the booksellers' messengers in Albemarle Street were said to have 'pressed without ceremony their obstreperous demands'. He himself was not able to share this happy reception. When he received his own copies, he was at first outraged, as any author must have been, by the manner in which some of his favourite stanzas had been mangled or omitted altogether. To Murray he wrote:

> I have received the Juans – which are printed so *carelessly* especially the 5th Canto – as to be disgraceful to me – & not creditable to you. – It really must be *gone over again* with the *Manuscript* – the errors are so gross – words added – changed – so as to make cacophony & nonsense. – You have been careless of this poem because some of your Synod don't approve of it – but I tell you – it will be long before you see any thing half so good as poetry or writing. – Upon what principle have you omitted the *note* on Bacon & Voltaire? and one of the concluding stanzas sent as an addition? because it ended I suppose – with –

'And do not link two virtuous souls for life
Into that *moral Centaur* man & wife? [']

Now I must say once for all – that I will not permit any
human being to take such liberties with my writings –
because I am absent. – I desire the omissions to be replaced
. . . If you have no feeling for your own reputation pray have
some little for mine. – I have read over the poem carefully –
and I tell you *it is poetry.* – Your little envious knot of parson-
poets may say what they please – time will show that I am
not in this instance mistaken. . . .

But gradually he was subdued: 'I read over the Juans – which
are excellent,' he was telling Murray in September – 'Your
Synod was quite wrong – & so you will find by & bye – I regret
that I do not go on with it – for I had all the plan for several cantos – & different countries and climes . . .' How long could he
hold back? The spectacle before his own eyes and the news
from London combined to intensify his ever rising political
impatience. By the middle of October he was writing to
Hobhouse in a much fiercer tone – no hint of the dilettante, no
touch of the coxcomb was left here:

I sent two more Poeshies to A[lbemarle] Street – *'Cain',* a
tragedy in three acts – 'a Vision of Judgement' by way of
reversing Rogue Southey's – in my finest ferocious Caravaggio style – and a *third* entitled 'the Irish Avatar' upon the
late Irishisms of the Blarney people in Dublin. – All which I
pray you to look at – I am mistaken if [these?] *two* latter are
not after your own radical heart. –
Your infamous Government will drive all honest men
into the necessity of reversing it – I see nothing left for it –
but a republic *now* – an opinion which I have held aloof as
long as it would let me. – *Come* it must – *they* do not see this –
but all this driving will do it – it may not be in ten or twenty
years but it is inevitable – and I am sorry for it. – When we
read of the *beginnings* of revolutions in a *few* pages – it seems
as if they had happened in *five* minutes – whereas *years* have

always been and must be their prologues – it took from eighty eight to ninety three – to decide the French one – and the English are a tardy people. – I am so persuaded that an English one is inevitable – that I am moving Heaven and earth – (that is to say Douglas Kinnaird – and Medea's trustee) to get me out of the funds. – I would give all I have to see the Country *fairly free* – but till I know that *giving* – or rather *losing* it – *would free* it – you will excuse my natural anxiety for my temporal affairs. –

Still I can't approve of the *ways* of the *radicals* – they seem such very low imitations of the Jacobins. – I do not allude to you and Burdett – but to the Major and to Hunt of Bristol & little Waddington &c. &c. – If I came home (which I never shall) I should take a *decided* part in politics – with pen and person – & (if I could revive my English) in the house – but am not yet quite sure *what* part – except that it would *not* be in favour of these abominable tyrants. – I certainly lean towards a republic – all history – and experience is in it's favour even the French – for though they butchered thousands of Citizens at first, yet *more* were killed in any one of the great battles than ever perished by a democratical proscription. – America is a Model of force and freedom & moderation – with all the coarseness and rudeness of it's people.

Apart from the rising invective against the abominable English government, it was the first time he had used the word 'democratical' with a favourable connotation. It was almost but not quite one of his last messages from Ravenna. He had an Italian greeting for Teresa, now arrived in Pisa – 'I embrace you *à la Corinne.*' He would soon be plucking up courage to advise the reading as a companion volume of Benjamin Constant's *Adolphe* – always a favourite with him but one not easily to be recommended to a mistress, unless the liaison was thoroughly understood on both sides. He would embrace Thomas Moore too, and maybe found with him, even at such a distance, a new kinship, based partly on his genuine admiration for Moore's light lascivious touch ('I am not quite sure that I shall allow the

Miss Byron's [legitimate or illegitimate] to read Lalla Rookh'),
partly because he knew him as a fellow author ('I would rather
Moore edited me than another'), but partly also because they
did share a common detestation of English arrogance. ('Here I
have my hands full with tyrants and their victims. There never
was such oppression, even in Ireland, scarcely!'). Even his ten-
year-old partnership with Murray was coming under strain. Off
and on through the year he had mentioned again to Moore the
possibility of starting a new English journal, where they could
say together what they wanted and what was needed:

> I see the way he and his Quarterly people are tending – they
> want a *row* with me, & they shall have it . . . But though
> backed by all the corruption, and infamy, and patronage of
> their master rogues & slave renegades, if they do once rouse
> me up, . . . It was all very well ten or twelve years ago, when
> I was a 'curled darling', and *minded* such things. At present I
> *rate* them at their true value; but, from natural temper & bite,
> am not able to keep quiet.

He left Ravenna at last in October, more justly anxious than he
had ever been in his life about how he might get printed what
he wanted, more passionately than ever, to say. It can become,
for some writers, the passion to drive out all others.

The last, the very last, major piece of writing which he
brought near to completion in Ravenna was a fine expression of
the rebellious mood now dominant in his mind. It was called
Heaven and Earth : A Mystery, and the epigraph, taken from Chapter VI of the Book of Genesis, might have been expected to
sound the alarm in Albemarle Street: 'And it came to pass . . .
that the sons of God saw the daughters of men that they were
fair; and they took them wives of all which they could choose.'
Such a theme, touched by Byron's wand, might have been
expected to tell the tale of some idyllic free-love society, in
which marital excitements left no scars. Here at least, once
again, Byron offered evidence of how he read his Bible so much
more diligently than most others: who else, even among long-
practising Calvinistic preachers, had ever chosen that potent

verse for his text? 'Byron, in his innocence', recorded another editor, 'had taken the verse . . . which records the intermarriage of the "Sons of God with the daughters of men".'* But Byron's innocence in biblical matters should never be assumed. Alternatively, it might have been assumed that he intended to perpetrate another *Cain*. Byron himself was aware of that peril and wanted to ward it off. It is, he told Murray, 'less speculative than *Cain*, and very pious'. Goethe preferred it to all the other of Byron's serious poems, and happily concluded: 'A bishop might have written it.' He did succeed, according to another editor, in making Noah, one of the principal characters, 'talk like a street-preacher'. So many varied vantage points of judgement might prepare the way for something which could be regarded, from Byron at least, as an attempt to match the sweetness and light which Swift could also offer. But it was nothing of the sort. *Heaven and Earth is* a sequel to *Cain*: several of its actual characters were direct descendants from Cain for a start, and had not taken any hint to improve their conduct. If *Cain* passed judgement on the politics of Paradise, this new work offered a no less direct and adverse verdict on the politics of the Deluge. Japhet, the new hero, was not in the same class as Cain as the Arch-rebel, but he did rebel none the less. Noah was accorded not quite so strong and objectionable a role as those combined authoritarian figures Adam and Eve. He counselled his obstreperous son to find some release in hypocrisy – surely in Byron's catalogue the worst sin of all:

> Peace, child of passion, peace!
> If not within thy heart, yet with thy tongue
> Do God no wrong!

But truly the case was even more serious. The moral of *Heaven and Earth* is that once again God was calling on men, and, even more especially in this instance, women, to accept a monstrously unjust dispensation. When the flood comes – described

* This reference is contained in Volume V of the Coleridge-Prothero edition of Byron's works; the McGann edition of these later poems was not available at the time of writing.

in what Hazlitt called 'a terrific scene' even though all have been expecting the crash throughout the whole play – it is the voices crying out against it, a mother's voice above all others, which rends the heavens:

> *A Mother [offering her infant to Japhet]*:
>   Oh, let this child embark!
>   I brought him forth in woe,
>   But thought it joy
>   To see him to my bosom clinging so.
>   Why was he born?
>   What hath he done –
>   My unweaned son–
>   To move Jehovah's wrath or scorn?
>   What is there in this milk of mine, that Death
>   Should stir all Heaven and Earth up to destroy
>   My boy

Another chorus, a chorus of those about to die, turns the anger to the powers on high.

>   But as we know the worst,
>   Why should our hymns be raised, our knees be bent
>   Before the implacable Omnipotent,
>   Since we must fall the same?
>   If he hath made Earth, let it be his shame,
>   To make a world for torture. – Lo! they come,
>   The loathsome waters, in their rage!
>   And with their roar make wholesome nature dumb!
>   The forest's trees (coeval with the hour
>   When Paradise upsprung,
>   Ere Eve gave Adam knowledge for her dower,
>   Or Adam his first hymn of slavery sung) . . .

And then again at the very end:

> *Woman*: Oh, save me, save!
>   Our valley is no more:

My father and my father's tent,
My brethren and my brethren's herds,
   The pleasant trees that o'er our noonday bent,
And sent forth evening songs from sweetest birds,
The little rivulet which freshened all
      Our pastures green,
      No more are to be seen.
When to the mountain cliff I climbed this morn,
     I turned to bless the spot,
   And not a leaf appeared about to fall, –
   And now they are not!
Why was I born?

Byron also had envisaged in his own mind, as he explained to a friend two years later, a sequel to *Heaven and Earth* in which again Japhet and Adah together strive 'with very strong arguments of love and pity, to take his loved one on board'.* Instead, in the end, 'the last wave sweeps her from the rock and her lifeless corpse floats past in all its beauty, whilst a sea-bird screams over it'. Byron had considered conveying the lovers to the moon or another planet and he rejected the resort, not because of any last-minute repugnance to the idea of salvation for the sinners, but because he did not believe his lovers could approve of the moon as a residence; no unknown world could be made more beautiful than this one: 'all human interest would have been destroyed which I have even endeavoured to give my angels.'

Byron arrived at the Casa Lanfranchi at Pisa, on the banks of the Arno, on 1 November 1821. Happy though he surely was to be restored to his Teresa, the first weeks and months of his instalment were notable also for his engulfment in politics, whichever way he turned. Back in England the storm over *Cain* was just starting and even Byron could not have foreseen that it would rise to the dimensions of a hurricane. He knew the

---

* This remark was made by Byron to Thomas Medwin and recorded in his memoirs. The book has some valuable references which do not appear elsewhere; however it should never be read or relied upon without reference also to Doris Langley Moore's castigation of Thomas Medwin in her *The Late Lord Byron*.

implications of *Heaven and Earth*, and was even ready to offer his timorous publisher some accommodating emendations. One increasingly persistent worry was the controversy with his publisher. Some of his attacks were skilfully parried by Murray: more often the quarrels, however repaired, left deeper wounds. No one in his publisher's circle, not even the amiable, pliant Thomas Moore, appreciated the strength of his political moods; some felt it was part of their mission to deflect his purpose. Taken individually, some of these complaints might have seemed to be no more than a writer's irritation. Taken together, they show how formidable was the scale of the choice mounting before him – especially for the author denied the right to proceed with his *Don Juan*. His fury suffused his writing and his reading and his correspondence:

> I have lately been reading Fielding over again. – They talk of Radicalism – Jacobinism &c. in England (I am told) but they should turn over the pages of 'Jonathan Wild the Great'. – The inequality of conditions and the littleness of the great – were never set forth in stronger terms – and his contempt for Conquerors and the like is such that had he lived *now* he would have been denounced in the 'Courier' as the grand Mouth-piece and Factionary of the revolutionists. – And yet I never recollect to have heard this turn of Fielding's mind noticed though it is obvious in every page.

To Kinnaird, on 19 January:

> . . . tell me – if 'the Deluge' has arrived at Murray['s] – it was sent on the 15th Decr. 1821 – I have several counts ag[ain]st Murray – 1stly he behaved shabbily – & uncivilly – in not th[anking] me for my very civil behaviour about *Galignani's* copyrights. – 2ndly Rogers says he went about affecting *not* to be the publisher of 'Don Juan' – &c. at the very time that he was pressing me to write more of it. – 3rdly. he has not been very magnifique about the letter on Pope – and 4thly. – you know how he has behaved about the rest – the *Juans* &c. – Pray press the publication of 'the Vision' – you will soon find a publisher.

And then again to Kinnaird a few days later:

> With regard to what I sent you a few days ago (the Mystery)
> and what I shall send you in a few days (the drama of 'Wer-
> ner') I shall publish them with another publisher. – and
> *anonymously* if you like. – Indeed – I am much surprized that
> you say nothing of 'the Vision' as you seemed delighted
> with it and eager to get it published. – Published it *shall be* –
> though even on my own account. – As I said before the
> profit is a *secondary* object – *pleasant* – if it comes – but to be
> borne without – if it does not. – If you cannot settle with any
> *English publisher* – forward them to Galignani – at Paris – &
> make any agreement you please – conditional for example –
> as each to share – or if he chooses to purchase the Copyright
> – or to divide profit or loss – what you please. – You can get
> my M.S.S. out of Murray's hand – the Pulci – &c. as I shall
> most likely collect the whole of what I have in M.S.S. and
> publish them at once – *My* object is not *immediate* popularity
> in my present productions which are written on a different
> system from the rage of the day. – But *mark what I now say* –
> that the time will come – when *these* will be preferred to any
> I have before written;

And then again, in an even stronger tone:

> I *[n]ever courted* the public – and I never will *yield* to it. – As
> long as I can find a *single* reader I will publish my Mind
> (while it lasts) and write whilst I feel the impetus. . . . But
> let this be as it may – I can assure you that I will not swerve
> from my purpose – though I should share the lot of all who
> have ever done good or attempted to instruct or better man-
> kind. – I can sustain their persecution – it is not the first time
> either, and console myself for their neglect – always
> employing my own mind to the best of my understanding.
>   I replied to your last letter – stating my reasons for quit-
> ting Murray as a publisher – and also my determination to
> continue to publish; – as to profit – that must be as it pleases
> the Gods – but I shall not give way to discouragement – as
> long as I do not feel my mind failing. – With regard to the

public I have expected *that* to *change* this many a good year –
but I may perhaps find a reader or two even yet in Germany
or America . . .

Momentarily, however, this idea of a break with Murray was
suspended by the thought that he might be unfair to one who
had endured much on his behalf, especially the beratings about
Cain.

> But now – all such things disappear in my regret at having
> been unintentionally the means of getting you into a scrape.
> – Be assured that no momentary irritation (at real or sup-
> posed omissions – or commissions) shall ever prevent me
> from doing you justice where you deserve it – or that I will
> allow you (if I can avoid it) to participate in any odium or
> persecution – which ought to fall on me only. . . . As to what
> the Clergyman says of 'Don Juan' you have brought it upon
> yourself by your absurd half and half prudery – which I
> always foresaw – would bother you at last. – An author's *not*
> putting his name – is nothing – it has been always the cus-
> tom to publish a thousand anonymous things – but *who* ever
> heard before of a *publisher* affecting such a Masquerade as
> yours was? – However – now – you may print my name to
> the 'Juans' if you like it – though it is of the latest to be of use
> to you. – I always stated to you – that *my* only objection was
> in case of the law deciding against you – that they would
> annihilate my guardianship of the Child. But now (as you
> really seem in a damned scrape) they may do what they like
> with me; so that I can get you out of it – but – Cheer up –
> though I have 'led my ragamuffins where they are well pep-
> pered' I will stick by them as long as they will keep the field.

Then, in February, this time to Thomas Moore:

> There is nothing against the immortality of the soul in
> 'Cain' that I recollect. I hold no such opinions; – but, in a
> drama, the first rebel and the first murderer must be made to
> talk according to their characters. However, the parsons are
> all preaching at it, from Kentish Town and Oxford to Pisa, –

the scoundrels of priests, who do more harm to religion than all the infidels that ever forgot their catechisms!

Then in March he bewailed his case to Thomas Moore, his fellow author, and one more likely to understand his afflictions than any publisher, banker or adviser, however close. Authors have their own favourites among their offspring, and the whole letter reveals, not in strident complaining tones, the deepening anxiety in his mind about what he was writing, how much attention he should pay to the world:

The unpublished things in your hands, in Douglas K.'s, and Mr John Murray's, are 'Heaven and Earth, a lyrical kind of Drama upon the Deluge, etc.'; 'Werner,' *now with you*; – a translation of the First Canto of the Morgante Maggiore; – *ditto* of an Episode in Dante; – some stanzas to the Po, June 1st, 1819; – Hints from Horace, written in 1811, but a good deal, *since*, to be omitted; several prose things, which may, perhaps, as well remain unpublished; – 'The Vision, &c. of Quevedo Redivivus,' in verse.

Here you see is 'more matter for a May morning;' but how much of this can be published is for consideration. The Quevedo (one of my best in that line) has appalled the Row already, and must take its chance at Paris, if at all. The new Mystery is less speculative than 'Cain', and very pious; besides, it is chiefly lyrical. The Morgante is the *best* translation that ever was or will be made; and the rest are – whatever you please to think them.

I am sorry you think Werner even *approaching* to any fitness for the stage, which, with my notions upon it, is very far from my present object. With regard to the publication, I have already explained that I have no exorbitant expectations of either fame or profit in the present instances; but wish them published because they are written, which is the common feeling of all scribblers.

With respect to 'Religion,' can I never convince you that *I* have no such opinions as the characters in that drama, which seems to have frightened every body? Yet *they* are

317

nothing to the expressions in Goethe's Faust (which are ten times hardier), and not a whit more bold than those of Milton's Satan. My ideas of a character may run away with me: like all imaginative men, I, of course, embody myself with the character while I *draw* it, but not a moment after the pen is from off the paper.

I am no enemy to religion, but the contrary. As a proof, I am educating my natural daughter a strict Catholic in a convent of Romagna; for I think people can never have *enough* of religion, if they are to have any. I incline, myself, very much to the Catholic doctrines; but if I am to write a drama, I must make my characters speak as I conceive them likely to argue.

As to poor Shelley, who is another bugbear to you and the world, he is, to my knowledge, the *least* selfish and the mildest of men – a man who has made more sacrifices of his fortune and feelings for others than any I ever heard of. With his speculative opinions I have nothing in common, nor desire to have.

With Moore again he protested his innocence of some of the fiercest charges levelled against him.

This war of 'Church and State' has astonished me more than it disturbs; for I really thought 'Cain' a speculative and hardy, but still a harmless production. As I said before, I am really a great admirer of tangible religion; and am breeding one of my daughters a Catholic, that she may have her hands full. It is by far the most elegant worship, hardly excepting the Greek mythology. What with incense, pictures, statues, altars, shrines, relics, and the real presence, confession, absolution, – there is something sensible to grasp at. Besides, it leaves no possibility of doubt; for those who swallow their Deity, really and truly, in transubstantiation, can hardly find any thing else otherwise than easy of digestion.

I am afraid that this sounds flippant, but I don't mean it to be so; only my turn of mind is so given to taking things in the absurd point of view, that it breaks out in spite of me every now and then.

His argumentative tone rose as the weeks passed – and this – on 2 May – may have been his first response to the February *Edinburgh Review* of his *Sardanapalus-Foscari-Cain* volume.

As to myself – I shall not be deterred by any outcry – they hate me – and I detest them – I mean your present Public – but they shall not interrupt the march of my mind – nor prevent me from telling the tyrants who are attempting to trample upon all thought – that their thrones will yet be rocked to their foundation . . .

Then later in May he wrote to Shelley about that favourite book contaning so much which Shelley had encouraged:

The only literary news that I have heard of the plays – (contrary to your friendly augury) is that the Edinburgh R[eview] has attacked them all three – as well as it could. – I have not seen the article. – Murray writes discouragingly – and says 'that nothing published this year has made the least impression' including I presume what he has published on my account also. – You see what it is to throw pearls to Swine – as long as I wrote the exaggerated nonsense which has corrupted the public taste – they applauded to the very echo – and now that I have really composed within these three or four years some things which should 'not willingly be let die' – the whole herd snort and grumble and return to wallow in their mire. – However it is fit that I should pay the penalty of spoiling them – as no man has contributed more than me in my earlier compositions to produce that exaggerated & false taste – it is a fit retribution that anything [like a?] classical production should be received as these plays have been treated. . . .

The *Edinburgh Review* hurt him deeply, despite all his protestations – 'it will do much harm – I have no hesitation in saying that the late volume contains by far the best of my writings, and the time will come when it will be thought so.' This is what he told Kinnaird on 27 May and what he reaffirmed to Murray at the same time: 'With regard to the late volume – the present run against *it* or *me* – may impede it for a time – but it has the vital principle of permanency within it – as you may perhaps one day discover. . . Please send me the dedication of Sardanapalus to Goethe – which you took upon you to omit – which omission I assure you I take very ill. . . .' When Byron talked so persistently of the quality of that particular volume, we can hardly suppose that it was the *Two Foscari* he had in mind; that was a lovely lament for Venice, but no more. It was *Cain* and *Sardanapalus* together which he strove to elevate to such a high place among his own writings. He was shaken by the ferocity of Jeffrey's attack, but soothed a little maybe by the glowing appreciation for *Sardanapalus*, the play, and Myrrha, the beauty. What would he have said if he had known that the damnation had been pronounced by Jeffrey and the soft words of benediction by William Hazlitt?*

Should he answer Jeffrey? He was certainly much tempted to do so: the invectives of the *Review* article still scorch today, and their heat must have seemed much fiercer then. If he was damned in such terms by the Whigs, what would the Tories say? What true defenders could be expected to rally in any quarter? Should he answer Hobhouse too: for *Cain* had provoked a private quarrel much rougher than any other between them, and Byron had once replied to him on this point: 'I forgive you as a Christian should do – that is I never will forgive you as long

---

* Byron made very few direct references to Hazlitt. We have no means of knowing how much he had read of his writings, and of course, it must be remembered that many of Hazlitt's essays, including some of the best, had been published anonymously. His Ravenna Journal did contain one shameful reference (dated 28 January 1821) when he compared Hazlitt with Wilhelm Friedrich Schlegel: 'He is like Hazlitt, in English, who *talks pimples* – a red and white corruption rising up (in little imitation of mountains upon maps), but containing nothing, and discharging nothing except their own humours.' It seems also that Byron had not read Hazlitt on Schlegel, who dealt with the topic more memorably and knowledgeably than Byron himself.

as I live.' Of course he did not mean that in those precise terms, and the old friendship was happily restored. No doubt these were the criticisms which cut nearest to the bone, the ones from his old allies and friends, the Whigs and the Reformers. But he did not abjure all self-criticism. Significantly his repentance referred to his past literary crimes, not the present ones. He wrote to Isaac D'Israeli, a new friend:

> At present I am paying the penalty of having helped to spoil the public taste, for, as long as I wrote in the false exaggerated style of youth and the times in which we live, they applauded me to the very echo; and within these few years, when I have endeavoured at better things and written what I suspect to have the principle of duration in it, the Church, the Chancellor, and all men – even to my grand patron Francis Jeffrey Esqre. of the E[dinburgh] R[eview] – have risen up against me and my later publications. Such is Truth! Men dare not look her in the face, except by degrees: they mistake her for a Gorgon, instead of knowing her to be a Minerva. . . .

Some of his answers may be considered tentative or even temporizing. *Werner or The Inheritance: A Tragedy* which he started soon after his arrival – reviving a theme which he had toyed with long before – cannot be regarded as a truly Byronic response worthy of his powers. Nor was *The Deformed Transformed: A Drama*, despite its considerable power, anything to be compared with his major writings. All through these months he was preparing for a return to *Don Juan*; the actual writing had been started several months before Teresa knew.

Two events – two mighty and tragic events in Byron's life – intervened that summer: the death of Allegra and the death of Shelley. Allegra died at the Bagno Cavallo on 20 April and Shelley was drowned in the Bay of Spezia on 8 July. It was a Byronic habit to seek comfort in composition, and he did so in the aftermath of both these occasions. He wrote *The Deformed Transformed* some time in the summer, and he re-started officially on *Don Juan* soon after he returned from his surveillance of the charred bodies of his friends.

However, on 8 July he had already written to Murray a notable letter on their relationship. Murray, as the later exchanges prove, might still have kept his famous author, but the political breach between them seemed widening every week:

Last week I returned you the packet of proofs. – You had perhaps better not publish in the same volume – the *Po* – and *Rimini* translation. – I have consigned a letter to Mr John Hunt for the 'Vision of Judgement' – which you will hand over to him. – Also the Pulci – original and Italian – and any *prose* tracts of mine – for Mr Leigh Hunt is arrived here & thinks of commencing a periodical work – to which I shall contribute – I do not propose to you to be the publisher – because I know that you are unfriends – but all things in your care except the volume now in the press – and the M.S.S. purchased of Mr Moore – can be given for this purpose – according as they are wanted – and I expect that you will show fair play – although with no very good will on your part. – With regard to what you say about your 'want of memory' – I can only remark that you inserted the note to 'Marino Faliero' – against my positive revocation and that you omitted the dedication of 'Sardanapalus' to Goethe (place it before the volume now in the press) both of which were things not very agreeable to me & which I could wish to be avoided in future as they might be with a very little care – or a simple Memorandum in your pocket book. – It is not impossible that I may have three or four cantos of D[on] Juan ready by autumn or a little later – as I obtained a permission from my Dictatress to continue it – *provided always* it was to be more guarded and decorous and sentimental in the continuation than in the commencement. – How far these Conditions have been fulfilled may be seen perhaps by and bye. But the Embargo was only taken off [upon these] stipulations. – You can answer at yr. leisure.

A few days later, with the full knowledge of the Shelley tragedy upon him, with a recollection of the injustice with which the world had treated him, with a fresh understanding of his own politics and his enemies:

I have written three more cantos of Don Juan, and am hovering on the brink of another (the ninth). The reason I want the stanzas again which I sent you is, that as these cantos contain a full detail (like the storm in Canto Second) of the siege and assault of Ishmael, with much of sarcasm on those butchers in large business, your mercenary soldiery, it is a good opportunity of gracing the poem with *** With these things and these fellows, it is necessary, in the present clash of philosophy and tyranny, to throw away the scabbard. I know it is against fearful odds; but the battle must be fought; and it will be eventually for the good of mankind, whatever it may be for the individual who risks himself.

What do you think of your Irish bishop? Do you remember Swift's line, 'Let me have a *barrack* – a fig for the *clergy*?' This seems to have been his reverence's motto ***.

I'll come to Swift and his shocking example in the next chapter – Swift was starting to take his place in Byron's reading alongside Pope. The name of John Hunt is no less significant in his story and it was in 1821 that he made his decisive entry on the scene. Authors without willing publishers, even famous ones, can lose their moment of opportunity. All the signs were that at last Byron was to be able to devote all his unimpeded energies and imagination to *Don Juan*, and that he would have a printer willing to print it. But obstacles, old and new, were still there blocking his path, unexpectedly but effectively.

TWELVE

Genoa

I am at this moment the most unpopular man in England.

Letter to John Hunt, Genoa, March 1823

Teresa had carried the day about *Don Juan* for a while: the truest testimony to her power. But the actual interval lasted for less than six months, reckoning from the first moment when he yielded to her entreaties to the most likely moment when he started, quite privately at first, to return to work on his masterpiece. Some things he had to say, when he had found the right way to say them, though the heavens might fall, however his friends might mobilize in protest, however Teresa might scream her objections – not that that was her normal style, despite his own occasional comparisons between her and Lady Caroline; hers was more an overpoweringly lovely lament. 'I would rather', he reported her as saying, 'have the fame of Childe Harold for THREE YEARS than an IMMORTALITY of Don Juan.' And if she did say approximately that, it shows that her guile had been successfully transferred from her lovemaking to literary criticism. But even that from her was not enough to stop him for long. *Don Juan* had a power stronger than any single love, even Teresa's, and she came to understand this part of his nature too. The circumstances in which the writing was renewed are especially sensitive and significant. They show how, at the supreme moments, politics drove him forward; they shatter, if any further demolition is necessary, the suggestion that Byron was a dilettante who didn't really care which way he moved as long as life could be made reasonably accommodating. If that had been the truth, no new cantos of *Don Juan* would have appeared; the great war scenes, the assault on English society, the revolutionary epic, would have stayed unwritten.

324

Such a multitude did believe that would have been better for Byron's fame, starting and ending with his most faithful and loving disciples, Hobhouse and Teresa. The only person who fought throughout for a different fate for his greatest poem was Byron himself. Of course, there have been examples, many such, when dissenters, poets in particular, have matched their own inspiration against the world's, and have lived or died to be vindicated. The pattern is common enough; but what is unique to Byron's case is that all the adulation and acclaim came in his youth when he was expressing not immediately popular doctrines – he never did that – but reputable doctrines which had the chance of winning a decent support among his patriotic countrymen. This was the Whig faith – if that is not too theological a term to apply to such devoted Erastians – of Charles James Fox to which he gave his allegiance, and all honour to him and to Fox. This was the way the very idea of English liberty was kept alive in perilous times, times of war when it is not easy to uphold such comparatively modern conceptions of individual freedom. Byron, in the last few years of his life, did something even more intellectually adventurous. He had already helped to keep the Foxite flame burning in the coldest of climates; but he knew also there must be a tremendous counter-attack into the enemy's camp. That was what the renewed *Don Juan* was to be. It was there within him, even while he bowed to Teresa's stricture.

The latest, most scholarly supposition about the time when he returned to *Don Juan* puts the date at January 1822, a few weeks only after he made the much-feared journey from Ravenna to Pisa.* One impediment he may have felt to the task or delight of re-starting to write, beneath Teresa's watchful eye, may have been due to the predicament in which he had left his hero in the Turkish harem, in the care of Gulbeyaz and her lord:

> Oh the heavy night!
> When wicked wives who love some bachelor
> Lie down in dudgeon to sigh for the light

* Jerome McGann's most indispensable volume of all of *The Complete Poetical Works*, Volume V.

Of the grey morning, and look vainly for
   Its twinkle through the lattice dusky quite,
To toss, to tumble, doze, revive, and quake
Lest their too lawful bed-fellow should wake.

The delicacy of the double awakening, of Dudù and Juanna, as he had now become, in no less than seventy-seven stanzas, is a miracle all its own: one, however, which could never have been accomplished, if the tale had been left to stand on its own, like Beppo's. The tide in the affairs of women, taken at the flood and leading 'God knows where', and giving such eager and varied honour to them in the process, could never have been traced without the voluptuous assistance from Teresa herself:

   All who have loved, or love, will still allow
Life has nought like it. God is love, they say,
   And Love's a God, or was before the brow
Of Earth was wrinkled by the sins and tears
Of – but Chronology best knows the years.

The whole canto might be thought at first reading to belie the claim of any abiding political interest in Byron's mind; rather it confirms his artistry. One spur which sent him back to *Don Juan* was his realistic reading in a recent report of what had happened at the Siege of Ismail a few years before. Henceforward from Canto VII onwards the poem was fully developed as a lecture, in all its ramifications, on 'the noble art of killing, Glory's dream unriddled':

   'Let there be light!' said God, and there was light,
   'Let there be blood!' says man, and there's a sea!

All too often the two walked together; God and man had to be made the target of the same challenge.

Once he was fully engaged with *Don Juan* again – in the summer of 1822 – the poem in its contrasting glories, the combined flow of wit and passionate debate with all assorted enemies, seemed to proceed more readily than ever before. It is doubtful whether Teresa's standards of a higher piety were attained or attempted, and not much more on that count was heard from him or her. 'I obtained permission', he told Thomas Moore, 'from the female Censor Morum of my morals to continue it, provided it were immaculate.' Few but Byron would have used the word in that context. Nothing could stop him now – not even the absence of an assured promise from a printer-cum-publisher. The wrangle with Murray continued, and it must have been especially galling for this uncertainty to bare itself just at the moment when his touch was most sure. 'The argument consists', he wrote on 24 August 1822, to Kinnaird, who became at this crisis his most trusted confidante, 'of *more* love – and a good deal of war – a technical description of a modern siege (in the style of the Storm in the 2d. Canto which is or was reckoned Good) with much philosophy – and satire upon heroes and despots and the present false state of politics and society.' Canto VI showed his touch at its gentlest; Cantos VII and VIII offered the most comprehensive, but not the last of his great assaults on the war gods, the victors and the vanquished:

Suwarrow now was conqueror – a match
   For Timour or for Zinghis in his trade.
While mosques and streets, beneath his eyes, like thatch
   Blazed, and the cannon's roar was scarce allayed,
With bloody hands he wrote his first dispatch;
   And here exactly follows what he said:–
'Glory to *God* and to the Empress!' (*Powers
Eternal!! such names mingled!*) 'Ismail's ours.'

Methinks these are the most tremendous words,
   Since 'Mene, Mene, Tekel,' and 'Upharsin',
Which hands or pens have ever traced of swords.
   Heaven help me! I'm but little of a parson:
What Daniel read was short-hand of the Lord's,
   Severe, sublime; – the Prophet wrote no farce on
The fate of Nations; – but this Russ so witty
Could rhyme, like Nero, o'er a burning city.

He wrote this Polar melody, and set it,
  Duly accompanied by shrieks and groans,
Which few will sing, I trust, but none forget it –
  For I will teach, if possible, the stones
To rise against Earth's tyrants. Never let it
  Be said that we still truckle unto thrones; –
But ye – our children's children! think how we
Showed *what things were* before the world was free!

That hour is not for us, but 'tis for you:
  And as, in the great joy of your millennium,
You hardly will believe such things were true
  As now occur, I thought that I would pen you 'em;
But may their very memory perish too! –
  Yet if perchance remembered, still disdain you 'em
More than you scorn the savages of yore,
Who *painted* their *bare* limbs, but *not* with gore.

Canto IX took him on his journey to the Empress's court in
Moscow, to mock the monarch whom even his friends the
Whigs would sometimes excuse or extol, but not before a
deeper radical, political note had been struck, a stronger strain
of scepticism – or 'some good sensible practical truths that you
don't see every day in the week', he joked to Kinnaird. 'The
principal object of Byron's satire in *Don Juan*,' wrote Professor
Grierson, with these verses in mind, 'as of Swift's in *Gulliver's
Travels*, is human nature as revealed in the bungled, cruel business of government and war.' And then he concluded, when he
recited them: 'The poet who wrote these stanzas was as much at
war with the world in which he lived and moved as the author
of *Prometheus Unbound* . . .' adding, 'and he was a more effective
fighter.' But why a competition between such mighty allies?

Just when he was despatching the first three of these new
cantos to London he heard the news of the death of Castlereagh,
and he struck off a special preface which gave as true an insight
into his raging spirit as the verses themselves. A rich anthology
of invective could be compiled with Castlereagh as its single
subject: somehow he best represented for the radical England of
the day the wickedness and the wretchedness of the post-1815

period. 'Castlereagh has cut his own throat and is dead,' wrote Cobbett to a political prisoner of the time; 'let that sound reach you in the depth of your dunjeon; and let it carry consolation to your suffering soul!' Shelley's verses on the same theme were to become the most memorable, although, through no fault of his, not printed at the time: 'I met murder on the way/He had a face like Castlereagh.' But Byron's Preface, which he used all his reputation to get published whatever the outcry, deserves to rank with the others. He dashed off a few squibs at once:

> So He has cut his throat at last – He? Who?
> The Man who cut his country's long ago. . . .

But the Preface throbbed with a much stronger note:

I am aware of nothing in the manner of his death or of his life to prevent the free expression of the opinions of all whom his whole existence was consumed in endeavouring to enslave. That he was an amiable man in *private* life, may or may not be true, but with this the Public have nothing to do; and as to lamenting his death, it will in time enough when Ireland has ceased to mourn for his birth. As a Minister, I, for one of millions, looked upon him as the most despotic in intention and the weakest in intellect that ever tyrannized over a country. . . . Of the manner of his death little need be said, except that if a poor radical, such as Waddington or Watson, had cut his throat, he would have been buried in a cross-road, with the usual appurtenances of the stake and mallet. But the Minister was an elegant Lunatic – a sentimental Suicide – he merely cut that 'carotid artery' (blessings on their learning) and lo! the Pageant, and the Abbey! and 'the Syllables of Dolour yelled forth' by the Newspapers – and the harangue of the Coroner in an eulogy over the bleeding body of the deceased – (an Anthony worthy of such a Caesar) – and the nauseous and atrocious cant of a degraded Crew of Conspirators against all that is sincere and honourable. In his death he was necessarily one of two things by the *law* – a felon or a madman – and in either case no great subject for panegyric. In his life he was – what all the world knows, and half of it will feel for years to come, unless his death prove a 'moral lesson' to the surviving Sejani of Europe. It may at least serve as some consolation to the Nations, that their Oppressors are not happy, and in some instances judge so justly of their own actions as to anticipate the sentence of mankind. – Let us hear no more of this man; and let Ireland remove the Ashes of her Grattan from the Sanctuary of Westminster. Shall the Patriot of Humanity repose by the Werther of Politics!!!

This is the real fact, as applicable to the degraded and hypocritical mass which leavens the present English generation, and is the only answer they deserve. The hackneyed and lavished title of Blasphemer – which, with radical, liberal, jacobin, reformer, etc. are the changes which the hirelings are daily ringing in the ears of those who will listen – should be welcome to all who recollect on *whom* it was originally bestowed. Socrates and Jesus Christ were put to death publicly as Blasphemers, and so have been and may be many who dare to oppose the most notorious abuses of the name of God and the mind of man. But Persecution is not refutation, nor even triumph: the 'wretched Infidel,' as he is called, is probably happier in his prison than the proudest of his Assailants. With his opinions I have nothing to do – they may be right or wrong – but he has suffered for them, and that very Suffering for conscience-sake will make more proselytes to Deism than the example of heterodox Prelates to Christianity, suicide Statesmen to oppression, or over-pensioned Homicides to the impious Alliance which insults the world with the name of 'Holy'! I have no wish to trample on the dishonoured or the dead; but it would be well if the adherents to the Classes from whence those persons sprung should abate a little of the *Cant* which is the crying sin of this double-dealing and false-speaking time of selfish Spoilers, and – but enough for the present.

This defence of the blasphemers, political and religious, was not just 'the last straw' which broke the back of Murray the publisher, but no doubt it helped. Who could believe that he would ever have dared to print these paragraphs over his name? Publication did not take place for a full year after Byron had completed the new cantos, eighteen months after he had re-started work on them. For the author, the interval must have been one of near-intolerable frustration, the more so since at times it was not at all certain whether the poem would ever be printed at all.

Byron had once called on John Hunt and his family in his house off the Edgware Road, soon after Hunt had been released from prison in 1813. He got an impression then of Hunt's sturdy independence of spirit which he never had reason to abandon. Customarily he would not find it necessary to distinguish between the two brothers; both had their similar qualities, both could be compared with the pamphleteers of the seventeenth century who would risk their ears or their necks to get the truth published. John had had another spell in prison in 1820 for publishing a pamphlet which was held to be an offence against parliamentary privilege. He had a directness which his brother sometimes lacked, and he soon won Byron's confidence again, both as a publisher and a man, even though he could never offer the sums which Murray had paid and even though the process of completing the terms between them took longer than might have been expected. John was also the principal agent engaged with his brother in preparing the new journal which Shelley and Byron had discussed in Ravenna. Leigh Hunt had come to Pisa for the express purpose of furthering the project. When some of Byron's friends had protested – not only Murray, but Moore and Hobhouse too – that dealings with such men would injure his reputation, Byron had retorted with all the fierce show of personal loyalty which came so naturally to him: 'With regard to L. Hunt – he stuck by me through thick and thin, when all shook and some shuffled in 1816.' Hunt had written a poem on Byron's departure which Hazlitt had hailed as one of his best. All the evidence of political interest and outlook suggested that the co-operation between the two men should be easy and beneficial. And John Hunt's role in the affair made it all the more appealing. His participation was one of the reasons why Byron considered, despite all the warnings, that the new venture should be backed and could succeed, and a reason further why a note, written from Pisa, on 21 September in the following terms, was attached to a letter from Leigh to his brother: 'Lord B as well as myself will be glad to have [Hazlitt] write in any work in which we are engaged, – so much so, that he mentioned it to me himself before your letter arrived. Remember me to him, and kindly, though tell him that I have often had bitter feeling upon a certain work when thinking of my lost friend.' Leigh Hunt was a true friend of Shelley, and he preserved his friendship with both of them in the teeth of Hazlitt's attack. And taking into account the auspices under which the idea had been launched, Leigh Hunt had every ground for objecting to the elaborate efforts made by some of Byron's friends to rupture the association even before it had been given any chance to fructify. Hobhouse had paid a special visit to Byron at Pisa to try to achieve just that. 'Mr Hobhouse', wrote Leigh Hunt later, with good excuse, 'rushed over the Alps, not knowing which was more awful, the mountains or the Magazine.'

Some other anticipations of what was being prepared at Pisa offer good reminders of Byron's reputation and how it might be thought that the Hunt brothers were not jeopardizing his respectability. A certain John Watkins had published earlier in the year a libellous biography of Byron – the first in a large library of similar concoctions – in which the biographer asserted that a set of writers were assembling in Pisa to produce a new journal, 'the proprietor and editor of the most seditious paper in England' (that is, Leigh Hunt) and others who would help to form 'an academy of blasphemy', and 'a poetical school of immorality and profaneness'. And such language was not confined to defenders of the faith who were summoned to assail his religious views. William Wordsworth had heard the same rumour, and he wrote to Landor to report that 'Byron, Shelley, Moore, Leigh Hunt . . . are to lay their heads together in some town of Italy, for the purpose of conducting a Journal to be directed against everything in religion, morals, and probably in government and literature, which our Forefathers have been accustomed to reverence.' The first number appeared on 15 October 1822, with Byron's *Vision of Judgement* as the first and principal item. 'I know one may be damned for hoping no one else may e'er be so'; that was one theme of the poem. Never did he speak more truly. Never was one man damned so soon and so universally for the crime of pleading forgiveness for his fellow sinners.*

If the tragedy had not intervened, if Shelley had been there to welcome his friend and mentor, to appease with his charm, as he so often could, irritations and incompatibilities between his associates, the bitter animosities which later arose between Leigh Hunt and Byron might well have been avoided. If the company assembled to produce *The Liberal* – Byron chose the title – could have had the chance to work together, each might have been better able to test the concealed or forgotten virtues of the others, both in London and in Pisa. Hazlitt might have been guided towards a reconciliation with Shelley, just as Leigh Hunt had sought some accommodation between Byron and Hazlitt. Byron and Hazlitt might have been better able to discover their common approach to so many political arguments and political practitioners – starting with Shelley. A political alliance between the Byron–Shelley circle and the much derided Cockney school was not such an unthinkable proposition, since on so many matters of governing importance they were agreed – the infamy of the post-1815 settlement, at home and abroad, in which England played the role of gaoler and executioner; the rising tide of a new revolution, now more truly irrepressible; the wickedness of the Holy Alliance; the exposure of all the canting methods whereby Church and State imposed

* *The Vision of Judgement* is discussed with much joy and perception by John D. Jump in his *Byron*, and he remarks how Andrew Rutherford, in his *Byron: A Critical Study*, describes *The Vision* as 'Byron's masterpiece, aesthetically perfect, intellectually consistent, highly entertaining and morally profound'. Who can dissent? However, great stretches of *Don Juan* qualify for the same tribute, or why not, more remarkably, the whole of it?

their will; the rejection of all Thanksgiving Odes for those evil times, whether preached by poets, parsons or Quarterly Liars. The very name 'Liberal' selected by Byron was to be applied to their causes as never before. And thanks in no small degree to John Hunt's participation the attempted union did bear some fruit and, in Byron's case especially, the chance to write as he wished with no impediment was kept open when it might have been stunted afresh or blocked absolutely.

To accommodate his new friends still branded by some of his older ones, to help ensure *The Liberal* would not disgrace his cause, to drive ahead with *Don Juan* now that the impetus was so strong, and to keep his insistence that nothing and nobody should be allowed to tamper with its inspiration: these were his purposes, this was the Byron of 1822 and 1823: not someone greater than the Byron of *Darkness* or *Sardanapalus* or the fourth canto of *Childe Harold* or the first cantos of *Don Juan*, but one who must have felt thwarted and challenged in saying what he wanted, one who was resolved more than ever to say it.

The Liberal was greeted with a scream of Tory anger and outrage, a manifestation even more remarkable than the famous fit of morality described by Macaulay which had accompanied Byron's departure into exile.* The mixture of politics and religion should be noted; that was always the high Tory's favourite brew. And Byron was the main enemy. It so happened that his *Vision of Judgement* was printed without the Preface designed to emphasize that Southey not George III was intended as Byron's victim, and he suspected some foul play on Murray's part in failing to hand over the manuscripts to Hunt. But, with or without this flimsy shield to deter them, the Tory newspapers would surely have attacked. They certainly thought they could exploit the association with the Hunts, as Hobhouse & Co. had prophesied. They jeered at the journal's 'bad grammar and Cockney English', and could even muster a touch of humour: 'We should think', said one, 'the (Hunt) children must have done the first part of *The Liberal*.' But much more important surely was the opportunity they seized to destroy Byron himself;

* A good account of the *Liberal* episode is provided by William H. Marshall in his *Byron, Shelley, Hunt and The Liberal*.

they knew in their black Tory hearts that he was their most dangerous enemy: kill him first, and the smaller fry could be massacred later. And somehow *The Vision of Judgement* hit them harder than might have been expected. Charles Lamb, no admirer of Byron, alas, said this piece was 'the one good-natured thing that Byron ever wrote'. But the *Courier* dealt with the new menace in proper terms. Leigh Hunt was 'a manufacturer of namby pamby poetics', his friend 'the infidel Shelley' to be dismissed only because he was incapable of future mischief. The 'master-hand' which guided *The Liberal* was Byron's:

> With a brain from heaven and a heart from hell – with a pen that can write as angels speak, and yet that riots in thoughts which fiends might envy – with the power to charm, instruct, and elevate – but with the ruling passion to provoke our loathing and deserve our scorn – this compound of rottenness and beauty – this unsexed Circe, who gems the poisoned cup he offers us, and exhorts our admiration of its rare and curious workmanship, while the Soul sickens at the draught within – seems to have lived only that the world might learn from his example, how worthless and how pernicious a thing is genius, when divorced from religion, from morals, and from humanity.

And just at that same moment, greeting that first issue a more serious critic, Thomas Carlyle, gave his private view:

> Byron's Magazine, or rather Hunt's, 'The Liberal' is arrived in Town; but they will not sell it – it is so full of Atheism and Radicalism and other noxious *isms*. I had a glance of it one evening; I read it through and found two papers apparently by Byron, and full of talent as well as mischief. Hunt is the only serious man in it, since Shelley died: he has a wish to preach about politics and bishops and pleasure and paintings and nature, honest man; Byron wants only to write squibs against Southey and the like. The work will hardly do.

335

The *Courier* understood well enough that the argument was not one about literary fashions. The *Gentleman's Magazine* understood too, but thought perhaps that the peril could better be averted by saying that Byron was 'becoming so dull': a charge which lost some of its force as they moved towards the peroration:

> that he abandoned the Christian Religion for the religion of Childe Harold; that he changed his disgust, at Mr Moore's too warm painting, for a taste indicated by the incestuous ravings of Manfred; that he resigned his respect for the free government of Britain, for a love of democracy which he has inculcated in theory, and a preference for Turkish or Austrian despotism, which he has manifested in practice; that, once the admirer of Milton, Dryden, Pope, he has become the associate of the Cockney Bluestockings, and the panegyrist of Lady Morgan; or to give one which comprehends all other degrees of metamorphosis and degradation, he has sunk from the station of an English nobleman, and the highest place in English literature, to be the colleague of Mr Leigh Hunt, the author of *Don Juan*, and a contributor to the Liberal.

Another Tory critic had suggested that some parts of 'the blasphemous parody, *The Vision of Judgement*, were more deserving of the notice of the Attorney General than the critic', and the hint was soon adopted. During the December Sessions, the Grand Jury in Middlesex indicted John Hunt after a charge had been brought by a body known as the Constitutional Association: 'Hunt being a person of wicked and malicious disposition, and wickedly and maliciously contriving and intending to injure, defame, disgrace and vilify, the memory, reputation, and character of his late Majesty King George the Third. . . .' Byron commented on these developments in a lengthy letter which he still thought it worthwhile to send to Murray. He felt his whole reputation was at stake, but as often, it was to *Don Juan* he turned for the instrument with which he could best defend himself. He wrote to Murray on 25 October 1822:

D[on] Juan will be known by and bye for what it is intended a *satire* on *abuses* of the present *states* of Society – and not an eulogy of vice; – it may be now and then voluptuous – I can't help that – Ariosto is worse – Smollett (see Lord Strutwell in vol 2d. of R[oderick] R[andom] ten times worse – and Fielding no better. – No Girl will ever be seduced by reading D[on] J[uan] – no – no – she will go to Little's poems – & Rousseau's romans – for that – or even to the immaculate De Stael – they will encourage her – & not the Don – who laughs at that – and – and – most other things. – But never mind – 'Ca ira!' – And now to a less agreeable topic, of which 'pars magna es' – you Murray of Albemarle St. – and the other Murray of Bridge Street – 'Arcades Ambo' (*'Murrays both'*) et *cant*-are pares – ye I say – between you are the Causes of the prosecution of John Hunt Esqre, on account of the Vision; – you by sending him an incorrect copy – and the other by his function. – Egad – but H[unt]'s Counsel will lay it on you with a trowel – for your tergiversifying as to the M.S.S. &c. whereby poor H[unt] (& for anything I know – myself – I am willing enough) is likely to be impounded. –

Now – do you see what you and your friends do by your injudicious rudeness? – actually cement a sort of connection which you strove to prevent – and which had the H[unt]s *prospered* – would not in all probability have continued. – As it is – I will not quit them in their adversity – though it should cost me – character – fame – money – and the usual et cetera. – My original motives – I already explained (in the letter which you thought proper to show –) they are the *true* ones and I abide by them – as I tell you – and I told L[eig]h H[un]t when he questioned me on the subject of that letter. – He was violently hurt – & never will forgive me at bottom – but I can't help that, – I never meant to make a parade of it – but if he chose to question me – I could only answer the plain truth – and I confess I did not see anything in that letter to hurt him – unless I said he was 'a *bore*' which I don't remember. – Had their Journal gone on well – and I could have aided to make it better for them – I should then have left them after my safe pilotage off a lee shore – to

make a prosperous voyage by themselves. – As it is – I can't
& would not if I could – leave them amidst the breakers. –

As to any community of feeling – thought – or opinion
between L[eigh] H[unt] & me – there is little or none – we
meet rarely – hardly ever – but I think him a good principled
& able man – & must do as I would be done by. – I do not
know what world he has lived in – but I have lived in three
or four – and none of them like Keats and Kangaroo
terra incognita – Alas! poor Shelley! – how he would
have laughed – had he lived, and how we used to laugh now
& then – at various things – which are grave in the
Suburbs. – You are all mistaken about Shelley – you do not
know – how mild – how tolerant – how good he was in
Society – and as perfect a Gentleman as ever crossed a
drawing room; – when he liked – & where he liked. –

. . . Mr J[ohn] Hunt is most likely the publisher of the
new Cantos – with what prospects of success I know not –
nor does it very much matter – as far as I am concerned – but
I hope that it may be of use to him – for he is a stiff sturdy
conscientious man – and I like him – he is such a one – as
Prynne – or Pym might be.

Again and again, and in wonderfully vibrant tones, he found
himself pitting his wit and strength against what he believed,
quite rightly, to be the deeply reactionary forces which were
taking control, in London and across the whole continent. If
any question is offered about what he was up against, note
should be taken of Murray's reply: 'You see the result of being
forced into contact with wretches who take for granted that
everyone must be as infamous as themselves. – Really Lord
Byron – it is dreadful to think of yr association with such out-
casts from Society.' And the same Murray in the same letter did
not refrain from a little gentlemanly blackmail: 'My name is
connected with your Fame, and I beseech you to take care of it
even for your sister's sake – for we are in constant alarm but she
should be deprived of her situation at Court. . . .' He marked, in
a note to Mary Shelley, the 'continual declamation against the
Liberal from all parties – literary – amicable – and political – I

never heard so persevering an outcry against any work – nor do I know the reason for not even dullness or demerit could authorize the extraordinary tone of reprobation. . . .'

Then to Kinnaird, Byron wrote, on 24 February 1823:

As to the run against me – I fully believe it – but what is a man good for if he cannot face such things? – Whatever motives may be attributed to me on the score of the Hunts – *you* know the only *real* one – viz. a wish to assist them in their distress. . . . I have now in all eight Cantos of D[on] J[uan] (one completed the other day and not yet copied) the thing in 'the Liberal' and one or two still in M.S.S. – If you find any one to bid on the whole – so – if not – no matter. – As to popularity – Voltaire was reduced to live in a corner – and Rousseau stoned out of Switzerland – and banished France. – I should never have thought myself good for any thing – if I had not been detested by the English. – You see I know this better than *you* – for when you wrote to me in *raptures* with the *success*!! of 'Heaven and Earth' I told you that your joy was kind but premature. – You can tell me nothing of hostile or oppressive from the English – which I have not contemplated – and such is my feeling towards their national meanness – that I would not wish it otherwise – except as far as it gives my friends pain. – But Courage! – I'll work them.

And then again a few weeks later, to a Kinnaird whom he started to suspect – wrongly perhaps – of being subdued by the same alarms which had afflicted the rest of the Murray circle:

If you mean to hint that the new C[ant]o's are inferior to the old – I say that they are equal – and in parts superior – you recollect the similarly obliging and erroneous anticipation of worthy friends about the 3d. 4th. and 5th. – Henry Fox says you are quite alarmed about them – you certainly were *not* so when you first received them. – *What* has changed you I do not know – but this I know – that you seem to have got into the very thick of Murray's well known endeavour to

destroy every publication of mine – which don't pass
through his own medium. – The advice to postpone the
publication till I had written a new Childe Harold forsooth!
– *could* only come from that quarter and I know it did – for
the Man gave out – that *he* perhaps would condescend to
publish *that*. – Lady Blessington says you have been a little
alarmed about 'John Bull' ever since that paper attacked
you for becoming the Queen's banker – are you afraid that
he should do as much because you are my friend? – If so – I
will say in the preface that you did your best to suppress the
publication – all that remonstrance will ever obtain from
me will be Canto on Canto as long as I can write – do you
suppose that I was to sit down and suppress my free
thoughts for the Edinburgh or Quarterly? they may have
enough of that – if I live to repay them.

These literary clashes also coincided with troubles behind the
scenes, sometimes magnified out of all proportion. The quarrel
with Leigh Hunt was a wretched and unedifying one, most
especially, it must be thought, when Leigh Hunt sought to pursue it in the most furious terms, when Byron was safely dead. By
the mere recital of the facts it is not difficult to expose uncon-
scionable insensitivities on both sides. Byron should have
treated Hunt's large family, poor Marianne and her Yahoo children, with more sympathy, and Leigh Hunt should have had
enough knowledge of the world to recognize that, if tact is discarded or despised, the bestowal of favours can leave deep sores
on both sides. But the detailed record of how the breach
between them cut ever deeper, day by day almost, should not be
allowed to hide the fact that each of them, after his different
styles, was not deflected from the job he had agreed to do. They
did still combine their efforts to produce *The Liberal* – for all its
commercial failure, no small contribution to English literature.
All Byron's contributions, it so happens, had not been
specifically written for the new journal, but they were none the
worse for that, and the original idea of the journal had been to
offer a new outlet for writings which might otherwise not be
published or be in danger of heavy censorship. And all the

while, in Byron's case, while he was engaged in hearing the news of *The Liberal*'s fortunes or misfortunes, he was writing much else, with a political zest never surpassed even according to his own high standard.

Some of the contributions by both Byron and Hazlitt to later issues of *The Liberal* offer tantalizing hints about their relationship. Hazlitt contributed five full-scale essays, all of them of a high quality and one of them higher still, *My First Acquaintance with Poets*. Even if he was offended by the sympathetic tone of the essay towards the Lakers, it is hard to believe that Byron would have read it without any appreciation whatever – especially, it might be added, if he had doubts about the authorship. It was second only to *The Vision of Judgement*, and the others had several brilliant Hazlittean touches to offer. Maybe Byron did not read any articles but his own. He *was* interested in an anonymous and generally favourable notice of his *Heaven and Earth* which appeared in the *Edinburgh Review*, and he made some inquiries to discover whether Jeffrey was the author. In fact, as we know now, a century and a half later, the writer of the most discriminating paragraphs was Hazlitt. He often wrote whole paragraphs which Jeffrey might incorporate in the final product, as he did, as we have surmised, with *Sardanapalus*. Hazlitt thought well of *Heaven and Earth*, and contrasted it most favourably with Thomas Moore's piece on the same theme. Moore had been nervous that he might be accused of impiety in his *Love of the Angels*; so he contemplated changing his Angels to Turks and his God to Allah. Byron had reason for his scorn: 'Are you *really* recanting, or softening to the clergy? It will do little good for you – it is you, not the poem they are at. They will say they frightened you – forbid it, Ireland. Believe me.' The Mooreish recanting revealed afresh the atmosphere in which they were writing; why Thomas Moore & Co. were so alarmed about Byron's association with the Hunts. Byron, it appears, never had the chance of discovering how the Hazlitt who had delivered the critical lectures at the Surrey Institution in 1818 was being weaned to fresh judgements by Japhet, by Sardanapalus and, most movingly perhaps, by Myrrha. Rather, it is sometimes assumed that the lecturer Scamp who makes a brief appearance in Byron's piece, *The Blues*, which he also handed on to *The Liberal*, was modelled on Hazlitt. When Byron released this piece to Hunt, he must have known that Hazlitt was writing for the same journal. He called *The Blues* a buffoonerie, and that was about right; it was certainly *not* a serious satire, such as Byron could now always achieve when he wished. Hazlitt himself made no reference anywhere to Scamp, and since he was always quite ready – before or after *The Liberal* – to take issue with the noble poet, it does appear that the model for Scamp may have been someone else altogether. It is sad, to repeat the point mildly, that they never met. Hazlitt, as we have seen, had a special skill for noting men's – and women's – voices. If they had talked, it is impossible to believe that Hazlitt would not have been charmed and that he would not have recorded for us his version of the voice with which the serpent tempted Eve.

Where they could not so readily have found agreement was in their estimate of contemporary English writers. Hazlitt could recognize, with perception and magnanimity, new signs of genius among the Lakers, for example, even while he detested their politics. Byron was inclined to be much more constricted and orthodox in his critical verdicts, still seeking to apply the precepts of his own most honoured model, Pope, in a world where new departures must be accepted. Byron's worst misjudgement was of Keats whom he continued to deride in unpublished (and unpublishable) terms almost till the end, only starting to attempt a new evaluation in the notable case of Keats's *Hyperion*. Hazlitt, the critic, could have taught Byron something here, but maybe he would have learnt much too; for the great Keatsean quality of disinterestedness, of negative capability, which Keats partly learnt from Hazlitt could be displayed by Byron too; not consciously or deliberately but predominantly in much of his later writing. Maybe their arms-length literary quarrels would have flared to something worse face to face; but more probably they would have found their common cause in tackling the Wordsworth who still preached of Carnage's daughter or the Southey who would despatch them to Botany Bay. The strongest tone of *The Liberal* was addressed magnificently against the ancient and modern Gods who threatened to plunge Europe into a new bloodbath. Hazlitt could summon Pope to his aid here no less than Byron, against

> Gods partial, changeful, passionate, unjust,
> Whose attributes were rage, revenge, or lust. . . .

Hazlitt could capture this mood in prose as Byron had done in verse:

> The great world has been doing little else but playing at make-believe all its lifetime. For several thousand years its chief rage was to paint larger pieces of wood and smear them with gore, and call them Gods and offer victims to them – slaughtered hecatombs, the fat of goats and oxen, or human sacrifices – shewing in this its love of shew, of cruelty, and imposture; and woe to him who would 'peep through the blanket of the dark to cry *Hold, hold*' – *Great is Diana of the Ephesians*, was the answer in all ages.

This indeed was the mocking answer of Byron no less than Hazlitt, each capable of quoting the Scripture to their purpose. And Alexander Pope, it should be noted, could be summoned with equal facility to sustain the sacred, secular cause of the true peacemakers. If Hazlitt had arrived in Pisa as John Hunt's emissary instead of his brother and his bunch of Yahoos, *The Liberal* could have lived. It could have enjoyed a success worthy of the journal which had published, along with other treasures, a satire as delicately savage as anything written by Pope, and an essay which can take its place as the best in the language.

The most overtly political piece produced by Byron at this time was *The Age of Bronze*, which he started writing over Christmas 1822, despatched to London in January, and which was published, anonymously, by John Hunt on 1 April 1823. Since it seemed to lack the ease and subtlety of *Don Juan* and *The Vision*, and was, as he himself acknowledged, a reversion to his early *English Bards* style, the poem has sometimes been deprecated as a rough political polemic and nothing else. Indeed, the

Tory writers in *Blackwood's* at the time sought to pillory Hazlitt and John Hunt as 'a pack of liars' for disseminating the suggestion that Byron was the author. For a while they pressed the charge – perhaps to infuriate Byron himself – that Hazlitt was the real author of the offending piece. The anonymity arose since Byron thought he was writing for *The Liberal*, and for these reasons, and some political reasons which still endure, *The Age of Bronze* has rarely received its due. By any test, it is far superior to *English Bards* – the targets are much clearer, more worthy of assault and more exactly hit, as fiercely attacked, at times, as one finds in the satire of Byron's first model Pope or, more comparably in this instance, as downright as Dryden. Possibly his contemporaries, like later critics, were misled by the opening verses which seemed to be treating with too much concern the humiliation and maltreatment of Napoleon on St Helena, a popular enough theme at Holland House and one which had fascinated Byron, but not one to touch the interests of peoples and nations who had to face the desolation of the 1820s. His critics should have been warned from the start:

> I know not if the angels weep, but men
> Have wept enough – for what? – to weep again.

He would not follow Napoleon's chariot for long:

> The king of kings, and yet of slaves the slave
> Who burst the chains of millions to renew
> The very fetters which his arm broke through.

It was the resurgent people in so many lands who stirred him: the Poles, the Italians, the Spanish, the Americans, the Greeks. He was among the first, if not the very first, to see and acclaim the common pattern of revolt across the continent.

> But lo! a Congress – What! that hallowed name
> Which freed the Atlantic! May we hope the same
> For outworn Europe?

Byron was not to be deceived by the statesmen and diplomats who assembled at Verona.

> Clap thy permitted palms, kind Italy
> For this much still thy fettered hands are free!

Verona was paying court to one whose political character Byron had studied with precision. His 'coxcomb Czar' deserves a place in the annals of invective alongside Dryden's Achitophel.*

> Resplendent sight! Behold the coxcomb Czar,
> The Autocrat of waltzes and of war!
> As eager for a plaudit as a realm,
> And just as fit for flirting as the helm;
> A Calmuck beauty with a Cossack wit,
> And generous spirit, when 'tis not frost-bit;
> Now half dissolving to a liberal thaw,
> But hardened back whene'er the morning's raw;
> With no objection to true Liberty,
> Except that it would make the nations free.
> How well the imperial dandy prates of peace!
> How fain, if Greeks would be his slaves, free Greece!
> How nobly gave he back the Poles their Diet,
> Then told pugnacious Poland to be quiet!
> How kindly would he send the mild Ukraine,
> With all her pleasant Pulks, to lecture Spain!

* So harsh or memorable was the portrait that one of Byron's most sympathetic editors – E. H. Coleridge, writing in Volume V of his 1901 edition of the Poetry – could not refrain from reminding his readers that 'Byron's special grudge against him at this time was due to his vacillation with regard to the cause of Greek Independence. But he is too contemptuous. There were points in common between the "Coxcomb Czar" and his satirist.' Such an outburst from such a normally acquiescent quarter nearly eighty years after *The Age of Bronze* was published suggests that the Czar Alexander had his friends in the England of the 1820s, or the England of the 1890s or probably both. But Byron did not share these Tory or Whiggish prejudices. And he was right about Greece. The Greeks must win their own freedom:

> How should the Autocrat of bondage be
> The King of serfs, and set the nations free?

How royally show off in proud Madrid
His goodly person, from the South long hid!
A blessing cheaply purchased, the world knows,
By having Muscovites for friends or foes.

Each of the other victorious leaders received their due, noble
Albion, for one:

Alas, the Country! How shall tongue or pen
Bewail her now *un*country gentlemen?
The last to bid the cry of warfare cease,
The first to make a malady of peace.
For what were all these country patriots born?
To hunt – and vote – and raise the price of corn?
But corn, like every mortal thing, must fall,
Kings – Conquerors – and markets most of all.
And must ye fall with every ear of grain?
Why would you trouble Buonaparte's reign?
He was your great Triptolemus; his vices
Destroyed but realms, and still maintained your prices;
He amplified to every lord's content
The grand agrarian alchymy, high *rent*.

The offence cut deep indeed and indiscriminately.

How rich is Britain! not indeed in mines,
Or peace or plenty, corn or oil, or wines;
No land of Canaan, full of milk and honey,
Nor (save in paper shekels) ready money:
But let us not to own the truth refuse,
Was ever Christian land so rich in Jews?
Those parted with their teeth to good King John,
And now, ye kings, they kindly draw your own;
All states, all things, all sovereigns they control,
And waft a loan 'from Indus to the pole.'
The banker – broker – baron – brethren, speed
To aid these bankrupt tyrants in their need.
Nor these alone; Columbia feels no less
Fresh speculations follow each success;

> And philanthropic Israel deigns to drain
> Her mild per-centage from exhausted Spain.
> Not without Abraham's seed can Russia march;
> 'Tis gold, not steel, that rears the conqueror's arch.

Or ruder still :

> (Where now, oh Pope! is thy forsaken toe?
> Could it not favour Judah with some kicks?
> Or has it ceased to 'kick against the pricks?')
> On Shylock's shore behold them stand afresh,
> To cut from Nation's hearts their 'pound of flesh.'

It is not easy to believe that fading poetic merit was the cause why *The Age of Bronze* was dismissed as an imitative failure or to forget that that same Pope's toe was kicking Teresa and her family from state to state in the Italy which the Holy Alliance had subdued. Or sometimes the counter-attack took a more circuitous route; was not Byron's rhetoric strictly defensive, offering no fresh spacious escape, and was not *The Age of Bronze* a final proof of the charge? Professor Grierson's retort to these excuses is still the best:

> Nor is his satire and eloquence disposed of by declaring that his conception of liberty was purely negative, for he was not a metaphysician but a poet and a politician. A free government, says Burke, is for practical purposes, what the people think so. The Europe for which Byron spoke knew well that it was not free, and understood and appreciated Byron's attacks on Holy Alliances and Congresses better than Shelley's metaphysics or Wordsworth's enlightenment.*

And better still, it may be added, than Wordsworth's thanksgiving. Byron gave the answer direct too in Canto VIII to Wordsworth's blasphemy:–

> 'Carnage' (so Wordsworth tells you) is God's daughter:
> If he speak truth, she is Christ's sister, and
> Just now behaved as in the Holy Land . . .

---

* Grierson: *The Background* (See page 259).

And that behaviour, be it not forgotten, was the mass slaughter of Moslems as they prayed to their Allah. Wordsworth's line, wrote Byron, was 'as pretty a pedigree for Murder as ever was found out by Garter King of Arms – What would have been said, had any free-spoken people discovered such a lineage?'

It is advisable always to remember what Byron was writing – and what he was reading. Many of the events in his eventful life, political affairs or love affairs, can acquire a new lustre and significance when it is noted how he translated them into poetry or discovered new meanings in old favourites. When, for example, did he first read Montaigne? He would soon be describing the whole of *Don Juan* as 'by far the most popular of mine' and one which would 'just show these fellows that I am not the boy to be put down by their outcry – I mean it for a poetical T. Shandy – or Montaigne's Essays with a story for a hinge.' The more one looks, the more apt the comparison. But when did he start with Montaigne and how deep did his interest grow? How the intimacy began is not clear, but certainly he went on reading him till the end.* Leigh Hunt, who could be jaundiced in his reports about Byron's reading as about most else, recorded what he had observed at Pisa – 'The only writer of past times, whom he read with avowed satisfaction, was Montaigne' – but no explicit confirmation is required. His whole temperament had a touch of Montaigne in it: the readiness to discuss sexual passion or sexual fiascos was only one of the signs. It is surely legitimate to suppose that he learnt about Montaigne first of all from his old mentor, Alexander Pope, and

* Much the best book on Byron and his books is Elizabeth Boyd's *Byron's Don Juan: A Critical Study*, first published by The Humanities Press, New York, in 1945, and again in 1958. She explores his 'much-tumbled' library with loving care and diligence and inspiration. But she cannot give us any detail about when the Montaigne enthusiasm started. No edition of Montaigne was in his library when it was sold. No copy is referred to in the elaborate index published by E. H. Coleridge in 1903. He did not, like Swift, give a copy of Montaigne to his Vanessa, or, so far as we know, to any of them. Quite conceivably Montaigne exerted his full influence in those months of 1822 when he was returning to *Don Juan*, even though Pope and Swift together had planted the first seed.

then from a newer one he was now discovering or re-discovering, Jonathan Swift. Both Pope and Swift paid particular honour to Montaigne; the foremost English Catholic of his age and the foremost English (or Irish) Anglican had both acknowledged the old Jewish sceptic as their master. And Hazlitt could have joined that company; he took Montaigne as a model, both for his doctrines and his forms, and never ceased to repay the debt. Byron's admiration was no less unconstrained and he naturally summoned Montaigne to his aid when he expressed his new-found or newly re-established scepticism more openly than ever before.

'*Que scais-je?*' was the motto of Montaigne,
   As also of the first Academicians:
That all is dubious which Man may attain,
   Was one of their most favourite positions.
There's no such thing as certainty, that's plain
   As any of Mortality's Conditions:
So little do we know what we're about in
This world, I doubt if doubt itself be doubting.

It is a pleasant voyage perhaps to float,
   Like Pyrrho, on a sea of speculation;
But what if carrying sail capsize the boat?
   Your wise men don't know much of navigation;
And swimming long in the abyss of thought
   Is apt to tire: a calm and shallow station
Well nigh the shore, where one stoops down and gathers
Some pretty shell, is best for moderate bathers.

'But Heaven,' as Cassio says, 'is above all, –
   No more of this then, – let us pray!' We have
Souls to save, since Eve's slip and Adam's fall,
   Which tumbled all mankind into the grave,
Besides fish, beasts, and birds. 'The Sparrow's fall
   Is special providence,' though how *it* gave
Offence, we know not; probably it perched
Upon the tree which Eve so fondly searched.

> Oh, ye immortal Gods! What is Theogony?
>   Oh, thou too mortal Man! what is Philanthropy?
> Oh, World! which was and is, what is Cosmogony?
>   Some people have accused me of Misanthropy;
> And yet I know no more than the mahogany
>   That forms this desk, of what they mean; – *Lykanthropy*
> I comprehend, for without transformation
> Men become wolves on any slight occasion.
>
> But I, the mildest, meekest of mankind,
>   Like Moses, or Melancthon, who have ne'er
> Done any thing exceedingly unkind, –
>   And (though I could not now and then forbear
> Following the bent of body or of mind)
>   Have always had a tendency to spare, –
> Why do they call me misanthrope? Because
> *They hate me, not I them*. – And here we'll pause.

Here Sardanapalus, the peace-loving emperor who scorned to adopt the methods of his enemies, reappears more convincingly than ever. That portrait was not some passing infatuation. It was intended to endure:

> And I will war, at least in words (and – should
>   My chance so happen – deeds) with all who war
> With Thought; – and of Thought's foes by far most rude,
>   Tyrants and Sycophants have been and are.
> I know not who may conquer: if I could
>   Have such a prescience, it should be no bar
> To this my plain, sworn, downright detestation
> Of every despotism in every nation.

And then:

> 'Tis time we should proceed with our good poem
>   For I maintain that it is really good.

And so it is. Always the unforgiveable offence seems to be, however unavoidable, the interruption of *Don Juan*'s matchless sweep. And then we should recall that when he wrote this canto he was still awaiting the publication of three earlier ones and had no assurance by whom and when these new ones would be published. It was not until 15 July 1823 that three cantos of *Don Juan* appeared under a new imprint: 'London, 1823, Printed for John Hunt, 38 Tavistock Street, Covent Garden and 22 Old Bond Street'. And this same John Hunt had published the year before, anonymously, Hazlitt's *Liber Amoris* or *The New Pygmalion*. To have been the publisher of both Byron and Hazlitt at the moment when each was inviting mortal – or immortal – defamation was a double service not easily measured to English politics and English literature.

But this was no more than half or less than half of *Don Juan*. Well before that notable publication day he had made arrangements to forsake, temporarily at least, the Italy which had given him refuge for seven years and such inspiration to write. As he made his arrangments to sail to Greece, he did not know what reception the new *Don Juan* might be given and whether and how the rest would be printed. 'As to the M.S.S.', he wrote to Kinnaird on 16 June, 'you really must publish them whenever I have sailed – my distance will diminish the hatred of my enemies.' He was the only person – with just two exceptions maybe, John Hunt and Kinnaird, but in a most qualified degree – who knew what the remaining seven cantos contained: not only the elaboration of his Montaigne-modelled creed in modern terms but the whole, magnificent assault, on English aristocratic society – its ideals, privileges, policies and crimes, and the pietistic religion in which it was draped, and the horrors of war and destruction which the two together were willing to impose. 'In all this', wrote Professor Grierson, 'Byron seemed to be the child, the defiant and rebellious child of Evangelical and Calvinistic Protestantism, feeling the power of the doctrine he defied, the reality of sin and evil, as Shelley never did.' And at no time can he have felt those childhood pressures so intensely, not knowing for sure whether he would be able to state his own case to the world.

But can we leave *Don Juan* on such a note? Canto X, we may recall, looked forward, not back and offered a tribute to the power of the poet which he would often affect to deny.

When Newton saw an apple fall, he found
　　In that slight startle from his contemplation –
'Tis *said* (for I'll not answer above ground
　　For any sage's creed or calculation) –
A mode of proving that the earth turned round
　　In a most natural whirl called 'Gravitation,'
And this is the sole mortal who could grapple,
Since Adam, with a fall, or with an apple.

Man fell with apples, and with apples rose,
　　If this be true; for we must deem the mode
In which Sir Isaac Newton could disclose
　　Through the then unpaved stars the turnpike road,
A thing to counterbalance human woes;
　　For ever since immortal man hath glowed
With all kinds of mechanics, and full soon
Steam-engines will conduct him to the Moon.

And wherefore this exordium? – Why, just now,
　　In taking up this paltry sheet of paper,
My bosom underwent a glorious glow,
　　And my internal Spirit cut a caper:
And though so much inferior, as I know,
　　To those who, by the dint of glass and vapour,
Discover stars, and sail in the wind's eye,
I wish to do as much by Poesy.

How then and where was Byron to take leave of *Don Juan*? Byron's own famous forecast was that he would 'make his hero finish as Anarcharcis Clootz – in the French Revolution', guillotined for his allegiance to freedom's cause in Robespierre's Paris. It was a bright, passing notion, and would have expressed Byron's own judgements about the Revolution – and before any latter-day Jacobin rushes in to cite this likely conclusion of the story as a sign of Byron's retreat from a final revolutionary posture, it must be recalled that Clootz's fate was so nearly that of Thomas Paine, against whom no such charges of revisionist or reformist backsliding are normally levelled. As it stands, and it is evident that Byron was not dissatisfied, the poem ends with a brilliant, devastating surprise, the woman's tide sweeping forward in a manner in which only Byron would have dared. The conclusion of Canto XVI is sometimes quoted as proof of his incurable cynicism or flippancy, whereas it is much more a stroke of his comic genius. However, it should also be noted that scattered through those last cantos, evidence is offered of the modern quality not usually attributed to him – Byron's acknowledgement of the trials to which his women and most others are subjected: his feminism, to use the word monstrously and anachronistically. The best case on this score, as I have tried to argue before, arises from the pleas of mitigation made by some of the women who knew him best – his mother, Lady Melbourne, Lady Oxford, and, of course, Teresa, till her dying day. She would illustrate how he had always loved her *à la Corinne*, and never *à la Adolphe*. But who can deny that he sometimes repaid the compliment of understanding?

> Alas! Worlds fall – and Woman, since she fell'd
>   The World (as, since that history, less polite
> Than true, hath been a creed so strictly held)
>   Has not yet given up the practice quite.
> Poor Thing of Usages! Coerc'd, compell'd,
>   Victims when wrong, and martyr oft when right,
> Condemn'd to child-bed, as men for their sins
> Have shaving too entailed upon their chins, –
>
> A daily plague which in the aggregate
>   May average on the whole with parturition.
> But as to women, who can penetrate
>   The real sufferings of their she condition?
> Man's very sympathy with their estate
>   Has much of selfishness and more suspicion.
> Their love, their virtue, beauty, education,
> But form good housekeepers to breed a nation.
>
> All this were very well and can't be better;
>   But even this is difficult, Heaven knows!
> So many troubles from her birth beset her,
>   Such small distinction between friends and foes,

The gilding wears so soon from off her fetter,
  That – but ask any woman if she'd choose
(Take her at thirty, that is) to have been
Female or male? a school-boy or a Queen?

'Petticoat Influence' is a great reproach,
Which even those who obey would fain be thought
To fly from, as from hungry pikes a roach;
  But, since beneath it upon earth we are brought
By various joltings of life's hackney coach,
  I for one venerate a petticoat –
A garment of a mystical sublimity,
No matter whether russet, silk, or dimity.

And lest these glances might seem too trivial, those last cantos contained also the vision of Aurora, renewing the aspirations which he would never suppress without chance of recovery:

And, certainly, Aurora had renewed
  In him some feelings he had lately lost,
Or hardened; feelings which, perhaps ideal,
Are so divine, that I must deem them real:-

The love of higher things and better days:
  The unbounded hope, and heavenly ignorance
Of what is called the World, and the World's ways:
  The moments when we gather from a glance
More joy than from all future pride or praise,
  Which kindle manhood, but can ne'er entrance
The Heart in an existence of its own,
Of which another's bosom is the zone.[*]

---

* Some of these views on Byron's irrepressible hopefulness are best presented by E. D. Hirsch in his chapter 'Byron and the Terrestrial Paradise' included in *From Sensibility to Romanticism*. The same chapter is included in a Norton Critical Edition of *Byron's Poetry*, selected by Frank D. McConnell. Here are to be found many other critical treasures not easily found elsewhere: for instance, the introduction, *Lord Byron's Pilgrimage* by Bergen Evans: 'High moral earnestness in belligerent abundance, absolute assurance that she knew all the ultimate answers to the riddle of the

Most anxiously, before he left for Greece, in July, he was waiting for the proofs of Canto XVI. He had to sail before they arrived. And when the edition did finally appear – on 26 March 1824 – it carried the thoughtful note from John Hunt: 'The errors in the press, in this Canto, – if there be any, are not to be attributed to the Author, as he was deprived of any opportunity of correcting the proof sheets.' Maybe he knew what an artistic achievement it was and why therefore he could sail for Greece with some serenity in the place he had truly fashioned for himself: his heart for every fate.

---

universe, and an evangelical zeal to subdue others for her convictions – these she had; but tenderness, laughter, playfulness, helplessness, absurdity, affection – the things Byron liked and needed in a woman – these she had not.' The writer was, of course, describing Lady Byron – I thought for a moment he was writing of Mrs Thatcher.

The most terrifying portrait ever drawn of Lady Byron – and the most indisputable, since it is composed of such a huge assembly of accurate detail – is that which appears in Doris Langley Moore's *Ada Countess of Lovelace*. In her previous volume on the subject Mrs Moore said that 'it is painful to watch a young, attractive and in many ways gifted woman allowing herself to be consumed with vindictiveness passing itself off as righteousness.' But this is what did happen, and mostly the manners and religion of the age assisted her in the exertion: the same age which damned Lord Byron, almost beyond recovery.

THIRTEEN

Cephalonia–Missolonghi*

> I have two constant sentiments, a love of
> liberty and a detestation of cant, and neither
> is calculated to gain me friends.
>
> In conversation with Lady Blessington.

Among the books which Byron took with him on the *Hercules*,
on the journey from Leghorn en route for Cephalonia and
Missolonghi, were the nineteen volumes of Sir Walter Scott's
The Works of Jonathan Swift, D.D., with *A Life of the Author* by the
same Sir Walter. The combination of subject and biographer
must have made an irresistible appeal to Byron. Sir Walter had
made friendly gestures to him from a distance at some of the
most awkward moments in his life; Byron had even dared to
dedicate his *Cain* to him, with no shattering response; and Sir
Walter's life of Swift was truly a determined and graceful effort

* My own introduction to this last period in Byron's life, which offers a
huge, vast literature of its own, was made through Harold Nicolson's
Byron: The Last Journey, published by Constable in 1924. Like some others, I
fear, I was not attracted by the approach to Byron of one who might have
been expected to be one of his most winning and faithful admirers, and
who, for me, had written so well on so many kindred topics – Benjamin
Constant, The Congress of Vienna, and much else. Nicolson seemed to
have some grudge against Byron, and seemed to suppose that he went to
Greece to cure his sourness. But if he did suffer from such a complaint, *Don
Juan* was the cure.

The most important book on the whole background is William St
Clair's *That Greece Might Still Be Free*. The most elaborate and instructive
comment on Byron's relationship with Swift is contained in A. B. England's *Byron's Don Juan and Eighteenth Century Literature*, some parts of
which are reproduced in John Jump's *Byron: A Symposium*, already noted
page 294. Professor England shows, with much excellent illustration,
how well Byron knew Swift, how he knew him in some respects better
even than he knew Pope.

to tackle the hero or villain of previous biographies more fairly than many who had attempted the task before and a multitude who came later. And even before the assistance of Sir Walter's kindly insight was offered, Swift had been taking a higher and enlarged place in Byron's literary Valhalla; not quite yet being accorded the same esteem as Pope, but not displaced from him very far. Often to ward off his own prudish, prurient assailants, Byron would invoke the shield of Swift, his fame or his infamy. He loved his rhyming, his ribaldry, his taste for irony, his touch of savagery; above all, his readiness to mix comedy and tragedy in the same deadly potion. To read Scott's *Life*, is to appreciate why Swift's appeal to Byron grew so steadily:

> His powers of versification [wrote Scott] are admirably adapted to his favourite subjects. Rhyme, which is a hand-cuff to an inferior poet, he who is master of his Art wears as a bracelet. Swift was of the latter description; his lines fall as easily into the best grammatical arrangement, and the most simple and forcible expression, as if he had been writing in prose.

These beautiful sentences in praise of Swift offer an uncanny comparison with Byron's own developed style. But the Swift they were writing about was the same of whom Dryden had written: 'Cousin Swift, you will never be a poet', and later critics were all too ready to adopt this judgement until Scott and Byron – and Hazlitt, it must be noted, before either of them – came forward to alter the general view. Often during his last voyage Byron talked of Swift. He emphasized the point to the incurable romancer, Trelawny, who had complimented him on the rhymes in *Don Juan*. 'If you are curious in these matters, look in Swift,' he replied, 'he beats us all hollow, his rhymes are wonderful.' For once, Trelawny may be believed without question or cavilling.*

* I read this comment in a review by Nigel Dennis in the *Sunday Telegraph* (October 1977) of William St Clair's *Trelawny: The Incurable Romancer*. 'Can we believe Trelawny made the remark?' asks Dennis, and he replies: 'Trelawny was much too foolish to have invented it.' William St Clair's volume, the best and most level-headed on Trelawny, confirms the Dennis verdict.

Swift and Scott together had to contend with some old rivals. Soon after his arrival in Cephalonia he found himself happily engaged in theological debate with Dr James Kennedy, the local physician and a Methodist who struggled to save his body and soul. Byron brought his natural courtesy and keen religious interest to the task in a manner which captivated Dr Kennedy at the time and has stirred much curiosity ever since, including Teresa's. She too could recognize her Byron in those debates, as charmingly reported by Dr Kennedy. He did not yield one inch of ground in defence of his own scepticism, but he recapitulated his case in a manner which carried no offence to Catholic or Calvinist:

> I am sure that no man reads the Bible with more pleasure than I do. I read a chapter every day and in a short time shall be able to beat the canters with their own weapons. Most of them are like Catholics who place the Virgin Mary before Christ, and Christ before God; only they have substituted the Apostle Paul for the Virgin, and they place him above Jesus, and Jesus above the Almighty.

No doubt Dr Kennedy was guilty occasionally, like others of his faith, of making these transpositions in the Holy Family hierarchy almost without noticing. And we must pause to wonder, too, how the Calvinist Dr Kennedy could have coped with Byron's compliment to the Pope: 'I like his holiness very much, particularly since an order, which I understand he has lately given, that no more miracles shall be performed.' Ever since his boyhood he had been willing to engage the authorities in argument about the absurdities and cruelties and injustices and horrific certainties which their religions were prepared to condone and propagate.* Along with the chapter of the Bible he

---

* Byron's religion or his rejection of religion became so dominant a theme that the preaching of his own brand of scepticism appeared ever more constant and assured. The book which tackles the subject most directly is *Byron as Sceptic and Believer* by Edward Wayne Marjarum, first published in 1938 and re-issued by Russell & Russell Inc. in 1962. The author strives to hold the balance – that is, between his scepticism and his belief – fairly

claimed to read every day – from the copy given him by Augusta – he would read now also an essay of Montaigne. And Montaigne's pupil, Alexander Pope, had not been displaced or removed to a subordinate place. Rather, Swift had now been elevated to the same pinnacle.

One other passage in Scott's pages we may imagine Byron reading with special delight dealt with some of his diseases and how eminent medical authorities had attributed some of them to 'habits of early and profligate indulgence'. Scott examined

---

and securely. But since Byron is allowed to speak for himself time and time again, his fury against whatever powers had decreed such a range of human suffering becomes well-nigh uncontrollable. It may be noted here, however, that in one of the most recent interpretations, *Byron's Don Juan*, Bernard Beatty argues that the poem was a religious one, or at least that it was moving powerfully in that direction, and that Aurora Raby appears at the end to provide what one reviewer called 'the improbable ascetic heroine'. The whole book is a closely argued one, but the final claim too ambitious. The author in turn directs the reader's attention to Jerome McGann's 'brilliant summary in *Fiery Dust* (pages 247–55) which establishes "the strange marriage of Socinianism and Catholicism in Byron's thought" and downplays the importance of Byron's Calvinism'. The pages are brilliant indeed; they do illustrate how Byron had disavowed his Calvinism, and how little it could be claimed that some other religion had been put in its place.

One of the best arguments about his religion – and one which points to a firm conclusion – was contained in Ernest J. Lovell Jr's *Byron: The Record of a Quest*. He illustrates how Byron's scepticism deepened as the years passed and considering how strongly Thomas Moore testified about its strength in the early years of their acquaintance, the conclusion seems to me unchallengeable. 'He never found a necessary faith to believe, consistently, that the natural order was essentially benevolent to man; and if not, what is then to be said of its Creator?' More and more he posed the question, and failed to receive an intelligible reply. 'This last period of his life,' Lovell continued, 'reveals more clearly than any other his preoccupation with a God who was not only cruel and unjust but even bloodthirsty.' And how could men and mankind face such a challenge with honour. 'He refused to escape into a Wordsworthian asylum of natural solitude, into Chateaubriand's land of the happy savage, or into anybody's dream of the Middle Ages or a future Utopia.' And Professor Lovell is, of course, the editor of those two volumes of Byron's conversations, *His Very Self and Voice* published in 1954. The voice is irrepressible.

these accusations with a scruple worthy of a later, more scientific age, and concluded with the sentence which combines his humanity and his wit: 'And, until medical authors can clearly account for and radically cure the diseases of their contemporary patients, they may readily be excused from assigning dishonourable causes for the disorders of the illustrious dead.' And this sentence which should be studied by all biographers tempted to offer their wisdom beside sickbeds or deathbeds has a peculiar, heightened Swiftian application. No great writer has been more plainly charged with and convicted of madness, and yet the charge, as all the modern evidence proves, is false. The main reason why so terrible a libel was so eagerly and persistently believed was that Dr Johnson had adopted and disseminated it, rounding off the tale, in his *Vanity of Human Wishes* verses, with the seemingly incontrovertible sneer that Swift spent his last years 'a driveller and a show'. Walter Scott was suspicious of Dr Johnson's treatment of Swift on other matters, but he had no means of repudiating the charge. So it stood for all to read, including Byron on the way to Greece. One day, amid his fevers, he said to his doctor, Julius Millingen, 'the apprehension of two things now haunt my mind. I picture myself slowly expiring on a bed of torture or terminating my days like Swift – a grinning idiot.'

The last hours, the last days were horrific enough, even if he was spared each of these particular afflictions. Considering how much life was still there, how modern medicine could easily have offered a cure, the whole scene was near enough to torture. The last months, so multifariously chronicled, with almost every single detail recorded and disputed, still present an argument. Even if the English establishment averted its gaze, the eyes of the rest of the world were soon riveted upon him, and he left, for our amusement and instruction, a wonderfully assorted bundle of legacies: the record of much practical aid and advice offered to his Greek comrades-in-arms; a few unpublished stanzas of *Don Juan*, as we have seen; a splendid renewed religious argument with the Calvinists routed as if by some modern Gideon; an exchange with his new publisher, essential for his later reputation; and a hint of a last love affair, the whole comprised in that last wonderful poem on his thirty-sixth year, part love song, part battle cry, holding the Byronic balance between the individual's freedom and the claims of a larger humanity. It may seem a sacrilege to tear out any single strand from this tapestry, and yet it is true that he had known what he was doing better than anyone else, and even at Missolonghi, after the fatal fever had struck him, it was the news of *Don Juan*'s health which could stir his spirit: 'They may say what they will of the work in question – but it will stand – and as high as most others in time.' It does stand indeed. He had been inspired to start it in the Venice of his adoption, and the last cantos were published only a few days before his death. He seemed to know, thanks to the good news received at Missolonghi of John Hunt's unfailing courage, that *Don Juan* would shake the world more even than *Childe Harold* had done. *Childe Harold* made him famous overnight and caught the ear of all Europe with a new, inescapable accent, but there was one defect in it, the egoism, the mood of posing melancholy in face of the world's trials which almost became identified with Byron himself: 'The man of loneliness and mystery/Scarce seen to smile, and/Seldom heard to sigh.' How nearly suffocated was he by that false picture; even some of his greatest contemporaries mistook what they saw. For this was never the real man, as the superabundant wit and worldly wisdom of the letters prove, and as *Don Juan* asserts more surely still. He made himself instead the poet of the Revolution, and the transformation was complete before he ever set sail for Greece a second time. *Don Juan* was Byron taking command of a stage greater even than that of Greek independence, one more spacious than all the continents across which Childe Harold had roamed. It was a one-man declaration of war on the Holy Alliance, and helped to breed many of the forces which led to its overthrow. It was his revenge not merely on the canting, cowardly English society which had driven him from our shores, but on all the principalities and powers of the age which had brought such a world of human misery in their train. This, for sure, was the same Byron who had been haunted by Swift's fate, and who spoke on these life-and-death matters to the same Dr Millingen:

It is with infinite regret I must state, that although I seldom left Lord Byron's pillow during the latter part of his illness, I did not hear him make any, even the smallest mention of religion. At one moment, I heard him say: 'Shall I sue for mercy?' After a long pause he added: 'Come, come, no weakness! let's be a man to the last.'

FOURTEEN

Aftermath

I never let anyone off in the end.

16 February 1821

The Byronic odyssey did not end with his death; the aftermath was even more adventurous and splendid. The news itself, of course, was sensational, in every sense of that debased word, and mourners and defamers everywhere started to measure the man afresh. Heinrich Heine, who could be justly seen as his most direct heir, both as a poet and a prose-writer, honoured his comrade-in-arms, as he called him, in proper fashion:

> So this great heart has ceased to beat! He was great, he had a heart, and not some little ovary of sentiments. Yes, this was a great man; his sorrow showed him a new world; he defied miserable men and their still more miserable gods like Prometheus; the fame of his name penetrated to the icebergs of ultima Thule and to the burning sands of the oriental desert.

Heine spoke for freedom-aspiring, revolutionary Europe, for the peoples to whom Byron appeared as liberator even more plainly than he knew.* A tumult of argument about the righteousness or wickedness of his cause – as if he were a kind of

---

* Compare Heine's *Adam der Erste*, 'Vermissen werde ich nimmer mehr.'

I shall never miss	I want the full liberty that is my due!
the realms of Paradise.	If I find it circumscribed in any way
That was no true paradise –	Paradise changes for me,
it contained forbidden trees	into a hell or a prison.

Translation from *Heine's Jewish Comedy* S. S. Prawer.

Professor Prawer's essential book on Karl Marx is referred to on page 383. The latest contribution with the most extensive references to the Byron-Heine connection is contained in his *Frankenstein's Island*.

363

one-man new religion on his own – was unloosed at once and has never finally subsided. The clash was symbolized by the way his body was brought home. Most of England's rulers, Whigs no less than Tories, more explicitly than at the graveside of any other of our greatest poets, felt it inadvisable even to modify their execrations on the man and his work. Westminster Abbey was not to be defiled by his ashes, with Byron himself concurring in advance; it was left to Hazlitt to record that if he had been lain there he would have got up again on his own exertion.*

The next scene, nearby Newstead and the Nottingham where his name was not forgotten by the men and women he had championed, was described by a young Mary Howitt:

> 7th Mo., 18, 1824. – Poor Byron! I was grieved exceedingly at the tidings of his death; but when his remains arrived here, it seemed to make it almost a family sorrow. I wept then, for my heart was full of grief to think that fine eccentric genius, that handsome man, the brave asserter of the rights of the Greeks, and the first poet of our time, he whose name will be mentioned with reverence and whose glory will be uneclipsed when our children shall have passed to dust, to think that he lay a corpse in an inn in this very town.

> . . . Nottingham, which connects everything with politics, could not help making even the passing respect to our poet's memory a political question. He was a Whig; he hated

---

* The placing of a plaque in the Poet's Corner of Westminster Abbey did finally occur in May 1968. The chief credit for this change must go to the Dean of Westminster at the time, the Very Revd Eric Abbott who approved a petition from the Poetry Society and responded to some earlier entreaties from a good Byronist, the late Lord Boothby. The previous appeal in 1924, the year of the commemoration of Byron's death, had been rejected by an earlier dean, despite backing for it from Thomas Hardy, Rudyard Kipling and three Prime Ministers: Balfour, Asquith and Lloyd George – none of these, it must be acknowledged, being better friends of the Church than Byron himself.

priests, and was a lover of liberty; he was the author of *Don Juan* and *Cain*. So the Tory party, which is the same as saying the gentry, would not notice even his coffin. The parsons had their feud, and therefore not a bell tolled either when he came or went. He was a lover of liberty, which the Radical Corporation here thought made him their brother; therefore all the rabble rout from every lane and alley, and garret and cellar, came forth to curse and swear, and shout and push, in his honour. All religious people forswore him, on account of his licentiousness and blasphemy; they forgot his *Childe Harold*, his *Bride of Abydos*, the *Corsair*, and *Lara*.

The next morning all the friends and admirers of Byron were invited to meet in the market-place, to form a procession to accompany him out of town. Thou must have read in the papers the funeral train that came from London. In addition to this were five gentlemen's carriages, and perhaps thirty riders on horseback, besides Lord Rancliffe's tenantry, who made about thirty more, and headed the procession, and were by far the most respectable; for never, surely, did such a shabby company ride in the train of mountebanks or players. There was not one gentleman who would honour our immortal bard by riding two miles in his funeral train. The equestrians, instead of following two and two, as the paper says they did, most remarkably illustrated riding all sixes and sevens.

'What a miserable failure they made of poor Lord Byron's funeral,' wrote Henry Milman, the incumbent Dean of St Paul's, with doubtless a touch of condescension towards the Westminster Abbey bunglers in his tone: ' – to bring him from Greece where he might have reposed with dignity, to be buried among all the other old Byrons at Huckley or Hockley in the Hole, with Nottingham weavers for the mourners, is really pitiful.' The presence of those Nottingham weavers, twelve years after the Luddite revolts, was the final, impious insult. Thus Byron's expulsion from his class continued after his death; he inspired horror and love in equal intensity.

William Hazlitt, second only to Byron, was the English writer whom Heinrich Heine most admired; how strange must his emotions have been when he saw the England of Church and State pursuing their victim even beyond the grave. Hazlitt himself would never alter his opinion to suit some popular fashion; but he would examine his deeply-embedded, hardly-wrought convictions afresh and bravely. And this is what he did in his revaluation of Byron, not suddenly but most memorably over the next six years of his own life.

Three months after Byron's death, after he had interrupted his splenetic essay on the subject, when the event had penetrated his own consciousness and the world's, he wrote of Shelley and Keats, but he offered too, another epitaph of his own on Byron:

> To this band of immortals a third has since been added! – a mightier genius, a haughtier spirit, whose stubborn impatience and Achilles-like pride only Death could quell. Greece, Italy, the world, have lost their poet-hero; and his death has spread a wider gloom, and been recorded with a deeper awe, than has waited on the obsequies of any of the many great who have died in our remembrance. Even detraction has been silent at his tomb; and the more generous of his enemies have fallen into the rank of his mourners. But he set like the sun in his glory; and his orb was greater and brightest at the last; for his memory is now consecrated no less by freedom than genius. He probably fell a martyr to his zeal against tyrants. He attached himself to the cause of Greece, and dying, clung to it with a convulsive grasp, and has thus gained a niche in her history; for whatever *she* claims as hers is immortal, even in decay, as the marble sculptures on the columns of her fallen temples!

Only a few could stir Hazlitt to such eloquence, and they were usually the men, women or idols he had learnt to love. Byron had never been included in that category.

A few months later Hazlitt set out on some travels of his own, not deliberately in Byron's footsteps but constantly finding himself confronted afresh, even disturbed, at first, by the abiding Byronic presence. He found Byron's poems 'stuck up all over Paris', and would not himself take this as a proof of French taste. He was much amused by one 'Elegy on the great man's death, written by his friend Sir Thomas More'. 'The loving bard had been confused with the old statesman,' said Hazlitt, and could not refrain from remarking: 'The author of Utopia was no flincher, he was a martyr to his opinions and was burnt to death for them – the most heroic action of Mr Moore's life is, the having burnt the Memoirs of his friend!' The old disputes about the publication of *The Liberal* still rankled, and most notably Thomas Moore's insulting part in them. For those misdeeds, neither Moore nor Byron would ever be finally forgiven. But Hazlitt's judgement did move, perceptibly if not avowedly. He found himself quoting Byron more and more frequently – almost always with Hazlitt the sign of a new literary affair. He never came to love him, as both Byron and Hazlitt did their own favourite authors, some of whom they held in common – Fielding, Montaigne, Scott, Sterne, Cervantes, Rousseau, Swift occasionally, the Bible. It is hard to calculate which knew the Scriptures better, the ex-Calvinist or the ex-Unitarian. Byron placed Pope at the head of his list; Hazlitt knew Pope as a critic but could never quite match Byron's state of adoration. And what of Shakespeare? Hazlitt honoured and loved him together before any other observer and, at last, without any rival. Byron would not bring himself to acknowledge such pre-eminence; but he knew Shakespeare, quoted Shakespeare, misquoted Shakespeare, consciously and unconsciously moulded him into all his thinking as did no one else – except Hazlitt.

Almost simultaneously with these fortunate convergences in mood and critical attention, an event occurred which could have ruptured them afresh. Leigh Hunt published his *Lord Byron and Some of His Contemporaries with Recollections of The Author's Life and of his Visit to Italy*: a book which purported to describe his relationship with all his famous poet friends, Byron the foremost, as the appealing title suggested, but the others as well,

Shelley, Keats, and Hazlitt too. Yet was not the real tone of the whole book embittered, whining, inexcusable? Such was the natural, legitimate verdict of Byron's friends at the time, with Thomas Moore and Hobhouse at their outraged head, and they, after all, had their still uncovered wounds from *The Liberal* disputes. But what should Hazlitt say? Past associations and present moods might combine to make him take Hunt's side. However, apart from other Hazlittean susceptibilities on which Hunt touched none too delicately, he had this curious comment on the Byron–Hazlitt relationship. The style, by the way, may strike the reader at once as affectedly ornate or circuitous, and this was by no means the way Leigh Hunt normally wrote:

Mr Hazlitt, habitually paradoxical, sometimes pastoral, and never without the self-love which he is fond of discerning in others, believed at the moment that a lord had a liking for him, and that a lord and a sophisticate poet would put up with his sincerities about the aristocratical and the primitive. It begat in him a love for the noble Bard; and I am not sure that he has got rid, to this day, of the notion that it is returned. He was taken in, as others have been, and as all the world chose and delighted to be as long as the flattering self-reflection was allowed a remnant to act upon. The mirror was pierced at Missolonghi, and then they could expatiate at large on the noble lord's image and their own! Sorry cozenage! Poor and melancholy conclusion to come to respecting great as well as little; and such as would be frightful to think of, if human nature, after all, were not better than they pretend. Lord Byron in truth was afraid of Mr Hazlitt; he admitted him like a courtier, for fear he should be treated by him as an enemy; but when he beheld such articles as the 'Spirit of Monarchy', where the 'taint' of public corruption was to be exposed, and the First Acquaintance with Poets, where Mr Wordsworth was to be exalted above depreciation,

'In spite of pride, – in erring reasons spite – ' (for such was Mr Hazlitt's innocent quotation) his Lordship could only wish him out again, and take pains to show his polite friends that he had nothing in common with so inconsiderate a plebeian.

No other records corroborate that Byron did speak of Hazlitt at this time in these highly offensive terms; and it was Leigh Hunt himself who had advised Hazlitt of Byron's readiness to welcome his contributions to *The Liberal*. And if Byron ever read those two Hazlitt essays, it is hard to believe he would not have been captivated by their brilliance, as the rest of mankind has been.

However, there the heavy charge stood starkly on the page and one well calculated to break for ever any incipient Byron–Hazlitt rapprochement; perhaps that was the Hunt calculation, and yet Hazlitt reacted in a manner which could hardly have been foreseen. He turned a reproachful, suspicious eye on his old friend, Leigh Hunt. Curiously or not so curiously, he did not review the whole book directly, as he might have been expected to do. What he did do in his *A Farewell to Essay Writing* (his own title), written at Winterslow Hut on 20 February 1828 and published, signed W.H. in the *London Weekly Review*, 28 March 1828, was to review, magically, his whole writing career and to recall, quoting Byron incidentally, when 'the credulous hope of mutual minds is o'er'. He was 'rather disappointed, both on my own account and his', that Hunt had not explained his own character more skilfully – that he was still 'puzzled to reconcile the shyness of my pretensions with the inveteracy and sturdiness of my principles'. Quite politely, but none the less devastatingly in the analysis of motive and character, he exposes the weakness in Leigh Hunt's criticism of himself, and thereby shows also how Hunt may have had some delusions in describing his other contemporaries. 'This transposition of motives makes me almost doubt whether Lord Byron was thinking so much of the rings as his biographer was.'

Maybe, Hazlitt felt this comment and conclusion were not quite fair to his friend Hunt; in any case, he wanted the friendship repaired. So when he saw Hunt's book on Byron set upon by others, he made another effort to come to his old friend's help and to defend the Cockney School from these Tory assaults. In the *London Weekly Review* of 17 May 1828, he wrote some general comments on the book, emphasizing some of the virtues of those parts of it which scarcely received any attention at all, the purely descriptive passages with no Byronic references within them. And at one point he puts the question: 'Pray did it never strike you that Lord Byron himself was a Cockney writer, if descending from the conventional to the vernacular is to be so.' Byron, for sure, would not have appreciated the compliment. What he could heartily have approved was the ferocity with which Hazlitt turned on their common tormentors, the practised liars of the Tory press – the equivalent of the modern *Daily Mail* or *Sun*: 'Belief is with them mechanical, voluntary: they believe what they are paid for – they swear to that which turns to account. Do you suppose, that after years spent in this manner, they have any feeling left answering to the difference between truth and falsehood?'

As the months passed, Hazlitt had the chance of reading *Don Juan* more acutely; it is not clear – indeed it is most improbable – that he could do what we can do and read it all right through. But his critical verdict changed. He told Thomas Medwin in Switzerland that *Don Juan* was his favourite among Byron's works. He wrote directly in 1829 a paragraph which Byron would have read with approval:

It has been made a subject of regret that in forty or fifty years' time (if we go on as we have done) no one will read Fielding. What a falling-off! Already, if you thoughtlessly lend *Joseph Andrews* to a respectable family, you find it returned upon your hands as an improper book. To be sure, people read 'Don Juan'; but *that* is in verse. The worst is, that this senseless fastidiousness is more owing to an affectation of gentility than to a disgust at vice. It is not the scenes that are described at an alehouse, but the *alehouse* at which they take place that gives the mortal stab to taste and refinement. One comfort is, that the manners and characters which are objected to as *low* in Fielding have in a great measure disappeared or taken another shape; and this at least is one good effect of all excellent satire – that it destroys 'the very food whereon it lives'. The generality of readers, who only seek for the representation of existing models, must therefore, after a time, seek in vain for this obvious verisimilitude in the most powerful and popular works of the kind; and will be either disgusted or at a loss to understand the application. People of sense and imagination, who look beyond the surface of the passing folly of the day, will always read *Tom Jones*.

'The great spirits of the eighteenth century', wrote Professor Grierson, 'believed in their fellow men'; Fielding was one of those spirits. *Tom Jones*, from the youngest days of those two mighty readers, Hazlitt and Byron, had been a friend who could do no wrong.

Then, a few weeks later, Hazlitt included a lively discussion about Byron in one of his Northcote's conversations; often he would put into Northcote's mouth his own second thoughts, his own striving for fresh formulations.

N: I see you place Sir Walter above Lord Byron. The question is not which keeps longest on the wing, but which soars highest: and I cannot help thinking there are essences in Lord Byron that are not to be surpassed. He is on a par with Dryden. All the other modern poets appear to me vulgar in the comparison. As a lady who comes here said, there is such an air of nobility in what he writes. Then there is such a power in the style, expressions almost like Shakespeare – 'And looked round on them with their *wolfish* eyes.'
H: The expression is in Shakespeare, somewhere in *Lear*.
N: The line I repeated is in *Don Juan*. I do not mean to vindicate the immorality or misanthropy in that poem – perhaps his lameness was to blame for this defect – but surely no one can deny the force, the spirit of it; and there is such a fund of drollery mixed up with the serious part. Nobody understood the tragi-comedy of poetry so well. People find fault with this mixture in general, because it is not well managed; there is a comic story and a tragic story going on at the same time, without their having any thing to do with one

another. But in Lord Byron they are brought together, just as they are in nature. In like manner, if you go to an execution at the very moment when the criminal is going to be turned off, and all eyes are fixed upon him, an old apple-woman and her stall are overturned, and all the spectators fall a-laughing. In real life the most ludicrous incidents border on the most affecting and shocking. How fine that is of the cask of butter in the storm! Some critics have objected to it as turning the whole into burlesque; on the contrary, it is that which stamps the character of the scene more than any thing else. What did the people in the boat care about the rainbow, which he has described in such vivid colours; or even about their fellow-passengers who were thrown over board, when they only wanted to eat them? No, it was the loss of the firkin of butter that affected them more than all the rest; and it is the mention of this circumstance that adds a hardened levity and a sort of ghastly horror to the scene. It shows the master-hand – there is such a boldness and sagacity and superiority to ordinary rules in it! I agree, however, in your admiration of the Waverley Novels: they are very fine. As I told the author, he and Cervantes have raised the idea of human nature, not as Richardson has attempted, by affectation and a false varnish, but by bringing out what there is really fine in it under a cloud of disadvantages.

Both Northcote and Hazlitt had re-read *Don Juan* or parts of it. The magic potion was at work, and one element in it was political, bringing Hazlitt and Byron together.* When Hazlitt set out

* Some of these comments are prompted by the excellent essay 'On Byron and William Hazlitt' written by James A. Houck, Associate Professor of English, Youngstown State University, who made this contribution to *Lord Byron and His Contemporaries: Essays from the Sixth International Byron Seminar 1982*, published by the University of Delaware Press. His conclusion is most just: that 'his [Hazlitt's] writings give a glimpse at least of a major critic changing his mind and moving toward an appreciation for and a recognition of what is now seen as one of the major literary productions of his time'. And Hazlitt, for sure, would have been both fascinated and convinced by the 1988 reception of Byron. No one has ever believed more faithfully in what he called 'the suffrage of posterity'.

to write his *Life of Napoleon*, he assured and reassured himself with the most estimable motto: 'I should be sorry if there were a single word approaching to *cant* in this work'; a considerable ambition for an impecunious journalist who knew, and was to know again, the rigours of the debtors' prisons, who was writing on a subject which he knew must involve him in reaching a host of unpopular verdicts at a moment when Sir Walter Scott, the same whom he did honour, was writing on the same subject and would be exploiting every advantageous patriotic reflection. It is hard to believe that Hazlitt did not happily set before him the sentences from Byron's writing in the Pope–Bowles controversy which he had extracted as 'the passage for which we forgive him':

> The truth is that in these days the grand primum mobile of England is *cant*: cant political, cant poetical, cant religious, cant moral; but always cant, multiplied throughout all the varieties of life. It is the fashion, and while it lasts will be powerful for those who can only exist by taking the tone of the times. I say cant, because it is a thing of words, without the smallest influence upon human actions; the English being no wiser, no better, and much poorer, and more divided among themselves, as well as far less moral, than they were before the prevalence of this verbal decorum!

These words had been written by Byron in the early months of 1822 when *Don Juan* had been proscribed by friend and foe – more particularly the former – and the Hazlitt who was shunned in decent company for his *Liber Amoris* wrote the commendation: 'These words should be written in letters of gold, as the testimony of a lofty poet to a great moral truth, and we can hardly have a quarrel with the writer of them.'

Hazlitt, in making his measurement of the man, wrote preeminently of Greece and the world did the same. Any other order of priorities would be an affectation. Greece embraced him as her special lover and champion, and no one should quibble about the claim. Everybody surely, and most certainly all who speak English, must now look on the plains of Marathon through Byron's eyes. His death at Missolonghi and a few immortal verses scattered through his vast outpourings *did* change the history of modern Greece. To the very last, Greece had inspired him.

Yet his love affair with Italy was more subtle, more tempestuous and languorous by turns, more adult and comprehensive. He had learnt to speak some Italian before he ever set foot on Italian soil, and the Italian poets ancient and modern, their accents, and their rhythms, and their political themes, shaped his own poetry more than any other of his literary forebears except the English. Every line of poetry which he wrote in the last eight years of his life – except those last immortal ones on his thirty-sixth year – were written beneath an Italian sun or Italian stars. Genoa, Pisa, Ravenna, Venice all acquired an enrichment from his presence, and he made the Italian cause his own as only a student of Dante and Ariosto and Rossini could. A main point of contention among Italian historians and critics would persist: to which of their new poets did he owe the most? But no one could doubt how deep was the general debt: Byron himself would never dream of denying it. 'He bade me seek first in Venice,' wrote John Ruskin, 'the ruined homes of Foscari and Faliero.' How many visitors to Venice, starting with his two pupils, Ruskin and Turner, who also helped teach each other, thanks to Byron, know more about the Doge who lost his head than all the rest, and thereby have been taught a revolutionary lesson. 'Even Shakespeare's Venice', wrote Ruskin, 'was visionary: and Portia as impossible as Miranda. But Byron told me of, and reanimated for me, the real people whose feet had worn the marble I trod on.' Ruskin could acknowledge 'his clear insight into men's foibles, his intense reach of pity, never failing, however far he had to stoop to lay his hand on a human heart'. But this same man had another contrasted gift, and the Italy of those times needed both: 'He is the finest, sternest seer of the nineteenth century. No imagination dazzles him, no fervour daunts him, and no interest betrays.' And one clear part of what the seer saw, much more clearly than Ruskin himself, was the unity of Italy which Dante had prophesied – or prophesied with such assurance, with Byron's help. The poetry of politics unleashed in Ravenna had within it a direct summons to Garibaldi's precursor and premonitions of Garibaldi himself. One day in January 1821 he recorded how, on his daily ride through the Ravenna woods, he had met some strange companions: 'Met a company of the sect (a kind of Liberal club) called the Americani in the forest, all armed and singing with all their might in Romagnole "Sem tutti soldat per la liberta". They cheered me as I passed.' Garibaldi was conducted through those same woods by the sons of Byron's Americani after his escape from Rome in 1849, and saved from his pursuers; he lay concealed for more than twenty-four hours. There Garibaldi's hut may be discovered by today's traveller near the same pine forest which Byron before him and Dante before them had made famous.

One voice, the purest and the most resonant in all the records of the Risorgimento, was that of Joseph Mazzini, and his hymn to Byron reverberated in the England of the nineteenth century even if it is sometimes submerged today, along with the submergence of Mazzini's own reputation. He knew something of exile himself; so his acknowledgement of what Byron wrote in his years of exile, in the land of his adoption, rang all the truer. He saw Byron as one of the master minds of the century, and he believed, with a prophetic gift, that the English people might come to see that too, at a time when Byronism and Byron were quite out of fashion. He dared to use the word 'democracy' before Byron; more assuredly, he knew the power of Byron's revolutionary appeal and how it would accumulate its force. The spirit of Mazzini merges with Byron's, especially in those months in Ravenna in 1822: 'Surrounded by slaves and their oppressors; a traveller in countries where even remembrance seemed extinct; never did he desert the cause of the peoples; never was he false to human sympathies.' These were Mazzini's words of Byron, but they might each have been writing of the other. 'At Naples, in the Romagna, wherever he saw or spoke of noble life stirring, he was ready for any exertion or danger, to blow it into flame. He stigmatized baseness, hypocrisy and

injustice wherever they sprang.' Mazzini, like many other political figures of his epoch, could write with a magniloquence
which offends modern taste, but the true reasons why Byron
spoke to him more movingly than any other Englishman of the
century are there for us to see and feel:

> Thus lived Byron, ceaselessly tempest-tossed between the
> ills of the present, and his yearnings after the future; often
> unequal; sometimes sceptical; but always suffering – often
> most so when he seemed to laugh; and always loving, even
> when he seemed to curse . . . Never did the 'eternal spirit of
> the chainless mind' make a brighter apparition amongst us.
> He seems at times a transformation of that immortal Pro-
> metheus, of whom he has written so nobly, whose cry of
> agony, yet of futurity, sounded above the cradle of the Euro-
> pean world. . . . The day will come when Democracy will
> remember all that it owes to Byron. England too, will, I
> hope, one day remember the mission – so entirely English,
> yet hitherto overlooked by her – which Byron fulfilled on
> the Continent; the European role given by him to English
> literature, and the appreciation and sympathy for England
> which he awakened amongst us.

Mazzini recruited another worthy successor for the Byronic
cause. Every freedom-lover driven from his native land would
be tempted to respond; Alexander Herzen found the truest com-
radeship among the Italian exiles. He discovered Byron in the
darkest days of his own defeats, and he learnt how to hand on
the sacred flame to Garibaldi, to the next generation of Italian
revolutionaries who carried the cause to victory, to his own suppressed comrades in Tsarist Russia, to the England which gave
him sanctuary. His whole temper is Byronic. 'He who frankly
avows his defeats feels that there is something in him that can
escape and resist his downfall; he understands that he can
redeem his past, and not only lift up his head but turn, as in
Byron's tragedy from Sardanapalus the effeminate into Sardanapalus the hero.' When Garibaldi arrived in Venice in 1864 to
celebrate the liberation of Italy he was greeted in the Piazza by

Alexander Herzen. Byron would have had as good a right as anyone to attend that night of rejoicing. He was one of the makers of Venetian freedom; he put his own liberating stamp upon it; his name becomes inseparable from many others, and each of them, it is not too much to claim, whatever their political divergencies, would never have disowned his repudiation of political and religious cant in every form and disguise: Ruskin, Turner, Hazlitt, Stendhal, Rossini, Heine, Mazzini, Manin, Garibaldi, Herzen, all carrying the same sacred flame, all caught in the same Venetian light, all drawing some of their strength from the burning Byronic oracle.

The interlocking causes of national resurgence and radical revolt derived in some degree from Byron, in Greece and in Italy; each had its unbreakable affinity. Across so many other lands in the rest of Europe, places where he had travelled himself or where Childe Harold or Don Juan had made the journey for him or, more customarily, where they had travelled together, his influence was hardly any less marked, then or thereafter: Spain, Portugal, Switzerland, Germany, France, Russia, Poland. Neither the poetry nor the history of these countries could be properly recited without an estimate being made of Byron's impact, and one feature of those estimates may be noted at once. Neither poets nor historians could imagine that his influence was moderating, laodicean, accepting established authorities in this world or the next. The Byron of (say) Henry James would have been found meaningless and incomprehensible in (say) the Poland of Adam Mickiewicz. In January 1822, Adam Mickiewicz, a boy in his teens, wrote from Vilna to a friend in Berlin how 'with a dictionary in hand I edged my way through Shakespeare like a rich man from the gospel entering heaven through the eye of a needle, but now for my pains it goes much easier with Byron, and I have made progress. I think I shall translate *The Giaour*.' Then in November: 'It is truly Byron that I read, and I throw away any other book written in another spirit, because I detest lies.' And then again two passages which show how Byron's words were deeds. Mickiewicz did translate *The Giaour*, and he wrote a preface:

Everyday the readers may become convinced about Byron's influence on contemporary literature, because they see the colour and the impress of this great poet in all the later poetical works. . . . Byron's characters are endowed with conscience. And that is what distinguished chiefly our author from the writers of the past century. The bygone age was a sophist, not knowing the difference between good and evil, it had only taken practice in petty reasoning, and its chief aim and ambition had been to find an explanation to everything, or to blab about everything. . . . Byron was the first poet who would not be satisfied with such sophistic condemnation of thought and feeling. He had always had before his eyes the great problems of the world, the problems of the fate of the human race and of the future life. He had tackled all the basic moral and philosophical questions, he had coped with all the cruxes and difficulties of dogmas and traditions, he had cursed and fumed like Prometheus, the Titan, whose shade he loved to evoke so often.

He lectured in Paris on the same subject in December 1842:

Byron begins an era of new poetry. He was the first to show the people that poetry is not a futile pastime, that it does not end in desires, that one should live up to one's writings. . . . This strongly felt need to make his life poetic, to bring the ideal near to the reality, is all the poetic value of Byron. . . . His poetical power was so great that it could be felt in a few words, that those few words had been able to wake and shock the souls, and to disclose to them what they were. . . . He was known to see through any political problems with his sharp eye, and to reach to the source of the chief mystery of human history. . . . Everything that tormented the minds of men, that had found response in the souls of the young people of our generation was faithfully given expression in Byron's writings and in his life. In the works of Slavic poets we may detect like feelings and like tendencies.

And when he died of cholera in 1888 in Turkey, organizing a

Polish Legion against Russia, he left an unfinished essay on Byron:

> As the minstrels in the Middle Ages, singing in the spirit of their times, had been well understood by their contemporaries, so the songs of Byron appealed to the broad European masses and created a host of followers. Just so a string of a harp when plucked, makes other, silent, but similarly tempered strings resound.

Byron and Europe were a combination which never seemed to lose its appeal and its power, from the day of his death till modern times. Paul Graham Trueblood, editor of the book of essays on Byron from which I gleaned the above extracts from Mickiewicz, gave fitting expression to the strength of this appeal at the end of the collection.*

In a fragment from his journal in Cephalonia, where he had come to aid the Greek cause, Byron told all of his heart:

* These extracts are taken from the essay 'Byron and Poland' by Juliusz Zulawski, which appeared in *Byron's Political and Cultural Influence in Nineteenth-century Europe: A Symposium*, edited by Paul Graham Trueblood. The whole book bears the most apposite epigraph: 'European nineteenth century culture is unthinkable without Byron, as its history would be without Napoleon', a sentence from Northrop Frye's *Fables of Identity*. Not all the pieces are quite as arresting as Zulawski's, but then not all the writers have a native Byronist as wonderful and devoted as Adam Mickiewicz.

The Byronic influence was not confined to Europe. When the poet Wilfrid Scawen Blunt, who had some Byronic blood in his veins, met Achmed Arabi, the Egyptian nationalist leader, Blunt was surprised to discover how much Arabi had learnt from his ancestor. And Blunt tried to repay the recognition by warning the British Government of the time: 'The Suez Canal', he wrote, 'cannot be better protected for England, as for the rest of the world, than by the admission of the Egyptian people into the comity of nations.' That was in 1882, and Byron, the anti-imperialist, would have strongly approved. How many tens of thousands of English and Egyptian soldiers and sailors were killed before – in 1956 – the Canal was taken over and run quite successfully by the Egyptians. The story of Wilfrid Scawen Blunt – his politics as well as his loves – is marvellously told by Elizabeth Longford in her *A Pilgrimage of Passion*.

The dead have been awakened – shall I sleep?
The World's at war with tyrants – shall I crouch?
The harvest's ripe – and shall I pause to reap?
I slumber not; the thorn is in my couch;
Each day a trumpet soundeth in mine ear,
It's echo in my heart. . . .

Then the writer added the sentence: 'The trumpet of liberty would not let Byron sleep.' A romantic inscription, but not one which Byron the realist would have sought to disown.

Sometimes it is complained that Byron and Byronism, the man and the myth, must be sharply distinguished; that Byron unloosed, or became associated with, a force in politics quite beyond his own intention or comprehension. But 'do men gather grapes of thorns or figs of thistles?' It is hard to believe such a sequence of events is conceivable, and only English observers might seem free to offer such verdicts. To measure the European reflection of his achievement, to add to the appreciation of the poets themselves, we should recall afresh the verdict of one who understood Byron as well as anybody, George Brandes, the Danish critic.* He wrote of his impact at the time of his death and then measured the reverberating influence across most of the European continent:

> The news of Byron's death raised the enthusiasm for the first war of liberation that had been fought since the Revolution to fever heat. A new ideal was conceived by the human mind. With Napoleon the glory of energy had passed away, and the heroes of action had for a time disappeared from the earth. Human enthusiasm was, as has been said, in the plight of a pedestal from which the statue has been removed. Byron took possession of the vacant place with his fantastically magnificent heroes. Napoleon had supplanted Werther, René, and Faust; Byron's Promethean

* See page 173. These two extracts come from Volume III of his *Main Currents in Nineteenth Century Literature.*

and despairing heroes supplanted Napoleon. Byron was in marvellous accord with the spirit and the cravings of the age. Orthodox dogmas had in the early years of the century overcome revolutionary and free-thinking principles; now orthodoxy was in its turn undermined and obsolete. There was at this moment no future for either thorough-going unbelief or thorough-going piety. There remained doubt, as doubt – *poetic* Radicalism, the thousand painful and agitating questions concerning the goal and the worth of human life. These were the questions which Byron asked.

But he did not ask indifferently. It was the spirit of rebellion which asked with his voice, and which through his voice made of the young generation in all lands one cosmopolitan society. They united their voices with his in the cry:

> . . . revolution
> Alone can save the world from hell's pollution.

In England, Bentham, the Radical philosopher, ashamed to see the reaction successful even in that most advanced of countries, had tried to undermine it by appealing to men's *interests*. Byron let loose all the *passions*. His attack was not directed at any one point; he aimed at revolutionizing men's minds, at awaking them to the sense of tyranny. The politicians of the Holy Alliance period believed that they had bound the spirit of the Revolution in everlasting chains, that they had broken, once and for all, the link which united the nineteenth century to the eighteenth. Then this one man tied the knot again, which a million of soldiers had hewn through. American republicanism, German freethought, French revolutionism, Anglo-Saxon radicalism – everything seemed combined in this one spirit. After the Revolution had been suppressed, the press gagged, and science induced to submit, the son of imagination, the outlawed poet, stepped into the breach,' and called all vigorous intellects to arms again against the common enemy. The restored monarchy does not really survive him. The principle of authority has never had a more inveterate opponent.

But what of his England which supposedly knew him best? There the testimony of his political enemies was swift and clear; the more Byron and all his works could be outlawed, the better for the health and morals of the nation. Byron himself could have applauded this response: he would have been happy to know that *Don Juan* was starting to do the work he had intended. But where were his political defenders, the true ones and the pretentious? The burning of the memoirs by the innermost clique of his closest friends must have appeared as a confession of guilt and therefore too a blow, a self-inflicted one almost, at his political creed. In 1828 came Leigh Hunt's book, one which should have been expected to assist the liberal cause in which they had joined; but the malice and the scandal achieved an exactly opposite result in a manner Hunt himself at his most malicious could hardly have calculated. Thomas Moore's book was published in 1830, and with this the Byronic charm, poetry and prose, began to reassert its own strength. However, Thomas Moore's volume, for all its shining merit as one of the best biographies in the language, was at its weakest when he trespassed into political arenas. No one knew that better than Byron himself; so sometimes Byron must have tempered his political outbursts to mollify his correspondent. Yet, as the record proves, Byron still had a plentiful store of political fervour available, and in Moore's case he often felt inclined to appeal to his Irish patriotism, so often insulted by English overlordship. Yet still Thomas Moore could not or would not grasp the full force of Byron's political imagination; how startled he would have been to read the burning tributes of Adam Mickiewicz or George Brandes.

One supposition is that Byron's political impact and influence, here in England, *did* fade almost at once after his death, and that when a new generation of critics in the 1860s and 1870s started to re-examine his poetry and his fame generally, it was not his politics in any real sense which they studied. Sometimes this view is accompanied by comparisons between Byron and Shelley, and one comparison between them which has gained a peculiar notoriety, appears in Franz Mehring's *Life of Marx*, where can be read the supposedly conclusive sentence:

'Referring to Byron and Shelley, he (Marx) declared that those who loved and understood these two poets must consider it fortunate that Byron died at the age of thirty-six, for had he lived out his full span he would undoubtedly have become a reactionary bourgeois, whilst regretting on the other hand that Shelley died at the age of twenty-nine, for Shelley was a thorough revolutionary and would have remained in the van of socialism all his life.' However, the attribution of this verdict to Marx has been questioned by one who is certainly the greatest authority on Marx's knowledge of English literature, Professor Prawer in his *Karl Marx and World Literature*. The quotation does not come direct from Marx but was relayed by his notoriously untrustworthy son-in-law, Edward Aveling. If Marx himself had read Shelley and had been so impressed, it seems inexplicable that he never once referred to him when he was so constantly referring to other literary figures, Byron included. Moreover, if Marx had been so constantly reading radical journals and pamphlets, he could have noticed for himself that Byron was being quoted more frequently than Shelley, and that none of these quotations would have had any offensively bourgeois associations. No doubt also, Marx discussed the matter with Engels; Engels wrote, most perceptively:

> It is the workers who are most familiar with the poetry of Shelley and Byron. Shelley's prophetic genius has caught their imagination, while Byron attracts their sympathy by his sensuous fire and by the virulence of his satire against the existing social order. The middle classes, on the other hand, have on their shelves only ruthlessly expurgated 'family' editions of these writers. These editions have been prepared to suit the hypocritical moral standards of the bourgeoisie.

The date when Engels wrote those words in *The Condition of the Working Class in England* is worth noting – 1845; twenty-one years after Byron's death, twenty-odd years before Marx's alleged remark to Aveling. Even on grounds of proximity to the event, the Engels estimate is much to be preferred, and it does underline how much Byron was being read by working-class readers all through a period when, thanks to the reticence of fastidious bourgeois critics, he was supposed to be neglected. The truth seems to be the exact opposite; workers who could read were doing everything in their power to get their hands on the forbidden documents, and no scrap of evidence exists that when they succeeded they were disappointed.*

The anti-Byronic revulsion did sweep across all different sections of English society and not solely among the leaders or the leadership against whom the final cantos of *Don Juan* had been directed, with all the withering effects recognized by Engels. One evidence of it, at once a proof of how deep was the opposition to the man and his works and an instrument which forced that hostility still deeper, was the review which Lord Macaulay wrote of Moore's biography in 1831. Macaulay might have been expected to offer some comfort to one who had espoused the Whig cause so openly and who had been so shamefully traduced by the Tories, and indeed the review contains, as we have seen before, the famous passage which immortalized the moment of Byron's exile: 'We know no spectacle so ridiculous as the British public in one of its periodical fits of morality.' But then, with one stroke after another, Macaulay painted the portrait of the gloomy, raging egotist, for ever at odds with himself, seeking to play the role of 'the great mover of an intellectual revolution' and utterly incapable of it. At some moments he seemed almost to be plagiarizing Hazlitt's *Spirit of the Age* portrait (quite a number of eminent Victorians did that – Walter Bagehot was another) but without accepting Hazlitt's own later and wiser qualifications; without even knowing they had been adumbrated. He pictured the time when 'whatever remains of that magical potency which once belonged to the name of Byron' would pass. He even composed an often-forgotten sentence which seemed to belie his earlier professions of tolerance: a condemnation of would-be followers of Byron who drew 'a pernicious and absurd association between intellectual power and moral depravity. . . . From the poetry of Lord Byron they drew a system of ethics, compounded of misanthropy and

* Felix Holt in George Eliot's novel, published in 1866, does express violent distaste, but that is George Eliot, twenty years on from Engels.

voluptuousness; a system in which the two great commandments were to hate your neighbour, and to woo your neighbour's wife.' Macaulay, like Byron, could not resist an epigram.
Seemingly, the British public had not quite overcome its fit of
morality. And Macaulay was ready to admit that he had read
Don Juan in full but with a rising distaste 'as Byron sank to the
level of his own imitators in the Magazines'. On his own essay
as a whole, he later confessed to his sister: 'I never wrote anything with less heart. I do not like the book; I do not like the
hero; I have said the most I could for him.' In fact, the corrosive
hostility was not in any way concealed. Macaulay did more
than anyone else to confirm the lineaments of the satanic
Byron, with the self-love indelibly emphasized at every turn
and so much else omitted or defiled: even the wit, the gaiety, the
love of truth, the love of liberty. Was there not a half- suppressed
fear that the Byronic message could be carried further until it
constituted a threat to all sacred things: sacred, not so much in
the religious sense – Holland House had never been a temple of
piety – but in terms of the established forms of political society?
Was it not extraordinary that Byron's gifts, his qualities, his
inspiration, should be denied at such a moment – the months
just before the passage of the great Reform Bill – by the rising
hope of the ardent, ambitious Liberals?* Byron had even given
them their name. Some disowned him even at the very
moment when he was bestowing such glory upon them.
Macaulay would not be beguiled. For him, most of *Don Juan*
was trash; the poem as degenerate as the man.

Another voice may be set alongside Macaulay's, one which
appears to confirm his prophecy and to carry forward the damnation to another epoch, a voice which, like Macaulay's, cannot
be dismissed as some demon spokesman of English Toryism,
Byron's natural enemy. Charles Kingsley wished to see the evils

* To prove that these questions are not farfetched – and for its own sake –
we may quote the judgement of one of Macaulay's countrymen. Professor
Grierson made a different estimate: 'Byron was the single-handed champion of European freedom in the days of the Triple Alliance, and he dared
Mrs Grundy at the time when her sway in England was almost at its zen-
ith, when she was preparing to take her place on the English throne.'

of Victorian society fought with Evangelical fervour, and he was ready to use all his considerable talents as a novelist, churchman and social reformer for the purpose. But somehow he, like Macaulay, felt it necessary to turn aside to repudiate – exterminate, if he could – the Byron–Shelley assault on that same English society. A quite unnecessary diversion, one might have thought: and Kingsley did not even have Macaulay's excuse of a book to review. However, even a first taste of Kingsley's anti-Byronism is enough to prove how genuine and potent a mixture it was, how much he felt that, with his pitiless exposure, he was performing a pious and patriotic duty. True, he considered Shelley to be an even more irredeemable sinner than Byron, one even more unconscionably engaged in the devil's work, and it is wonderful to note, in passing, how – in contrast with Karl Marx's judgement about what role each poet might have played, and as a final proof of Shelley's ineradicable wickedness – he sees him 'probably ended in Rome, as an oratorian or a Passionist'. But on Byron's head, he unloosed a deluge of eloquence:

> Words thrown off in the heat of passion; shameful self-revealings which he has written with his very heart's blood: ay, even fallacies which he has put into the mouths of dramatic characters for the very purpose of refuting them, or at least of calling on all who read to help him to refute them, and to deliver him from the ugly dream, all these will, by the lazy, the frivolous, the feverish, the discontented, be taken for integral parts and noble traits of the man to whom they are attracted, by finding that he, too, has the same doubts and struggles as themselves, that he has a voice and art to be their spokesman. And hence arises confusion on confusion, misconception on misconception. The man is honoured for his dishonour. Chronic disease is taken for a new type of health; and Byron is admired and imitated for that which Byron is trying to tear out of his own heart, and trample under foot as his curse and bane, something which is not Byron's self, but Byron's house-fiend, and tyrant, and shame.

This, and more, and much more.

How demented they could make him appear; a man possessed of unknown devils and unable to discover any cure. Kingsley's combined hatred and fear of what Byron stood for, the eloquent expression which he gave to their views of so many of his outraged countrymen thirty and forty years after his death, adds an ironic interest to the Byronic references which appeared in one of his most notable books. In *Alton Locke* he purported to write the autobiography of a Chartist poet, grappling with the evils of the England he saw all around him and the mysteries of the universe. He has the honesty to admit how much Byron meant for his hero in the moments he could snatch for his self-education at the London bookshops. He continued to hurry through *Childe Harold*, *Lara* and *The Corsair* – 'a new world of wonders for me. They fed, those poems, both my health and my diseases.' The whole passage glows with the excitement which a young reader may feel in making his own first discoveries. Charles Kingsley no doubt understood that sentiment; but he also took precautions, even in that first comparatively innocuous reference, to implant the suggestion that Byron carried some political virus – 'the innocent, guilty pleasure grew on me day by day. Innocent because human – guilty, because disobedient.'

The story and character of Alton Locke were based on Kingsley's knowledge of the real Chartist poet, Thomas Cooper, who in turn had described how copies of *Childe Harold* and *Manfred*, picked up from the second-hand bookshops, had 'seemed to create almost a new sense within me. I wanted more poetry to read from that time; but could get hold of none that thrilled through my nature like Byron's.' Thomas Cooper, of course, was an exception; he was striving almost from childhood to make himself a poet, and to make his poetry serve his politics, and he succeeded. He played his full part in the Chartist activities of the late 1830s, suffered two imprisonments for his principles, came near to being transported, and lived to become one of the chief recorders, in the journal which he founded in the early 1850s and in his later autobiographical writings and poems, of the whole Chartist movement.

What leaders and followers chose to read, what inspired them to act, was a subject of supreme importance for the time. Shelley was at last receiving his due as a revolutionary guide and philosopher. Some of his poems never published in his lifetime – *The Masque of Anarchy*, for one – now became favourite anthems to be recited or sung at Chartist rallies, and Byron was enlisted to serve the same purpose. Indeed some of the evidence suggests that he was read in such circles much more even than Shelley, and, if that were true, it would hardly be surprising. Many more copies, original or pirated, of Byron's writings must have been available, especially in the second-hand bookshops, and most of them were easily comprehensible even by the casual reader. Some of Shelley's poems, and some of the greatest, demanded deeper study. And sometimes, as the Charles Kingsley explosion proved, the two poets were placed in the same dock, charged with criminal participation in the same conspiracy. Thomas Cooper sustained the common tradition which Richard Carlile had once kept alive in Dorchester gaol, and helped to hand it on to an even greater exponent.

A good case can be made for the claim that another Chartist leader, George Julian Harney, was the most assiduous and influential of all Byron enthusiasts, having started to read him in his boyhood, like Thomas Cooper, and enlarging his interest, literally, till his dying day. He was born in 1817 and he died in 1897, and he summoned Byron to his side in so many arguments, at every crisis in his life. He was at one period the chief advocate of the 'physical force' Chartists in their crucial debates with 'moral force' champions, although he himself came to acknowledge that his opponent in the debate, William Lovett, must be accepted as the 'first in honour' among all the Chartist leaders. He was also the first working-class leader in the English context who saw that democracy and socialism must be an international creed. The strength he drew from Byron assisted him in each of these major debates, but in the Fig Tree Lane rooms in Sheffield, for example, where the home-made banners carried the names of their heroes, from Wat Tyler to Byron and Shelley, he could turn other discussions in a Byronic direction. When some sectarian dispute was raised suggesting that political purity should be applied to sexual matters, he happily replied: 'but we are not of that number: the *Giaour*'s love is the love for us.' And when he was asked to indulge too deeply in some philosophical flight of fancy, he adopted Byron's reply to Coleridge:

> Explaining metaphysics to the nation –
> I wish he would explain the Explanation.

He was as horrified as Byron by the hyprocisy he saw all around him. 'It is not pleasant to have to confess but the truth is that England is, *par excellence*, the land of cant and humbug. Queen Victoria rules over the Britannic Empire, but Mrs. Grundy rules over British society.' And again: 'The perseverance of Englishmen in taking their pleasures gravely, under the most adverse meteorological circumstances, cannot be too highly commended, especially by doctors and undertakers.' Then, a few years later, he wrote even more directly: 'His poetry is still an inspiration. He is the poet emphatically of Freedom – freedom of thought, freedom political and social. He is not of that order of phrasemongers who with the name of Liberty on the lips have tyranny in their hearts, and who aspire to overthrow ancient Privilege that they may on its ruins build up their own more intolerable despotism.' From this considered conclusion, it looks as if Harney, a real revolutionary, had studied deeply – as deeply as any modern academic – the mighty arguments about the way revolutions may be betrayed, and how the preparations for them must be mounted afresh. Most of all, right to the end, on the supreme question of how a man should comport himself in face of the odds, he was a true follower of his guide. When he himself was set upon by some of the baying patriots who hated his internationalism, he replied with Byron's lines often wrenched to serve a different purpose:

> I wish men to be free
> As much from mobs as kings –
> from you as me

So Byron became a symbol of his own life, 'dear to Pessimists who see the wrong rampant which they know they cannot conquer, but which they will not tamely endure'. Those, Harney's own words as he looked back across the un-Byronic, anti-Byronic century, showed how his spirit had not been cowed.*

One other *political* figure – leave aside the poets or publicists, for a moment – showed a consistency and devotion in his Byronism to match Harney's; indeed Harney would print considerable extracts from his writings alongside the great stretches from Byron himself in the Chartist paper, the *Northern Star*. Harney could discern how true was the discipleship of Benjamin Disraeli; it had started in his cradle or at least in the library where Disraeli confessed or boasted he had been born. He was instructed there by his own father, whose books had occasionally drawn glowing tributes from Byron, and that was enough for Benjamin. Anyone who honoured his father would be honoured in turn; here was an added enticement, but, anyhow, Byron became for a while the very air the young Disraeli breathed. At the age of nineteen, along with one of his very first manuscripts he sent a letter to John Murray with the request that if it wasn't suitable 'the sooner it be put behind the fire the better, and as you have some small experience in burning MSS, you will perhaps be so kind as to consign it to the flames'. The historic burning in Albemarle Street had taken place just two months before, and maybe the impecunious young Disraeli's relations with the prestigious publisher never quite recovered from that barb. Byron indeed placed a special Byronic mark of his own on every book Disraeli wrote. *Vivian Grey*, published

---

* Much the most important discussion of Byron's contribution in this field is contained in *Thomas Cooper, The Chartist: Byron, and the 'Poets of the Poor'* by Philip Collins, Professor of English Literature, University of Leicester, in the Nottingham Byron Lecture which he delivered in 1969. Most of the Harney references come from A. R. Schoyen's *The Chartist Challenge* published in 1958, a monograph worthy of Harney and Byron. I had read of the Philip Collins book in John D. Jump's *Byron* (see page 294), but had great difficulty in obtaining a copy. It was found for me by Lucy Edwards, of the Byron Society in Nottingham. I owe her a great debt for so much help on so many comparable matters.

two years after Byron's death, celebrated with a full romantic flourish 'the most splendid character which human nature can aspire to', and some side-glances revealed a more individual appreciation: he could celebrate too the great man's 'strong, shrewd commonsense; his pure, unalloyed sagacity'. A year later *The Young Duke* caught 'Byron bending o'er his shattered lyre, with inspiration in his very rage'. *Contarini Fleming* was hailed as 'a *Childe Harolde* in prose', and Heinrich Heine would not accept the general verdict that Disraeli's attempt to follow in the Byronic footsteps was so palpable a failure. Byron and his fate and his pitiless pursuit by 'the British public in one of its periodical fits of morality' continued to haunt Disraeli for a decade or more. True, the phrase and its elaboration were plagiarized from Macaulay but the theme was no less passionately felt. Indeed the young Disraeli could write on such themes with a more intimate knowledge and anxiety than Macaulay; he was truly a disciple of Byron in deed as well as word. An ambitious young politician could have been excused if he kept reasonably quiet on the subject. Instead, he wrote *Venetia*, no literary masterpiece, but a brave, reckless apologia not only for the libertine Byron but, for good measure at the same time, for the atheist and republican Shelley. Shelley was allowed to summon to his defence a host of witnesses, Shakespeare, Dante 'and old Montaigne for me', and one other too, above all the rest, Don Quixote, 'the best man who ever lived'. Don Quixote, incidentally, was second only to Rousseau's classic, *La Nouvelle Héloïse*, a Bible among the romantics, a challenge to Toryism all on its own. 'But what do you think of the assault on the windmills?' Shelley was asked in Disraeli's account, and Shelley's answer was firm enough: 'In the outset of his adventures, as in the outset of our lives, he was misled by his enthusiasm, without which, after all, we can do nothing. But the result is, Don Quixote was a redresser of wrongs, and therefore the world esteemed him mad.' But *Venetia*, it may be objected, was an essay in Byronism written by a Disraeli who had not been contaminated by membership of the House of Commons, much less a Tory Ministry. How much could this mood survive a period in office? One answer is provided by Thomas Cooper, who after his release from gaol took his courage in his hands and called on Disraeli at his house in Grosvenor Gate. Thanks to the guidance given there, the prison poem, *The Purgatory of Suicides*, by Thomas Cooper, the Chartist, was properly printed. 'Nay sir,' said Cooper to his sceptical publisher, 'I shall not strike the Chartist out. Mr. Disraeli advised me not to let anyone persuade me to strike it out, and I mean to abide by his advice.' And just as he resisted 'cutting and slashing' on behalf of others, he doubtless took the old Byronic lesson to heart for himself. One of his last novels, *Lothair*, mostly written in Downing Street by the sixty-six-year-old, gout-ridden, asthmatic Tory Prime Minister, had for its leading figure a Byronic heroine. It is Theodora, 'the divine Theodora' with the look of a Maenad and a voice vibrant with the Marseillaise, the champion of a doctrine which knows that 'the necessities of things are sterner stuff than the hopes of men', who speaks of another Rome, 'that country which first impressed upon the world a general and enduring form of masculine virtue; the land of liberty, and law, and eloquence, and military genius, now garrisoned by monks and governed by a doting priest'. No chink of doubt is left by the author about Theodora's pre-eminence and glory. She shapes the plot; she directs Lothair's destiny; she stirs from him the ecstatic confession: 'Had it not been for you, I should have remained what I was when we first met, a prejudiced, narrow-minded being, with contracted sympathies and false knowledge, wasting my life on obsolete trifles, and utterly insensible to the privilege of living in this wondrous age of change and progress.' *Lothair*, or *Theodora*, as it might better have been titled, is an anthem of the Roman Republic, not of ancient times, but the Republic of Mazzini and Garibaldi, of the Italian Risorgimento, presented with an exhilaration and richness worthy of Byron himself:

She spoke to the men in all the dialects of that land and of many languages. The men of the Gulf, in general of gigantic stature, dropped their merry Venetian stories and fell down on their knees and kissed the hem of her garment; the Scaramouch forgot his tricks, and wept as he would to the Madonna; Tuscany and Rome made speeches worthy of the Arno and the Forum; and the Corsicans and the islanders unsheathed their poniards and brandished them in the air, which is their mode of denoting affectionate devotion. As the night advanced, the crescent moon glittering above the Apennines, Theodora attended by the whole staff, having visited all the troops, stopped at the chief fire of the camp, and in a voice which might have maddened nations sang the hymn of Roman liberty, the whole army ranged in ranks along the valley joining in the solemn and triumphant chorus.

However, it may be protested – both in Harney's case and Disraeli's – is it not absurd to cite their later defences of their hero? Had the century not by that time seen the restoration of Byron to his proper place, undertaken by the great critics? Is not the attempt to set such store on these eccentric voices quite superfluous? It must be retorted at once that the real dates speak rather differently.

The world had had to wait to see justice done from these lofty heights. John Morley wrote his magnificent essay anointing Byron as 'the poet of the Revolution' in December 1870; no one else, he claimed, was as effective an interpreter of the moral tumult of the epoch. Swinburne wrote his no less magnificent defence in 1866 and his wretched retraction nearly twenty years later. Matthew Arnold wrote his even more famous reassessment, placing Byron along with Wordsworth 'first and pre-eminent in actual performance' in *The Poetry of Byron* in 1881, and the volume in which he made his selection was still not allowed to be stained by more than a few isolated verses from *Don Juan*. However, when these and several more wrote about 'resuscitating Byron', Harney's reply was the most apt and he had a better right than anybody to make it: Londoners in a fog, he said, 'might just as well speak of resuscitating the sun'. The burning oracle in all its power and glory had always been there for men and women who wished to see and feel it.

A special pride of place must be accorded to the Morley lecture, since he combined in his own comprehension an historian's knowledge of the French Revolutionary epoch and the liberal politician's awareness of how the Byronic ideas retained their power throughout the ensuing decades and how they needed, from age to age, to be revived. It must be emphasized that he felt himself swimming against the floods: 'We cannot help perceiving that generations are arising that know not Byron.' A deep psychological reason was responsible for the neglect: Victorian distaste for the licentiousness of *Don Juan* and its author was allied with the revolutionary impulse which Byron could excite more passionately and faithfully than anyone else. To bestow the title of Poet of the Revolution with such full honours was a brave act in itself in a country where the name of the Revolution was more and more associated with all forms of social upheaval, wickedness and infidelity. And Morley, in this limited aspect of the matter, as on the grander theme, knew what he was doing: 'As for Great Britain,' he wrote, 'she deserved *Don Juan*. A nation, whose disrespect for all ideas and aspirations, that cannot be supported by a text, nor circulated by a religious tract society, was systematic, and where consequently the understanding is least protected against sensual sophisms, received no more than a just chastisement in "the literature of Satan".' But this was always the lesser strand in the mightiest of all political themes: 'Nowhere else', he wrote, 'do we see drawn in such traits that colossal figure which has haunted Europe these four-score years and more, with its newborn passion, its half-controlled will, its constant cry for a multitude of unknown blessings under the single name of freedom, the one known and unadulterated word of blessing.' True surely: all the other words have been adulterated. That word freedom retains its strength and beauty still today, and the preservation of its qualities during some of the darkest times owes much to Byron: more than to any other poet. 'The magic still works', wrote Morley. 'It is as though some mysterious and potent word from the gods had gone abroad over the face of the earth.'

Of all the recipients of the legacy left by Byron, the most incongruous – and the most eloquent – was John Ruskin. He had *Don*

Juan read to him as a child by the same loving, evangelist parents who taught him the Bible, and he recognized how one great prophet – as great as Homer or Milton, he would say – had the foresight and courage to see the way the world was moving, in defiance of all the words of comfort and deception with which lesser men and women were content. He felt the power of what he called Byron's 'volcanic instinct of justice; conviction that about ninetynine hundredths of whatever at present is, is wrong, conviction making us declarers of political doctrine monstrous to the ears of mercenary men'. If Byron had lived into the full years of the nineteenth century, he would have denounced with all his splendid wrath the worship of money and wealth-making as ends in themselves. He would refuse to be cowed, browbeaten, or silenced:

> And I will war, at least in words (and should
>   My chance so happen – deeds) with all who war
> With thought . . .

His sincerity was one obvious quality; so how was he disbelieved? How was the tale ever told that he was always engaged in some kind of masquerade? 'The first thing you have to do, in reading Byron to purpose,' said Ruskin, 'is to remember his motto, "Trust Byron". You always may; and the more that he takes some little pleasure at first in offending you.' But these good instruments – the courage, the honesty, the mockery – would not have availed if the cause itself was not the very greatest – to serve humanity at large, not in some abstract form or in the guise of some golden calf but in the flesh and blood of the real world of men and women – and of animals too.* 'The

---

* The best writer on Ruskin is Ruskin himself. But a good lecture on the subject was delivered by R. W. Chambers in November 1925 on 'The English Association'. Among other aspects of the matter which might be missed without him, is this revealing paragraph on Venice and dogs. The Scott concerned, of course, is Sir Walter.

> Scott, Byron, and Ruskin are the three greatest dog-lovers of English literature. Hence their sympathy. For it is easier for a camel to go through the eye of a needle, than for one dog-lover to believe that

thing wholly new and precious to me in Byron', wrote Ruskin again, 'was his measured and living truth – here at last I found a man who spoke only of what he had seen and known and who spoke without exaggeration, without mystery, without enmity and without mercy.' Not the customary tribute, not a single feature from that familiar caricature. Note that word *only* in Ruskin's final verdict; he wrote only what he had seen and knew. And that is the tribute which Byron would most have treasured. He prided himself on his common sense, his knowledge of reality, his readiness for action. That is what Byron was *and is*, the poet of action: more than any other in our language, the poet who cannot watch the fearful human scene without incitement to protest or revenge or perpetual Promethean counter-assault. And it was all these virtues and passions, raised to their highest pitch, which made him the poet who exposed most faithfully what was truly meant by modern war in all its manifestations. He saw the futility of it, combined with the vanity and the pretensions of the great military commanders – before Stendhal, before Tolstoy. 'He was', wrote Ruskin again, 'the first great Englishman who felt the cruelty of war, and, in its cruelty, the shame.' Quite a claim, for sure, considering the vastness of the subject, its supposed grandeur and its human wretchedness. Jonathan Swift, I suppose, by the way, must be

---

another dog-lover could ever do anything very wrong. Every one knows the story of Byron's dogs, particularly of Boatswain, whose epitaph declares him to possess 'all the virtues of man without his vices'. Before Byron went abroad he arranged that he, his dog, and his old servant Joe Murray should rest in the same tomb. 'If I was sure his lordship would come here, I should like it well enough,' said old Joe (perhaps fearing the rival claims of Westminster), 'but I should not like to be alone with the dog.' 'If Byron were only in Venice now,' wrote Ruskin in 1869, 'I think we should have got on with each other.'

Of course they would: they would have told each other dog stories, and Ruskin would have carried off Byron to the Scuola degli Schiavoni to inspect Carpaccio's picture of St Jerome's dog 'watching his master translating the Bible, with highest complacency of approval, though not, of course, understanding the full import of his master's literary work'.

excluded from the reckoning as an Irishman, for he had certainly written of the cruelty and the shame of war with the same vehemence, and Byron learnt much directly from Swift, and was turning to him again, as we have seen, on the boat to Greece; how much of his own fame would Byron wish to have entwined with his furious, sustained cry of anguish and hatred against the warmongers of every breed and age, and most especially of his own. He changed the way he wrote, to serve his grand objective; what other poet has shown so resolute, so revolutionary, a political will? It was thus that he made *Don Juan* the greatest anti-war epic in our language or, maybe, any other. In that cause, he had Swift for his master and Ruskin for his pupil, and through the latter spoke to a later century when the bloodletting would outpace anything even he could imagine and when the establishment of peace became an imperative for the survival of the race. Byron foresaw that too. He told in *Darkness* how warring creeds could destroy the universe: the claim is not too high. He strove in *Sardanapalus* to tell us again what the holocaust might be. And he applied himself to the task in *Don Juan* more freshly than ever before. He wrote with all his wits about him, and with a contempt for contemporary restraints which transfigures his whole life. He knew what he was doing, and would not allow anyone or anything to stop him. Such courage and such imagination can save us.

APPENDIX I

Byron's maiden speech in the Lords on the Frame-work Bill, 27 February 1812

'My Lords, the subject now submitted to your Lordships for the first time, though new to the House, is by no means new to the country. I believe it had occupied the serious thoughts of all descriptions of persons, long before its introduction to the notice of that legislature, whose interference alone could be of real service. As a person in some degree connected with the suffering county, though a stranger not only to this House in general, but to almost every individual whose attention I presume to solicit, I must claim some portion of your Lordships' indulgence, whilst I offer a few observations on a question in which I confess myself deeply interested.

To enter into any detail of the riots would be superfluous: the House is already aware that every outrage short of actual bloodshed has been perpetrated, and that the proprietors of the frames obnoxious to the rioters, and all persons supposed to be connected with them, have been liable to insult and violence. During the short time I recently passed in Nottinghamshire, not twelve hours elapsed without some fresh act of violence; and on the day I left the county I was informed that forty frames had been broken the preceding evening, as usual, without resistance and without detection.

Such was then the state of that county, and such I have reason to believe it to be at this moment. But whilst these outrages must be admitted to exist to an alarming extent, it cannot be denied that they have arisen from circumstances of the most unparalleled distress: the perseverance of these miserable men in their proceedings tends to prove that nothing but absolute want could have driven a large, and once honest and industri-

ous, body of the people, into the commission of excesses so hazardous to themselves, their families, and the community. At the
time to which I allude, the town and county were burdened
with large detachments of the military; the police was in
motion, the magistrates assembled; yet all the movements, civil
and military, had led to – nothing. Not a single instance had
occurred of the apprehension of any real delinquent actually
taken in the fact, against whom there existed legal evidence
sufficient for conviction. But the police, however useless, were
by no means idle: several notorious delinquents had been
detected – men, liable to conviction, on the clearest evidence, of
the capital crime of poverty; men, who had been nefariously
guilty of lawfully begetting several children, whom, thanks to
the times! they were unable to maintain. Considerable injury
has been done to the proprietors of the improved frames. These
machines were to them an advantage, inasmuch as they super-
seded the necessity of employing a number of workmen, who
were in consequence left to starve. By the adoption of one frame
in particular, one man performed the work of many, and the
superfluous labourers were thrown out of employment. Yet it is
to be observed, that the work thus executed was inferior in
quality; not marketable at home, and merely hurried over with
a view to exportation. It was called, in the cant of the trade, by
the name of "Spider-work". The rejected workmen, in the
blindness of their ignorance, instead of rejoicing at these
improvements in arts so beneficial to mankind, conceived
themselves to be sacrificed to improvements in mechanism. In
the foolishness of their hearts they imagined that the maintenance and well-doing of the industrious poor were objects of
greater consequence than the enrichment of a few individuals
by any improvement in the implements of trade, which threw
the workmen out of employment, and rendered the labourer
unworthy of his hire. And it must be confessed that although
the adoption of the enlarged machinery in the state of our
commerce which the country once boasted might have been
beneficial to the master without being detrimental to the servant; yet, in the present situation of our manufactures, rotting
in warehouses, without a prospect of exportation, with the

demand for work and workmen equally diminished, frames of this description tend materially to aggravate the distress and discontent of the disappointed sufferers. But the real cause of these distresses and consequent disturbances lies deeper. When we are told that these men are leagued together not only for the destruction of their own comfort, but of their very means of subsistence, can we forget that it is the bitter policy, the destructive warfare of the last eighteen years, which has destroyed their comfort, your comfort, all men's comfort? That policy, which, originating with "great statesmen now no more", has survived the dead to become a curse on the living, unto the third and fourth generation! These men never destroyed their looms till they were become useless, worse than useless; till they were become actual impediments to their exertions in obtaining their daily bread. Can you, then, wonder that in times like these, when bankruptcy, convicted fraud, and imputed felony are found in a station not far beneath that of your Lordships, the lowest, though once most useful portion of the people, should forget their duty in their distresses, and become only less guilty than one of their representatives? But while the exalted offender can find means to baffle the law, new capital punishments must be devised, new snares of death must be spread for the wretched mechanic, who is famished into guilt. These men were willing to dig, but the spade was in other hands: they were not ashamed to beg, but there was none to relieve them: their own means of subsistence were cut off, all other employments pre-occupied; and their excesses, however to be deplored and condemned, can hardly be subject of surprise.

It has been stated that the persons in the temporary possession of frames connive at their destruction; if this be proved upon inquiry, it were necessary that such material accessories to the crime should be principals in the punishment. But I did hope, that any measure proposed by his Majesty's government for your Lordships' decision, would have had conciliation for its basis; or, if that were hopeless, that some previous inquiry, some deliberation, would have been deemed requisite; not that we should have been called at once, without examination and without cause, to pass sentences by wholesale, and sign death-warrants blindfold. But, admitting that these men had no cause of complaint; that the grievances of them and their employers were alike groundless; that they deserved the worst; – what inefficiency, what imbecility has been evinced in the method chosen to reduce them! Why were the military called out to be made a mockery of, if they were to be called out at all? As far as the difference of seasons would permit, they have merely parodied the summer campaign of Major Sturgeon; and, indeed, the whole proceedings. civil and military, seemed on the model of those of the mayor and corporation of Garratt. – Such marchings and countermarchings! – from Nottingham to Bullwell, from Bullwell to Banford, from Banford to Mansfield! And when at length the detachments arrived at their destination, in all "the pride, pomp, and circumstance of glorious war", they came just in time to witness the mischief which had been done, and ascertain the escape of the perpetrators, to collect the "*spolia opima*" in the fragments of broken frames, and return to their quarters amidst the derision of old women, and the hootings of children. Now, though, in a free country, it were to be wished that our military should never be too formidable, at least to ourselves, I cannot see the policy of placing them in situations where they can only be made ridiculous. As the sword is the worst argument that can be used, so should it be the last. In this instance it has been the first; but providentially as yet only in the scabbard. The present measure will, indeed, pluck it from the sheath; yet had proper meetings been held in the earlier stages of these riots, had the grievances of these men and their masters (for they also had their grievances) been fairly weighed and justly examined, I do think that means might have been devised to restore these workmen to their avocations, and tranquillity to the county. At present the county suffers from the double infliction of an idle military and a starving population. In what state of apathy have we been plunged so long, that now for the first time the House has been officially apprised of these disturbances? All this has been transacting within 130 miles of London; and yet we, "good easy men, have deemed full sure our greatness was a-ripening", and have sat down to enjoy our foreign triumphs in the midst of domestic calamity. But all the

cities you have taken, all the armies which have retreated
before your leaders, are but paltry subjects of self-congratula-
tion, if your land divides against itself, and your dragoons and
your executioners must be let loose against your fellow-citizens.
– You call these men a mob, desperate, dangerous, and ignorant;
and seem to think that the only way to quiet the *"Bellua
multorum capitum"* is to lop off a few of its superfluous heads. But
even a mob may be better reduced to reason by a mixture of conciliation and firmness, than by additional irritation and
redoubled penalties. Are we aware of our obligations to a mob?
It is the mob that labour in your fields and serve in your houses,
– that man your navy, and recruit your army, – that have enabled you to defy all the world, and can also defy you when neglect and calamity have driven them to despair! You may call the
people a mob; but do not forget that a mob too often speaks the
sentiments of the people. And here I must remark, with what
alacrity you are accustomed to fly to the succour of your distressed allies, leaving the distressed of your own country to the
care of Providence or – the parish. When the Portuguese suffered under the retreat of the French, every arm was stretched
out, every hand was opened, to enable them to rebuild their villages and replenish their granaries. And at this moment, when
thousands of misguided but most unfortunate fellow-country-
men are struggling with the extremes of hardships and hunger,
as your charity began abroad it should end at home. A much less
sum, a tithe of the bounty bestowed on Portugal, even if those
men (which I cannot admit without inquiry) could not have
been restored to their employments, would have rendered
unnecessary the tender mercies of the bayonet and the gibbet.
But doubtless our friends have too many foreign claims to
admit a prospect of domestic relief; though never did such
objects demand it. I have traversed the seat of war in the Penin-
sula, I have been in some of the most oppressed provinces of
Turkey; but never under the most despotic of infidel governments did I behold such squalid wretchedness as I have seen
since my return in the very heart of a Christian country. And
what are your remedies? After months of inaction, and months
of action worse than inactivity, at length comes forth the grand

specific, the never-failing nostrum of all state physicians, from the days of Draco to the present time. After feeling the pulse and shaking the head over the patient, prescribing the usual course of warm water and bleeding, – the warm water of your mawkish police, and the lancets of your military, – these convulsions must terminate in death, the sure consummation of the prescriptions of all political Sangrados. Setting aside the palpable injustice and the certain inefficiency of the Bill, are there not capital punishments sufficient in your statutes? Is there not blood enough upon your penal code, that more must be poured forth to ascend to Heaven and testify against you? How will you carry the Bill into effect? Can you commit a whole county to their own prisons? Will you erect a gibbet in every field, and hang up men like scarecrows? or will you proceed (as you must to bring this measure into effect) by decimation? place the county under martial law? depopulate and lay waste all around you? and restore Sherwood Forest as an acceptable gift to the crown, in its former condition of a royal chase and an asylum for outlaws? Are these the remedies for a starving and desperate populace? Will the famished wretch who has braved your bayonets be appalled by your gibbets? When death is a relief, and the only relief it appears that you will afford him, will he be dragooned into tranquillity? Will that which could not be effected by your grenadiers be accomplished by your executioners? If you proceed by the forms of law, where is your evidence? Those who have refused to impeach their accomplices when transportation only was the punishment, will hardly be tempted to witness against them when death is the penalty. With all due deference to the noble lords opposite, I think a little investigation, some previous inquiry, would induce even them to change their purpose. That most favourite state measure, so marvellously efficacious in many and recent instances, temporizing, would not be without its advantages in this. When a proposal is made to emancipate or relieve, you hesitate, you deliberate for years, you temporize and tamper with the minds of men; but a death-bill must be passed off-hand, without a thought of the consequences. Sure I am, from what I have heard, and from what I have seen, that to pass the Bill under all the existing circumstances, without inquiry, without deliberation, would only be to add injustice to irritation, and barbarity to neglect. The framers of such a bill must be content to inherit the honours of that Athenian law-giver whose edicts were said to be written not in ink but in blood. But suppose it passed; suppose one of these men, as I have seen them, – meagre with famine, sullen with despair, careless of a life which your Lordships are perhaps about to value at something less than the price of a stocking-frame; – suppose this man surrounded by the children for whom he is unable to procure bread at the hazard of his existence, about to be torn for ever from a family which he lately supported in peaceful industry, and which it is not his fault that he can no longer support; – suppose this man – and there are ten thousand such from whom you may select your victims – dragged into court, to be tried for this new offence, by this new law; still, there are two things wanting to convict and condemn him; and these are, in my opinion, – twelve butchers for a jury, and a Jeffreys for a judge!'

APPENDIX II

Byron and Pope

Byron wrote two elaborate essays or letters in defence of his hero, Pope, each having been provoked by an opponent who might not be regarded as worthy of his attention. However, the Reverend W. L. Bowles in his *Strictures on the Life and Writings of Pope* felt himself to be expressing the views of many others, including most of the Lakers, headed by Coleridge, and Byron seized the opportunity offered by the publication of Bowles's work to say much of what he believed needed to be said on larger questions. One passage commanded the ecstatic support of Hazlitt, and may still command no less enthusiastic support today (see page 373). No other proof is needed of the significance of what he said and why he said it. The whole controversy is worth reading on its merits and also for the fresh evidence which it offers of how Byron could devote time, energy, skill, application on an inordinate scale to the causes in which he believed, and the defence of 'the little Queen Anne man' qualified for that inclusion. But Byron also provoked a notable reply from Hazlitt which appeared in the *London Magazine* for June 1821. This too can easily be read in full. Hazlitt naturally and readily sides with Byron on some aspects of the debate. 'There is some *good hating*,' he insists, in the way Byron tackles some of Bowles's associates in the defamation of Pope, such as Southey, and some proper exposure of Bowles's editorial inquisition into Pope's moral character – 'a pure piece of clerical priggism'. However, there are other main points of dispute to be carried back into Byron's camp. Hazlitt would not agree with Byron in his seeming depreciation of the role of the imagination or when he 'clownishly chooses to consider all poetry but what relates to ethical or didactic truth as "a lie" '. And then he asks: 'Is Lear a lie?' The argument at least is not so plain as Byron would have it and maybe he has accorded to Pope an impossible pre-eminence.

By the time he wrote this article Hazlitt felt himself able to tackle any opponent on his own critical ground. He had his own praise of Pope which was also not the full portrait:

> He lived in the smiles of fortune, and basked in the favour of the great. In his smooth and polished verse we meet with no prodigies of nature, but with miracles of wit; the thunders of his pen are whispered flatteries; its forked lightnings pointed sarcasms; for 'the gnarled oak', he gives us 'the soft myrtle': for rocks, and seas, and mountains, artificial grass-plats, gravel-walks, and tinkling rills; for earthquakes and tempests, the breaking of a flowerpot, or the fall of a china jar; for the tug and war of the elements, or the deadly strife of the passions, we have
>
> Calm contemplation and poetic ease.
>
> Yet within this retired and narrow circle how much, and that how exquisite, was contained! What discrimination, what wit, what delicacy, what fancy, what lurking spleen, what elegance of thought, what pampered refinement of sentiment! It is like looking at the world through a microscope, where every thing assumes a new character and a new consequence, where things are seen in their minutest circumstances and slightest shades of difference; where the little becomes gigantic, the deformed beautiful, and the beautiful deformed. The wrong end of the magnifier is, to be sure, held to everything, but still the exhibition is highly curious, and we know not whether to be most pleased or surprised.

But has not Hazlitt also manipulated his microscope a little too assuredly? It is not clear that he was as well aware as Byron of the fights in which Pope had to engage to make his voice heard and what a giant he truly was.

BIBLIOGRAPHY

The three main sources for modern Byron students are:

1. *The Complete Poetical Works*, edited by Jerome J. McGann, Oxford University Press, 1980 onwards. Volumes 1 to 5 are so far published. A single volume in the Oxford Authors Series, 1986, contains both the complete *Childe Harold* and the complete *Don Juan*. Two other McGann volumes are cited below.

2. *Byron's Letters and Journals* in twelve volumes edited by Leslie A. Marchand, London, John Murray, 1973–1982. *Byron – A Biography*, by Leslie A. Marchand, 3 vols., London, John Murray, 1957. *Byron – a Portrait* by Leslie A. Marchand, London, John Murray, 1971. *Byron's Poetry: A Critical Introduction*, by Leslie A. Marchand, Boston, Riverside Studies, 1965.

3. The various works of Doris Langley Moore – *The Late Lord Byron*, London, John Murray, 1961. *Lord Byron – Accounts Rendered*, London, John Murray, 1974. *Ada, Countess of Lovelace*, London, John Murray, 1979. Two other particular treasures should be added to this list: *The Great Byron Adventure*, published in *The Sunday Times* in February and March 1959, in which the author described her discoveries when she became the first independent author to examine the Lovelace Papers in the possession of Lady Wentworth, Byron's only great-grandchild. The second treasure: *My Caravaggio Style*, the novel by Doris Langley Moore, published by Cassell in 1959, and soon to be republished.

For Hazlitt, the main sources are:
The Complete Works of William Hazlitt in the twenty-one volume Centenary Edition; edited by P. P. Howe, J. M. Dent, 1935.

The best *Life* is still P. P. Howe's, first published by Martin Secker in 1922, revised in 1928, and republished later by J. M. Dent, Hamish Hamilton and by Penguin. Penguin have also published the best single selection of his writings in the edition edited by Ronald Blythe in 1970.

The most important critical judgement is contained in *Hazlitt: The Mind of a Critic* by David Bromwich, Oxford University Press, 1983.

My own views of the subject were elaborated in an essay contained in *Debts of Honour*, London, Davis-Poynter, 1979.

I add the others which I have found most helpful; references to several of these are contained in the footnotes.

Ashton, Thomas L., *Byron's Hebrew Melodies*, London, Routledge & Kegan Paul, 1972

Blackstone, Bernard, *Byron, A Survey*, London, Longman, 1975 |

Blessington, Marguerite, Countess of, *Conversations of Lord Byron*, London, 1834; Princeton, 1969

Bold, Alan, *Byron: Wrath and Flame*, London, Vision & Barnes Noble, 1983

Bostetter, Edward E., ed., *Twentieth Century Interpretations of Don Juan: A Collection of Critical Essays*, Prentice-Hall, 1969

Boyd, E. F., *Byron's Don Juan: A Critical Study*, New Brunswick, 1945

Brandes, George, *Main Currents in Nineteenth Century Literature*, 6 vols., London, Heinemann, 1923

Burnett, T. A. J., *The Rise and Fall of a Regency Dandy: The Life and Times of Scrope Beardmore Davies*, London, John Murray, 1981

Butler, Marilyn, *Romantics, Rebels and Reactionaries*, Oxford, 1981

Buxton, John, *Byron and Shelley – The History of a Friendship*, London, Macmillan, 1968

Byron Journal, The, published each year since 1973 (London, Byron House). An invaluable collection of modern Byronic commentaries.

Calvert, William J., *Byron: Romantic Paradox*, Chapel Hill, 1935

Chew, Samuel C., *Byron in England*, New York, 1924

Cline, C. L., *Byron, Shelley and Their Pisan Circle*, London, 1952

Coleridge, E. H., *The Works of Lord Byron: Poetry*, 7 vols., London, John Murray, 1898–1904

Collins, Philip, 'Thomas Cooper, the Chartist: Byron and the Poets of the Poor' (Byron Foundation Lectures), Nottingham, 1969

de Vere White, Terence, *Tom Moore, The Irish Poet*, London, Hamish Hamilton, 1977

Drinkwater, John, *The Pilgrim of Eternity*, London, Hodder & Stoughton, 1925

Elwin, Malcolm, *Lord Byron's Wife*, London, Macdonald, 1962

Fleming, Anne, *Bright Darkness*, London, Nottingham Court Press, 1983

Foot, Paul, *Red Shelley*, London, Sidgwick & Jackson, 1981

Galt, John, *The Life of Lord Byron*, New York, 1830

Gamba, Count P., *Lord Byron's Last Journey to Greece*, London, 1825

Gleckner, Robert F., *Byron and the Ruins of Paradise*, Baltimore, The Johns Hopkins University Press, 1967

Graham, Peter W., *Byron's Bulldog: The Letters of John Cam Hobhouse to Lord Byron*, Ohio State University Press, 1984

Grierson, Herbert, *The Background of English Literature*, London, Chatto & Windus, 1925 and 1934

—— *Essays and Addresses*, London, Chatto & Windus, 1940

—— *A Critical History of English Poetry* (with J. C. Smith), London, Chatto & Windus, 1944

—— *Cross Currents in English Literature of the Seventeenth Century*, London, Chatto & Windus, 1929

Grylls, R. Glynn, *Claire Clairmont – Mother of Byron's Allegra*, London, 1939

—— *Trelawny*, London, 1950

Guiccioli, Teresa, *My Recollections of Lord Byron*, 2 vols., London, 1869

Gunn, Peter, *My Dearest Augusta*, London, The Bodley Head, 1968

—— Ed., *Selected Letters and Journals*, London, Penguin Books, 1984

Hobhouse, John Cam (Lord Broughton), *Recollections of a Long Life*, London, 1909–1911

Holmes, Richard, *Shelley – The Pursuit*, London, Weidenfeld & Nicolson, 1974

Howell, Margaret J., *Byron Tonight: A Poet's Plays on the 19th Century Stage*, Springwood Books, 1982

Hunt, Leigh, *Lord Byron and Some of His Contemporaries*, London, 1828

Jenkins, Elizabeth, *Lady Caroline Lamb*, London, 1932; paperback, Routledge & Kegan Paul, 1974

Jump, John D., *Byron*, London, 1972

—— Ed., *Byron: A Symposium*, London, Macmillan, 1975

Joseph, M. K., *Byron the Poet*, London, Gollancz, 1954

Kelsall, Malcolm, *Byron's Politics*, London, Harvester Press, 1987

Kennedy, James, *Conversations on Religion with Lord Byron*, London, John Murray, 1830

Knight, G. Wilson, *Lord Byron: Christian Virtues*, London, Routledge & Kegan Paul, 1952

—— *Lord Byron's Marriage*, London, Routledge & Kegan Paul, 1957

—— *Byron and Shakespeare*, London, Routledge & Kegan Paul, 1966

—— *Poets of Action*, London, Methuen, 1967

—— *The Poetry of Pope*, London, Routledge & Kegan Paul, 1958

—— *Neglected Powers*, London, Routledge & Kegan Paul, 1971

Longford, Elizabeth, *Byron*, London, Hutchinson & Weidenfeld, 1976

Lovelace, Ralph Milbanke, Earl of, *Astarte – A Fragment of Truth Concerning George Gordon, Sixth Lord Byron*, London, 1905, republished 1921

Lovell, Ernest J. Jnr., *Byron: The Record of a Quest*, Connecticut, Archon Books, 1966

—— *Captain Medwin*, London, Macdonald, 1962

—— *His Very Self and Voice: Collected Conversations of Lord Byron*, New York, 1954

McGann, Jerome J., *Fiery Dust: Byron's Poetic Development*, University of Chicago Press, 1968

—— *Don Juan in Context*, London, John Murray, 1976

Marjarum, Edward Wayne, *Byron as Skeptic and Believer*, Princeton, 1938

Mayne, Ethel Colburn, *The Life and Letters of Anne Isabella, Lady Noel Byron*, London, 1930

Medwin, Thomas, *Journal of the Conversations of Lord Byron at Pisa*, London, 1824, Princeton, 1966

Moore, Thomas, *Letters and Journals of Lord Byron, with Notices of his Life*, London, 1830

Nicolson, Harold, *Byron – The Last Journey*, London, Constable, 1934

O'Leary, Patrick, *Regency Editor, Life of John Scott*, Aberdeen University Press, 1983

Origo, Iris, *The Last Attachment*, London, Jonathan Cape and John Murray, 1949

Page, Norman, *Byron, Interviews and Recollections*, London, Macmillan, 1985

Parry, William, *The Last Days of Lord Byron*, London, 1825

Prothero, Rowland E., *The Works of Lord Byron: Letters and Journals*, 6 vols., London, 1898–1901

Quennell, Peter, *Byron: A Self Portrait: Letters and Diaries*, London, John Murray, 1950

—— *Byron – The Years of Fame*, 1935

—— *Byron in Italy*, London, 1941, republished 1967 and 1974

—— (With George Paston) *'To Lord Byron'*, Feminine Profiles, based upon unpublished letters, London, John Murray, 1939

Raphael, Frederic, *Byron*, London, Thames & Hudson, 1982

Ridenour, George M., *The Style of Don Juan*, New Haven, Yale University Press, 1960

Robinson, Charles E., *Shelley and Byron: The Snake and The Eagle Wreathed in Fight*, Baltimore and London, Johns Hopkins University Press, 1976

—— Ed., *Lord Byron and His Contemporaries: Essays from the Sixth International Byron Seminar*, University of Delaware Press, 1982

Russell, Bertrand, *History of Western Philosophy* (Chapter on Byron), London, 1946

Rutherford, Andrew, *Byron: A Critical Study*, Edinburgh and London, Oliver & Boyd, 1961

—— *Byron: The Critical Heritage*, London, Routledge & Kegan Paul, 1970

Steffan, Thomas Guy, *The Making of a Masterpiece* (A Variorum Edition), Austin, University of Texas Press, 1957

—— *Lord Byron's Cain*, Austin, University of Texas Press, 1968

Stowe, Harriet Beecher, *Lady Byron Vindicated*, Chicago, 1968

Strickland, Margot, *The Byron Women*, London, 1974

Thomas, Gordon Kent, *Lord Byron's Iberian Pilgrimage*, Brigham Young University Press, 1983

Trelawny, Edward John, *Records of Shelley, Byron and the Author*, London, 1858, paperback, 1973

Trueblood, Paul Graham, *Byron's Political and Cultural Influence in Nineteenth Century Europe. A Symposium.* London, Macmillan, 1981

Vassallo, Peter, *Byron: The Italian Literary Influence*, London, Macmillan, 1984

Vulliamy, C. E., *Byron*, London, Michael Joseph, 1948

West, Paul, *Byron: Critical Essays*, Prentice-Hall, 1963

—— *Byron and the Spoiler's Art*, London, Chatto & Windus, 1960

INDEX